VOLTAIRE

VOLTAIRE
(From a Drawing Made About 1790)

VOLTAIRE

Volume One

GEORG BRANDES

FREDERICK UNGAR PUBLISHING CO.
New York

Translation by
Otto Kruger
and
Pierce Butler

Republished 1964

First published 1930

Printed in the United States of America

Library of Congress Catalog Card No. 64-15687

CONTENTS

VOLUME ONE

OVERTURE

I

OVERTURE

1

SOME writers are of importance in literary history. The greatest, mark epochs in the literature of their country.

A very small number, at most a few dozen, are important in world history.

Voltaire is one of these.

* * *

Once upon a time a bundle of nerves, charged with electricity, captivated Europe and enlightened it.

Once upon a time there was a man who was regarded as the supreme embodiment of human wit while still young, and who retains this reputation even to this day.

Once there was a demon whose intellect was fire and whose ideas were lightning, whose heart was warm in devotion and friendship, while his mind shone cold and clear as a northern light. The art of his natural simple eloquence has rarely been equalled and never surpassed. It was conversational, not oratorical; he never made speeches.

Once upon a time there was a man of the world, a business man, a courtier, a landowner, a poet, a scientist, a historian, a hermit, whose nature was will, whose desire was honor, whose ambition was action, whose manner was charm, whose support was a rare memory, whose intellect was a genial vigilance, whose commendation, meaning distinction, was sought as eagerly by Pope as by actress, by King as by poet, and whose mockery left a stigma for centuries.

Before his time only Marcus Tullius Cicero held such a central position in Europe's literature; Vol-

3

taire therefore looked back at Cicero admiringly, as at a model, and his favorite rôle was that of Cicero, in his own play, *Rome Sauvée*. Nevertheless, Cicero did not compare with him in wit and vigorous satire.

As a satirist famed in all courts and in all circles he had a predecessor; Pietro Aretino, equally dreaded and equally wooed.

But while Aretino was a pamphleteer—at times obscene, at times sanctimonious—with tribute and luxury as his only aim, so that posterity speaks of him with nothing but contempt, Voltaire's glory after death is far greater than during his life.

By his avid intellectual curiosity and inexhaustible inventive faculty, by his dynamic energy, he accomplished nothing less than embodying a nation, a continent and a century.

Goethe, at first Voltaire's opponent and, later, his admirer, said of him that he was French like no other Frenchman, even called him "the first outstanding writer in France, the one who corresponds best to the nation." And in our own day two of Voltaire's uncompromising opponents among French critics, his opposite, Brunetière, and his hater, Faguet, said the same: No name is more French, none reflects better the French nature.

Thus, Voltaire summarizes a nation.

And, likewise, a century. The eighteenth century is, in truth, Voltaire's century.

Finally, Voltaire summarizes a continent—even more than a continent. For in the territory of the mind he made conquests, like Alexander and Napoleon in the outer world, and by intellectual means reigned as unquestionably as they. And his reign has proven to be far more lasting. For, there are still Voltairians. But where today is one to find an adherent of Alexander or Bonaparte?

Voltairianism represents a new reformation two hundred years after Calvin and Luther. A proclamation of freedom of research (deceptive, because it stopped at the Bible) was first issued in France in Voltaire's time, and spread from France all over the earth.

2

No one has been so maligned as Voltaire. Few important personalities have served as a battleground for more stubborn quarrelling.

Lessing, who spiritually had been his disciple, and humanly had been guilty of a minor offense against him—seldom excused by the guilty—wrote after Voltaire's death the following epitaph:

Hier liegt—wenn man euch glauben wollte,
Ihr frommen Herrn!—der längst hier liegen sollte.
Der liebe Gott verzeih aus Gnade
Ihm seine Henriade
Und seine Trauerspiele
Und seine Verschen viele:
Denn was er sonst an's Licht gebracht,
Das hat er ziemlich gut gemacht.

Voltaire, who highly esteemed Pope, was in turn greatly esteemed by Byron, sincere admirer of Pope. In *Childe Harold* the poet composed these lines to his memory:

The one was fire and fickleness, a child,
Most mutable in wishes, but in mind
A wit as various—gay—grave—sage—as wild—
Historian, bard, philosopher, combined;
He multiplied himself among mankind.
The Proteus of their talents: But his own
Breathed most in redicule,—which, as the wind
Blew where it listed, laying all things prone,—
Now to o'erthrow a fool, and now to shake a throne.

In Germany, Wieland was a poet in Voltaire's spirit and therefore liked by the Göttingen poets, the German romantics, who embody the reaction against the philosophy of the eighteenth century, were far more hostile to Voltaire than Lessing had been.

3

Voltaire came from a country and lived in an age in which the intelligence of the best educated was refined, while political and social conditions were barbaric. As a writer he was therefore outlawed. As a satirist and reform-writer he was put in the Bastille repeatedly and all through his life was in constant fear of being jailed.

For that reason, the most famous man of French literature spent comparatively few years of his life in Paris, where his stay was either forbidden or too dangerous. Even at the age of eighty-three years, when, after twenty-eight years' absence, he dared to set foot in the French capitol, Louis XVI would have liked to have him arrested, and had him advised to disappear as quickly as possible—advice made unnecessary by his death.

Thus, Voltaire spent his days in exile, either on foreign soil—in England, Holland, Prussia, Switzerland—or as near as possible to the borders of France—in Cirey, Ferney—whence he could flee at a moment's notice.

In this outlawed situation, he wrote almost always anonymously. Indeed, this did not by any means protect him since his style was known; and besides, much was ascribed to him that he had not written at all. Thus, for his safety's sake, he disowned his writings again and again, lied about being responsible for them, and not a few he permitted to remain unprinted for an age. When they were published it was seldom at his instigation.

Nearly all his writings met with the same fate; their sale was forbidden.

Several of his most valuable works, as the *Philosophic Letters* on England, were burned by the hangman. He worked unceasingly, but in constant fear of being robbed of his freedom.

Nevertheless, when about forty years old, he was hailed by the most powerful and gifted men and women of his time—by Kings, Empresses, aristocrats and soldiers, by thinkers, poets, and by the scientists of the age, as their spiritual leader.

Finally, respect for him became so pronounced that the most prominent in the field of literature, the highest society of all countries, saw in him not only the most famous and renowned writer of the age, but also a personality which exemplified liberalism and toleration, high humanitarianism and abhorrence of cruelty: to the extent that a man like Franklin, the champion not only of the new North America, but also of freedom of the people, inventive faculty, theoretical understanding and practical sense, brought his grandson to him and asked for his blessing. Voltaire said: "God and Liberty!"

Men and women of his time were fired by the rays of his brilliant intellect. Not a few of the most cultured openly worshipped.

Innumerable letters to Voltaire show the ardor and gratitude of their devotion. Typical, for instance, are the first letters of Frederick the Great, written when he was Crown Prince.

On the other hand, to those who clung to old-fashioned piety and to the die-hard conservatives, and above all to the dull, Voltaire was the mocker and destroyer. To the superstitious, he was the devil. To the malicious and the envious, he was the object of hatred and slander.

During his long life he gave to one generation after another the consciousness of right and the strength of reason. Never was he himself cold when he thought he had detected some truth. It flamed up in him, and he threw it into the remotest spaces, now like the beam from a lighthouse, now like a grenade from a mortar, now like the transmission of electrical energy in charged cells.

As Condorcet observed: For him the truth was no secret to be whispered among the initiate. To him it was like food prepared freshly and in the most appetizing manner; or like medicine which, not to be refused, should please the palate; a banner to be raised, a watchword to be called.

His greatest work of art is no one of the numerous tasks completed during his life, but his life itself.

This life has many stages of development, many more than that of the insect, which at first is larva, then pupa, and finally butterfly. The insect has ugly moments. There is nothing nice about a larva. But Voltaire's life has this rare thing in common with the insect to which Psyche has given wings—that its last phase is the most wonderful.

Voltaire, at first fashionable poet, playwright and wit, in the view of his time something like a national poet, began on English soil to turn into an enlightener, awakener of ideas, reformer, implacable foe of obsolete prejudice and long-established abuses. In the course of time, he emerged as historian, naturalist, lyricist, dramatist, novelist, political economist, philosopher, agitator. The most brilliant point in Voltaire's metamorphosis is reached when the game-cock turns into the commander-in-chief, the wag becomes the scientist, the homeless, aimlessly roaming courtier develops into the responsible patriarch, the settled lord and benefactor of a whole region. At that time he took a bold and aggressive stand against fanaticism and everything else that stood in the way of right and justice. He became a protector of the oppressed and maltreated—a figure never to be forgotten.

The satyr was transformed into Pan.

Voltaire's spirit is universal. His sane and practical knowledge included even sanitary regimen and serum treatment. He plead for cleanliness, proposed the establishment of public baths. He was the first to teach man the pollution caused by cemeteries inside a city or church, letting the dead slaughter the living. And in France he was the first to recommend vaccination against small-pox. On top of this, this same man was the first Frenchman who was not satisfied to ask himself the most vital intellectual questions, but even answered them. Is the Christian tradition historically true? Is the Christian doctrine inspired by God and intellectually probable? Without hesitation he answered: the tradition is full of fables and improbabilities; the Church is the first evidence of a decline from the higher civilization of heathen antiquity. Its doctrine is incomplete at its best, a gloomy and tyrannical superstition at its worst.

4

It is true that in the Europe of the eighteenth century France was next to England in enlightenment.

Judged by modern standards, however, this enlightenment was a dreadful barbarity, far worse than that of Russia during Czardom. The penal laws were in chaos. New laws were passed revoking the old; they were often contradictory and always trickily and speciously phrased. Almost every disposition of the judge could be enforced and justified under some law. Hence the judge's power was unlimited.

Judiciary appointments were for sale. Children, incapable of administering their own affairs—hardly out of school—were given the arbitrary power of making or breaking full grown men and women within their jurisdiction.

La Bruyère, in the fourteenth chapter of his book *Les Charactères,* says: "The judge's duty is to practice justice, his profession is to strain it." Had they only been content to stop at that!

Attorneys in the provinces had farmers arrested on a trumped-up charge of theft or carrying arms, and held them prisoners until paid. Woe to him who had a judge for an enemy! The village-mayor of Puissieux sentenced a certain Carlier to be tortured and broken upon the wheel, just because he hated him. It was quite simple: Carlier owned a brick-yard. There was an assessor named Frillet who yearned for just such a brick-yard. It was not difficult to persuade Frillet to accuse Carlier of murder and to have him broken upon the wheel. Two men who protested Carlier's innocence were hanged for false testimony. When this matter had been disposed and the court had sentenced him to die, Louis XV commuted his sentence to ten years of exile in—Burgundy. Upon another judge who had forged documents a fine of fifteen francs was imposed.

La Bruyère says: It is not absolutely impossible for a man who has influential friends to lose a law-suit.

The old-French criminal law was summarized in the penal code of 1670. There was no general penal law. The judges could at any time dig out some old and inhuman decree. Even though the Danish law of 1683 was far from modern, it was many steps in advance of the French.

In the France of the eighteenth century was to be

found the same cruelty as existed two hundred years before. Stake and wheel were introduced from Germany in the time of Francis I, in 1535, as a deterrent to robbers and highwaymen, and this penalty (at that time) was scarcely too severe, since the robbers tortured their victims dreadfully. But later its use was not limited to punishing highway robbers.

There were five favorite methods of inflicting the death penalty: quartering, the stake, the wheel, the scaffold and the gallows. These five were variously combined in the punishment of the many kinds and degrees of crimes. Thieving, no matter how petty, was punishable by the gallows. A maid who had stolen a few napkins was hanged. It was the universal belief that the torture of the criminal was necessary to satisfy a demand, and the demand was of God, according to the conception of the time. Not only ecclesiastic, but also secular justice imposed punishment in the name of God. And the criminal had to do church-penance.

All power was in the hands of Church and King.

As late as the year 1780 a teacher of criminal law, Muyart de Vouglans, divides the crime of offending the Divine Majesty into three groups: the first contains: blasphemy, atheism, sorcery, witchcraft; the second: heresy, apostasy, schism; the third: desecration of holy things, i.e., desecration of churches, sacraments, graves, crucifixes, images of saints.

Since the Revocation of Edict of Nantes, Protestants in France had been outlaws. Louis XV, in 1724, forbade the Protestants to practise any other religion than the Roman Catholic or to gather at any other divine service.

Death at the stake was the penalty for sorcery, blasphemy, heresy, desecration of churches, incest, parricide, and homosexuality.

A sentence to the galleys for even a limited time was really a life sentence, for the prisoners were held after their time had expired. The galleys were the means of maintaining French naval power in the Mediterranean. The rowing benches had to be filled. When the suicides among the galley-slaves became too frequent, it was, at the time of Colbert, proposed

that some of those who had served their time be released. Sometimes if the convict had rich relatives,
a Turkish slave might be bought from the Knights of
Malta, as his substitute.

Life in the galleys was like this:

On twenty-five or thirty double benches sat three
hundred rowers shackled five or six to an oar. Naked
to the waist, they sat on the bench from which they
were never unchained, winter or summer, day or
night. They ate and slept on it. Moreover, they were
constantly exposed to the cruelty of the keepers who,
whip in hand, circulated among them.

Most cruel was the treatment of the Protestants
who, after the Revocation of the Edict of Nantes,
were sentenced to the galleys. Their life was one
of continuous torture Jeanne Pierre Espinas was
sentenced for life to the galleys and was chained to
one spot, half-naked, for twenty-three years, because
he had given supper and a night's lodging to a Protestant clergyman.

Literature enjoyed no legal protection. Justice, the
supreme distinction between right and wrong, was
assumed to reside naturally in the King. The judges
passed sentence because the King had delegated to
them the power divinely his, and the law did not affect him in any way. His will was law and he had the
right to break down every obstacle. Where no law
had been violated, yet an arrest was desired, the one
interested simply procured a *lettre de cachet,* a secret
warrant countersigned by the secretary of state and
bearing the royal seal. It ordered the person named
in it to go to a certain prison or into exile, either
abroad or in a certain town within the borders of
France. The *lettres de cachet* robbed of their freedom
persons who, like Voltaire, had done nothing for
which any legal accusation could be lodged against
them. There was no indictment, hence no trial. The
victim stayed in prison or exile for an undetermined
period. He could not clear himself, since he had not
been accused.

After Damien's attack upon Louis XV the situation
of literature was regulated by the law of 1757, as follows: any one against whom evidence was brought,

as author, creator, or even buyer, of writings attacking religion, disturbing the peacefully inclined or undermining the order and peace of the State, was sentenced to die. The same penalty was imposed upon pedlars of the writing. Furthermore, authors and distributers of printed matter, who did not follow the rules prescribed to the Press, were sentenced to the galleys.

A comparatively light penalty was the destruction of the printed matter; this was, at the demand of the prosecuting officer, torn to pieces and burned by the hangman.

It is no slight honor to have led the opposition against such legal conditions.

Voltaire's fight for a reform of the criminal law is the center of a movement which, in the latter half of the eighteenth century, was launched against the old criminal code and which during the revolution led to its complete breakdown. This movement became widespread through the efforts of Voltaire. Wherever it was strategically important to declare war upon obsolete medieval forms, he appeared on the scene to assume the leadership.

Whoever wrote against the old legal system sought association with Voltaire and strove for his approval. Every one who was oppressed by the harshness of this system or by the distortion of justice resulting from it, saw in him his protector and savior. In the decade from his death to the outbreak of the revolution, the platform he advocated gains more and more powerful and more and more widespread support, but not a plank, not a doctrine is added. All keep within the limits of Voltaire's aims. All threads start from and lead back to him.

For, by numerous volumes, by hundreds of pamphlets, by ten thousand letters, he influenced, in every civilized country, the princes and princesses, the royal favorites and royal mistresses, the cardinals and abbés, the field marshals and officers. In fact, the whole writing public that developed after him was influenced by him and continued his work, even where it tried to disagree with him.

Diderot, perhaps the most prominent of his dis-

ciples, often irked by Voltaire's limitations as a deist
and by the narrowness of his conception of good
taste, wrote in the midst of his annoyance that all
were so deeply indebted to him, that, whatever he
might say or do, everything must be forgiven.

5

Voltaire was not made of the same stuff as those
creatures of whom Paludan Müller writes in the introduction to his *Adam Homo*: "the unarmoured heroes with the naked throats." He is at the same time
God and rogue, Zeus and Scapin. At his inmost core
he is the mocker. When he is completely serious,
bombast and pathos are far from him. He can gnash
his teeth in exasperation, but he never declaims (in
his own name). He does not thunder, he sneers. Literature is no longer an art but a weapon. He bran-
dishes his weapon, his deadly power of mockery. He
was in one sense an especially cunning and careful
person, as John Morley said of him, too clever ever to
throw away a shield. But he felt that once he had
drawn his sword he could not, as long as he lived,
put it back in its sheath, and though he did not (like
Horatio) throw away his shield, he threw away his
scabbard. The hiss and flash of his blade in its brilliant, cutting strokes inspired awe in those who encountered him.

Ambitious as Voltaire was and high as he raised
himself above his class, he was not able to maintain
his personal dignity as a writer. From the start he had
literary opponents and enemies. He answered them
too often, never let them out of his sight, but continued the feud to what seems a tiresome length to
present-day readers. Thus against his will he made all
of them immortal. Their names like choruses repeat
themselves in hundreds of places in his work where
one would think him occupied with anything else
rather than with them.

His self-assertiveness never took aristocratic form.
Constantly irritated and provoked, he could, with his
touchy nervous system, his oversensitive temper and

his wasplike instinct, never resolve to let his opponents have the last word. Incessantly he searched for and took revenge, was at all times the warrior, unmerciful, sometimes cruel. As a rule, his assailants were malicious, small, unworthy, envious. They wanted to rise, earn glory and ingratiate themselves with the rulers of the Church, attacking him now from this, now from that ambush. Some of them were only haughty clerical pedants. But their attacks embittered him so much that he at times—unmindful of his fight for the freedom of speech—demanded for them the Bastille, the prison in Fort l'Evèque, even the galleys, and actually had one of them, as a penalty for libel, sent to the Bastille for some time.

Far as he was in advance of his time and its prejudices, he nevertheless possessed some of these prejudices. Again and again he who himself belonged to the middle-class insults his enemies with their inferior origin, and where it serves to expose them to ridicule and contempt, he does not mind departing from strict truth.

His habit, created by the reign of lawlessness in France, of denying the authorship of his works—and he denied at times almost all of them except the Henriade and the poems on the battle of Fontenoy—had an unfavorable effect on his character. He gradually looked on his lies as fully justified for self-defense.

On September 19, 1764, he wrote to D'Alembert with reference to the *Dictionnaire philosophique*: "As soon as the slightest danger comes up kindly notify me so that I may disown my writings in the public papers with my habitual frankness and innocence."

This weakness in his character naturally lessened the respect paid him by his contemporaries.

Nevertheless, he was and remained the Olympic Zeus in the minds of the most prominent men and women of his time. To literature indeed a Zeus, whose Olympic shock of hair, whose Ambrosian curls, were the wig affected by the fashion of that age. But with the wig removed he seemed like Houdon's marvelous statue, with the contours of his head more clearly visible, more wonderful than ever.

He had, like Heinrich Heine fifty years later, something of the tiger's lust to tear to pieces whomsoever
challenged him, combined with the melodious rich-
ness of the mocking-bird and the charm of the ga-
zelle.

In addition he had a winning way of suddenly
dropping his anger at its highest pitch, as soon as the
object of his wrath got in trouble and appealed to his
heart. Just as he was moved and won over by the
father of a man who had sold libels against him and
therefore deserved punishment, he was willing to
open his arms to Jean Jacques Rousseau, soon after
he had published his *Lettres de la Montagne* against
Voltaire, when a rumor (which, by the way, was
false) induced him to flee to Ferney.

Voltaire's life work is an orchestra in which poetic
spirit holds the soprano, a geniality founded upon
the history of culture takes the alto, while hatred,
meant in the first place for all cruelty and all prejudice, takes care of the instrumental music. The personal polemic is represented by the piccolo.

Bolingbroke said of Marlborough: "He was such a
big man that I have forgotten his vices." Unfortunately, the historian cannot talk that way.

6

Voltaire takes root in France's classic seventeenth
century. He believes in the literary and political
greatness of this century, and in all substantial matters he pays homage to its taste. It is surprising how
much remains in him of the almost frantic adoration
of King and Nobility. The classic kingdom and its
aristocracy were based on the idea that through them
a state of perfection was reached, therefore any demand for change appeared arrogant rebellion against
the divine purpose with which the world was established. This conception had its majestic high priest
in the person of Bossuet.

The playwrights of that time were forbidden the
use of living questions in their dramas. While after
the death of Louis XIV all discussion was concerned
with the important questions of the day, one did not

speak openly of religion and world history, of politics and finances, of war and diplomacy, as one spoke in the reign just ended of the latest tragedy and the latest novel.

Voltaire enlivens the style of the time, which was lofty but academic. To the lightly spoken word he gives relief and the stamp of permanence.

He knew just what of the admired seventeenth century would captivate posterity. Surely not what occupied the contemporaries most: Louis XIV's elegance, his appetite, his change in mistresses, his shifting to dreadful intolerance, his plundering generals, his ailment of a fistula. What Voltaire deemed the substantial thing of his time was the literature: Racine, Molière and Boileau, Corneille and La Fontaine, but above that a genius, not a Frenchman, who under the appletree in Woolsthorpe and later under the elms in Cambridge formed the modern civilization founded by Copernicus, Tycho Brahe, Kepler and Galileo: Isaac Newton.

When in the first half of the nineteenth century Voltaire had become the object of general contempt and his poetry was called obsolete and his critical ability limited, outside of France his belittlement of Shakespeare was cited again and again as it is expressed in his letter to the French Academy. It was not mentioned that this letter had been written when he was eighty-two years old and that it was the expression of senile stubbornness and zeal; it was never mentioned that it had been none other than Voltaire who in his youth had introduced Shakespeare to France and had translated and annotated his works. Regardless of its exaggerations this letter of Voltaire corresponds exactly to Goethe's essay *Shakespeare und kein Ende,* written at an advanced age. And nothing else made Voltaire so popular in France.

Shakespeare he could criticize. To Newton he bowed unconditionally. In France he was the first to be filled with enthusiasm for Newton and to make his work understood; likewise he was the first of all to appreciate what the accomplishment of awakening natural science meant.

Henceforth natural phenomena were to be explained not as miracles but as the working of natural laws. And facing the rising sun of science, specters and ghosts dissolved. It extinguished the pyres on which heretics, Jews and witches had been burned alive. It broke the chains of the insane and of the negro. It conquered the earth differently and with more thoroughness than any Roman Emperor or King of Huns. But if one asks where in Europe's best literature one first meets a correct conception of science, the answer from the lips of scientists, even from those of a Dubois-Reymond, will be: "First in Voltaire."

France at the time of Voltaire was a hundred years behind England in sciences. When Newton, in 1686, brought his *Principia* before the Royal Society, Voltaire's meritorious predecessor, Fontenelle, was revising in his famous discussion *La Pluralité des Mondes,* Descartes' theories which Newton had gone far beyond. Forty years later Fontenelle defended this doctrine in his speech to the memory of Newton. In France, that is, in Versailles and Paris, it was standard for the academicians and Jesuits who were in charge of instruction.

As remarkable as Descartes' results had been in mathematics and pure philosophy, to physics as regards the causes of gravity, the nature of light, and floods and tides he brought a guess only. The effects of magnetism he associated with the windings of screw-like molecules.

Voltaire wrote *Eléments de la Philosophie de Newton*—not as an extract from Newton's *Principia,* but as an independent description of his discoveries in optics and astronomy. The chancellor d'Aguesseau refused him permission to print this work. It was published in the Netherlands. Voltaire captivated the court, the ladies and the abbés, who to that time had done homage to Fontenelle, explained the new conception of the law of gravity, of the refraction of the rays of light, and did away with a great many errors, thus preparing the way for d'Alembert and Lavoisier.

As a scientist he had an even surer eye for the nature of phenomena than had Réaumur and Euler, and in his forecasts and prophecies was far ahead of his time. The limited extent of his research was to be expected on account of the crude knowledge of chemistry of the time and the impossibility of exact measurement of energy or mass. With absolute intellectual independence he raised himself above the scientific and metaphysical errors, the advocates of which at that time bore the most prominent names, as Descartes and Leibnitz. Plain common sense, developed to genial open-mindedness, enabled him to perceive and destroy phantoms, and to build on experience alone.

His limitations, in the realm of the sciences, are to be detected in points at which common sense, even at its acme, does not suffice. He could raise himself above Buffon, where the latter believed in a certain fantastic primeval procreation, and poured his mockery on that species of eel which it was said could be created from a mixture of flour and mutton-gravy. On the other hand, in his excessive inclination to believe in the obvious as the only fact, he got to the point where he regarded petrifactions as accidental formations. Their true nature had been known much earlier by the genial potter of the Renaissance, Bernard Palissy. In his doubt of the biblical story of the Flood, which was supposed to be proven by shells found on mountains, he misunderstood the true geological conception which previously had been so clear to Leonardo and later to Goethe. But, in sharp contrast to Goethe, he had a fine feeling for Newton's mathematical physics and argued in favor of the inductive method.

In the numerous instances where Voltaire rejected the correct theory his error was due to the fact that for the refutation of his objections a century of research was necessary; thus he rejected the doctrine of the conservation of energy because energy disappears after the collision of rigid bodies, and because energy is formed in the animal. So his contemporaries as well as he failed to find the source of the energy when a spark creates fire.

In Cirey, Voltaire had a physical apparatus and the chemical equipment then known, a laboratory and a dark-room. He was the first to carry out a not un-

important optical experiment suggested by Newton.
His observation that the same amounts of different
liquids at a different temperature do not adopt the
average temperature brought him very near to the
discovery of the specific warmth of the physical body.

Had he developed a little further his ideas of the
calcination of metals and of the compound nature of
air, he would have been the first to discover oxygen
and the reduction of oxygen, which actually was discovered by Scheele, in 1774, forty years later. Not
without reason have the great scientists of the nineteenth century paid the highest respect to Voltaire's
chemical researches.

It was science that enabled him to note the difference between the war history of his time and the
history of civilization. In hundreds of his critical
studies and letters he expressed courageously and
clearly the fundamental ideas of science. As historian
and poet, thanks to his intellectual suppleness, he saw
events alternately from the general, human standpoint (as in his *History of Charles XII*) and from the
super-human standpoint from which the earth is seen
as one heavenly body among the others (as in his
Essai sur les Mœurs and in *Micromegas*).

A study of history founded like that of Voltaire on
science, shows the wretchedness of the hitherto existing war history of man—this account of incessant
fighting for a few strips of land—and the unworthi-
ness of its ecclesiastical history—this fabric of man's
feverish dreams about abodes and manifestations of
superior beings, camouflaged with the name religion.

Since Erasmus' time there had been no one to hate
and abhor war as much as Voltaire.

He has told us of the circumstances which led him
to the philosophy of history. One day Madame de
Châtelet told him that she (who was so expert in
mathematics and physics) was actually disgusted
with history. "What good is it to me, a Frenchwoman,
living at her country-seat, to know that in Sweden
Egil succeeded Hakon or that Ottoman in Turkey
was a son of Ortogul? With pleasure I read the history of the Greeks and Romans, which offers me great
and attractive pictures. But never have I been able

to finish reading the history of a modern nation: a mess of unimportant events without connection, a lot of battles that don't mean anything."

Voltaire answered that the study of history would not be a waste of time, if one would dismiss the particulars which are so boring and unbelievable, and retain the fundamentals which are hidden by these particulars. That in this way chaos would be transformed into an intelligible picture. Instead of a motley multitude of names, dates and fables we would produce history itself.

For him laws, art, literature and customs were the main goals of the historian; the inconsequent details were an unnecessary ballast which had to be removed. Thus he became the creator of the modern history of civilization.

Not as a historian, but as a poet Voltaire was esteemed most highly by his contemporaries. He was a born poet; from his boyhood he wrote excellent verse, and this gift stayed with him until he was an old man. No one has surpassed him either in prose or in poetry in that main virtue of writers which is called conciseness—moreover, there is in his best verse a certain melody akin to that with which a hundred years later Lamartine won all hearts.

By his contemporaries Voltaire was overestimated as a poet. To Frederick the Great as well as to Catherine II he appeared a greater epic poet than Homer, the equal of Vergil and Ariosto. Nowadays he hardly counts as epic poet. As a lyric poet his contemporaries put him on a plane with Horace with whom he can hardly be compared. What we today esteem most are his short epigrammatic verses. These and the short philosophical novels, his witty and phantastic rogueries in the form of stories, tales or letters, are the most perfect things he did. That portion of his work will continue to survive.

Immortality will probably be allotted to *Candide* also, with its keen satire of Pope's and Leibnitz's smug contentment with the system of the world, with its impudent description of the fate of the Confident and the Faithful.

As a tragedian and in general as a dramatist Vol-

taire represents the transition from Racine to Victor
Hugo. After passing through the period of tragedies
in his youth his plays become more and more eloquent melodramas like those of Hugo, but in the classical style. Great as was Voltaire's comic talent, abun-
dantly rich in wit as he could be outside of the stage,
he lacked real talent as a writer of comedy. He did
not produce one comedy of any value. Whoever seeks
pleasure in his incomparable wit must not look for
it in his theatrical works.

Horace Walpole said: "The world is a comedy for
him who thinks, a tragedy for him who feels."

Since Voltaire thought as well as felt, his satirical
humor changed to terror at the sight of the crimes
of tyrannical fanaticism.

As the inconsiderate and shameless mocker with
the devilish wit which metamorphosed to the Angel
of Light, the great Lucifer himself, he inspired respect even in men and women of little sensitiveness.

When in Petersburg Catherine of Russia stepped
into the room where Voltaire's books, which she had
bought after his death, were kept, she bowed deeply
before his portrait and said to her secretary Wag-
nière: "This is the man to whom I owe all I know and
all I am."

To the Prince de Ligne she said a few years later:
"I wanted to profit from intercourse with your ingenious men ending with *-istes* (the encyclopedists); I
have tried them; I had them come to me; sometimes
I wrote to them; they bored me and didn't understand me. Just one was my good protector, Voltaire.
Do you know that it was he who taught me in modern
fashion? He afforded me the pleasure of reading his
works, and taught me much, while at the same time
he entertained me."

To her Voltaire was the trumpet of glory personified.

7

To be sure, he was not great like Michel Angelo, or
deep like Spinoza, or filled with the human understanding of Molière.

But compare him with Luther! Even today Luther attracts by his vigor, his viewpoint of the people, his unchanging aim to discover the truth. But he was and remained a superstitious peasant. Voltaire was free from superstition. Luther was essentially intolerant and became more and more so. Voltaire is, in spite of his passion for reform, not second to Luther, the great advocate of tolerance. Luther, with all his appeal to the right of Nature as opposed to the Catholic asceticism which was contrary to Nature, had no notion of science. Voltaire was a scientist of the first order.

Luther made a deeper impression upon the popular mind, but the impression was limited and limiting. Luther freed. Voltaire still frees.

In the public consciousness Voltaire is still the great mocker. But in the second half of his life those around him looked upon him with different eyes. The Countess de Genlis, who as a devout Catholic had a deep aversion for Voltaire, but nevertheless, visited him in Ferney, wrote of him: "His portraits and busts resemble him very much. But no artist has reproduced his eyes. I expected to find them gleaming and fiery—and they really have the most spiritual expression I have ever known. But at the same time there is something velvet-like in them, an indescribable mildness."

The same lady, after having seen the grounds near Ferney, wrote: "He is here greater than in his books; for everywhere one notices a genial kindness. One cannot imagine that the same hand which has written so much that is godless, false and malicious should have created so much that is noble, sensible and useful. He showed us his estate, explained to us in a simple, natural manner everything he has built or started to work on, and by no means seemed to pride himself upon it. I don't know any one else who could do it."

Is it not strange that Voltaire ends as seventy years later Goethe's Faust dreamed to end, "a great lord blessing everywhere the inhabitants of a free and happy colony of which he is the founder"?

If one stands in the foyer of the Théâtre Français,

that room which for centuries has been one of the
focal points of intellectual Europe, one sees excellent
busts of all the more or less prominent dramatists of
France, in rows along the walls, a whole army of the
intellect, in marble. In the first large hall, opposite
the mirror in front of which stand the busts of Corneille and Molière, there is a single dominating statue,
Houdon's famous sitting Voltaire. It towers above
the busts, with his indescribable smile and that clever
hand grasping the back of the chair.

Such was not the lot of the man in life. Abhorred
by Louis XV, he actually was banned from Paris
much of his life and when, during his last visit to
Paris, he died, permission to have him buried there
was refused. He had always feared that his body
would be thrown in the carrion-pit. In his youth,
when the clergy refused a grave to his good friend,
the great and noble actress Adrienne Lecouvreur,
he wrote these famous lines:

> Ah, verrai-je toujours ma faible nation,
> Incertaine en ses vœux, flétrir ce qu'il admire,
> Nos mœurs avec nos lois toujours se contredire
> Et le Français volage endormi sous l'empire
> De la superstition!

When he died he, too, was denied a grave, and the
slim, little corpse escaped the danger of being thrown
into some hole in a waste field, thanks only to a
nephew who had him brought in deepest secrecy to
the Abbey Scellières in Champagne, in the cellar of
which the simple coffin was hid. Later the prior of
the abbey was dismissed because he had permitted
the coffin to remain there.

In this abbey the coffin stayed for thirteen years,
nameless. Then, in July of the year 1791, during the
revolution, the sarcophagus, drawn by twelve white
horses, made its solemn entry into Paris. He received
an ovation that Paris has never before or since accorded the remains of King or Emperor. When, fifty
years later Napoleon's coffin was brought home from
St. Helena, the enthusiasm was trifling in comparison.

In the year 1814, however, some young reaction-
aries broke into the Panthéon at night, gathered

Voltaire's bones in a sack, took them through night and fog to a dump heap, and buried them in a place where they could never again be found.

Thus, on the dump heap ended the earthly remains of one who had been adored by his contemporaries as their genius, who during the revolution had passed for more than a demi-god and in whom posterity sees a mighty figure belonging not merely to literary history but to world history.

II

CHILDHOOD

1

FRANÇOIS MARIE AROUET was born on November 21, 1694, in the parish of Paris, Saint-André-des-Arts, the fifth and last child of an able and honest man, François Arouet. From 1685 to 1692, that is from his twenty-sixth to his forty-third year, his father held the position of notary in the Châtelet in the Department of Justice, and soon afterward was promoted to the distinguished and profitable position of Receiver of Court-Fees, Fines and Taxes, of the Chamber of Accounts.

François Arouet, who in the course of time became to his son a hard and stubborn father, was in reality a reasonable, strictly honest, educated Parisian, socially inclined, with a taste for good literature and refined social life.

His family—tanners, cloth-merchants and farmers —can be traced as far back as 1523, to a master-tanner named Helenus Arouet, in Poitou. In the course of centuries the Arouets raised themselves from the level of artisans to the upper middle-class, were given the then especially prized honor of having their burying-places assigned in the community churches, allied themselves by marriage with lawyers and tradesmen, became themselves owners of large drapers-shops and added their names to the landed gentry. They were considered notables in their districts, and became landowners of Pas-de-Cygne, and La-Motte-au-Fées. In Paris they were drapers.

Voltaire's father was in constant connection, as attorney, with the most prominent names of France; he was notary of the Duke de Bethune-Sully, of the Duke de Praslin and of the Duke de Saint-Simon, and it is said that these great lords treated him less as a legal advisor than as a friend.

In the few passages of his memoirs in which Saint-Simon deigns to mention Voltaire, he does not forget to refer to the relation between Voltaire's father and his own: "He was the son of my father's notary, and I often saw him delivering papers for signature. He never could make anything of this freethinking son of his whose freethinking has in the end made his success under the cloak of the name Volterre."

Two contemporaries of Voltaire's father, the Dukes of Saint-Simon and of Richelieu, were godfathers to Voltaire's older brother Armand.

In June, 1683, François Arouet the father had married a cheerful, lovable young girl who, like himself, came from Poitou, but was of noble family. Marie Catherine Daumart de Mauléon was related to the first families of the province. Of charming appearance, she had, according to the assertion of her famous son, all the intellect which could be found in her family. Her father and brother were office-holders, her father what nowadays would be called record-keeper (*greffier criminel*) in the Parliament. Her brother, who was Controller-General of the Royal Guard, had early introduced her at court where she got an impression of the gilded superficial society that crowded the drawing rooms of the palace at Versailles. She brought the elder Voltaire no dowry, but probably it was to her that he was indebted for his influential acquaintances, not only those just mentioned, but such powerful families as the Caumartins, the Nicolais and the Chateuneufs. It was she, too, who made her house the rendezvous of the wits of the time.

The family Daumart had its escutcheon: a silver tower on an azure field. When, in 1696, an escutcheon was bestowed upon Marie Daumart's husband, mainly for the reason that the revenue office collected taxes on such distinctions, he was given permission to add three red flames in a gold field to the silver tower. In *l'Armorial* of 1696 he figures as *François Arouet, conseiller du roy, receveur les épices à la chambre des Comptes porte d'or à trois flammes de gueules.*

Madame Arouet's was a youthful, natural, lively nature. A good friend of Ninon de Lenclos, she liked the frank, gay tone she found at Ninon's house. Her husband was Ninon's notary. She was not altogether free from aristocratic prejudices, and it was no doubt she who induced Arouet to apply for heraldic colors. He was so far from vain about it that he jokingly remarked the escutcheon was rightly due him, since he had paid for it. She loved the gay social life of a young married woman and was very popular; and, since she had friends among the talented, worldly men who visited her house, she did not seem to have escaped becoming, about the year 1700, the subject of gossip which was, however, more frivolous than malicious. Her husband never made complaint.

She brought five children into the world, but lost two at an early age.

The eldest son was altogether different from the younger. Rather heavy, taciturn, reserved and a little clumsy, he had that kind of talent which felt itself drawn to theology, and he studied, not unsuccessfully, in the seminary of the Oratoire. In contrast to his younger brother, he was a family man, attentive to all his relatives, dutiful towards his father who, indeed, was highly satisfied with this son and according to the custom of the time made a will bequeathing his office of fee and fine collector to the boy after his death. In their boyhood the two brothers got along fairly well, and, in spite of his slower temper, Armand, the elder by more than ten years, did not lack good ideas, when the friends of the family amused themselves by egging on the brothers to play practical jokes on each other. But before long an estrangement took place, presumably because of the more brilliant education of the younger and the distinguished acquaintance he had already begun in his boyhood to build up. The attachment quickly became an aversion. At home the younger played the rôle of the prodigal son who thought himself rejected and disdained, the elder became the good son and father's darling. But it never came to pass that the father relented and killed the fatted calf for the prodigal.

Armand appeared to his younger brother, who in frivolous spite always called him the Jansenist, as the type of the dull, pious fanatic. Did he not become an enthusiastic adherent of a certain deacon Pâris, one of the most prominent exponents of Jansenism, a man whose pretended miracles had attracted general attention, caused considerable excitement and resulted in police prosecution? Armand himself was under arrest for a short time. At the time of his boyish pranks Voltaire had never turned to his brother to soothe his enraged father. He would prefer any one of his friends in the house. One mitigation of these strained relations took place, lasting only a short time. When both were elderly and Armand (in December, 1739) had an apoplectic stroke, Voltaire was so deeply moved that he offered to travel to Paris in case his brother wished to see him. But when the latter improved the atmosphere of reconciliation came to an end.

As a young boy François bore the nickname Zozo, and we still have a letter of the year 1704, written by Armand, but signed by both: Zozo, Arouet.

A sister born eight years before Voltaire, Marguerite-Catherine, who married François Mignot, an official of the chamber of accounts in Paris, died in September, 1726. She was a simple and dignified woman who exhausted herself in her maternal duties; neglected at first, but after her death grievously mourned by her wandering poet brother, who did all he could for the children she left behind. It was not at all easy for him to win over the oldest daughter; in 1738 she came to Cirey, where he married her to a Captain Denis, an honorable and able man, a Knight of Saint-Louis. Widowed in the year 1744, she became the housekeeper of her uncle. She was a sister-in-law of the abbé Mignot, a good-hearted and at the same time practical man, who collected sinecures, got his income from the abbey in Scellières and held the position of a senator in the Parliament of Paris, but who is remembered chiefly because, after Voltaire's death, he removed the poet's body and thereby saved it from insult.

Among the guests of the Arouets there was a Monsieur de Lesseville whose ancestor owed his success to a unique incident and had been ennobled. One day he loaned King Henry IV, when the latter was in great embarrassment, the sum of 20,000 livres without accepting a promissory note. His descendants had enriched themselves, become members of Parliament, affected escutcheons and liveried servants, held big hunts and spent a great deal of money. Patiently Madame Arouet listened to the hunting-stories of M. de Lesseville, found it flattering to receive such a mighty senator and had hopes that the acquaintance would set her younger son upon the pathway to glory and honor. She arranged for François to be a school-mate of a nephew of M. de Lesseville, who was meant to become a town-councillor. She hoped that joint studies would result in a joint profession. But she died too soon to see her ambitions realized, and when her husband assumed them the exacting father and his free-souled son were immediately and impossibly antagonistic.

The beautiful and lively mother died in July, 1701, at the age of forty, when her famous son was not seven years old. He suffered an immense loss. One can see from his intellectual stamp, that he was in want of the influence and tenderness of a mother, although he never speaks of this privation.

2

The house in the diocese Saint André des Arts, in which Voltaire was born, is unknown. Gone, too, is the house which, shortly after the birth of the child, was assigned to his father as his official residence, a spacious apartment in a big building which was situated where the rue de Jérusalem and the rue de Nazareth crossed. The largest room had a beautiful ceiling of vaulted arches.

This house in which Arouet's youngest son spent his boyhood was situated opposite the house of

Nicolas Boileau Despréaux. In 1683, the notary had, together with a colleague, drawn up Boileau's will, and their connection did not end with that piece of business. The poet was a frequent guest of the family Arouet, and during his vacations Arouet with his wife and little son not infrequently visited the house in Auteuil, of whose garden and gardener Voltaire speaks in his poem *Epître à Boileau*. It does not seem, however, that the famous Despréaux succeeded in entertaining the young wife; she said of him: Good book, but stupid man (*Bon livre mais sot homme*). True, Boileau was thirty-five years her senior.

Arouet knew a still more famous French poet, the great Corneille himself, as a frequent drinking companion. But from what his son says, Pierre Corneille succeeded no better in entertaining the husband than had Boileau in entertaining the wife. Voltaire writes: "He told me the great man was the most boring mortal he had ever seen, and his conversation the dryest" (letter of September, 1761).

Among the gifted men who were intimate friends of the family and who took a friendly interest in the little boy, the Abbé de Chateauneuf must be mentioned. He and his brother, the Marquis, were Savoyards who had made their fortunes in Paris. The marquis had been French Ambassador to Constantinople and to The Hague and was an educated and sensible man. The Abbé, best known as Voltaire's godfather, received a yearly income from an ecclesiastical property and was a merry worldling and a fellow of the circle which gathered in Le Temple around the Archprior of Vendôme, that descendant of Henry IV and Gabrielles d'Estrés, who, according to the description of Saint-Simon, possessed all the vices of his brother, the duc de Vendôme. He was excessive in every natural and unnatural way, devoted to drinking, and "dishonest to the core which, by the way, was rotted with venereal disease." But in his youth he had been a rather nice fellow and remained all through his life extraordinarily clever and entertaining. About the prior's best friend, the Abbé de Chateauneuf, the same Saint-Simon has only good to say. He calls him "a man of good companionship, sought-after in the best circles." A friend of the much loved Anacreonic poet Chaulieu and of Ninon de Lenclos, he might have made through the latter the acquaintance of the family Arouet. Just as warmly received in the house was the noble lyricist Rochebrune, whose bastard Voltaire calls himself jokingly in a poem to the Maréchal de Richelieu.

Another of the intimate circle of the aging Ninon, as well as one of the closest friends of the house Arouet, was the Abbé Nicolas Gédoyn. He is said to have shared with Chateauneuf the honor of being the last lover of Ninon. After having been a Jesuit for ten years he left the order and freely took part in social life, lived on the income from a canonship of the Saint-Chapelle, which the Court had granted him, and had, as Voltaire says, "no other home than ours." He was a fine and learned man, a good narrator, entertaining, but often too passionate in disputes. He had been one of the most eager to support Boileau in his battle for the acknowledgment of the superiority of the writers of antiquity over the moderns to whom Perrault dared give the palm. Gédoyn would have liked to canonize Vergil and Horace and cited their excellences with an uncontrolled fire which highly pleased Madame Arouet and which Rochebrune did his best to arouse in order to amuse the lady of the house.

As a child Voltaire certainly learned many things from Gédoyn; but Zozo's real teacher was the Abbé de Chateauneuf. The first qualities the boy displayed were an attentive liveliness, and a susceptibility to impressions which struck sparks of wit and rouguery from him. Chateauneuf, who, like the whole circle, was irreverent, amused himself by letting the four-year-old child learn by heart verses from Lourdet's impious *Moïsiade*. This mockery of the Bible was taught the child at a tender age, and his mother seems to have found this a good joke.

Entranced by the charm and liveliness of his little god-child, Chateauneuf brought him up in his own way, using the admiration the child naturally would feel for the older man.

He introduced Zozo at the house of Ninon de Lenclos. Voltaire insists that, at that time, he was thirteen, but that is an impossibility, for by that time Ninon had been dead two years. He visited her at the age of ten or eleven, and it is certain that the verses written by the little boy aroused her interest. He wrote verse before prose. Verse was his natural language.

There can be no doubt that these verses which procured his admission to Ninon's house are "The Petition of an Old Soldier"—which in several editions of Voltaire is postdated. One day the old soldier came to the school which little François attended and asked one of the teachers, Father Porée, to write for him a petition to the King's son (le Grand Dauphin) in whose regiment he had served. As Father Porée for the moment was busy, he told the invalid to apply to little François Arouet who, after half an hour, handed him the following enchanting petition in verse:

Noble sang du plus grand des rois,
Son amour et son espérance,
Vous qui sans régner sur la France
Regnez sur les cœurs des François;

Pourrez-vous souffrir que ma veine,
Par un effort ambitieux,
Ose vous offrir une étrenne,
Vous qui n'en recevez que de la main des Dieux?

La nature en vous faisant naître,
Vous étrenna de ses plus doux attraits
Et fit voir dans vos premiers traits
Que le fils de Louis était digne de l'être.

Tous les à l'envie vous firent leurs présents;
Mars vous donna la force et le courage,
Minerve, des vos jeunes ans,
Ajouta la sagesse au feu bouillant de l'âge,

L'immortel Apollon vous donna la beauté,
Mais un Dieu plus puissant que j'implore en mes peines
Voulut me donner mes étrennes
En vous donnant la libéralité.

Nobody will deny that this as the product of a ten-year-old boy is extraordinary.

One could wish that Voltaire in his report of his

visit to Ninon had a friendly word for her and had not restricted himself to a description of her resemblance to a mummy. The anecdote which he tells of Chateauneuf and Ninon (which, on the other hand, is ascribed to Gédoyn, and not Chateauneuf, by the author of the *Vie de Mademoiselle de Lenclos*), seems to be invented to show how she was able to attract her suitors. Chateauneuf wooed her; she let him languish for some time and then set a certain day. When he asked why she had chosen that special day, she answered that she wanted to celebrate her seventieth birthday. In reality at seventy she had long abandoned all gallantry. Her house was a place where youths met to learn good taste. Such strict judges as Saint-Simon and Madame de Sévigné speak of her with the highest respect. To transfer the anecdote to Gédoyn is still more absurd, since he had not been introduced to her before 1694, when she was seventy-four years old. With him she would have had to celebrate her eightieth birthday.

It is true that Ninon was pleased with the bright boy brought by Chateauneuf, so much pleased that she willed him two thousand francs to buy books. There is something alluring and drolly surprising in this friendship of the eighty-four-year-old Ninon and the ten-year-old Voltaire. The abdicating queen of beauty and of free eroticism, the friend of Molière, did homage to the young heir to the throne of the mind. Many times Voltaire recalls with warmth the benefactor of his childhood.

In contrast to the mischievous tone in which he speaks of her in *Défense de mon Oncle* is, first of all, the pretty play *Le Dépositaire,* performed in the provinces in 1767, which was written solely for her glorification. It is taken from an anecdote told by the Abbé Chateauneuf in his *"Dialogue on Ancient Music."* Moliére is reported to have said that no one ever had so keen a sense of the ridiculous as Ninon de Lenclos, and that when he read to her his *Tartuffe* (probably the first three acts) she told him something that had happened to her with a gentleman whom she described so vividly that his own Tartuffe seemed to him pale by comparison. Her friend Gourbille had entrusted part of his property to the gallant and philosophical Ninon, and another part to a man supposed to be very pious. The latter kept the deposit for himself, while she who had not been supposed to be very conscientious returned her part intact. In the play Ninon is thirty-five to forty years old and is pictured as a lady of good breeding who sees through the character of the other trustee.

A finer and more impressive description of her is in the dialogue *Madame de Maintenon et Mademoiselle de Lenclos*. It contains an entire philosophy of life: Madame de Maintenon and Ninon, who had been friends at school, had lost touch after Madame de Maintenon had become so important a person at court. Madame de Maintenon, weary of a life spent in splendor and luxury at the side of a King who is no longer capable of amusement, visits Ninon and asks her to give up her free habits to come to court, and give her the companionship she missed. In Ninon's refusal there is a gentle, Horatian epicureanism in which she expresses her preference for a modest but free existence.

Finally, the letter dated 1771, *Sur Mlle. de Nenclas,* is an account of the still fresh traditions of Ninon, of anecdotes about her, of verses written against her by rejected adorers, or in her honor, by accepted. The famous Dutch astronomer Huyghens wrote that epigram which is rather frivolous for an astronomer:

Elle a cinq instruments, dont je suis amoureux.
Les deux premiers ses mains, les deux autres ses yeux . . .

We must not fail to mention another frequent visitor to the house on the corner of the rue Jérusalem: it was the Intendant of Finance, Louis Urbain Lefèvre de Caumartin, Marquis de Saint-Ange, descended from a family famous in the times of Louis XIII. In the circle of poets and musicians which met in Madame Arouet's house he felt at home and like the great gentleman he was, seems to have gained young Voltaire's confidence to an unusual extent. It was he who interposed between father and son at their quarrel after Voltaire's violent love affair in

Holland in 1714. He, too, was the first to encourage
the young poet to write his *Henriade*. It was Caumartin who supplied him with most of the material used
in *The Century of Louis XIV*. Saint-Simon calls him
an especially mild-tempered man, socially inclined,
who, despite his courtierlike tone and his haughty
attitude, found pleasure in making himself oblig-
ing. He knew all the anecdotes of the old court and
related them charmingly from a memory that retained everything read or seen. Voltaire, in 1716, paid
him homage in his poem to the prince of Vêndome:

> Caumartin porte en son cerveau
> De son temps l'histoire vivante;
> Caumartin est toujours nouveau
> A mon oreille qu'il enchante;
> Car dans sa tête sont écrits
> Et tous les faits et tous les dits
> Des grands hommes, des beaux esprits;
> Mille charmantes bagatelles,
> Des chansons vieilles et nouvelles,
> Des ridicules de Paris.

His brother, the Abbé Caumartin, who later became Bishop of Blois and a member of the French
Academy, was one of the stars in the notary's house.
He was one of the noblest and most ingenious men
in France. No one understood so well as he how
to give an appropriate answer, to judge correctly,
to phrase a compliment with a hidden sting, to lull
into a feeling of security, to penetrate a secret or
to observe an eloquent silence. His teasing wit was
sometimes almost prophetic of Voltaire, only less
sharp, less powerful, though no less subtle.

3

Although the imagination of the little boy was not
—like that of Victor Hugo a century later—centered
on his scenic and architectural surroundings, one of
Voltaire's earliest deep impressions must have been
of the Paris about him.

The Paris of that time was that of Louis XIV who
died when Voltaire was twenty-one.

The architecture of Louis XIV is a triumph of classical dignity and loftiness, a world of regular and imposing mansions, gardens, bridges, churches and triumphal arches. It breaks with every national tradition, despises everything gothic. It satisfied taste by observing the rules which can be derived from the Antique, i.e., the Greek-Roman, still, as by Voltaire, considered to be one style, although it included eight centuries and two countries of profound inner differences. Hence the style of Louis XIV has its monotonous impressiveness, its obliteration of everything domestic and native, its uncompromising fight against local character.

Catherine II was so great an admirer of Louis XIV that she could not bear to hear the least belittlement of him. One day, the Prince de Ligne said to her: "Your Majesty at least might admit that this great King, whenever he wanted to take a walk on the bank of a canal, had to have an absolutely straight avenue, a hundred and twenty feet wide. He did not know, as you do, what a narrow bridge, a brook or a meadow meant."

To get an idea of the taste of the time take a collection of engravings of the old Paris, say by Perelle, and eliminate whatever partakes of the architecture and intellectual life of the Middle Ages, eliminate all points and spires like the wonderful Sainte Chapelle and the mighty Notre Dame, with its rich, temperamental world of fantastic figures. There is a transformation of Nature into Art in all things, every flower-bed is transformed into arabesques ingeniously flourished, every meandering brook is canalized to the regulated splendor of a fountain. The cave becomes a grotto, the castle a mansion with long horizontal lines and flat roof, the citadel a palace. While the fort-like construction on the main part of Chantilly, erected under Francis I, was really its chief claim to beauty, the aim in Fontainebleau is majesty combined with charm. This applies even more to Versailles, built in revolt against Nature in a desolate region.

The Paris of the Renaissance revealed itself in the *Place Royale* begun in 1604 by order of Henry IV.

There still stood the original bronze statue of Louis XIII—later replaced by another. The horse was the work of Daniele de Volterra, the figure of the King the work of Biar (1639).

The old Paris, with whose slang Voltaire shows himself most familiar, had its center on the "Island" where the symmetrical and harmonious structures of the Place Dauphine had raised their heads ever since the day of Richelieu, over a crowd of pedestrians, sedans and spirited horses drawing carriages. The carriages were heavy things, but beautiful, belling out at the top and looking like little houses with windows and roofs.

The great meeting places at that time were the Seine bridges as were a century later the galleries of the Palais Royal, and still another half century later the inner Boulevards.

The statue of Henry IV on the Pont Neuf was a center of the Paris of that day, and presumably it made a grave impression on the little Zozo. Henry IV soon became his hero. It was largely through Voltaire that this King subsequently became France's national hero, for at that time his memory was overshadowed by that of the Roi Soleil.

The Pont Neuf itself looked altogether different from any of the Seine bridges today. The Pont Neuf, Pont St. Michel, Pont au Change, Ponte Notre Dame, Pont Marie, Pont Saint Landry were not far apart, and several of them were built upon, like the Ponte Vecchio in Florence of today.

In the Place des Victoires stood, not the present equestrian statue, but Louis XIV on foot, crowned by the Goddess of Victory. Vanquished soldiers in chains surrounded the base.

On the boulevards could be seen Louis' heavy triumphal arches which are still there, with their cold trophies and allegories, the Porte Saint Denis and the Porte Saint Martin (1673 and 1674).

What the Court was to the people, Versailles was to the city of Paris. For a moment Madame Arouet won a foothold there, as later her son was to win a foothold and fight desperately to keep it.

Versailles was the pride of France as well as of

the King. It was the center of the empire; from an intellectual point of view, indeed, the center of Europe. It was a small world which represented the finest that could be extracted from the greater world without. How near and yet how out of reach it stood, the Palace of Versailles, object of admiration, home of mercy, with vestibules and courts, with vast cultivated parks with avenues and galleries instead of garden-walks, with Thetis' grotto in which Apollo the Sun God rests at Thetis' side. As Charles Perault suggested: "like the king who comes to Versailles to rest, after having done good to all mankind." There were lakes and cascades, there was the fountain of the pyramide filled with Tritons and Delphins, there was Latona's basin, neatly raked walks; nicely cultivated lawns, nicely raked beds, nicely pruned trees, nicely curry-combed horses, nicely powdered noblewomen, nicely peruked noblemen, the whole a sanctuary with its Holy of Holies, the place where the sovereign lived and breathed, blessing France and its vicinity. Here was the hall, where he took his meals, sitting alone at the table, dining—as told by Elizabeth Charlotte—on four plates of different soups, a whole pheasant, one partridge, a big dish of salad, mutton with garlic and gravy, a plate of pastry, then fruit and marmalade. Here, finally, was the Holiest of Holies, the bedroom where he slept, every inch a king.

It is very instructive to turn the pages of one of the traveler's guides to Paris of that time, and to see what was considered most worth while. Here is, for instance, one of 1727, the first year of Louis XV. It contains six to seven hundred pages in two thick volumes, is composed by a certain J. C. Nemeitz, Privy Councillor to the Prince of Waldeck, and is entitled: *Séjour à Paris, c'ést à dire instructions fidèles pour les Voyageurs de condition comment ils se doivent conduire, s'ils veulont faire un bon usage de leur temps et argent durant leur séjour à Paris.*

One arrived at Paris either by the common diligence or by the mail-coach. The postilion directed the traveler to an inn, and, if one gave him a tip, commended one to the favorable notice of the host. Those

who came to Paris to study the language did well to
take up their residence in the Faubourg St. Germain,
the resort of all foreigners, where most language
teachers lived and where were the riding schools.
There were theaters in this suburb and the opera was
not far.

One should be warned against the fallacy that he
could count on being served good food everywhere
in Paris. If one could not afford to employ his own
cook, it was best to take his meals at the regular
tables of the landlords. Of intellectual nourishment
the studies of French, mathematics and drawing were
fashionable for foreigners. The chief ambition in
studying the language was to be able to write a letter
in correct French. Models regarding style were Voi-
ture, Bussy-Rabutin and Fontenelle.

The wise traveler did well to keep a certain reserve in his intercourse with the countesses and mar-
quises whom he met at the hotels; otherwise: rapid
disappearance of the money that was to have paid
the costs of his stay. There was no want of recreation. The gardens in the Tuileries were a nice prom-
enade, also the park of the Luxembourg. However,
the latter was supposed to be healthier, since where
the Seine flowed past the Tuileries evil vapors arose.
The Palais Luxembourg, then called also Palais
d'Orléans, was freer of access and easier to inspect
then than it is now.

The sensible stranger took only moderate part in
balls, and masquerades, also was moderate in gambling. There was gambling everywhere, and the game
offered an opportunity of meeting prominent ladies
and gentlemen. There were also more innocent enter-
tainments. The traveler should by no means miss the
public festivals, the ecclesiastical processions. About
Easter time there was a good Passion concert, and
choral singing, especially in the cloister Val de Grâce
(finished in 1669), the vaults and decoration of which
were of interest.

Molière himself sang of it in a poem in which,
typical of his age, he classed Pierre Mignard with the
greatest painters of the Italian Renaissance. These

were mentioned in a most curious sequence:

Et Jules, Annibal, Raphael, Michel-Ange,
Les Mignards de leur siècle.

Les Ténèbres, as the Passion was called, was played beautifully by the royal orchestra.

On Maundy Thursday the King washed the feet of twenty-three boys and gave them food. Princes of the Blood waited on them and each boy was served thirteen courses. On the first of May the procession with the reliques of the Holy St. Denis took place. On the third day of Whitsuntide the young people of Suresnes (near Paris) amused themselves at a game which consisted in pulling off the neck of a goose.

On the eves of all important holidays the King, after receiving the Sacrament, touched with his hand several hundred sick who were brought to him by the charity physicians. He touched their cheeks, made the sign of the cross, and said: The King touches you, may God heal you!

Thus, there were plenty of public attractions. The park at Versailles was never closed. One could stroll about there as much as one pleased, save when the King promenaded.

4

When little François Arouet was nine years old, his father took him (in October, 1703) to the school of the Jesuits who at that time were in charge of the famous Collège Louis-le-Grand, directly behind the Sorbonne. In its time it was vigorously opposed by the University, but had only gained thereby. Famous Jesuits had lectured there to as many as three thousand students. When under Louis XIV the Jesuits gained complete control at Court and after the King, in 1674, had attended the performance of a tragedy produced in the classical manner by their pupils, he permitted them to put his name on their façade, and over-night the inscription *Collegium Societatis Jesu* became *Collegium Ludovici Magni*.

At the beginning of the eighteenth century this college was more fashionable than any other. The most prominent families of the aristocracy sent their sons there. After every vacation the street Saint Jacques was jammed with carriages in which arrived elegant young men with sword in belt, and when they descended, the street rang with the calls of their lackeys announcing their arrival: *Monsieur le comte de Guiche! Monseigneur le prince de Rohan! Monseigneur le duc de Montmorency!* Here Voltaire made a number of acquaintances who later were to prove of much use and great joy to him.

The Jesuits had early acquired a reputation as teachers and educators. They considered it highly important to instill self-confidence into their pupils. Their Christianity was, a half century before Grundvig, a happy Christianity. They tried to avoid the mistake the Jansenists had made, of suppressing eagerness and energy by their insistence on the fundamental corruptness of human nature damned by its sin; on the contrary, the Jesuits tried to cultivate energy, to prevent despair, to encourage ambition and the proper use of the intelligence. Moreover, they always knew how to capture the attention of their pupils, to instruct and at the same time to entertain and amuse them. They were never loath to arrange public contests and plays, to further the physical and mental development of the youths.

Naturally, the lessons given in 1703 in the College Louis-le-Grand were not of the modern type. The curriculum included mathematics, physics, chemistry, rhetoric, grammar and elemental philosophy. Latin was the foundation of the whole course. Whatever the pupils learned in general education was taught in Latin and was concerned with Latin authors. The object—as strange as it may seem—was to enable the pupils to write Latin verses and to deliver Latin orations. French was taught only as the knowledge of it fell like crumbs from the richly covered table of the Latin language. A knowledge of French was necessary in order to translate. Greek, it is true, was on the schedule, but was rather neglected. Hence, Voltaire never became a good Hellenist, but was an excellent Latinist.

So deeply rooted was the domination of Latin that for centuries the tragedies and comedies in which the Jesuits let their French pupils act for their entertainment and the strengthening of the memory were written in Latin. It was even regarded as a dangerous radical gesture, when Father Porée, at the time Voltaire went to school, permitted purely French plays to be given in French. It became customary for the Latin tragedy to have its stage in the court-yard of the school, where an immense tent protected the spectators seated in a horseshoe in three rows and in the windows leading to the court. On the day the prizes were distributed a ballet and a tragedy were given, the expenses were met by the King. The "Little Comedy" (ludi priores) was written in French and was played in a second court; a screen was put up to isolate the theater, the stage of which faced opposite the library. Later a play by Père de Cerceau was so successful that its reputation went as far as the Court and the students had to go to the Tuileries and give it in the Galérie des Ambassadeurs.

Besides the plays there were mock-trials. The pupils conducted "law-suits," that is, made speeches in defense of medicine, rhetoric, poetry, philosophy, architecture, etc.—a rather childish idea of the good fathers! But even these sham trials were preferable to the horrible debates held at that time in the University of Copenhagen, and they fulfilled their purpose of training future orators for the bar or for public life.

The students boarded and lodged in the school. Of the more noble each had his spacious room. It seems that in the daytime the little Arouet shared a room with four others and had the same teachers as they, while at night he had his own cell.

The bright youngster, like other vivid children, was not only very inquisitive but unusually precocious, besides being mischievous and unruly; a true Til Eulenspiegel. He also knew how to interpret the meaning of a half-sung song. His mind was active, vivid, satirical, full of unexpected ideas, never tired

and always daring, as promptly ready for attack as
for pert retort, fond of teasing, irritating, pointing
out mercilessly the weaknesses of teachers and fellow
students. At the same time he was warm-hearted as a
friend and pupil, and at an early age made himself
agreeable by a polite and courteous behavior, which
all his life was a characteristic of nearly every letter
and every verse of this man who before all things
understood the art of pleasing.

5

There was only one teacher whom little François
disliked, Father Lejay. Lejay spoke slowly and with
difficulty; taught rhetoric, but was himself as unelo-
quent as can be conceived. Fond of mocking and teasing as the boy was, he mimicked this teacher and
earned his enmity.

There are many anecdotes illustrating Voltaire's
early developed tendency to criticize dogma and
theology. Nevertheless, Father Lejay's reported out-
burst seems hardly probable: "Wretch! Some day
you'll become the standard of deism in France!"

But for the rest, it is astonishing what warmth of
feeling he showed for his teachers as well as for his
comrades.

As regards the teachers, there are numerous references to permanent attachments on the part of the
pupil, attachments that passed occasionally through
rough weather, but which were sincere and deep. Of
course there was no lack of people who saw in them
only calculated hypocrisy, since there are numerous
writings of Voltaire in which the Jesuits are shown in
an especially disadvantageous light.

However, one is not justified in drawing from this
any unfavorable conclusion as to Voltaire's honesty.
The fundamental Jesuit idea of complete sacrifice
of the individual for a system which eliminates and,
as far as it can, destroys freedom of thought and of
personality, was bound to provoke Voltaire's hatred.
Nevertheless, he preferred the humane moral code
of Jesuitism to the rigor of Pascal and the Jansenists.

Certain as it is that there are intolerable and fanatic personalities among the Jesuits no less than among other men in the Roman Church and outside of it, the noisy and pugnacious are rarely met with among them. No one who has been in touch with Jesuits from the different sections of Europe, be they English, French, Polish or Italian, could help being attracted by their unselfishness, their good breeding, their fineness and sincerity of character. They were at their best as teachers. They were not pedants. They knew how to arouse children's interest, and they had a rich enough knowledge of a variety of subjects to satisfy the curiosity they excited.

If one compares Jesuits as educators with Lutheran theologians, the scales swing violenty in favor of the Jesuits.

There can be no doubt that Voltaire felt the appeal which the Jesuit conscientiousness, gentleness and charm exert upon the impartial, and he has expressed his gratitude for the education they gave him, in strong words. At the age of fifty he writes in a letter dated February 7, 1746, to Father de Latour: "I was educated for seven years by men who took unrewarded and indefatigable pains to form the minds and morals of youth. Is it credible that anyone should fail to have some feeling of gratitude toward such teachers? How? It should be natural for a man to feel pleasure at the sight of the house in which he was born or of the village where he received the paid-for care of a foster-mother; so is it surprising that we should have a heart-felt love for those who gave us unselfish guidance during our first years? If the Jesuits on the Malabar islands have an action pending against Capuchins, what do I care? Is that any reason to be ungrateful toward the men who gave me an appreciation of good literature, who awakened feelings that to the grave will be the consolation of my life? Nothing can erase from my heart the memory of Father Porée who is equally dear to all who have studied under him. Never has anybody made a study more lovable by what he brought to it himself. His lectures were for us such an unmixed delight that I wish it had been the custom in Paris, as in

Athens to attend such lectures at any age; in that case I would have returned often to profit by them. I was so fortunate as to come under the tutelage of more than one Jesuit of Father Porée's character, and I know that his successor was worthy of him. If, finally, I were to be asked what I saw during the seven years I lived in the house of the Jesuits, I should say this: the most diligent, simple and regular life; every hour devoted either to the care of their pupils or to the exercises demanded by their strict confession of faith. I call to witness the thousands educated by them, as I was; there is not one who would belie my words."

All through Voltaire's life one can observe his continued attachment and gratitude to the teachers of his early youth. In 1738 he writes to Father Tournemine: "My very dear and most reverend Father, is it true that my *Mérope* has pleased you? Have you found in it any of the exalted feelings that you have planted in me in my youth? *Si placet, tuum est* (if you like the play it is yours). I always say that when I talk of you and Father Porée."

Apropos of his tragedy *Mérope,* he writes in the following year from Cirey to his friend Thiriot who deserved his friendship so little:

"Hurry in God's name to Father Brumoy; try to see some of these Fathers, my former teachers; they must never become my enemies. Talk with tenderness, with force! Father Brumoy has read *Mérope,* he is satisfied with it; Father Tournemine is enthusiastic about it. God grant that I have deserved their praise! Assure them of my unswerving devotion; I owe it to them; they educated me. He is a monster who does not love those who have fertilized his mind."

In 1729, he sends his *Henriade* to Father Porée with a letter which begins:

"If you, my reverend Father, recall a man who all his life will remember you with the tenderest gratitude and fullest respect, accept this work with some indulgence, and regard me as a son who after an absence of several years presents to his father the fruit of work in an art first learned from him. From the preface you will see what fate this work has had, and I want to learn what fate, in your judgment, it deserves."

Among other things Voltaire asks whether he has spoken of religion "as he should." He writes with the same warmth in the letter of 1738 to Father Tournemine, on the same question—in his fear of hurting and grieving his old benefactors:

"If in several other works, which I carelessly let slip in my youthful hot-headedness and which were never meant for publication, works which have been cut and falsified and which I have never endorsed, if in such works there are remarks of which one can complain, my answer is short: I am ready to discard mercilessly whatever might cause anger, no matter how innocently it may be meant. It does not cost me anything to improve myself and my works."

Even though one must not take Voltaire literally, there can be no doubt that the feeling for his educators was sacred to him.

It was Father Tarteron who first gave the child Horace and Juvenal to read at a tender age, in carefully expurgated editions to be sure. Père de Tournemine was one of the most learned teachers of the institution, as much at home in mathematics as in philosophy, equally skilled in Greek as in Hebrew. He was Voltaire's first guide in literature and we have seen how flattered and happy he felt later at the admiration of his old teacher for his *Mérope*. Tournemine combined a vivid imagination with the purity of mind of a child. He admired the brilliant promise of his pupil, wishing only that he could "break him to the bridle." How attached young Voltaire was to him is shown when during the naïve love episode of his adolescence he wrote to his beloved Olympe, in Holland: "The first thing I want to do when I get back to Paris is to win over to you Father Tournemine."

Father Paullou was the boy's confessor and enjoyed, as letters of his school days show, the heartiest love of his pupil. Among the more or less reliable estimates of the young François, the following made by Father Paullou is accepted universally: "This child is consumed with thirst for fame."

The youngest of the teachers and at the same time the one for whom Voltaire preserved such a fondness that all his life he never said a slighting word about him, was the cultured Father Thoulié who changed his name by means of an anagram and became famous as Abbé Olivet. He translated Demosthenes and Cicero, became an influential member of the French Academy and wrote its history. Voltaire felt a tenderness for him, which was mutual. For Voltaire he is Quintilian reborn, and Olivet for his part never hesitated to take the side of his former pupil in his numerous and often very bitter quarrels as, for instance, with J. B. Rousseau and with Desfontaine. There were coarse elements, there was even a certain rudeness in Olivet's nature; nevertheless, Voltaire in his letters addresses him thus: *Elegans et sapiens Olivete, vir doctissime! Vale dilige tuum amicum, tuum discipulum!*

To the most famous pupil of that institution, the dearest of all his teachers was, and remained, Father Porée. Porée was the born educator, such an accurate physiognomist that the character and abilities of each of his pupils were evident to him, and he could accordingly prescribe lessons to suit the special needs of each. His temper was even, his manner pleasant. He possessed an unbounded, contagious serenity, was indulgent and likeable. The peace in his soul was mirrored in his face. He loved good literature passionately and imparted this passion to his favorite pupil.

François did not live like the young nobles in the school, but led a quiet, reflective life. He worked assiduously, not with the diligence of the dull grind tied to the book, but more in his spare time than in class. He took no part in the games and dawdlings of his comrades, but eagerly drew his teachers out and held endless discussions with them. He investigated everything, sought enlightenment on philosophy, religion, literature, history, statecraft, natural science. Even subjects that ordinarily lie beyond the horizon of a schoolboy were not beyond his: current events, politics, the government of France and other countries. As Father Porée wrote of him: "He liked to weigh Europe's interests on his little scale."

Even as a boy he appreciated good food and good wine, nice clothing and a certain personal elegance. He was never an ascetic. Since he was unusually frail, he dreaded cold weather.

It was a custom in school to spend the free hours in the courtyard as long as the water in the font of the chapel was not frozen. As the door to the chapel was open during the day, Voltaire used, as often as he had a chance, to put ice in this sacred vessel, so he would not have to leave his corner by the stove.

Every grade had its honor bench which was reserved for the best pupils. On the bench the most highly prized seat was not the first, but in winter that which was next the stove of Dutch tiles. For this grim battles were fought. One day, the freezing Voltaire tried to push a comrade from this seat, exclaiming: "Away with you, or you'll get a push that will enable you to warm yourself next to Pluto!" "Why don't you say: in Hell?" "Bah, one is no more believable than the other!"

There is another anecdote on the subject of Heaven. It was first told by his biographer Paillet de Warey (1824). A boy seated next to him insisted that Voltaire had hid his glass. Another called: "Arouet, return it, you are a trouble-maker who'll never go to Heaven!"—"What does he say about his Heaven?" responded the boy. "Heaven is the world's great dormitory."

6

Young Arouet passed through school without ever having been exposed to humiliating punishment. His comrades were not always so fortunate. The Marquis d'Argenson tells in his memoirs that he and the young Duke de Boufflers, Colonel of the regiment which bore his name and Hereditary Governor of Flanders, were whipped in presence of the whole class in punishment for a trifling prank. They had blown peas at Père Lejay from a tube. The Maréchal du Boufflers complained of this to the King and took his son out of the school. The Marquis d'Argenson describes how embarrassing it was for him and his brother, both of whom were later ministers, to wear the coarse, black uniform of the Jesuit pupil. Before their entrance to college they had led the lives customary among young gentlemen, attended plays and social affairs, visited restaurants and women. Once, during a school comedy, his intimate friend, the young Prince de Soubise, entered the amphitheater wearing his resplendent cloak. The young Marquis, in his student uniform, was too mortified to look in his friend's direction.

At a distribution of prizes, in 1710, young Arouet and Jean Baptiste Rousseau saw each other for the first time. Rousseau heard Arouet called twice, and asked who the young man was. Père Tarteron replied that he was a boy who had an astounding talent for poetry, and proposed to introduce him, which he did. Rousseau found the face unpleasant—this, however, was not put on record before a bitter enmity had arisen between the older and younger poet—but the expression was vivid and bright and his behavior that of a very polite young man.

Notable among the friendships of his school days, one which lasted all his life, and became of the utmost importance to Voltaire, was that with the little Duke de Fronsac—he who was later so famous as Duke and Marshal de Richelieu but was best known as a conqueror of the other sex. Even the Duke de Lauzun hardly (although he, too, became famous in this regard) enjoyed such a reputation. Richelieu, like Lauzun, kept his attraction for women until his death. He lived to the age of ninety-two years (Lauzun died at ninety-one) and in the last year of his life he proved to the Court his skill in breaking young horses.

To the ladies Richelieu was an idol. Merely to be mentioned with him was held an honor. All showed themselves compliant, the coquettish and the prudes, princesses and women of the middle-class. They fought for his favor, sometimes even with fire-arms.

Madame de Polignac and the Marquise de Nesle, exchanged pistol-shots for his sake. The admirers who delivered his notes to other women kissed his hand for this favor; those whom he dismissed came back. Each morning he was given a packet of love-letters. Often he did not have the time to read them all, did not even open them and wrote with pencil on the envelope: "Letters I had not the time to read." At his death there were found on his table five billets-doux from prominent ladies who on one and the same day were asking for "one hour of his night." At that time he was ninety-two years old.

In school, Voltaire's acquaintance with the Duke —who left the institution early—was not intimate; but they often met in their youth at the houses of the Cardinal of Auvergne, the Duke de Sully, the Marshal de Villard and of Lord Bolingbroke. Even though the friendship was not helpful to Voltaire during the time of the Regency, when Richelieu was identified with the plot of the Church against the Regent and the conspiracy of 1718 to give up Bayonne to Philip V of Spain, later it was of great advantage. Apparently these two prominent, bewitching and arrogant personalities had a strong attraction for each other. They were equally elegant and equally impertinent. Not even the fact that Richelieu once had a trifling affair with the Marquise de Châtelet before Voltaire met her could harm this friendship. One should not believe Voltaire's detractors, such as Faguet, who try to make it appear that Voltaire's part in this relationship was that of a sycophant. On the contrary, when there were differences between them, he stood up against Richelieu as power against power. In the year 1722, that is, a little over a decade after the Duke left school, Voltaire writes to his friend, Thiriot:

"I am astounded at Richelieu's peevishness. I esteem him too highly to believe he could have spoken to you about me unpleasantly, as if I had denied to him what I owe him. I owe him friendship only, not submission, and if he has demanded that, I don't owe him anything. . . . I advise you not to see him again if you expect to hear him reproach me; it

befits him as ill to give a reprimand as it would
befit me to deserve one."

The numerous poems and still more numerous letters to the Duke, which cover a space of more than
fifty years, prove the firmness of the friendship. A
letter of the Marquise de Châtelet to the Duke, at a
time when she devoted herself entirely to Voltaire
and when the Duke had married a second time, contains a passage which does credit to him and to her.
She writes:

"I believe that I really am of some value since I
can count upon your true friendship. . . . You know
my heart; you know how completely it is filled. I am
happy to love in you the friend of my lover. . . .
This feeling would glorify the joy your friendship
gives me, if I myself had not poisoned it. I can not
forgive myself for having nourished passing ill-feel-
ing, no matter how slight. Now the character of my
friendship must strive to make up for this fault, and
in case it should be this fault to which I owe your
friendship, I want to say in spite of all my remorse:
'Happy crime!' (O felix culpa!)'"

7

To return to Voltaire's other school friends. Special
attention must be paid the brothers d'Argenson.
Their father was Lieutenant-General of Paris under
Louis XIV and thereafter Keeper of the Seal (Minister of Justice). Both sons rose to high positions.
The older, the Marquis d'Argenson, the same age as
Voltaire, remained his friend to the last day of his
life. He became Foreign Minister of France. The
younger, Count d'Argenson, with whom Voltaire was
less friendly but who employed Voltaire in a diplomatic mission to the King of Prussia (1743-1747),
became Minister of War under Louis XV. Because
d'Argenson relied at Court upon Jesuit influence,
Voltaire's attitude to him was cooler, even though in
his letters to the older brother he likes to recall memories of school with their walks all three together in
the "black allée."

With none of his friends did Voltaire keep up such a close friendship as with his real intimates among his school comrades. First of all there is Fyot de la Marche. The letters to him were published by Henri Beaune. His relations with Voltaire show respect as well as hearty attachment between the two men. But since Fyot de la Marche was a pious Catholic, the intimacy which denotes full mutual understanding is lacking. In contrast to this Voltaire was altogether hearty and confident with Cideville, senator in the Parliament at Rouen. The last letter to Cideville is dated August 30, 1765. He lived fifteen years longer, but became a bigot.

Among his lifelong friends are to be mentioned the two brothers Fériol, the Count d'Argental, and the Count de Pont-de-Veyle. Of these a little the less intimate was the stout Pont-de-Veyle, the epicurean, for whom it was hard to leave Paris to make a visit to Ferney. Doubtless Voltaire was more attached to d'Argental, who in letters is addressed: "My angel, my beloved angel, adored angel, divine angel"; but if he were writing to both brothers it is always just: "My angels!" There are extant letters to Pont-de-Veyle from the years 1736-1743, to d'Argental from 1734-1778. D'Argental is not only Voltaire's constant confidant but also, where it is necessary, his champion, e.g., in regard to Baculard d'Arnaud's ingratitude and slander. In the first sketch of Voltaire's *Septième Discours de la Vraie Vertue* are to be found the following lines:

Tendre et fidèle ami, bienfaiteur généraux
Qui peut te refuser le nom de vertueux?
Jouis de ce grand titre, ô toi dont la sagesse
N'est point le triste fruit d'une austère rudesse,
Toi qui, malgré l'éclat dont tu blesses les yeux,
Peux compter plus d'amis que tu as d'envieux.

One of the most heartily loved friends of those early years was Jean René de Longueuil, Marquis des Maisons, who died at thirty-two. His grandfather had been chancellor of Anne of Austria. He was five years younger than Voltaire and, like him, very precocious; at the age of twelve he found pleasure in reading the

Roman poets. At fourteen he became passionately absorbed in the study of physics, but did not neglect his law studies, which he was compelled to take up by the terms of his father's will. Jean was still a child when his father died. Louis XIV promised him his father's position as President of the Parliament of Paris, "hoping he would serve the King with the same fidelity as his father." When Maisons was eighteen the Regent gave him the right to take the chair of Parliament and to conduct the sessions. He fulfilled this duty to everybody's satisfaction. He was a friend of literature and of scientific research. He was an excellent chemist, and discovered a Prussian Blue which excelled all others. His garden contained the rarest plants. Here the coffee bean was for the first time successfully grown in France.

As Maisons' mother was the older sister of the Marquise de Villars, Voltaire doubtless through her met the great Marshal, and his wife, for whom as a young fellow he felt desperate and unreturned passion. It was during a visit of Voltaire's to the Castle of Maisons, in 1732, that he was taken ill with small-pox which then raged in Paris. His host and hostess showed him a touching solicitude; the great actress, Adrienne Lecouvreur, came to visit him and sat on his bed in defiance of the danger of infection. The exiled English statesman Bolingbroke visited him. In the opinion of the patient the physician Gervasi saved his life (see Voltaire's Epître xxv, A M de Gervasi). Voltaire had hardly left the Castle (December 1, 1723) when a fire started in the room in which he had been lying. Today the traces of this fire are still shown. In the poem in which Voltaire expresses his joy at being returned to life, he says:

Je reverai Maisons, dont les soins bienfesants
Viennent d'adoucir ma souffrance
Maisons, en qui l'esprit tient lieu d'expérience
Et donc j'admire la prudence
Dans l'âge des égarements.

Maisons was like an older brother, an honest, severe, sometimes sharp critic of his work, and when he died, Voltaire expressed his grief in a letter to Cideville (September 27, 1731). The letter begins: "My dear friend, the death of M. de Maisons has thrown me into a despair which borders on stupefaction. I have lost my friend, my support, my father. He died in my arms, not because of the ignorance of the physicians, but because of their neglect. I shall never be able to console myself for this loss, or for the cruel way it struck me." The same year he gave his friend a permanent monument in his poem *Le Temple du Goût*, in which he sees his shadow after death. The passage begins:

O transports? ô plaisirs? ô moments pleins de charmes!
Cher Maisons! m'écriai-je en l'arrosant de larmes,
C'est toi que j'ai perdu, c'est toi que le trépas,
A la fleur de tes ans, vint frapper dans mes bras.
La mort, l'affreuse mort, fut sourde à ma prière,
Ah! puisque le destin nous voulait séparer,
C'était à toi de vivre, à moi d'expirer.

Although there has been mention of so many aristocratic acquaintances and friendships founded in youth and kept up in later years, Voltaire's attitude toward friends from the plain middle-class was no less hearty. It is sufficient to mention Thiriot. It increases our respect for the poet that, when in his later life, even after thirty years, he saw again his school comrades, who had suffered reverses, the old feeling found vivid expression. So it was with Le Coq, an unknown Bohémian, who one day presented himself emaciated to a skeleton, with sunken cheeks, unkempt beard and dirty linen. Voltaire, deeply touched, recognized him under his rags and gave him help (letter to Cideville of October 28, 1741).

III

EARLY YOUTH

1

Young Arouet was in his seventeenth year in 1711 and his best and most intimate friends had left school. He could hardly bring himself to look into the rooms they had inhabited. The birds had flown, the nests were deserted. He longed for them and longed to fly away as they had. He was weary of the monastic life of the college, of the Latin and Greek. That desperate melancholy came over him, common to all those who have outgrown school and to whom it means no longer a life of development, but of confinement.

But his father demanded that he pass his final examination; he passed it in May, 1711. Now all he had to cope with was the examination which would give him the degree of a Master of Arts. Though not required, that was helpful as an introduction to law studies. He sat at his books all through the summer and tortured himself with the study of the Sceptics, and Aristotle, and ethics, without passing the examination, until he got such a headache that his father relented and let his son free.

During the vacations, his friend Fyot introduced him to his relative, the Marquis de Mimeure, and this laid the foundation of the friendship between the poet and the clever Marquis de Mimeure, who became his protector. M. de Mimeure was a pleasant Mæcenas to the literati, and the hospitality Arouet enjoyed in his house increased his passion for a life of intellectual fresh-air.

The working-year began. The moment had come to choose a profession. At the announcement of the young man that he did not wish to become anything other than a writer his father answered that this meant simply that he would be useless to society, a burden to his family, exposed to starvation.

Highly reluctant, young François started to hear lectures. They were held in a big barn of a building, for the law-students of that time were not spoiled. The tedious method of instruction, the useless stuff with which they wanted to burden his brain, enraged him so much that he felt himself drawn more than ever to literature. He thought more about Racine and Chaulière than about the *pandects*, rather of Madame de Mimeure than of the barbaric university Latin. He was not solemnly inclined, and patience he lacked altogether. He never completed his law studies. His father offered to buy him a position as Royal Attorney in Paris, but he declined.

Relations between father and son became more and more strained. "Tell my father," he said to a friendly would-be mediator, "that I don't care for honored positions which are purchasable; I shall earn respect without having it bought for me." On June 22, 1739, he wrote to the Marquis d'Argenson: "Since I entered this world without any particular standing, I was immodest enough to think I could as well as the next one make a place for myself if it was possible by will and work. I threw myself into the fine arts, which always carry with them a certain humiliation because one cannot by means of them become royal senator. Money can make one State Recorder of Petitions, but money cannot write a poem, and I wrote one." He was determined not to become a member of any profession and much as he craved power, knowledge, fame and the luxury of pleasure, he prized independence more highly.

2

The Court of Louis XIV, once the most brilliant in Europe, had in the King's latter years become the dullest and most somber. Yet, the person of the monarch was surrounded by splendor, in spite of the defeats of his armies and navies, in spite of the raised taxes, the shrunken treasury, the increased loans, the general misery of the people. But under the dominance of Madame de Maintenon the King had become so pious and morally strict that the Court held no more feasts or plays and only an occasional stiff reception. The last time a ballet was danced before the King was in the year 1681, and the last opera in Versailles was staged in 1694. About the year 1711 the King hardly ever showed himself, for Madame de Maintenon no longer left her rooms, where she spent her time with two or three ladies-in-waiting who were as pious as herself. A few times a day the King visited her and worked with his ministers in her apartment. It scarcely seemed possible that this could be the same Court that forty years ago had been the home of youth and gallantry. A lowering cloud of depression rose in Versailles and spread its heavy pall over France.

There was bound to be a reaction against the scrupulous morality, the solemnity, the deadly boredom of the Court in the last years of Louis XIV; it came in the regency of Philippe of Orléans, in the form of a spirit of refined licentiousness, a sensuous, effeminate elegance.

One place of refuge for the relaxation of intelligent men and Anacreontic worldlings of Paris was *Le Temple,* the residence of the Grand Prior of Vendôme, who was expelled from Paris from 1706 to 1714 because of his excesses. He was a younger brother of the Duc de Vendôme, the famous general of whose frightful cynicism Saint-Simon gives a vivid sketch.

The Grand Prior's friends and companions assembled at his house in the Hôtel de Boisboudrand around the blythe, lyric poet Abbé de Chaulieu, the leading guest. Chaulieu lived in *Le Temple.*

Here the young man, fresh from school and university, was introduced by his godfather, the Abbé de Châteuneuf, at the age of twelve. Here he met not only Chaulieu, but also Abbé Servien, the uncle of the young dukes of Sully, about whom there was nothing priestly except his garb. Here, likewise he met Caumartin, the Abbé de Bussy, son of famous

Roger de Bussy Rabutin and in Voltaire's judgment
wittier and more natural than his father; the Marquis de La Fare, known for a few good verses; the
Duke of Aremberg; the President Henault, Madame
du Deffand's friend many years later; Maximilien
Henri de Béthune-Sully, who at first was the closest
possible intimate of Voltaire, until his indifference
to his friend's desperate illness broke relations between them.

The supper-parties of this group were intellectual
orgies over which Bacchus reigned, while the Graces
were not exactly too formal. Here the young man
with the burning, sarcastic glance felt flattered to
have a place among thoroughly experienced gentlemen and not inexperienced ladies. Here he sat, the
newly discharged schoolboy, among princes and men
from France's proudest aristocracy, and bewitched
them by his nimble brain, his dextrous mockery, his
imperturbable poise, his roguery, the charm of which
none of them could approach. From the first day he
treated them as equals. Just as almost a hundred
years later Napoleon and his brothers sat on the
thrones of Europe as though they had been born for
that purpose and as if no one had ever doubted their
right, so this half-grown Voltaire, blandly ignoring
the strong spirit of caste existent in that day, treated
men of the first families of France as if unquestionably he were quite as important as they.

Now and then there were envy and rivalry to be
overcome, as with Chaulieu himself. Voltaire's first
appearance as satiric poet had made Chaulieu ec-
static and he rewarded the young man for the poem
Le Bourbier with a little composition which begins
thus:

> Que j'aime ta noble audace,
> Arouet, qui d'un plein saut
> Escalades le Parnasse,
> Et tout à coup, près d'Horace,
> Sur le sommet le plus haut
> Brigues la première place.

But later when Voltaire won applause as dramatic
poet, he wrote a well-known epigram against the
young man. Nevertheless, one can see, from Voltaire's

works, the cleverness and artfulness with which he won them all over.

One reads, for instance, the long letter, written in mixed poetry and prose, to the Abbé de Chaulieu, dated July 15, 1716, which begins with the little verse:

A vous, l'Anacréon du Temple;
A vous, le sage si vanté
Qui nous prêchez la volupté
Par vos vers et par votre exemple,
Vous dont le luth délicieux,
Quand la goutte au lit vous condamne,
Rend des sons aussi gracieux
Que quand vous chantez la tocane,
Assis à la table des dieux.

This letter, which fills three large printed pages, consists of verses, smooth, fluent verses scribbled just before departure of the mail and is of an incomparable grace, the more remarkable since it was meant only for the eyes of a seventy-seven-year-old man.

One finds again, in Voltaire's *Le Temple du Goût* (written fifteen years later) the same roguishness, the same nice skill and the same assurance in his descriptions of the frivolous masters of his youth.

Thus, first, of Chaulieu:

Je vis arriver en ce lieu
Le brillant abbé de Chaulieu
Qui chantait en sortant du table,
Il osait caresser le dieu
D'un air familier, mais aimable.
Sa vive imagination
Prodiguait, dans sa douce ivresse,
Des beautés sans correction.

Of Bussi, after a few disparaging remarks about his father, he says:

Mais sons fils, son aimable fils
Dans le temple est toujours admis,
Lui qui, sans flatter, sans médire,
Toujours d'un aimable entretien,
Sans le croire, parle aussi bien
Que son pere croyait écrire.

With droll impudence he writes of La Fare:

La Fare, avec plus de mollesse,
En baissant sa lyre d'un ton,
Chantait auprés de sa maîtresse
Quelques vers sans précision,
Que le plaisir et la paresse
Dictaient sans l'aide d'Apollon.

One should read, too, the jocular, friendly *Epître à M. le duc de Sully* (1720), in which Voltaire erects a monument to the palsied old Chaulieu, shortly before Chaulieu's death.

L'éternel abbé de Chaulieu
Paraîtra bientôt devant Dieu,
Et si d'une muse féconde
Les vers aimables et polis
Sauvent une âme en l'autre monde,
Il ira droit en paradis.

This circle increased young Voltaire's abhorrence of stupidity, his aversion from asceticism and his love of the good things of life. The inclination to pleasure so characteristic of this clique was not in his nature. The old gentlemen who in *Le Temple* originally assembled around the Prince of Vendôme belonged to the time when it was good form to drink the clear and sparkling Vin d'Ay until they rolled under the table. They had no shame whatsoever about going to bed drunk every night. They belonged to the jolly, careless retinue of the Wine-God. Each was a Silenus or a Satyr.

Voltaire, who sat among them and received their blessing in foaming champagne, which corresponded to the wit and exuberance of his wilful young nature, was representative of a younger generation which no longer looked to wine for inspiration. His drink was not wine but coffee, that sobering beverage, which clears the mind instead of clouding it, which does not cause vague dreams, but a clear sight before which shines the truth.

The old and the old-fashioned still liked to accompany their drinking with song. Voltaire substituted conversation, which became a fine art now for the first time because now for the first time the crackle of ideas became audible in the newly founded cafés.

Cafés were introduced in England in the year 1669, in France in the year 1671, but while they never flourished on British soil, except in London, by 1720 there were three hundred of them in Paris, and comparatively as many in the provincial towns. The café killed the old-fashioned inn with its drunkenness and quarreling.

Coffee-drinking engendered wit, intelligent discussion and laughter, not the raucous guffaw of the drunkard, but the infectious laughter that denotes a keenly appreciative sense of humor.

It was said of Voltaire that he lived on fifty cups of coffee daily, and died because of these fifty cups of coffee. This probably originated from the eulogy of Frederick the Great after Voltaire's death, in which he speaks of the pains Voltaire took in writing his last tragedy. "He spent whole nights working it over, and, whether to fight off sleepiness or to stimulate his brain, he unquestionably overdosed himself with coffee. Fifty cups hardly sufficed him."

When Voltaire shortly before his death announced before the French Academy his plan of a dictionary, he drank, five times, two and one-half cups of coffee.

It is certain that coffee symbolizes Voltaire, not wine, still less beer.

3

One can easily imagine what the honest and dignified father Arouet, former notary, now high official, had to say about this idle and aimless life of his younger son, and his company of poets and dukes. Instead of sticking to his law-studies and looking out for his future, the black sheep left the house in the forenoon and did not return until the wee, small hours.

He was the prodigal son in every respect. There is an anecdote, not all of which is reliable but which can safely be trusted this far: the young man had received one hundred *louis d'ors* for a literary work, at that time a fortune in his eyes. Walking through the rue Saint Denis he chanced to notice at an auction sale a carriage, two horses and several liveries. He bought the complete outfit, employed servants to fill the liveries, had the horses hitched up and put in a blissful day driving about showing his splendor to his friends, until near nightfall the coachman overturned the coach by the rue du Long-Pont. The next day he had to discharge his lackeys and sell carriage and horses to a hackney coachman for half what he had paid for them.

Another entirely credible story tells how his father, exasperated over the night reveling of his son, one evening ordered the house door to be locked and the key to be brought to him. Early the next morning young Arouet comes home from a merry party and finds the door closed and locked. The doorman can give him no better suggestion than to make himself comfortable for the night in a carriage standing in the courtyard. He does so, curls up as well as he can on the seat, and falls asleep. In the morning two very young senators from the Parliament pass by, notice young Voltaire, whom they know, and have him carried by two porters to a café, where the bad jokes of the servants and guests awaken him.

4

It is not surprising that the old man finally saw no other way to rescue his son from all these youthful follies, than to remove him from Paris. So he asked his old acquaintance the Marquis de Chateauneuf (brother of the Abbé, now dead) who was just about to start on a mission to the States-General in The Hague, to take the young man along as some kind of attaché. The unmanageable son had already been sent away to Caen, in Normandy, where his reputation as a poet at once opened for him the way to the best society in town. After a few months at Caen the eighteen-year-old found himself on the way to The Hague.

The Hague was flocked with fugitive Huguenots. Among them was a Madame Dunoyer who with her two daughters had left her husband, after ruining his respectable position by her folly. He had been a captain in the army, senator, state-deputy, finally grandmaster in charge of state-owned rivers and forests in Languedoc. Madame Dunoyer, though not a beauty, was not the less erotic, the real adventuress, bright, enterprising and bold. Previously, in England, she had lived on an income for which she begged; now in Holland she was trying to make her living by the publication of a periodical called *La Quintessence,* which gave a so-called Chronique of Paris and the Court, and which, though there was hardly one true word in it, did contain various amusing items of gossip and petty scandal. Her older daughter she had married very young to an old man. The younger, Olympe, called Pimpette, still lived with her.

Olympe had a broken engagement in her history. Jean Cavalier, one of the leaders of the rebellion in the Cevennes, suppressed by the Maréchal de Villars, was received with splendor in England and had been caught by Madame Dunoyer. When it came out that he not only had no money but was also deep in debt, she enabled him to pay his debts to the officers of his regiment by selling the diamonds she had taken when she left her husband. He became engaged to Olympe and gave the mother a signed marriage-contract. But after an engagement of two years, he disappeared and made a better match with an English girl.

Soon after his arrival in The Hague young Arouet was introduced in the very open house of Madame Dunoyer and immediately fell passionately in love for the first time. Olympe promptly reciprocated and did not let her young admirer yearn in vain. They saw each other daily and were both very happy.

The practical mother knew at once that this nineteen-year-old Arouet, without position and without income, was no husband for her Pimpette, and could only compromise her and make a later marriage more difficult to arrange. As soon as she got wind of the affair she went at once to the Ambassador and asked him to stop the damage that the over-frequent visits of the young attaché would undoubtedly do her daughter's reputation.

The Marquis de Châteauneuf decided to take the matter in hand at once, partly because he respected Madame Dunoyer's nuisance-value as a scandal-monger in *La Quintessence,* partly because he was afraid that the States-General might see an uncalled for proselytism in the eagerness of his Catholic page to win this Protestant girl; the more so because it was known that M. Dunoyer was interested in restoring his daughter to the Catholic faith.

In the evening when the young François Arouet came home, he was told that the Ambassador wanted to see him at once. Without any preparation he received the shocking intelligence that he was to return instantly to France. With difficulty he was able to gain a delay of twenty-four hours and that only on condition that he should not leave the house.

In spite of the alarming suddenness of it all he at once resolved not to give in. All night his fertile mind was working out a plan: he would get a note into Pimpette's hands proposing that they elope together and join M. Dunoyer in France. First of all it was important to ascertain a means of corresponding in the short time left the lovers.

By a strange bit of luck we still possess fourteen of the letters young Arouet wrote Olympe—perhaps all he wrote—in spite of the urgent plea expressed in each of them that they be burned. This is explained by the fact that Olympe's enterprising mother, after doing everything in her power to break up the attachment of the two young people and after getting possession of the letters, resolved to turn them to some use and, in 1720, that is, seven years later, published them in the fifth volume of her collection *Lettres Historiques et Galantes,* omitting only the unflattering references which the young lover in his exasperation and contempt had made to herself. When we recall that the reason at the bottom of this severe treatment of the nineteen-year-old youth was the French Ambassador's fear of the poisonous pen of Madame Dunoyer we must admit that she amply justified this fear.

It is fortunate that these letters have been preserved. Here, and here only, we become acquainted

with young Voltaire as a lover and as a lover so
young and so naïve that he has not the slightest
doubt his love will endure all his life. What is quite
touching, is that the young woman to whom he feels
himself so passionately drawn, is just as much in love
as he and just as desperate at the prospect of their
separation. How much it means that this young passion could not survive a forced separation!

These letters are all the more interesting in that
they are the only love letters of Voltaire left. Madame
du Châtelet collected no fewer than eight quarto volumes filled with Voltaire's letters to her. According
to Abbé de Voisenon there can hardly be any doubt
that Saint-Lambert burned those letters after her
death, in posthumous jealousy—as he later burned
the letters of Jean Jacques Rousseau.

We can follow the mind of the young lover during
that first night of the calamitous news, in 1713. Three
letters of introduction he must have from Olympe,
one to her father, one to her uncle, and one to her
married sister. Above all, the one to her sister is absolutely essential. The bearer of these letters to Voltaire is to be Olympe's family shoemaker. He must
hold a last in hand to explain his coming, as though he
had to repair the young man's shoes. He must bring
him a note from Olympe and her portrait. She must
induce her mother to hand it over. It would be safer
in his hands than in those of her ill-disposed mother.
The servant he is sending is absolutely dependable.
In order to be admitted he will pretend to be a manu-
facturer of tobacco cases and as he is a Norman he
will act his rôle excellently. Now François must bring
his letter to a close. On oath he protests his tenderness toward her, the tenderness she fully deserves.
He knows well that even the least faithful lovers
speak that way; but their love is not, like his, founded
upon absolute respect. . . .

"Once more, farewell, my dear beloved! Think a
little of your unhappy lover, but don't think of him
in a way that will make you sad; take care of your
health if you want to have me keep mine. Above all
things, be very careful, burn my letters, and all letters which you receive from me in the future; it is

better to have less tenderness for me and more cautiousness for yourself. Let's console ourselves with the hope of seeing each other again soon and let's love each other all our lives!"

The journey was put off for a short while; they could not find at once a suitable companion and guard for the young man; but he was held prisoner in the Embassy in the name of the King. The next day he wants to try to see her; they can rob him of his life, but not of the love he has for her. "Yes, my adorable beloved, I want to see you tonight, even though I may have to lay my head on the block." He will steal out of the house, he will rent a carriage, he will meet her when the moon shines, and they will drive like a gale, to Scheveningen.

Nothing came of it. Both were too carefully watched. But the next day a new plan: about midnight he will climb out of the window; she will at the same time, under the pretense of a natural desire to be alone, leave her mother's bed (the poor girl slept in the same bed as her mother) and they will meet at any spot she designates. Neither did anything come of that.

But the following day he has thought up a new and still better scheme. She must send Lisette to him at three o'clock. He will have prepared a package containing a man's suit. If then she will be so gracious as to allow a poor prisoner, who adores her, the favor of seeing her, she will come at dawn to the Embassy and he may hope to receive her in his little residence. The joy of being her slave will then make him forget his imprisonment. He has thought of everything; since his clothes are known, they must not be seen. He adds an overcoat under which she can hide his tightly fitting coat and cloak her face. She must mistrust everybody, her mother, even herself. But she must trust him without the least reservation. He will pull her out of the abyss, etc.

This plan succeeded, and the next letter rings with jubilation and wanton delight, like a love scene from Shakespeare. They forget their danger and their imminent separation in their happiness at being able to kiss and embrace each other in perfect secrecy.

"I don't know whether to call you Monsieur or
Mademoiselle; you are charming in woman's attire,
but you are also a most delightful cavalier, and our
doorman, who is not in love with you, considers you
a charming boy. The next time you come he will give
you an excellent reception. You achieved the fiercest
as well as the most graceful aspect of the cavalier,
and I almost fear that you drew your sword on the
street to make the young man complete." This brings
to his mind the disguised Viola in *Twelfth Night*. In
his joy the poet turns to semi-mythological verses, ac
cording to the custom of that time:

> Enfin je vous ai vu, charmant objet que j'aime,
>   En cavalier déguisé dans ce jour;
>   J'ai cru voir Vénus elle-même
>   Sous la figure de l'Amour.
>   L'Amour et vous, vous êtes du même âge,
>   Et sa mère a moins de beauté;
>   Mais malgré ce double avantage
>   J'ai reconnu bientôt la vérité.
>   Olympe, vous êtes trop sage
>   Pour être une divinité.

And he disparages gods and goddesses, just to show
how high she stands above them.

That same evening he wants to jump out of the
window to be at the appointed place at dawn. His
servant will come at four o'clock. "If I am not there
by then I am absolutely prevented from coming."

But no, he surmounted all obstacles, he came and
they saw each other once more.

The next letter, however, contains the bitter suspicion that the meeting of the previous day had been
found out. M. de La Bruyère has gone to her mother
and blabbed. And now, because of his fear that it may
hurt her reputation, it is impossible for him to see
her again before his departure. Nothing is left to
them but correspondence. He will write to her by
every mail to a certain safe address; his own address
is: A M. Arouet, *le cadet, chez M. Arouet, Trésorier de
la chambre des comptes, cour du Palais, à Paris.* Then
follows a great deal of advice as to how she should
deal with her mother: how allay her suspicions, how
never mention his name, how lull her into tranquil-

lity of mind until the day of liberation should arrive: "My dear Pimpette, just follow my advice now and compensate yourself all the rest of my life, I promise always to obey you."

But all hope is not gone yet. François Arouet had been misinformed. This we learn from the only letter of Olympe Dunoyer which is still in existence.

"Uncertain as I am whether I shall have the pleasure of seeing you tonight, I inform you that it was not M. de La Bruyère, who was at our house yesterday. It was an error of the shoemaker's wife, who alarmed us very inopportunely and without reason. My mother does not know that I spoke to you, and believes—thank Heaven!—that you have already departed. I don't want to speak to you about my health; that troubles me least of all, and I think far too much of you to have the time to think about myself. I assure you, my dear heart, that, were I able to doubt your tenderness, I would welcome illness; my dear child, even life itself would be a burden to me, if I had not the sweet hope of being loved by the one dearest to me in this world.

"Do what you can so I can see you tonight. Just go down to the shoemaker's kitchen and I guarantee you will have nothing to fear; for our quintessence manufacturess thinks you half-way between here and Paris. So, if you want, I'll have the pleasure of seeing you tonight; and if this can't be done, let me go to Mass in the Embassy. I then will ask M. de La Bruyère to show me the chapel; ladies are privileged to be curious. Then I'll ask him, quite incidentally, if nothing had been heard of you and when you went away. Don't deny me this favor, my dear Arouet, for I ask you this in the name of the greatest tenderness, that is in the name of the love which I feel for you. Farewell, sweet child! I adore you and I swear to you that my love will last as long as my life. Dunoyer."

As one can see, Olympe speaks as if she were the older of the two, which, however, was not the case, and her words give evidence of her keen resolve and honest affection.

There are still in existence a number of warm letters addressed to Pimpette from the road and from

Paris, and we can follow the numerous steps which
young Voltaire undertook to enable Olympe to leave
her mother and come back to her father. But how
little a dependent young man of nineteen years can
do! How little, especially under paternal surveillance
and under the judicial conditions of that time!

When he had scarcely arrived in Paris, young
François was informed that a letter had preceded
him from the Marquis de Châteauneuf, written "as
if it were concerned with a criminal." François'
father, to whom this was the last straw, secured a
lettre de cachet for the arrest of his son. He had to
go into hiding until his friends succeeded in calming
the first storm of paternal ire. He writes to Olympe
that at first his father wanted to send him to the
West Indies; later, however, he changed his mind;
but his friends cannot shake his father's determina-
tion to disinherit him. For Olympe, writes her lover,
there is only one thing left to do: depart as soon as
she gets her father's order: "You love me, my dear
Olympe, and you know how I love you; my love
surely deserves to be returned. . . . If you were
cruel enough to fling all my bad fortune in my face
by stubbornly staying in Holland, I should kill myself
at the first word of it."

5

The strict father wasted no time; he put his poetic,
love-sick son to work in a lawyer's office. Maître
Alain had his office in the rue Pavée-Saint-Bernard
near the Place Maubert. Meanwhile, the elder Arouet
intercepted Olympe's letters, the angry mother in The
Hague those of François. For the next succeeding
months the two young people changed their receiving
addresses constantly. Then the grand passion lost
one of its principals. Olympe fell in love with a seventeen-year-old Frenchman in The Hague, Guyot de
Merville, who twenty years later became one of Voltaire's most ardent opponents. An extreme case of
retro-active jealousy.

Merville, however, was just as unsuitable a match

as Arouet. Madame Dunoyer now began to move mountains to pave the way for a provident marriage for her daughter. She shortly succeeded in making Olympe the Countess Winterfeld. But since the mother's ambition, not the daughter's heart, brought about this union, the young countess soon left her husband and, having no other refuge, returned to her mother. Shortly afterward (1719) the mother died, whereupon the Countess Winterfeld left Holland and went to her relatives in France.

Voltaire was so far from bearing any grudge against his fickle first love that in 1721 he secretly helped her out of a pecuniary embarrassment. Wherever he mentions her in his later works it is with respect and warmth.

Her fortunes improved. Her father left her nothing but debts, but her uncle was very rich, and when he died she inherited his fine house in the Faubourg St. Antoine and bought herself a country estate.

Replying to La Beaumelle's slander of her, Voltaire wrote, in his *Supplement to the Century of Louis XIV*: "She gets a pension from the King and lives most of the time at her estate where she takes care of the poor of the vicinity. Her age, her meritorious life, her virtues, the large and honored family of which she is a member, and her high connections should protect her from the infamous slander of this foolish scoundrel."

The last mention of her name occurs in two letters written by Voltaire from Cirey, dated respectively July 16 and 30, 1736, in which he asks his friend the Abbé Moussinot to purchase a little writing-table with a screen and have it sent in his name to Madame de Winterfeld, rue Platrière, near the Sisters of St. Agnes.

Thus the forty-two-year-old man tried by a little gift to recall himself to the memory of the lady whom as a fiery nineteen-year-old boy he had loved.

Apparently the stay in a lawyer's office, boring as it was for the young poet, was not lost time. His extraordinary brain easily absorbed the greater part of judiciary methods, also judiciary tricks and subterfuge, ignorance of which would have been a drawback to the future businessman. Later, when he amassed with such speed and assurance a very considerable fortune, he probably owed it to his early acquired familiarity with this kind of judicial practice.

At the law-office he found a young colleague who became his constant companion for the longest part of his life. Nicolas Claude Thiriot remained, to the time of his death in 1772, Voltaire's most intimate and familiar friend, his trusted helper in many youthful affairs. There may have been some charm about his personality. Certain it is that he has nothing of this appeal for posterity. Few people in history have known as well as he how to make a paying thing of friendship with a celebrity. Voltaire's letters to him extend from 1721 to 1772, and during all this time he showed himself to be lazy, undependable, dishonest, treacherous, even fraudulent, and deviously extortionate in the price he set on every little service. Yet in 1769, fifty-five years after the beginning of their acquaintance, he turned to Voltaire with a request for financial support. To posterity, his name is connected indissolubly with that of his famous friend.

6

In this period comes Voltaire's first contact with the theater and its world. He had written the first draft of his tragedy *Œdipe,* a rather curious work for such a young poet, and now his obsession was his hope of seeing the play accepted at the Théâtre Français. The way to accomplish that was first to ingratiate himself with the actors and actresses. The latter had the stronger attraction and the greater influence. But because of his knowledge of the old Greek tragedy and out of a sane poetic and critical disinclination to inject into the play any modern love element, he purposely omitted sex interest. His play was declined by the actors, who could not see beyond this defiance of an old tradition.

His attempt to win over one of the young leading ladies, Mademoiselle Duclos, was a complete failure. She preferred the Count of Uzès. There was nothing to do according to the custom of the eighteenth century but to take his defeat lightly and to make a joke of it.

In his epistle to Madame Monbran-Villafranche, 1714, he says:

Nous semons pour autrui. J'ose bien vous le dire,
  Mon cœur de la Duclos fut quelque temps charmé;
L'amour en sa faveur avait monté ma lyre;
Je chantais la Duclos; d'Uzès en fut aimé;
  C'était bien la peine d'écrire.

In his letter of July, 1715, he is bolder: "By the way, talking of theatre ladies, I must report that La Duclos hardly acts any longer; every morning she takes a few pinches of mustard and cinnamon, every night a few pinches of the Count d'Uzès." He could not abstain from making a malicious allusion to the health of the lady. This he couches cleverly in the following verse:

Belle Duclos,
Vous charmez toute la nature!
Belle Duclos,
Vous avez les dieux pour rivaux;
Et Mars tendrait l'aventure,
S'il ni craignait le dieu Mercure,
Belle Duclos.

The beautiful and noble Adrienne Lecouvreur succeeded La Duclos as the object of his adoration, and for a short time became more than a friend.

To her he dedicated the earliest of his *Contes en vers* which had been written in the first place for La Duclos: *l'Anti-Giton,* a satire on homosexuals directed against a certain prominent man, the Marquis de Courcillon. These individuals later formed an influential group, as they did in Germany about 1900. To Lecouvreur he also dedicated his 29th epistle, which glorifies her as an actress; he has Melpomene contribute her taste, sensitivity, pathos and delicacy, Venus donates her charm and graciousness and finally Cupid bestows the capacity for love, the active capacity for love and only with this last gift does she become perfect as an actress. To her, furthermore, he addresses in 1719 the short poem, a farewell, which seems to

contain a hint of her passion for some one else, and
that in a way which equally honors Voltaire and her:

> Faites le bien d'un seul et le désir de tous;
> Et puissent vos amours égaler la durée
> De la pure amitié que mon cœur a pour vous!

In 1730, he wrote the touching poem, *La Mort de
Mlle. Lecouvreur,* in which he expresses his bitter
hatred of French prejudice and French cruelty as
evidenced by the refusal of a grave to the great
artist.

In addition to being turned down by the Théâtre
Français and scorned by Duclos, the young man met
a third depressing rebuff. This was from the French
Academy, which made him bow the first time, but
not in the end.

In the year 1712 L'Académie Français had instituted a contest for a prize, first offered by Louis XIII
and renewed by Louis XIV. The prize was for the
best lyric poem in the form of an ode on the performance of the chorus of Notre Dame de Paris. This
problem cannot be called exactly alluring; it required a glorification of the King's piety; consequently it was bound to lack poetic appeal. Surely no
one will try to maintain that this theme was suited
to the poetic gift of young Arouet who was induced
by his ambition to try for the prize.

He had composed just one ode in all his life. That
was when, at the age of fifteen, he performed the
exercise of translating into French verse one of his
hated teacher Father Lejay's Latin hymns to St.
Géneviève. Curiously enough, he later wished to disown this little work which does credit to his skill at
verse making. The ode he now composed in honor of
the two Louis on the chorus of Notre Dame is written in the same high and mighty style which Jean
Baptiste Rousseau had introduced in his equally cold
and pompous religious hymns.

In its melody as well as in its cadence this ode an-
ticipates Victor Hugo's first *Odes et Ballades,* except that Voltaire's work is damaged by those hide-
ous allegories—those infernal allegories that weigh
down every eighteenth century art, even including

sculpture: allegories such as Peace, Piety, Faith, Malevolence, Insolence and Rebellion—no matter how mellifluous the verse, the image is killed by them.

Even so, it is no exaggeration to say that this ode by a youth of eighteen is as good as any that were composed at the time. It has the same significance in Voltaire's life that Goethe's *Gedanken über Jesu Christi Höllenfahrt* has in his.

Two full years passed before a decision was reached. In the year 1714 the young poet was informed that the prize had been awarded by the well-known Academician, Monsieur de la Motte-Houssard to the old Abbé Dujarry, whose verses certainly could not even approach those of Arouet. They were flat and prosaic until they attempted to soar, when they became simply ridiculous. For example, the Abbé whose *forte* was obviously not geography, maintains that the South Pole is hot as the North Pole is cold.

Poles glacés, brûlants, où sa gloire connue
Jusqu'aux bornes du monde est chez vous parvenue.

Although Voltaire joked about his defeat and would not admit that he felt hurt by it, that he was hurt is clearly proved by his next violently exaggerated satire, *Le Bourbier,* in which he roasts La Motte with a ferocity which he found reason to regret when he saw La Motte's unresentful and indulgent attitude toward him. The sneering bitterness in this satire, resembles that of Byron in his *English Bards and Scotch Reviewers,* which overshot the mark just as far and which was passed over with similar indulgence by those it attacked.

Those narrative poems written by Arouet in his early youth (1714-1716), the already mentioned *L'Anti-Giton,* and *Le Cadenas* and *Le Cocuage* are very doubtful works of art when we look at them today, were it only because of their style of attack. Similarly distasteful to many modern readers is the poet's careless worldly manner. For his contemporaries, however, the wit of these verses gave them justification. These poems are analogous to those written by Goethe at eighteen, a little over fifty years later, in his collection *Annette*. The only difference is that Voltaire's poems touch upon indecent matters in the most delicate language, while those of Goethe, more sensual and rather doctrinal, postulate frivolity as a rule or duty. But, although these poems found favor in the eyes of the frivolous society of the Court, to the poet's father they were final proof that his errant son was completely degenerate.

7

In these circumstances it was fortunate that the young genius had a protector. It was the distinguished and highly gifted Urbain de Caumartin who by entreaty got his father's permission to take the young man to his château of Sainte-Ange, near Fontainebleau. Here François moved in the best society of the time. Here he wrote some of his first, keen poetic epistles in which he nonchalantly treats France's most prominent men as his comrades, flattering and scolding them at the same time, regardless of the fact that they were a half-century his seniors. To this Sainte-Ange period belongs the *Epistle to the Prince of Vendôme* in which he describes how the gallant King Francis I, who had in his time amused himself in this garden with Diane de Poitiers and with la belle Ferronière, appeared before him clad in laurel and myrtle and without any other crown than that which is awarded by an illness proceeding from Venus.

> Quelque lauriers sur sa personne,
> Deux brins de myrte dans ses mains
> Etaient ses atours les plus vains,
> Et de vérole quelques grains
> Composaient toute sa couronne.

But the amazing part is the description which young Arouet has Francis I give of the Grand Prior of Vendôme. The King draws the Prior's attention to all the things they have in common, without failing to mention a detail: Love of the fine arts, abhorrence of bigotry, dependability in every field except the erotic, and finally the disease which, he hopes, will not bring death to the prince, as it has him, but will yield to a few ounces of mercury.

> Il aime comme moi les arts
> Et les beaux vers par préférence;
> Il sait de la dévote engeance
> Comme moi faire peu de cas;
> Hors en amour, en tous les cas
> Il tient, comme moi, sa parole;
> Mais enfin, ce qu'il ne sait pas,
> Il a comme moi, la vérole.

The young Duke de Sully had, as mentioned before, an uncle, Abbé Servien, who was one of the veterans of the epicurean circle and apparently was honestly admired by Voltaire for his cheerfulness, grace, liberalism, and freethinking although on the other hand the young man was disgusted by the old man's unbecoming, sometimes perverted passions. Servien had exhibited a certain spitefulness by protesting vigorously against an over-nasty insinuation in a prologue performed in honor of the old Louis XIV at the Opera where he was, hands and nose buried in his muff, a regular spectator. The result was a *lettre de cachet* which expelled him from Paris. Soon after he had been allowed to return, another *lettre de cachet* reached him and this time it sent him to the prison of Vincennes for a term of twenty months. What was back of this second *lettre de cachet* is unknown, but undoubtedly it was some unsavory sexual excess. He was freed only after the King's death, when the Regent took over the government and called to the young Duke de Sully who had come to do him homage: "I did not forget about the Abbé."

From this period there are two poems of Voltaire's on Servien. The long epistle consoles him most charmingly over his imprisonment and recommends to him a brave philosophy of life: "The philosopher is free, even in chains." Here it is surprising that the young poet dares to glorify Fouquet, the great financier who had been removed from office because of his frauds. At this time Voltaire still regarded him as

martyr to the fickle temperament of autocracy. The
second poem *A M. l'abbé de . . .* by which Servien
is understood, has as a subtitle: "who mourned the
death of his beloved."

In a lightly satirical and jesting vein it advises the
epicurean man of God with the triple chin, not to
take so deeply to heart the death of his beloved, that
he himself must eventually go to the grave, and it
expresses the Anacreontic philosophy of life, which
is not high-minded but honest.

> Voila comme on doit sans cesse
> Faire tête au sort irrité:
> Et la véritable sagesse
> Est de savoir fuir la tristesse
> Dans les bras de la volupté.

The abbé did not have much occasion to profit by
these suggestions: he died the following year, 1716.
He had been a typical figure among the steady guests
of *Le Temple,* of whom so many, from the Grand
Prior and Chaulien down to the Abbé de Servien
were libertines in both the meanings the word had
at that time. High livers as well as freethinkers, but
freethinkers in theory only, who, far from wishing
the destruction of the Church, received their income
from it. They mocked its religion but grabbed its
money and jumped at the ecclesiastic sinecures that
bought them worldly luxuries.

8

It is sometimes said that at the accession of the
Regent, the spirit of *Le Temple* became the spirit of
France. This, however, would give us too narrow a
view of the new times.

Louis XIV died on September 1, 1715. This King,
whose name had been celebrated like no other French
one, toward the end of his reign so squeezed his
country that the report of his death was welcomed
with joy and his burial gave rise to scandalous cele-
brations. He left a country, strangled and bled by the
Church, with a national debt of two billions of livres,

with a foreign policy that produced nothing but defeats, and a system of domestic government that bred
helplessness.

The Regent, Philippe d'Orléans, who (as guardian
of the five-year-old heir to the throne) succeeded
him, the son of Monsieur, Louis XIV's vicious brother,
and of the Bavarian princess Elisabeth Charlotte,
was thoroughly competent. He had shown unusual
courage in his youth during the war with the Netherlands. He had during the War of the Spanish Succession held the chief command in Italy and in the years
1707 and 1708 the high command in Spain. He lost
the latter when it developed that he sought the Spanish crown for himself. In spite of the fact that he had
not been mentioned in the will of Louis XIV he was
recognized by the Parliament as Regent with full
royal power.

But if France was to be put on her feet again it
would require a fundamental revolution which was
resisted with all their power by the upper classes and
which the people could not force, weakened by misery and held down by the tax-free classes as they
were.

The first essential move would have been to call
back the banished Protestants; they were industrious,
reasonable and prosperous. They would have brought
with them a stream of gold and what, as Michelet
says, would be still better: a stream of young blood.
But it proved impossible. None in the circle of the
Regent wished to be taken for a protector of heresy,
or to assume the burden of a general hatred. Not
even the Jansenists, who had been supplanted by the
Jesuits and suppressed by Louis XIV, showed the
least sympathy for the Protestants. Even so enlightened a man as the Duke de Saint-Simon, who was very
close to the Regent, hedged about with his conservative and Catholic prejudices, had nothing but con-
demnation for the expelled Huguenots.

Just as impossible of accomplishment proved to
be any adequate financial reform. Colbert had already proposed a progressive income tax. But the
idea of collecting taxes from nobility and clerics
seemed so extremely insolent that even the common

people were aroused against it by the privileged class.

In these dire straits it was resolved to hold a strict investigation of all outstanding loans. The Prime Minister, the Duc de Noaille, founded a *Chambre de Justice*. Charges brought before this tribunal disclosed the fact that financiers had done business with the late king as usurers do with young men of prominent families: they had loaned him sums at interest up to four hundred per cent; but as though that were not bad enough, the accounts had been so poorly kept that there were a large number of duplicate items, double bills. The tax collectors withheld their collections from the internal revenue-office under the pretense of expenses incurred and gambled with the money in the stock market.

The Regent's demand for at least enough money to give the soldiers their pay was agreed to, but the promise was not kept; and when finally the Regent lost patience and threatened torture and the scaffold, it appeared that a large number of prominent men and fine ladies were interested in the finances. The ladies showed themselves especially active and the Regent had to give in.

More successful was an extensive revision (*le grand visa*) of securities, interest-bearing papers, etc.; it was made by four keen financiers, the brothers Pâris, whose name often recurs in the histories of these times, especially frequently in Voltaire's.

The elder Pâris used to keep an inn, "A la Montagne," at the foot of the Alps, in the management of which he was helped by his four stalwart sons. When, in the year 1710, a commissary of provisions sought a short passage over the Alps in order to bring victuals to the Duc de Vendôme in Italy, the father told him that his sons knew every mountain pass and would deliver the provisions. This was done and as a reward they got positions in the commissary department. Since they had inborn business acumen, were active, and congenial and like the brothers Rothschild a hundred years later, acted in conformity to a common plan, they were successful.

For a period they were completely supplanted by John Law, but after his downfall they rose again.

In 1722 the oldest, who called himself Pâris-Duverney, was made Royal Treasurer. He was an extraordinarily able banker. Put under the ministry of the Duke de Bourbon, he made the mistake of allying his fate to that of the Duke's and that of the Duke's mistress, Madame de Prie. So when Bourbon fell into disgrace, he fell with him. In the year 1730 they again won the royal favor. The oldest brother became the founder of the military school in Paris, while the youngest, Pâris de Montmartel, gained such power as treasurer and Court banker that for the next generation he conducted the finances of the kingdom all by himself. No finance official could be employed or discharged without his consent.

But we have run far ahead of our story.

By 1716 the brothers had succeeded in reducing the national debt by half. Simultaneously the dissolute but skilled Abbé Dubois eliminated the threat of war with England. France abandoned the forlorn cause of the Old Pretender and in November, 1716, France and England formed an alliance which later was joined by Holland. Dubois earned his coveted reward—a cardinal's hat.

At the same time he made another—soon widely known—alliance with the Scotchman John Law, the financial wizard of the age, a combination of the magician and the gambler, generously endowed by Nature with the qualities of both. He had the resourceful brain which finds simple but amazing solutions for every difficulty. Gracious, winning, extremely handsome, with an almost feminine beauty, he had absolute confidence in himself. A regency of eighteen months had used up all of Philippe d'Orléans original zeal for reform; but John Law had will-power enough for them both.

He founded a bank which demanded of its stockholders only one-quarter of their subscription in gold; for the balance it accepted the paper *billets d'Etat,* which had been almost worthless since their issue. Industry and commerce now began to look up. The notes issued by his bank became of constant value, not subject to the ruinous fluctuations of most other French money. The stockholders conducted the bank in a businesslike manner. Not more than fifty million notes were issued in the course of two years.

In August, 1717, the State went to this bank for direct help and expressed the desire to take it over. The Regent appealed to Law for support, dreamed of extortions, coercive proceedings, sequestrations such as the Austrian Government had resorted to in founding the Austrian State bank. Law wouldn't hear of such a thing; instead he planned to exploit the new France. Canada and Louisiana, and he organized *La Compagne d'Occident*. But though this company was founded with a nominal capital of 100,000,000 livres the subscription was paid in state notes so far below par that the total was worth only about 25,000,000. And he did not receive even this amount, but a yearly payment of four million, which was to be paid for the first year only. In the second year this four million was to be divided among the stockholders. It was remarkable about this prophet of the stock market, this "Ossian of Finance," that at bottom he was dependable and sound; he saw beyond money and securities, he knew perfectly well that the wealth of a country is fundamentally dependent upon its natural resources and the industry and prosperity of its population. He wanted to go to work practically and slowly. But all the ventures which he proposed and undertook, and whose successful execution demanded time, were precipitated because of the desperate financial condition. He himself was robbed of everything when the members of the house of Condé asked for and secured the sudden withdrawal of their huge investment. In the year 1600 the house of Condé had an annual income of twelve thousand livres; by 1700 this had become one million, eight hundred thousand livres and in 1718 over and above all this it received immense yearly pensions.

On more than one occasion Law was the victim of virtual betrayal, as for instance when d'Argenson, the father of the two contemporaries of Voltaire, who had posed as Law's friend, went over to his enemies and allied himself with a commercial company which was a competitor of Law. D'Argenson, to be sure, did not have the effrontery to enter commercial transactions in his own name while he was minister; but under the name of his valet he transferred to himself the salt-taxes and the interest on state funds.

There was only one step left: complete transfer of Law's bank into the hands of the State. The King made himself banker and flooded the country with paper money which was forced upon the population as were the *assignats* later under the Revolution. This took place in December, 1718.

Law had seen his dream realized: abolition of the terrible tax system and of the scavengers who misappropriated the state income, dismissal of at least forty thousand superfluous officials, and finally the taking over of the state debt under a plan by which he would lend the State fifteen hundred million livres at three per cent and pay its creditors with his stock; for this was still rising and would have realized, had it been sold a month later, a very considerable surplus. Hardly had he been made Controller-General when he submitted a plan to the Council of State to force the clergy to sell everything they had acquired within the last one hundred and twenty years. This idea was a complete revolution in itself, a 1789 seventy years before its time.

One can imagine what tremendous forces were set in motion to bring about his downfall, and what a little push was needed to topple over his house of cards. A run on the bank with the people standing in a queue the whole length of the rue de Richelieu, a run on Law, with the blunt Duke de Bourbon, France's future ruler, demanding twenty million livres of him within one month, for his friend Madame de Prie. He was abandoned by the Regent, who now had a permanent headache, caused by nightly carousals and an apoplectic stroke which left him in such a lassitude that he could no longer be aroused even by the greedy women who offered themselves to him.

But still Law held his head above water, and still proved his usefulness, by doing away with all tariff walls between the various provinces of France. Corn and merchandise were shipped duty-free. No longer was grain to rot in one province while in the next was famine. Also an artisan was permitted to settle wherever he chose. A carpenter from Lyons was henceforth at liberty to practise his trade in Paris.

But what good was all this when the bottom was slipping from under everything and when the artificially inflated stocks began to fall and fall. All the mortal enemies he had made, the pious to whom he was the Anti-Christ, the members of the Parliament who loathed him because he had spoken against the sale of offices and against the Sovereign's right of life and death, all these stirred up a storm of hatred against Law, who was called the cause of France's ruin. They wanted to hang him, to tear him to pieces. Unselfish, as he had always been, he had established a trust fund for his wife, equal to the income from the money he had originally brought with him to France. For himself, he rescued nothing. He fled in poverty, in 1720, to save his life, and six years later, in Venice, he died—still in poverty.

9

Voltaire, being in intimate touch with all the enemies both of the Regent and of Law, naturally viewed the Scotchman and what he called his system in an unfavorable light. Numerous passages in both verse and prose furnish evidence of this.

In the epistle to the Duke de Sully he says:

> Je me fais un plaisir extrême
> De parler, sur la fin du jour,
> De vers, de musique et d'amour,
> Et pas un seul mot du système,
> De ce système tant vanté,
> Par qui nos héros de finance
> Emboursent l'argent de la France,
> Et le tout par pure bonté!

In a letter to Thiriot, written in 1725, Voltaire quotes a number of verses he had composed on the Duke d'Orléans and on the Marquis, which he intended to weave into the sixth canto of his *Henriade* but they never were inserted. Among them are the following lines:

Philippe, garde-toi des prodiges pompeux
Qu'on offre à ton esprit trop plein du merveilleux,
Un Ecossais arrive et promet l'abondance;
Il parle, il fait changer la face de la France,
Des trèsores inconnus se forment sous ses mains,
L'or devient méprisable aux avides humains,
Le pauvre qui s'endort au sein de l'indigence,
Des rois, à son reveil, égale l'opulence,
Le riche en un moment voit fuir devant ses yeux
Tous les biens qu'en naissant il eut de ses aïeux.

In the third canto of the *Pucelle* Voltaire again strikes at Law. Even as an old man (1769) he speaks in his *Epistle to Boileau* with stiff hatred of the Scotch financier:

Un maudit Ecossais, chassé de son pays,
Vint changer tout en France, et gâta nos esprits.

In his *Précis du Siècle de Louis XV* he describes how Law drew public attention away from politics by awakening an inordinate desire for money, and thus broke the opposition against the Regent. The gambling fever drove out ambition. Law became the savior of the Regent. Law actually did contribute something. He was responsible for the foundation of vast commercial enterprises, and brought about the regeneration of the Transoceanic Trading Company which had been founded by Colbert and later destroyed by the war. Even though many private ventures failed, the nation as a whole entered with more confidence into large affairs and thus increased its wealth.

Voltaire gives a dispassionate account of how Law founded his bank and united it with the Mississippi company, how the public, taken by the prospect of quick profits, bought and bought these stocks, which rose immensely, and how France became wealthy on paper. In all walks of life one could attain a certain luxury. When the King took over the bank the stock rose to as much as twenty times its par value. But intoxicated at the success of his system, Law issued so many certificates that the supposed value of the stock in 1719 exceeded by eighty-fold all of the money current in France. Law himself, meanwhile, had turned from a Scotchman into a Frenchman, from an adventurer into a powerful landowner, from a banker into a state minister. "I myself," says Voltaire, "have seen him enter the halls of the Palais Royal, accompanied by dukes and peers, by bishops and marshals of France."

Then Voltaire bestows his praise upon the four brothers Pâris, who after Law's disappearance restored order to the finances of France.

10

The Grand Prior of Vendôme had returned to Paris without waiting to receive permission. So confident was he that he set out as soon as he had heard of the death of Louis XIV. Directly after his arrival he again became the center of his old circle. His first act was to send a summons to the Abbé de Chaulieu; then he gathered all his friends and drinking companions around him in *Le Temple*. All of these were old men, except a few like young Arouet, who quickly became intimately acquainted with the Prince; but age meant nothing to these creatures of iron and fire. It was a free-thinking, hard-drinking, copper-stomached crowd of *bon vivants* that gathered in *Le Temple*—although most of them held clerical titles and made their living by the altar which they did not serve. They could drink and make merry all night long without any bad effect on their health. And amid all this drinking and ribald joking came frequent disputes over literature and poetry in which they showed the finest judgment and surest taste.

Voltaire, who had been working two years on his tragedy *Œdipe,* read it after supper to these gentlemen and derived profit from their criticism. On June 20, 1716, he writes to Chaulieu:

"I well remember the critical objections raised by the Grand-Prior and yourself at the time of a certain dinner given by the Abbé de Bussy. This dinner was of great help to my tragedy, and I believe that all I need to insure the success of anything I am writing is to drink four or five times with you."

The young Prince of Conti, too, gave him good advice, as Voltaire tells us in the fifth of the letters which comprise the introduction to *Œdipe*:

"I must confess that it is to Monseigneur le Prince de Conti that I am indebted for the keenest and finest criticism. If he were a private person, I would be content to admire his judgment, but since his rank as well as his wit make him outstanding, I am venturing to ask him to protect literature."

It was at a dinner given by the Prince, who could write a neat stanza, that young Arouet, not forgetting to emphasize his equality, exclaimed, "Are all of us princes or all of us poets?"

The younger members of this circle advanced quickly in rank; in 1712, the Duke de Sully came into his family estates. At the same time the Abbé de Bussy, who "had no other fault than that he did not believe in God," was made a bishop.

11

The Regent was open-minded and with him a new attitude began to prevail, a battle against the cruel and stupidly pious inquisition of the former Government. He wanted to bring the basic qualities of human beings into their rightful position. In the beginning of his reign he spoke nobly of his desire to have about him not subjects who had to obey blindly, but thinking beings to whom he could explain the underlying motives of his orders, and prove that they were just and essential. What he had in his inmost heart was the real French spirit. This vicious man with his fatal weakness for women and wine was made of the same stuff as Montaigne and Molière.

His reign marks hypocrisy's downfall and liberalism's accession to the throne in more than one sense of the word. All that frivolous and shallow eroticism which before had been kept secret, and practised in the *"petites maisons"* by candle-light, was now performed openly, without shame, in one's own house. The late King had once nicknamed Philippe d'Orleans *"fanfaron de vice,"* one who makes himself out worse than he is.

Certainly in spite of all his debauches he was morally superior to the men and women of highest rank who played the pimp to achieve their own ends, bringing to his bed now comely, experienced sirens, now innocent and charming young girls. The first type he declined with a sort of horror, and from the latter refused to accept any kind of favor unless the young girl offered herself to him freely and willingly.

Louis had forced Philippe of Orléans to marry one of his illegitimate daughters, the Duchess de Blois. It was impossible to refuse anything to the King; he wanted to see his female bastards married to nobility. But when the Duke broke the news to his mother, Madame Elisabeth Charlotte, known in Germany by the pet name Liselotte, she was so enraged by this insult that she slapped her son's face hard enough to shake the furniture and to be heard in other rooms of the Palace of Versailles. This wife became the torture of his life. Always in league with his enemies, she spied for Madame de Maintenon, and disclosed his secrets at every opportunity.

The mistresses of the Duke, who followed each other in rapid succession, the pleasant and unselfish actress, Mlle. Desmares, the Duchess de Mouchy, the Comtess de Parabères, etc., aroused his sensuality, tenderness, generosity, but never his passion. Passionately he loved only one woman in all his life, and she was—tragically enough—his own daughter.

The offspring of the inharmonious union, the young Duchess de Beri, was beautiful, alluring and half-crazy. At her death it was found that her brain was abnormal. From her grandfather, the Sodomite, she had a part of her perverted inheritance; from her grandmother, who, though a healthy animal herself, came from the Bavarian Royal family which was full of insanity, she inherited a haughtiness that almost bordered on the insane. At the same time she was extremely sensual, very touchy and easily moved to tears. Educated by a debauched chambermaid, she abhorred her mother and always lived near her father. The latter studied, etched (a number of

voluptuous etchings, Daphnis and Chloe), received
alchemists, financiers, statesmen, and beautiful courtesans, and was as sensitive as his daughter. When
he felt too unhappy about his marriage they cried
and got drunk together. She was his only friend and
companion. When she was an over-developed girl
of fourteen and he prematurely surfeited at thirty-
five, passion flamed up hotly between them. He
always remained her devotee and her slave, and
when Louis XIV died she felt herself queen. She
was as gifted as she was mad and as mad as she
was witty. She took one lover after another, first
her Master of the Horse, then her Captain of the
Guard, Rion, whom—in spite of the tremendous dis-
parity in position—she wanted to marry. Rion was a
stout, conceited, beardless doll, who with the consent of the Duchess appeared as her official lover—
husband in all but name. The Regent, to teach him
patience, appointed him governor of Cognac and
presented him with the best regiment of the army.
Rion, however, was a nephew of Lauzun. And had
not Lauzun, in spite of every obstacle put in his way
by Louis XIV, married the great Mademoiselle? To
the duchess Rion was as good as Lauzun, and at her
castle La Muette she let him play the rôle of lord of
the house.

For the decoration of this castle the Regent gave
her the best he had, the best France had: Watteau,
appointed painter to the King in 1717 with the official
title *peintre des fêtes galantes*. His bewitching love
gardens and delicately sketched figures embarking
for Cytherea must transform this little castle in the
environs of Paris into a worthy shrine for the daughter of the Regent. From Watteau's paintings we learn
among other things the costumes of these days. The
old, stiff bodice into which, in the time of the old
King, women squeezed and laced the upper half of
their bodies, while their lower parts disappeared in
a hoop-petticoat, had been replaced by loose, light
garments which could easily be flung off.

The fountain-head of all intrigues and attacks
against the Regent was the Duchess de Maine, grand-
child of the famous Condé, who had married the son

of Louis XIV and Madame Montespan. She was a
witty and spiteful little lady, Voltaire's protector all
her life, but filled with a most vigorous hatred of
the Duke d'Orléans. Her husband, who was appointed
Regent in Louis XIV's will, had been set aside by
Parliament in favor of Orléans. Another member of
this circle was the Marshal de Villars, whose wife
shortly afterward made a deep impression on the
young poet.

It was probably to please the ladies of the little
circle in Sceaux and in the castle Villars near Melun
that Voltaire wrote his first witty and poisonous
verses against the Regent and his daughter. For, the
Duchess de Maine was indefatigable in circulating
pamphlets, drawings, caricatures and street-songs, in
order to sling mud at her rival and his daughter.
From her circle came *Les Philippiques,* written by
Lagrange-Chancels, odes which took furious flings
at the supposed incest. The scandal reached its
climax when, in 1718, the Duchess de Berri became
pregnant. Not in Sceaux only but all over Europe
it was whispered that, even though Rion was supposed to be the father, it was not so. Meanwhile the
haughtiness of the young Duchess had developed to
an insane degree. She increased her household to
eight hundred officers and servants. In the Luxembourg she had a throne built, three steps high, on
which she wanted to receive the foreign ambassadors.

That Voltaire in writing his *Œdipe* had in mind
the Regent and the Duchess, is betrayed in his first
epigram:

> Ce n'est point le fils, c'est le père;
> C'est la fille, et non point la mère;
> A cela près tout va de mieux.
> Ils ont déjà fait Etéocle;
> S'il vient à perdre les deux yeux,
> C'est le vrai sujet de Sophocle.

Here he is anticipating events, for the Duchess
had not yet given birth to a child; and when
finally it did come it was not a male, so that the
name Etéocles is out of place. However, his reference to the danger to the Regent's eyesight has better

foundation. He could hardly see out of one eye, and during a very nasty erotic scene which cannot be told, but in which it seems he was not to blame, the pious young Madame d'Arpajon, lying stretched out in front of him, had kicked him in the eye with her heel.

The other epigram, addressed to the Duchess de Berri, runs:

> Enfin votre esprit est guéri
>   Des craintes du vulgaire;
> Belle duchesse de Berri,
>   Achevez le mystère!
>
> Un nouveau Lot vous sert d'époux,
>   Mère des Moabites:
> Puisse bientôt naître de vous
>   Un peuple d'Ammonites.

Of course these epigrams were anonymous and Voltaire never admitted that they came from his pen, as without doubt they did. He even went so far as to deny these satirical poems, in a very impertinent poem to the Regent himself.

Nevertheless, they were in circulation under his name, and such insults demanded punishment. The Regent himself was so indifferent to gossip and adverse criticism of his person that he never called for the punishment of those responsible; he interfered only when the police proved to him that to let them go untouched was to encourage his enemies. So Voltaire was merely banished from Paris. The place to which he was first exiled was Toul, a boring little town; but at the intercession of old Arouet, François was sent to Sully-sur-Loire where there were family relatives who the father thought would keep some watch over the unruly young man. But from the first day he became the guest of his friend, de Sully, and lived at his family castle, surrounded by the whole circle of epicures and mockers who had settled in this lovely home and made it into a bewitched and bewitching fairy palace. Among the guests were Roussay, Lespar, Périguy, Guiche, the Duke de la Vallière, Madame de Gondrin, née Noailles, the younger Comtess de Toulouse, and Madame de Vrillière, Venus in person.

Among Voltaire's poems, read the beautiful little verse addressed to Madame de Gondrin when her life had been in danger on the Loire. The whole company living in the castle is depicted. Read a second little poem, *Sleepless Night in Sully*, which expresses the poet's joy at having been exiled to such a beautiful castle and in such charming company. One enjoyed conversation; one courted; one went hunting; and the young poet was very happy and at the same time worried at the thought that the world might never hear of his happiness and hence his exile might never be revoked. The only drawback to this stay was that it was compulsory. To prove his innocence he sent the Regent the following impudent verse:

> Non, Monseigneur, en vérité,
> Ma muse n'a jamais chanté
> Ammonites ne Moabites;
> Brancas vous répondra de moi,
> Un rimeur, sorti des jésuites,
> Des peuples de l'ancienne loi
> Ne connaît que les Sodomites.

This "Brancas" is Duke Louis Antoine de Brancas-Villars, to whom Voltaire sent a nice letter in which he begged his protection and politely requested him to deliver the long *Epître à Monsieur le duc d'Orléans*, in which by his dignity and his cleverness he tried to put himself in the best light to the Regent.

In the beginning of the epistle he warns the Duke not to hope for universal acknowledgment, in spite of his truly great qualities:

Prince, chéri des dieux, toi qui sers aujourd'hui
De père à ton monarque, à son peuple d'appui;
Toi qui, de tout l'état portant le poids immense,
Immoles ton repos à celui de la France;
Philippe, ne crois point, dans ces jours ténébreux,
Plaire à tous les Français que tu veux rendre heureux.
Aux princes les plus grands, comme aux plus beaux ouvrages,
Dans leur gloire naissante il manque des suffrages.

The Regent should not let himself be discouraged by spiteful critics, but neither, on the other hand, should he let his dull flatterers win him over; he should recognize their selfish motives and remember that his glory does not depend upon them nor upon the artists glorifying him. Voltaire enumerates all Philippe's attractive qualities, and then interrupts his enumeration to ask how it was, that a man with so many great qualities as the Duke could have lost his fine sense of justice long enough to let himself be persuaded to believe the worst about the humble petitioner. From this epistle the Duke could see how he thought and wrote. How could he think to recognize Voltaire's style in the crude jingles, which the adroit slander of his rivals had ascribed to him?

At the end of the year 1716 he again was given his freedom.

12

The use he made of it was foolish. In his epistle to the Regent he made himself out his adorer; as a matter of fact, the mild and even rather pleasant punishment he had undergone rankled so bitterly that he could hardly mention the Regent's name without anger. Even this would have been all right, if he had only been more careful to whom he spoke; but he was too young not to be talkative and too inexperienced to know that he was surrounded by spies.

He fell in with a very cunning and dangerous police spy and without a suspicion unburdened his heart to him. This was an officer by the name of Beauregard whom he had picked up in his café but whom, to be quite fair, it would have been perfectly possible for him to have met in more select society. With boyish vanity Voltaire not only boasted of the satires he really had written, but also, according to the police record still existing, made himself out as the author of various other poignant *pasquinades* in French or Latin, only one of which was actually from his pen. Circumstantial evidence became all the stronger against Voltaire when, in answer to Beauregard's question as to what the Duke had done to him to cause such hatred, he answered: "What? You don't know what that rascal did to me? He exiled me from Paris because I let the public know that his daughter, Messalina, is a loose woman."

The satirical poem, which thanks to this careless remark was ascribed to him, was entitled *Les J'ai vue,* and its real author was one Antoine Louis Lebrun who was fourteen years older than Voltaire. In it the poet laments the injustice that he has met with everywhere he goes: the prisons filled with good citizens, freedom a thing of the past, righteousness persecuted, people in chains, soldiers in despair and starvation, officials torturing and maltreating whole cities, a devil in woman's attire (Madame de Maintenon) making the laws, etc. That the author was a Jansenist was betrayed by his unrestrained indignation over the demolition of the cloister Port-Royal:

> J'ai vu le lieu saint avili,
> J'ai vu Port-Royal démoli,
> J'ai vu l'action la plus noire
> Qui puisse jamais arrivèr:
> L'eau de tout l'Océan ne pourrait la laver,
> Et nos derniers neveux auront peine à la croire.

Still more outspoken was his hatred of the Jesuits:

> J'ai vu l'hypocrite honoré,
> J'ai vu c'est dire tout, le jésuite adoré.

The poem finishes: "I have seen this shocking state of affairs and I am not yet twenty years old." Voltaire at that time was about twenty-two and the real author thirty-six; but it was regarded as certain that this poem was his work, as well as the short Latin inscription *Regnante puero.* The latter expresses sincere and bitter hatred, but doubtless comes from Voltaire.

Regnante puero, Veneno et incestis famoso Administrante, Ignaris et instabilibus sonciliis, Instabiliore religione Aerario exhausto, Violate fide publica

When a boy was king and his Regent known as a poisoner and incestuous lover, when the council was ignorant and unstable and religion even more uncertain, when the treasury was empty, the public confidence violated, etc.

It seems that this poem, "What I Have Seen," angered the Regent most particularly, although it criticized the former Government for which he was not responsible. One day, during a stroll in the garden of the Palais Royal, young Arouet crossed his path. The Regent called to him and said: "Monsieur Arouet, I bet that I'll let you see something you've never seen before."—"What's that?" asked the young man.—"The Bastille," replied the Regent.

The next day Philippe d'Orléans wrote to M. de la Vrillière:

"It is the order of His Royal Highness that Sieur Arouet fils be arrested and taken to the Bastille.
This 16th day of May, 1717
PHILIPPE D'ORLEANS."

The same morning, Voltaire's bedroom was filled with police who escorted him to the Bastille, as he himself humorously described it in the poem *La Bastille:*

The advantages of the lodging were praised to him: sunlight never intruded here annoyingly; these ten-foot-thick walls were assurance of a pleasant coolness. He should admire how solidly everything was fastened with threefold doors and triple locks: "This is done for your safety." At twelve o'clock he was given warm egg soup, a dish which did not exactly appeal to him. But he was told: "Eat in peace; here nobody will hurry you."

It was of no avail that he wrote to the Duke de Sully on the same day: "My innocence assures me your protection." He had been arrested and did not know why. It had been the father of his two comrades d'Argenson, the commissioner of police of Paris, who had him arrested, but he was merely carrying out his orders.

The first things Arouet missed (he was fastidiously neat) were his toilet articles, the second, his books, which he was always reading. Only five days after his arrest he asks that the following things be brought to him: two volumes of Homer, in Latin and Greek, two lace-trimmed handkerchiefs, a small cap, two collars, one night-cap and a small bottle of carnation perfume.

There was nothing left for him to do except to

try to pass the time by working. What M. de Caumartin had told him had started him on the idea of a long historic and national poem, whose hero was Henry IV. So it happened that the first half of the work, which at first was entitled *La Ligue,* later *Henriade,* was written in prison. Not only was the place none too inspiring for creative effort in poetry, but aside from that the conditions were difficult: during his eleven months' confinement in the Bastille he was not allowed writing paper. This accounts for the fact that, in the tower called *tour de la Basinière,* he wrote his composition between the lines of a printed book.

Not until April 11, 1718, were the gates of the Bastille opened for him, and as state imprisonment was always followed by exile, he was sent to Châtenay, where his father owned an estate. Hardly freed, he wrote to Minister Maurepas asking him to assure the Regent of his innocence. He said that he was not the author of that detestable inscription, that he had never even laid eyes on it. He never dreamed that his confession to Beauregard was in the hands of his enemies and thought he had been arrested merely on suspicion. At the same time he requested the permission for a few days' leave in Paris, to enable him to give proof of his innocence.

Baron Louis de Breteuil took it upon himself to forward the petition. Young Arouet was granted his request for a few days in Paris: the duration of this stay was extended one month, however, on October 12, 1718, he was declared free to live wherever he pleased.

13

The following lines appear in Voltaire's poem *La Bastille:*

> Me voici donc en ce lieu de détresse
> Embastillé, logé fort à l'étroit,
> Ne dormant point, buvant chaud, mangeant froid,
> Trahi de tous, même de ma maîtresse.

This fragment was written in 1717, in the deepest bitterness.

When he was living on the country estate of the Duke de Sully, he had met a young girl of good family, whose uncle, a prominent man, was hereditary mayor of the town of Sully, and was on terms of intimacy with the family at the château. The girl's full name was Suzanne Cathérine Gravet de Corsembleu de Livry; she was called Mlle. de Livry.

On the second floor of the château there was a private theater and the strikingly beautiful twenty-four-old Suzanne with her swan's neck and her magnificent complexion had an ardent desire to appear on the stage. Young Arouet was the perfect instructor for her, having instructed actors and actresses all his life, and himself played so many rôles. But before long the relations between teacher and pupil developed into something else, something flaming and mutual. The happy lover engaged Largillière to paint his portrait for Suzanne—the famous portrait of the young Voltaire.

The well-known epistle, *Les Vous et les Tu,* describes the further development of this affair, in Paris. The happy pair drove in a hackney-coach and had a frugal supper for two, which by Suzanne's presence became ambrosia. At times they were a trio. Voltaire had an intimate and admired friend, young Lefèvre de la Faluère de Genonville, who was present at the meals of the young pair, shared their amusements and listened to their songs.

While Voltaire was in the Bastille it was very natural that his friend should take his place and presumably the understudy had "gone on" for his principal even on earlier occasions. As it goes in the epistle *Les Vous et les Tu:*

> Contente d'un mauvais souper
> Que tu changeais en ambroisie,
> Tu te livrais, dans ta folie,
> A l'amant heureux et trompé
> Qui t'avait consacré sa vie.

As always when shoved to the back corner of the best-friend-best-girl triangle, Voltaire was anxious not to lose his friend. His thoughts always went through this cycle: first envy, anger, grief, fury; then

forgiveness, reconciliation, fast friendship. In epistle
XVII to Genonville he says:

> Tu sais combien l'amour m'a fait verser de larmes,
> Fripon, tu sais trop bien,
> Toi dont l'amoureuse adresse
> M'ôta mon unique bien;
> Toi dont la délicatesse
> Par un sentiment fort humain
> Aima mieux ravir ma maitresse
> Que de la tenir de ma main.
> Tu me vis sans scrupule en proie de ma tristesse
> Mais je t'aimai toujours tout ingrat et vaurien.

Later on he tried, in the spirit of his time, to regard
it as an unimportant matter, to look on infidelity as
a trifle, since the erotic instinct was nothing more
than a trifle itself.

So he says in an epistle to the Duke de Sully:

> Je sais que par déloyauté
> Le fripon naguère a tate
> De la maîtresse tant jolie
> Dont j'étais si fort entêté.
> Il rit de cette perfidie
> Et j'aurais pu m'en courroucer;
> Mais je sais qu'il faut se passer
> Des bagatelles dans la vie.

Apparently he soon made it up with Suzanne. In
the poem to the physician Gervasi he describes how
her image appeared to him when he thought himself
near death.

> Hélas! en descendant sur le sombre rivage
> Dans mon cœur expirant je portais son image;
> Ses amours, ses vertus, ses graces, ses appas,
> Les plaisirs que cent fois j'ai goûtés dans ses bras
> A ces derniers moments flattaient encore mon âme.

But still more eagerly he made it up with Genonville, whose early death was a hard blow to him. In
his poem to Gervasi he grieves over the fact that the
medical art had proved unable to help his dear
friend Genonville and keep him alive for his friends.
In his poem, *Aux Manes de M. de Genonville*, he even
recalls with melancholy joy his simultaneous association with his friend and Suzanne:

Il te souvient du temps, ou l'aimable Egérie
Dans les beaux jours de notre vie
Nous nous aimions tous trois. La raison, la folie,
L'amour, l'enchantement des plus tendres erreurs
Tout réunissait nos trois cœurs,
Que nous étions heureux! même cette indigence,
Triste compagne des beaux jours,
Ne put de notre joie empoisonner le cours.
Jeunes, gais, satisfaits, sans soins, sans prévoyance
Aux douceurs du présent, bornant tous nos désirs,
Quel besoin avions-nous d'une vaine abondance;
Nous possédions bien mieux, nous avions les plaisirs.

Suzanne was not content with having shone on the little private stage of the Duke de Sully; she wanted a career with the Théâtre Français and counted upon Voltaire to give her the entrée there; for at last the stage had admitted him and the rehearsals of his *Œdipe* were under way.

She wished to play Jocasta, and also comedy rôles; but for all her persistence she met with no success. Finally she went with a troup of French actors to England. When the company failed and the poor troupers had to strike out and each make his own living, Suzanne found refuge in London, at a newly opened café owned by a Frenchman. He was a good man who, moved by the well-bred appearance, the beautiful figure and the sad situation of the poor, unprotected girl, pitied her and spoke of her to his guests. This situation Voltaire has portrayed with such warmth in the play that attacks Fréron—*L'Ecossaise,* in which Lindane represents Suzanne.

A rich and prominent Frenchman, the Marquis Charles Frédéric de la Tour du Pin de Gouvernet, saw Suzanne in the café and fell passionately in love with her. It was so serious that he offered to marry her. In her pride the poor girl refused his offer—she would not have it said that marrying her he had made a mesalliance. She refused the presents he tried to give her. All he could get her to accept were a few tickets of the state lottery. So the Marquis allowed a reasonable time to elapse and then gallantly had a false list printed, showing one of Mlle. de Livry's numbers as winner of an immense sum. All her friends, among them Voltaire, learned of this good news with interest; she herself, in the belief that she had become a wealthy woman, married the Marquis and entered upon a life of splendor and magnificence. The marriage was performed in 1727.

When Voltaire called on her at her home in Paris, he received a snub from the porter at her door; evidently the Marquise no longer knew Monsieur Arouet. The contrast between this reception and the welcome Suzanne always had for him a few years before suggested the idea for that charming epistle in which the formal "vous" of the present replaces the intimate "tu" of the old days. "All the diamonds and pearls that deck her now are not worth one of her kisses of the old days."

From 1721 to 1778 Voltaire and Suzanne never saw one another. Meanwhile she had become a widow, and pious, and fifty-seven years older. When Voltaire returned to Paris at the age of eighty-three his first visit was to his young love, the Marquise de Gouvernet, who, at eighty-four, had no longer any hesitation about receiving him. The meeting filled him with emotion. "Oh, my friends," he said when he came back, "I have just crossed and recrossed the Styx!"

14

The rehearsals of *Œdipe* took their course. The Duchess de Maine and her set regarded this tragedy as a slap at the Regent and the Duchess de Berri; they could hardly wait for the first performance; they licked their chops at the thought of the Duke d'Orléans and his daughter in attendance, writhing like the King and Queen at the play in *Hamlet*.

Hardly out of prison, Voltaire had asked the Regent if he might dedicate the play to him. This was a piece of his foolhardiness. Later he had the impudence to dedicate to the Pope his *Mahomet*, a play of the impostor in the rôle of founder of religion. Now he tried to dedicate to the Regent his *Œdipe,* a play of incest. He had to be content with dedicating it to the Regent's mother, Elisabeth Charlotte.

This dedication is memorable, not for its wording,

which is no more than the conventional flattery of
the period, but for its signature: *Madame de votre
altesse royale le très humble et très obéissant servi-
teur Arouet de Voltaire.*

This, in 1718, is the first appearance of the name
that was soon to take the place of his own family
name altogether, and that was to serve Voltaire for
the next sixty years. Jean Louis Balzac discarded the
unattractive name of Guez, and Molière got rid of
Poquelin. For the same reason Voltaire from now on
dropped the Arouet from his signature. He can no
longer bear to have it used and (in his letters to Jean
Baptiste Rousseau) he gives as his reason for his
aversion that he had often been confused with Roy,
who was not only a bad poet but an enemy. Nevertheless, he preserves it in his new name Voltaire, which
is an anagram of Arouet le jeune. At the time Voltaire was known only as a distinguished graduate of
the Jesuit school, a witty young dandy and street-
arab, a brilliant poet and no less brilliant social
figure, whose saucy tongue and pen had forced the
Regent to lock him up for a year in the Bastille.
However, it was known that the opponents of the
Regent, the old Marshal de Villars and his beautiful
wife, and the whole little court in Sceaux expected
great things of him.

So on November 18, 1718, the gentlemen and ladies
of the court turned out in force for the première of
the drama, primed for a little scandal, the ridiculing,
perhaps even hissing of the Regent.

But the Regent and the author won over the audience.

A good-natured, benevolent spectator, Philippe
d'Orléans sat and listened to the play; being near-
sighted he could hear only. His weak eyes increased
the resemblance to the blind Œdipus. With more
pride than any queen the Duchess de Berri made her
entrance—Jocasta in person. She was exuberantly,
radiantly beautiful. Young as she was, there seemed
something forceful in her magnificence; her pregnancy had progressed considerably. With her suite of
thirty ladies-in-waiting, her attendants, and her
guard, she filled the larger part of the amphitheater.

She had even had a canopy built above her seat,
which was something new in a French theater.

The play could please either faction. Its composition is exemplary. It is filled with attacks on the
clergy; but the clergy is allowed to win in the end.
In *Œdipe* the priesthood is hostile to the King; and
one of them remarks:

Tremblez, malheureux roi, votre règne est passé.

The criticisms of religion are never put in the
mouth of the leading actor, but are always voiced by
a character shown in the end to be wrong. A minor
character named Araspes utters the warning against
belief in miracles; another minor figure, Philoctetes,
is suspicious of priests. He speaks like a Frenchman
of the eighteenth century, a supporter of the King
against the Pope's power. He offers to help his opponent and rival, Œdipus:

Contre vos ennemis je vous offre mon bras;
Entre un pontife et vous je ne balance pas.
Un prêtre, quel qu'il soit, quelque Dieu qui l'inspire,
Doit prier pour ses rois, et non pas les maudire.

The best known quotation from the play has become a proverb in France:

Nos prêtres ne sont point ce qu'un vain peuple pense,
Notre crédulité fait toute leur science.

These and similar lines called forth storms of
applause. Voltaire must surely have taken the deepest satisfaction in writing them, in using them, though
they have nothing to do with the theme or action of
the play, to give expression to his hobby.

How little he was moved in his Till Eulenspiegel
nature by the performance was shown by the fact
that, just for the fun of it, he went on the stage near
the end of the play, in the rôle of a trainbearer to the
high priest.

The play was written and acted in such a way as to
make Œdipus a sympathetic character. It aroused
no aversion to him, nor to the man in the royal stall
with whom the whole audience was comparing him.
Œdipus touched the heart. Where he sinned it was

fate that made him sin. He was a good and harmless
sovereign who honestly tried to govern his people
for their own greatest good. Dufresne, a very popular young actor, played the part. And the charming
Desmares, who was making her farewell performance before the Regent—whom she had loved
tenderly and unselfishly—gave a gracious and natural performance of Jocasta. The sad scene between Œdipus and Jocasta made a deep impression
on the audience. They broke into tears when those
lovely lips moved, and that tragically beautiful voice
poured out Jocasta's last words to him:

> Si tant de maux ont de quoi te toucher,
> Si ta main, sans frémir, peut encore m'approcher,
> Aide-moi, soutiens-moi, prends pitié de la reine!

The incest itself could not horrify the spectators
regardless of how terribly it was punished in the
tragedy.

They had become familiar with Oriental customs
through numerous writers. In Europe itself incest
was not unusual.

It was common knowledge that the bishop de
Tencin had been living in incest with his sister,
Madame de Tencin (the mother of d'Alembert), and
it was known that Kings of ancient Egypt had done
likewise.

Foreigners in Paris followed this example: According to Saint-Simon's assertion the Prince of Mont-
belliard married his son to his daughter. According
to the memoirs of Elisabeth Charlotte, the Duchess
von Württemberg's lover was none other than her
own son.

The play, then, was enthusiastically received by the
majority of spectators. When the author showed
himself in the box of the Marshal de Villars, between
the Marshal and his pretty wife, the public called in
chorus to her: "Why don't you kiss him!" And, in
the general enthusiasm, she did.

The Regent, too, got an ovation, supercilious, self-
indulgent, and vicious as he was. With his fine intellect and his keen appreciation he had of course
missed nothing of the play's contemporary applica-

tion or its allusions to himself. But he never batted an eyelid, didn't in the least feel hurt or embarrassed. He applauded, had the author called to him, and granted him an annual income of twelve hundred livres, roughly equal to twelve hundred dollars today.

A few days later, Voltaire accepted a very pleasant invitation to dine with the Duke. "Monseigneur," he said to his host, "I am highly gratified at having Your Royal Highness provide my meals. But I implore Your Royal Highness not to provide me again with lodging at your expense."

For the first time young Arouet had attracted public attention and had earned a reward deserved by one who refused to be discouraged or tried even by calamity but had kept on indefatigably and with undeniable talent. Later, in a letter dated October 22, 1759, he writes d'Argental: "I am supple as an eel, lively as a lizard and industrious as a squirrel." He was so known since his earliest youth.

Œdipe was an extraordinary success. The play was given forty-five times in succession, which was something hitherto unheard-of. It pleased the reading public as well as the playgoing public. The censor, La Motte, upon whom the publication of the play depended, could not content himself with the dry formula of approval that the censor's report had to give or withhold; and although he had been maliciously attacked in *Le Bourbier,* he described the author in his report as a worthy successor of Corneille and Racine. This angered old Chaulieu and provoked him to write the epigram quoted earlier in this book.

Voltaire, however, did not let the play speak for itself. It came out, as you might say, in seven coats of armor. Besides a regular introduction and dedication, it was introduced by no less than seven letters to M. de Genonville. The first protests that he was not the author of the poem *J'ai vu,* and contains his thanks to the actors; in the following he criticizes Sophocles' *Œdipus* by pointing out the improbability that the King should be so slow to recognize his fate in spite of all hints and signs; after that he considers

Corneille's *Œdipus* and criticizes the dull episode of Theseus' love-affair with Dirce, which as it goes on obscures the interest in the fate of Œdipus; finally he reviews his own tragedy and very frankly draws attention to the improbabilities inherent in the theme, which he has been able to cover up only, not eliminate. He also points out the flaw in the disappearance of Philoctetes after the third act. On the other hand, he stoutly defends the plausibility of a passion aroused again in Jocasta for Philoctetes. He demonstrates the falsity of the common eighteenth century assumption that Jocasta was sixty years old. He shows why she must actually have been about thirty-five, and as he says humorously but no less truly: "Women would be very unhappy if at that age they could no longer arouse any carnal feeling."

Among the men to whom Voltaire sent his tragedy was Jean Baptiste Rousseau, who at that time was in Vienna. Rousseau answered in a pleasant, hearty letter, which overflows with praise and reveals the sincere admiration of the older poet for the younger. Reading this letter one thinks what a pity that, through fault on both sides, this friendly relation should later turn into the most bitter and relentless animosity.

An acquaintance of importance met by Voltaire about this time, was the noted, or perhaps notorious Baron Görtz, the powerful minister of Charles XII. They met at the home of the rich Swiss banker Baron Hoguère, who entertained frequently in Paris, and who must be identical with the Högger mentioned by Fryxell as having loaned money to Charles XII in Turkey. As unbelievable as it sounds, considering the difference in age, Görtz and Voltaire became intimate friends; there is even a story that Görtz wanted to take the bright young man with him to Sweden. Apparently Görtz, with his adventurous blood and with the gift of managing people, which enabled him to have a constant influence on the otherwise intractable Charles XII, had felt in Voltaire something akin to his own nature. It is strange that Voltaire, who had criticized Law so relentlessly, did not see the resemblance between Law and Görtz, a resemblance

which did not stop at the fact that both of them had
issued paper money. Just then Görtz was cherishing
far-reaching political plans, the aim of which was to
put an end to the hostility between Peter the Great
and Charles XII by an alliance, plans which affected
all Europe, but which were tragically disrupted by
the death of Charles. At the end of the same year in
which Voltaire and Görtz met in Paris, Charles XII
fell in the battle near Frederikshald, and Görtz was
taken to Stockholm and beheaded.

There is no doubt but that it was the contact with
Görtz that had awakened Voltaire's interest in the
Swedish adventurer and hero, and led him to write
his *Histoire de Charles Douze*.

15

Precocious as Voltaire was mentally, he had an
equally precocious appreciation of the value of
money. One simply had to have money to lead the
kind of existence without which life did not seem
to him worth living. In his early youth, because of
the dissatisfaction of his father with his way of living,
and because of the unprofitableness of his art, he was
compelled to visit money-lenders and usurers, of
whom he has left us some humorous descriptions.
We marvel at his being summoned, during his stay
in Sully, in 1719, because of a promissory note for
five hundred francs which he had made at the age
of thirteen to a woman named Thomas. He refuses
to pay on one ground because he is still a minor, he
lacks one month to maturity, i.e., twenty-five years;
on another ground because he insists that he has
returned the money, and has been assured by the
woman that she has burned the note.

In 1719 Voltaire was living in a modest lodging
in the rue de la Calandre. He was constantly invited
out for lunch and supper; but of course he wanted
to lead a life in keeping with his position. The humiliating and dependent status of writers repelled and
disgusted him.

In the previous century, writers had lived on the

bounty of a wealthy patron. Corneille had known such poverty that in his old age he owned but one pair of shoes. He dedicated his *Cinna* to the financier Montauron, who paid one hundred gold pieces for the honor, and in that dedication compared him with the Emperor Augustus. La Fontaine had to go from door to door, to Bouillon and Herwart and to Madame de Sablière, to beg for food, lodging, and clothing. Colletet was so poor that as Boileau says, "he sought his bread from kitchen to kitchen." In the eighteenth century Allainval, a dramatist whose plays were frequently performed, was so completely lacking in means that he hadn't a roof over his head. Writers lived like parasites. How pitiful was La Bruyère during his stay at the house of Duke Louis de Bourbon, where he had been first teacher, and then companion, but always in a menial position! We cannot, either, forget how his fellow-servant, the poet Santeuil, died: from a pinch of tobacco which the Duke put in his glass—the droll fellow!

It was well known that Madame de Tencin, a lady who was very affable, and who never intended to humiliate anyone, every New Year gave two yards of velvet for new trousers to each writer who sat at her table. Voltaire heard of it and resolved that he would never come to any such pass. He had business sense and meant to be independent.

Even more than this: He won independence for writers as a class; he acquired also the freedom for authors to say openly all that poverty or gratitude had hindered his predecessors from saying. He separated the two conceptions scribe and parasite which until then had been synonymous.

As related before, the Government of Philippe d'Orléans, in need of money, founded in 1716, a tribunal called the *Chambre de Justice,* modeled after the tribunal of the same name, founded fifty years before. Its purpose was to investigate the origin of the fortunes of financiers, and to determine arbitrarily the taxes. No less than 4,410 wealthy men were alarmed, and the tribunal succeeded in extorting a sum of one hundred and sixty million livres from them. However, no more than seventy million of this reached the state treasury. The rest went into the pockets of the Regent's court, part into those of the ladies and part into the pockets of those whom he jokingly called his *roués*. When, for instance, the treasurer of the military police, Paparel, was sentenced to death for dishonesty in office and his entire fortune confiscated, the Marquis de la Fare, Paparel's son-in-law, succeeded in having the Regent transfer to him Paparel's immense fortune. The father-in-law was pardoned but had no sou returned to him.

Justice was not always had, even when the *Chambre de Justice* did its best. But of course the fury of the financiers was centered on this tribunal and still more on the informants who provided it with material for indictments. For this reason Voltaire wrote his ode, *La Chambre de Justice*, which brands this tribunal as infamous. It expresses indignation over the demand that families be compelled to give information as to the origin of their fortunes:

> Une ordonnance criminelle
> Veut qu'en public chacun révele
> Les opprobres de sa maison;
> Et, pour couronner l'entreprise,
> On fait d'un pays de franchise
> Une immense et vaste prison.

Furthermore, the ode expresses a justifiable contempt for the informants motivated by selfishness, envy, and spite:

> Le délateur, monstre exécrable,
> Est orné d'un titre honorable
> A la honte de notre nom;
> L'esclave fait trembler son maître;
> Enfin nous allons voir renaitre
> Les temps de Claude et de Néron.

According to gossip of the day, which Maurepas helped to circulate, this ode was written at the request of two financiers, Pâris and Héron. Certainly Pâris later showed gratitude. Indeed it was he and his brothers whom Voltaire had to thank for the greater part of his fortune aside from what he won in a lottery.

At his father's death (on January 1, 1722) Voltaire

did not inherit a great fortune. When he took office, the elder Arouet put up a sum of 240,000 livres as a bond. This did not represent his whole fortune. His daughter, Madame Mignot, received as dowry two houses in Paris. Voltaire's brother Armand, who inherited the father's office, was unable to pay Voltaire his share, i.e., one half of the 240,000 livres, and Voltaire was not satisfied with the interest on his share. This led to differences between the brothers, which continued for years. But Voltaire had a yearly income of 4,250 livres, granted him by the Regent.

From a letter which he wrote in 1718 to Madame de Bernières, the wife of the President of the Parliament, it can be seen that at the age of twenty-four he was engaged in business transactions which at that time were considered natural and justified. Today they would be called rather shady. He writes that his letter had been interrupted by a delegation which proposed to put him at the head of a newly founded company. "I, Madame, prefer your company, which is the most pleasant I know, to the Indian Company in which I have invested a good deal of my fortune. Let me assure you that I am thinking more of the pleasure of visiting you at your country estate than of the business we are going to transact."

He acted as intermediary at the closing of deals or the renewal of leases and found it a profitable occupation. "The Regent has given his word," he writes. "And as the person (apparently a woman) who has received his consent has also given me her word I have no fear of their using some other intermediary. I can even go so far to say that, should these people try to leave me out of it, I have enough influence to put the whole scheme on the rocks. . . . You tell me that if I am not in Paris on Thursday I will be dropped out of the business. You know these gentlemen, so you can just tell them for me that they alone can be the losers, as I was given the concession, and as long as I have it I choose whatever company I please." In the next letter he declares that he has got hold of an even bigger proposition, and that it is a sure thing: "The party (you know the one I mean) is on the right side of the Regent and he'll get the pick of the business."

A year later he made an amazing killing. Dining one evening at the house of Madame de Dufay, he listened to one of the guests—it was the brilliant libertine Condamine—making fun of the Comptroller General, Lepelletier-Desfort. It seems that the comptroller, in order to pay off the notes issued by the municipality, had instituted a lottery which could be worked for a win by a simple calculation. Voltaire owned some of the tickets, and, astounded by the correctness of the calculations, which he promptly checked, used it and won 500,000 francs. The comptroller, angry over his own shortsightedness, sued him but lost the suit. From that day on, Voltaire had no more worries over money.

16

The Duchess de Villars was so charmed by Voltaire's *Œdipe* that she at once invited the young poet to stay with the Marshal and herself at Villars. He accepted the invitation and—fell passionately in love. He was twenty-five, and she was thirty-four, very beautiful, adored by her circle, and incidentally by her husband, whom this passion for his own wife made somewhat ridiculous in the eyes of his contemporaries. Although his renown as Field Marshal helped him to live it down. The duchess praised and flattered and pampered Voltaire impossibly; but nothing more. She was fire and flame for his art; for him she was simply a good friend. Not that she was without sentiment; there was an Abbé de Vauréal to whom she showed a marked partiality. But for once in his life Voltaire suffered so keenly from a love denied that he lost his zest for work, neglected whatever literary plans he had, and was in a constant feverish fret.

The Marshal showed a sincere liking and a great admiration for his young guest. Again and again he calls him France's first poet. When the young man, in order to get over his passion, retired for a while from the château, the Marshal wrote him very pleasantly to come back to them. The good man disposes of all of Voltaire's false excuses for not returning, without for a moment suspecting his real reason.

To his friend, the Marquise de Mimeure, Voltaire confided that he was resolved not to go again to Villars; the Marquise seems to have approved of this. But he was easily persuaded to break his resolution again and again.

Only when he realizes that any kind of work becomes for him impossible does he make up his mind firmly to tear himself away. He uses the same trick he uses all his life: he is dying, terribly low, and his physician (this time it is Vinache) strictly forbids any visitors to see him. As a typical example of the style and tone of a great lord and important general of that time, a few extracts from a letter written Voltaire by the Marshal on this occasion are worth looking at. One should take into consideration the fact that the writer is a Duke, and forty-one years older than the young man whom he invites so impressively:

"If you want to take my advice, then don't entrust yourself to the care of Vinache, don't be taken in by his seductive speech, his art of trying to relate the combined influence of the seven planets and minerals to the seven vital organs of the human body.

"Come to us and eat good soup at regular times, don't take more than four meals a day, and go early to bed! Keep away from paper, ink, dice and lansquenet! I permit you to play checkers. Two months of such diet are far better than Vinache.

"I owe you a thousand thanks for the information you have given us. The Marquis (his son) has been grieving over the closing of our theatre and has resolved to return to his regiment. My coach which will bring him to Paris on Saturday will bring you back here on Sunday.

"Now we have opened a theatre of our own. The Marquise (his daughter-in-law) took charge of it with an ardor which is worthy of her, she was the daughter of Marshal de Noailles; she undertook to make up two soldiers from the King's regiment, for the rôles of Pauline and Stratonice, and although she applied more paint to their faces than there is on a carriage, she found it still was not enough.

"Mlle. Ludière, who is bashfulness personified, was in a bad scrape when she had to wrap crinoline around the naked hips of the two grenadiers because . . .

"What you tell us is more interesting than all the news we can tell you. One of the servant girls has fallen passionately in love with a gardener. Her mother, a worse dragon than Madame Dumay and married a second time, is opposed to the marriage. Madame la Maréchale has interfered in this matter; but she preferred to scold the mother rather than to pay the dowry herself, which is not like her usual generosity. . . .

"Here, my dear poet, you have all I can give you in bad prose in return for your verses. A thousand regards to the Duke and Duchess de Sully, both of whom I wish good health so that you may undertake the journey to us. Right now we have good and numerous company; we are twenty-two at the table, but most of them will depart tomorrow."

As can be seen, this letter was written in the age of politeness.

Voltaire was much sought after. Now he stayed at the castle of Duke de Richelieu, now in Maisons at the home of his friend, the President, or again, in spite of himself, at Villars, where at that time Fontenelle's *La Pluralité des Mondes* was being studied. There was great popular interest in events transpiring on the planets Saturn and Jupiter, which in default of a better instrument, were observed through opera glasses. Voltaire humorously describes this:

Le soir, sur des lits de verdure,
Lits, que de ses mains la nature,
Dans ces jardins délicieux
Forma pour une autre aventure,
Nous bouillons tout l'ordre des cieux:

Nous prenons Venus pour Mercure,
Car vous saurez qu'ici l'on n'a
Pour examiner les planettes,
Au lieu de vos longues lunettes,
Que des lunettes d'opéra.

One of the houses in which the young poet felt at home was that of the Marquis de Mimeure. The Marquis was a member of the French Academy, a fine intellect and a straightforward and agreeable gentleman. His wife formerly a beauty, and even now in her forties quite a handsome figure, had always liked to make her home the center of the literary and artistic life of Paris. Since the year 1714 Voltaire had been received there with open arms. He corresponded with the Marquise as an intimate friend. Nevertheless, it was hard for him to make himself congenial with the different wits to whom the house was open: Roy, whom he abhorred and who hated him, was one. Another was Piron who, like the master of the house, came from Bourgogne and was received with distinction as the merry, witty gipsy he was. At first he behaved very politely toward Voltaire, but, hurt by the latter's harsh attitude, he became his bitter enemy and opponent.

From the time when Voltaire began to feel strongly attracted by the beautiful wife of the President, Madame de Bernières, and especially after she in turn began to show a jealous interest in him, Voltaire lost interest in Madame de Mimeure. Madame Bernières became so unreasonable as to forbid him to visit the poor Marquise who had just had her breast amputated as the result of a grave disease.

Doubtless Madame de Bernières wished to have her young friend on hand as much as possible; she wished him to live at her home, to eat at her table. After 1723 a whole apartment was kept at his disposal in her house. In a letter of January 15, 1722, he writes her that he realizes more and more clearly that "she alone was his true friend." Bernières was President of the Parliament of Normandy, Madame de Bernières, thirty-five years old and very pretty, was rather dictatorial in her behavior, and she carried it off successfully by force of her husband's high rank and very considerable fortune.

Voltaire was as much at home at her country seat Rivière-Bourdet as in her house in Paris. But in order not to sacrifice his independence he paid for every stay. That this was the case was shown several

years later. Desfontaines, among many other nasty
libels against Voltaire, charged him with having
sponged on the President de Bernières. The latter's
wife made it known that Voltaire had paid the sum of
1,800 francs to cover expenses consequent upon his
visit.

At the estate of Richelieu Voltaire felt thoroughly
comfortable. From there, in 1720, he writes to his
friend Thiriot:

"At present I am living in the nicest château in
France. No Prince in Europe has such beautiful
statues in such great number. Everything here re-
minds one of the greatness of Cardinal de Richelieu.
The town is built like the Place Royal. The Château
is immense, but what pleases me most is the Duke de
Richelieu, whom I like with inexpressible tenderness
—no more, though, than you."

The young Duke had just finished seventeen
months in prison for his conspiracy to deliver the city
of Bayonne to the Spaniards. The Regent remarked
that for what Richelieu had done he deserved to lose
four heads if he had that many. However, the Regent's daughter, Mademoiselle de Valois, obtained
pardon for him. She loved him madly, and to save
his life she accepted the suit of the Duke de Modena
whom she had till then refused to marry.

17

One of the country places which young Voltaire
not infrequently visited was La Source, the estate of
Henry Saint John, Lord Bolingbroke. Voltaire little
suspected that what he learned there was an invaluable preparation for the future. There Voltaire met
for the first time a young Englishman almost perfectly equipped with the attributes of a great man.
For the first time he met a remarkable political and
parliamentary genius, and for the first time he came
in contact with an English aristocrat who, besides
being a thoroughly experienced statesman, was the
champion of the most advanced English freethinking
of that time, stood out for the highest English culture

of that epoch, and set an example of true political
originality.

Bolingbroke's renown as a politician is still fresh:
Lord Beaconsfield saw in him his first political ideal.
In his early published *Vindication of the English
Constitution* Disraeli said of him: "Lord Bolingbroke
brought into his party clearness and connection of
thought. He had that fiery imagination which, with its
incessant fertility, its endless resourcefulness, is just
as essential to a great statesman or a great general
as to a great poet. He was the ablest writer and the
most perfect speaker of his time."

Bolingbroke, sixteen years Voltaire's senior, had a
very active life behind him at the time the young poet
was introduced to him. After a frivolous youth he
was, ever since his election to the House of Commons
in 1701, recognized as a splendid orator, as a man
of penetrating mind and keen judgment. Although
a Tory, he became at the age of twenty-six Minister
of War under Marlborough. He held this position for
four years only, as the Whigs forced him out.[1]

In the Tory ministry he was appointed Foreign
Minister, and it was he who dictated the terms
of the Treaty of Utrecht with Louis XIV under such
easy conditions that the War of the Spanish Succession ended without humiliation for worn-out
France.

In 1714 he had just been given the task of forming
the new ministry when the death of Queen Anne
forced his resignation. Threatened with a charge of
high treason, i.e., communication with the Pretender
James Stuart, he fled to France. For seven years after
the Pretender's unsuccessful landing in Scotland—
from 1716 to 1723—Bolingbroke lived in France until
the Duchess of Kendal obtained for him permission
to return to England.

After 1719 Bolingbroke bought and lived on an
estate in Anjou amidst delightful surroundings. Here
he had a house which he never tired of arranging and

---

[1] When Bolingbroke became Minister of War the courtesans
of London said to each other: "Bolingbroke gets 8,000
guineas yearly, and all for us!" (Voltaire, letter of April 24,
1769.)

decorating and to which he gave the name La Source, from a fountain which started in his forest, a fountain which he insists in his letters to Swift is the most brilliant and the clearest in Europe.

Here he lived with his mistress, who soon became his wife, a French lady, widow of a certain Marquis de Villette, a brave naval officer and a cousin of Madame de Maintenon. The Marquise had become a widow at the age of forty-two and it was not until almost ten years later that Bolingbroke met her. But in spite of her age he loved her with a flaming jealous passion, and when the two joined their fates they lived in a constant state of delight.

From a letter of Voltaire to Thiriot, dated January 2, 1722, and written after his first stay at La Source, one can see how deeply impressed he has been by Bolingbroke's family life.

"I must describe to you the enduring enchantment of my visit at La Source in the house of my Lord Bolingbroke and Madame de Villette. I have found in this famous Englishman all the calm of his countrymen and all the politeness of ours. Never have I heard our language spoken more correctly or more forcefully. This man who has kept active all his life at recreation or at public work, has nevertheless found time to study and to retain everything. He knows the history of ancient Egypt as well as that of England. He knows Vergil by heart as well as Milton; he has a taste for English, French and Italian poetry; but he enjoys them in different ways because he knows very well how to appreciate the varying genius of each of these literatures."

Naturally, Voltaire could not resist reading his *Henriade* to this couple.

As his relations with the Regent had become more favorable when the latter had discovered that Voltaire was not the author of various attacks on him, the composer of the *Henriade* entertained the idea of dedicating the poem to the Duke on its completion. In 1718 he wrote the Regent a letter on the matter. When the epic was finished in 1720 and the Regent had in the meantime spoken to Voltaire about literature, had among other things called particular attention to the great talent of Rabelais whom Voltaire always underrated, the poet asked his friend Thiriot to make a copy of the first nine cantos for the Regent.

Now he had the joy of having the *Henriade* praised in the most glowing terms by Bolingbroke and his wife. He mentions this in his letter to Thiriot:

"After the description I have given of Lord Bolingbroke it may seem immodest on my part to say that Madame de Villette and he are infinitely pleased with my poem. In their enthusiasm they rated it above anything else in French poetry. I know very well, of course, that I must deduct a great deal from this exaggerated praise. But I want to spend three months polishing it until it is worthy of at least a part. I believe that if I further improve this work it will finally achieve a logical form."

It requires a certain understanding of the feeling and method of thought of the early eighteenth century, especially its poetic standards, to comprehend this enthusiasm for a work which today, even in the author's native land, has lost all interest. It is certain that even before its publication it interested the better circles. From La Source Voltaire writes to Madame de Bernières: "Let me know what social success my son (Henry IV) has won, if he has made himself many enemies and if it is generally acknowledged that I am his father."

Even before the *Henriade* was published, legends sprang up about it. It seemed that a really great epic, like the Æneid of old, had almost been burned, but was rescued at the last minute by a friendly hand. As Augustus is supposed to have saved from burning the Roman epic condemned by Vergil, so had President Hérault at Castle Maisons snatched from the flames the manuscript of Voltaire who, angered by the criticism of his audience, had thrown the treasure into the grate. This anecdote has been confirmed from too many sources not to be true. However, the probability that a copy existed can hardly be called negligible.

While Voltaire was developing himself as an epic poet, he suffered—as was perhaps to be expected after

the unusual luck he had with his maiden effort
Œdipe—a severe check as a playwright. His next
tragedy, *Artemire,* was received so unfavorably at
its first performance on February 15, 1720, that the
irritable author jumped from his theater box onto
the stage and started a personal argument with the
audience. When it became known who the speaker
was the spectators became quiet, as he spoke so
adroitly, so warmly and eloquently, that he was rewarded with enthusiastic applause. Unfortunately he
had been foolish enough to give an important rôle
to Mlle. de Livry in which she greatly displeased.
The play itself was weak and was unable to overcome
the original poor impression, although it aroused the
enthusiasm of Adrienne Lecouvreur, and although
she played it with her engaging spirit.

Voltaire realized that it was hopeless to continue
his battle on such unfavorable territory. He withdrew the play after its eighth performance, in spite
of the wish of the Regent's mother to see it again.
He used a few verses from it in his later tragedy,
Marianne, which is on a similar theme: a woman
tortured by the cruel jealousy of a man whom she
does not love.

18

About this period there crops up for the first time
in Voltaire an ambition which he retained many
years but which was never really satisfied, the aspira-
tion to a diplomatic career. Since the majority of
Voltaire's biographers have been hostile, they have
seized on every unsuccessful ambition to ridicule
him and to emphasize his weaknesses. There are only
a few historians and essayists who have not criticized
his inclination for diplomatic activity. Much of the
unruly part of his nature had to be tamed before
he could be of use as a diplomat; on the other hand,
he had in marked degree many of the qualities that go
to the make-up of a successful one: tact, affability,
winning personality. I am backed in this opinion by
no less an authority than Frederick the Great. In his
introduction to the *Henriade* he says: "Such a uni-

versal genius, such an outstanding mentality, such a
diligent man as M. de Voltaire could have achieved
a dazzling success in almost any line, had he chosen
to abandon the field of fine arts in order to devote
himself to those activities which are usually called
the serious professions, requiring zeal and ambition.
However, he preferred to follow the irresistible urge
of his genius toward art and science."

In 1721 Voltaire wrote his *Epître au Cardinal Dubois,* which in the style of the time flatters the unworthy minister in a shameless manner even going
so far as to call him a greater man than his predecessor, Cardinal de Richelieu. May 28th of the following year he wrote to Dubois offering to go on a
secret mission to Vienna, ostensibly to visit Jean
Baptiste Rousseau, really to bribe a certain Solomon
Levi to betray secrets of the Empire that would be
valuable to France. Dubois, not because he was too
narrow minded to employ a poet in the diplomatic
service—he had sent the dramatist Destouches as
Ambassador to England—was not attracted by Voltaire's offer, and the thing never came off. It was not
until Dubois was replaced by Cardinal Fleury as
Prime Minister and Frederick the Great had succeeded Frederick William on the Prussian throne,
that Voltaire was given his chance at diplomacy.

About this time occurred an embarrassing incident,
a precursor of similar ones which were to have a
marked influence on his life. Dining one day at the
home of the Minister of War, Le Blanc, it happened
that Voltaire was placed at the same table with Captain Beauregard. He had, of course, found out long
ago whose denunciations had sent him to the Bastille. It must have been either his intimate friend
d'Argental, or the police-spy masquerading as a gentleman. Voltaire, justly angered, and unschooled in
keeping silent, said: "I knew that spies were paid,
but I did not know that they were rewarded by the
privilege of eating at a Minister's table." After dinner Beauregard asked the Minister's permission to
chastise Voltaire. The Minister gave his consent, on
the condition that nobody should witness the affair.

Beauregard lay in wait for Voltaire's coach on the Sèvres bridge, pulled him out and caned him.

Voltaire obtained a warrant from the local magistrate, but Beauregard had hastened off, and rejoined his regiment. Voltaire, with a thirst for revenge, brought suit against Beauregard before the Châtelet Tribunal and pursued the case relentlessly. Moreover, he went all the way to the Sologne himself in a vain effort to find his enemy and obtain personal satisfaction. Meanwhile the law case proceeded with the usual aggravating slowness. In a letter to Madame de Bernières, dated January 15, 1723, Voltaire writes that he had hunted the man and had others hunt him, to no avail, but that he was fully determined never to give up the suit. Some months later Le Blanc was dismissed and exiled. He had been found out in certain stock market deals, besides Madame de Prie did not like him. In his place M. de Breteuil became Minister of War. Then at last Voltaire had the satisfaction of seeing Beauregard clapped in prison and kept there for some time.

Had Beauregard been of noble birth he would doubtless have got off scott-free, like the Count de la Feuillade some time before.

The Count resented the satire *Tart à la Crême* in Molière's *Critique de l'École des Femmes*. One day in Versailles, as the poet was bowing to him, the Count seized his head and rubbed it so vehemently against his coat buttons that the poor poet's face swam in blood. However, he did this only after he had asked the King: "Sire, can Your Majesty do without Molière?" And Louis XIV, understanding perfectly, returned the rather unkingly answer: "La Feuillade, I beg your indulgence for Molière."

19

His grace and intellect, his insouciant elegance, his readiness with a witty retort, and that presence of mind which was never at a loss for a sharp word or a neat bit of flattery, made young Voltaire a charming companion. But over and above these qualities, it

was that inner sparkle, that gushing spring of fresh
ideas lending such a sure spontaneity to his own
prose, and influencing the prose of his contemporaries, that made him irresistible.

Women were just as susceptible to this as men and,
although Voltaire gave up all eroticism at a comparatively early age, for a long time he stayed young
enough to make conquests among the fair sex, as was
the fashion in this century of gallantry, not through
the heart but through the mind.

A famous auburn beauty, the Countess Marie Marguerite Elizabeth de Rupelmonde, proposed to Voltaire that they go together on a journey to the Netherlands. He did not decline. So far he had seen no
part of the world but France. Besides, he had something very definite to do in the Netherlands. Didn't
Jean Baptiste Rousseau, his elder brother poet, live
in Brussels? They had exchanged polite letters of
praise for years and Voltaire wished to meet him.
However, he and his seductive companion made no
special haste to reach this goal.

The Countess Rupelmonde, if we believe her admirers, was as beautiful as Aphrodite, and if we believe her detractors, was as without regard for virtue.
She was the daughter of Marshal d'Aligre and, in
1705, had been married to Maximilian de Récourt,
Count de Rupelmonde, who was killed near Villa
Viciosa in 1710. Friends and adorers of this famous
lady found in her a strong inclination to tenderness
and great doubts on the serious questions of life.
At the time the two set out on their journey, in 1722,
Voltaire was twenty-eight, she thirty-seven, which is
an age at which a woman ravishes the adolescent.

The travelers made their first stop at Cambrai. A
Peace Congress had just begun, one of those affairs
where half the time is spent in getting through ceremonies and the other half without getting anywhere.
In a letter to Cardinal Dubois from Cambrai, Voltaire
writes that it looks as though all the deputies and
cooks in Europe were met. The German delegates
did nothing but drink their Kaiser's health. Of the
Spaniards, one heard mass twice a day and the other
directed a company of actors. The English sent many

swift couriers to Champagne, but few to London. Voltaire asserts that he is writing this letter to His Eminence at the special request of a beauty, and he does not forget to mention who the beauty is. His tone with the Cardinal is surprisingly familiar and easy.

Fête followed fête in Cambrai, and the diplomats vied with one another to pay the most flattering honors to the visiting pair from Paris. Hardly had the marriage of the Infante Don Carlos to the Princess de Beaujolais become known, when the Count de Saint-Estevan arranged a banquet with a ball and public fireworks, and opened two fountains of wine for the populace. Whereupon Count von Windisch-grätz honored his Emperor in a manner not to be outdone in splendor and magnificence. And everywhere the two travelers from Paris were guests of honor. At a dinner a unanimous wish was expressed in the poet's presence to see *Œdipe* the next day. But as the program had been arranged for Racine's comedy *Les Plaideurs,* at the special request of Windischgrätz, Voltaire addressed a petition to His Excellency in Madame de Rupelmonde's name:

> Seigneur, le congrès vous supplie
> D'ordonner tout présentement,
> Qu'on nous donne tragédie
> Demain pour divertissement.
> Nous vous le demandons au nom de Rupelmonde etc.

He delivered the petition in person, was promptly granted it, and informed his irresistible companion with the following lines:

> L'amour vous fit, aimable Rupelmonde,
>   Pour décider de nos plaisirs.
> Je n'en sais pas de plus parfait au monde
>   Que de répondre à vos désirs.
> Sitôt que vous parlez, on n'a pas de réplique;
> Vous aurez donc *Oedipe,* et même sa critique.
>   L'ordre est donné pour qu'en votre faveur
>   Demain l'on joue et la pièce et l'auteur.

The play should be played and likewise a joke on the author: that is, a travesty on *Œdipe* should be presented: Dominique's *Œdipe travesti.*

A letter of Voltaire to Thiriot reveals that he was by no means constant to the fair Rupelmonde. A poem, *Les deux Amours* (*A Madame la marquise de Rupelmonde*) was written to declare before the world that his love for her is pure and therefore steadily grows. This poem must be taken with a grain of salt, like so many of the rhymed gallantries of that age, at which Voltaire had no peer. Another little poem of this journey, addressed to the Comtesse, has been preserved, which shows some real feeling in spite of the style of the time. It begins with a passage in which Apollo and the Sea God succeeded so well in disguising themselves as human beings that nobody recognized them, while Venus, disguised as the lady whom we know, was lamentably unsuccessful.

> Mais c'est en vain qu'abandonnant les cieux
> Venus comme eux veut se cacher au monde;
> On la connaît au pouvoir de ses yeux
> Dès que l'on voit paraître Rupelmonde.

All these, however, are trifles. The only thing of lasting value among the poems written during this journey is the *Epître à Uranie*. In Holland she had told him about her religious doubts and her intellectual helplessness. Since he could not openly develop his thoughts in verse without laying himself open to danger, he wrote, like Pierre Bayle before him, both sides of the argument at once. Hence the title *Le Pour et le Contre*. There is no question which of the views the poet prefers, and here we have expressed for the first time in concise verse, Voltaire's early philosophy of life.

For ten years he let the poem lie unprinted. Then it appeared anonymously. It was not until full fifty years later, in 1772, that he dared to give it a place in his works. It begins with the explanation that she had demanded an answer from him, as if he were a second Lucretius:

> Tu veux donc, belle Uranie,
> Qu'érigé par ton ordre en Lucrèce nouveau,
> Devant toi, d'une main hardie,
> Aux superstitions j'arrache le bandeau;
> Que j'expose à tes yeux le dangereux tableau

Des mensonges sacrés, dont la terre est remplie,
    Et que ma philosophie
T'apprenne à mépriser les horreurs du tombeau
    Et les terreurs de l'autre vie.

Next he sketches briefly and clearly the contradictions and absurdities of the biblical tradition, its God who makes people sin in order to have the right of punishing them, who gives man the capacity for pleasure and then damns him to eternal torment for using it. This God creates man in His Own Image, and rues it instantly. Blind in His benefactions and blind in His wrath He has no sooner created man than He wishes to destroy him with the Flood. Then, after drowning the fathers, he wishes to die for the children:

Je veux aimer mon Dieu, je cherche en lui mon père:
On me montre un tyran que nous devons haïr.
Il créa des humains à lui-même semblables
Afin de les mieux avilir.
Il nous donna des cœurs coupables
Pour avoir droit de nous punir;
Il nous fit aimer le plaisir,
Pour nous mieux tourmenter par des maux effroyables
Qu'un miracle éternel empêche de finir.
Il venait de créer un homme à son image,
    On l'en voit soudain repentir,
Comme si l'ouvrier n'avait pas du sentir
    Les défauts de son propre ouvrage.
Aveugle en ses bienfaits, aveugle en son courroux
A peine il nous fit naître, il va nous perdre tous.
Il ordonne à la mer de submerger le monde.

.   .   .   .

Va-t-il dans le chaos plonger les éléments?
Ecoutez, ô prodige! ô tendresse! ô mystères!

Il venait de noyer les pères,
Il va mourir pour les enfants.

For the first time, Voltaire also mentions the Christian tradition. It strikes him as the height of absurdity that God's son, God Himself, let Himself be born in a superstitious and ignorant little nation, the conquered and despised dependency of other nations.

Le fils de Dieu même, oubliant sa puissance
Se fait concitoyen de ce peuple odieux;

> Dans les flancs d'une Juive il vient prendre naissance
> Il rampe sous sa mère, il souffre sous ses yeux
> Les infirmités de l'enfance . . .

Then the poet tells the story of Jesus' life and crucifixion according to the Gospels, and calls special attention to the fact that even the death of the Redeemer is insufficient to appease God's anger:

> Quoi! Dieu voulut mourir pour le salut de tous,
>   Et son trépas est inutile!
> Quoi! l'on me vantera sa clémence facile,
> Quand remontant au ciel il reprend son courroux.

He dwells with particular emphasis on the absurdity of the so-called Original Sin and of the notion that peoples who have never even heard of Christianity should be punished as non-Christians:

> Ayant versé son sang pour expier nos crimes,
> Il nous punit de ceux que nous n'avons pas faits.
> Ce Dieu poursuit encore, aveugle en sa colère
> Sur ses derniers enfants l'erreur d'un premier père.
> Il en demande compte à cent peuples divers
>   Assis dans la nuit du mensonge;
>   Il punit aux fonds des enfers
> L'ignorance invincible où lui-même il les plonge,
> Lui qui veut éclairer et sauver l'univers.

20

It was with similar ideas that he had written the poem at which he worked so long—it was then called *La Ligue*—later it was entitled *Henriade*—a weak contribution to literature, but a great deed for all time to come. How recently the most liberal minds of Louis XIV's reign had approved, or at least excused, the celebration of Eve St. Bartholomew! How few years since the gentlest of men, like Fénélon, the best-hearted, like La Fontaine, the cleverest, like La Bruyère, even women like Madame de Sévigné, had countenanced the banishment of the Huguenots from France, had even applauded it! Bossuet rejoiced when the promise of tolerance was repealed: "Let us hail this the most glorious event of our lives! Let our hearts overflow at Louis' piety and let our joy ring to heaven!"

The *Henriade* is today looked on as a very minor poetic effort; but in Voltaire's time it was considered positively breath-taking. Frederick the Great said in the preface that the passage describing the dream of Henry IV was worth more than the whole of the *Iliad*. In this poem Voltaire probed, with a keenness unsuspected at the time, the vital problems of humanity. He exposed the folly and horror of the religious wars. Frederick's critical faculties were carried away by his enthusiasm. The "fire of imagination" that he speaks of is conspicuous by its absence according to modern critics. But Frederick is sound in this, he points out the incalculable service Voltaire rendered man in showing the folly of his forefathers so clearly as to make an eloquent warning against its repetition.

While Voltaire polished and corrected this composition, religious mania for blood still had a hold on Europe. During the year 1721, in a single little Spanish town (Granada), nine men and eleven women were burned alive. There was a big scaffold on which four stakes could burn human flesh at the same time. Two years later, just after the *Henriade* had been completed, Philip V celebrated the arrival in Madrid of the little French Princess, his bride, by the burning alive of nine human beings, so that the Princess might enjoy their cries and the smell of their burning flesh. We need not admire the *Henriade* today, but when we consider that it was to put out these pyres that it was written, we cannot but admire its author.

Up to that time, if there were any pity felt, it was not for the heretic but for the supposedly offended Host. During the dragonades, when Louis XIV's cavalry were billeted on Protestants to torture them and ravish their women, it was done out of pity for the poor Host, which suffered intensely when the damned Huguenots devoured it. In the *Henriade,* which is really a poem of the Eve of Saint Bartholomew, it is man who becomes the object of pity.

The poem, to be sure, was first inspired by an admiration for Henry IV, awakened in Voltaire's mind by Caumartin. The deeper inspiration of the *Henriade,* however was the indignation felt at the imbecile cruelty of the religious views, and fury at the senseless lust for blood, on the part of the people. He did not know that the day of the epic poem had passed, that the form had become lifeless.

Homer, in Voltaire's eyes, was vivid but childish, Vergil a master of composition—in which, therefore, he must be slavishly imitated—and an elegant stylist. He thought the *Æneid,* however, suffered from the fact that the hero was saccharine and uninteresting besides being unhistoric. He, Voltaire, was not childish—this was his least fault—and he had a great, sympathetic hero, a mighty King, a figure of unquestionable historical importance.

He did not know that anecdotal, rhymed history was far from being the same thing as narrative poetry; moreover, with all his lack of naïveté he confused gallantry with love, and allegory with lofty poetic style.

He discovered a hero who had been completely forgotten, who had been put in the shade by the dull, pompous Louis XIV, forgotten as the original Protestant, forgotten as the enemy of Spain, now France's ally by marriage, forgotten, finally, as the great lover, *le vert galant.* One whose virtues and whose faults even made him a more suitable French national hero than Louis. Even if the *Henriade* is no longer read today, it made Henry IV the Hero of France for all time.

Today the work is deservedly forgotten, loaded down as it is with rhetoric and declamation, with abominable allegories, with imitations of Vergilian models, which have a cold, false effect. The wonders that appear in it are boring, as when the besieged see Henry in the clouds on a triumphal chariot of victory. The belief in God, which pervades the work, has an irritating effect by its senseless irrationality, as in the description of the murder of Henry III:

La mort impatiente attendait sa victime,
Et pour perdre Valois Dieu permettait un crime.

Or in the tenth canto at Aumale's death in a duel, which is explained by the fact that he did not believe in God:

> J'attends tout de mon bras,
> C'est de nous que depend le destin des combats.

By today's standard it is almost comic when St. Louis appears to Henry and, in a bad imitation of the sixth book of the *Æneid,* shows him Hell on the gates of which dull allegories stretch their tired limbs. Envy, Haughtiness, Weakness, Ambition, Hypocrisy, each has its own peculiar attributes which are picturesque, indeed, but never give form to the figures. On the whole it seems too bad that Voltaire, with the complete approbation of his contemporaries, should have accomplished with this work the one thing that is not in the least like him and which was furthest from his aim: to be utterly, profoundly boring.

With poor rationalism St. Louis explains to the hero of the poem how God's paternal heart forbids him to make the Punishment of Hell endless:

> Ne crois point, dit Louis, que ces tristes victimes
> Souffrent des chatiments qui surpassent leur crimes!

God makes use of Infinity when he rewards, but not when he takes revenge:

> Sur la terre on le peint l'exemple des tyrans;
> Mais ici c'est un père qui punit ses enfants.

Henry, who surely had a crying need of divine indulgence on one score, is really quite absurd when he is reminded by St. Louis that God does not punish minor amusements so terribly:

> Il adoucit les traits de sa main vengeresse;
> Il ne sait point punir des moments de faiblesse
> Des plaisirs passagers, pleins de trouble et d'ennui,
> Par des tourments affreux, éternels comme lui.

Two hundred years ago such a consolation was both original and welcome.

A still more difficult task for Voltaire than the explanation of Hell to the rational believer, was to fur-

nish a satisfactory definition of Salvation. Of the
dwellers in heavenly abode, however, he says very
nicely:

> Ils désirent sans cesse, et sans cesse ils jouissent,
> Et goûtent dans les feux d'une éternelle ardeur
> Des plaisirs sans regrets, du repos sans langueur.

Given a place here with other heroes and heroines
is a woman, whose reputation Voltaire later represents as hardly so well-deserved, but who is mentioned with all honor in the *Henriade* and later in his
Essai sur les mœurs. Jeanne d'Arc is represented as
the support of the French throne and as one whose
death brings shame upon the English:

> et vous, brave Amazone,
> La honte des Anglais et le soutien du trône!

There are eloquent and able passages in the *Henriade,* as, for instance, the description of St. Bartholomew's Eve in the second canto.

At some portions of the poem the reader will be
surprised and pleased. The passage in which St.
Louis describes the firmament (into which, apparently at the last revision of the work, the poet has in-
jected Newton's doctrine of the attraction of celestial
bodies) is executed with exemplary simplicity and
clearness. Of the sun he says:

> De lui partent sans fin des torrens de lumière;
> Il donne en se montrant la vie à la matière,
> Et dispense les jours, les saisons et les ans
> A des mondes divers, autour de lui flottant,
> Ces astres asservis à la loi qui les presse
> S'attirent dans leur course et s'évitent sans cesse,
> Et servant l'un à l'autre de règle et d'appui,
> Se prêtent les clartés qu'ils reçoivent de lui.

Next to a eulogy on the English Parliament, one
comes upon the following amusing mockery of the
States-General at Blois, whom Voltaire uses to sym-
bolize idle parliamentary discussion:

> De mille députés l'éloquence stérile
> Y fit de nos abus un détail inutile;
> Car de tant de conseils l'effet le plus commun
> Est de voir tous nos maux sans en soulager un.

The composition, however, is handicapped by the academic-classical style; a superfluity of high-sounding expressions kills all vividness and force. The description of Henry does not contain one significant and memorable feature; there is not one quality in his friend Mornay that would not apply well to the confidant of any tragic hero of that time. The figures of speech lose by borrowing from classical mythology, as, when Henry's charge of the enemy is compared to a landslide, or the valley into which he breaks is personified by its nymphs.

There are no natural surroundings, there is no scene, there is no blade of grass mentioned in the work. As I once put it: "There is no fodder for the horses." The winds are zephyrs, the peasants are shepherds. Voltaire's circumlocution to avoid the use of the word dog is almost burlesque:

Tels au fond des forêts précipitant leur pas,
Les animaux hardis, nourris pour les combats,
Fiers esclaves de l'homme et nés pour le carnage,
Pressent un sanglier, en raniment la rage,
Ignorant le danger, aveugles, furieux,
Le cor excite au loin leur instinct belliqueux.

Far ahead of his times as Voltaire was in other respects, in this he is on the level with his contemporaries, thoroughly dominated by the false ideal of classicism, and by that idol, "good taste," which is even more sacred to that age than the great God of Deism, the Shadow-God whom he had retained.

Voltaire guards and protects this God, useful now as a bugaboo against the dangerous instinct of the crowd, now to furnish a Creator for an imagination incapable of conceiving the creation of the world without a personal omnipotent Creator. However, he always does him homage with striking coldness.

Good taste, on the other hand, he worships with real enthusiasm. That taste was developed out of the finest efforts of the time of Louis XIII and the Augustinian age of Louis XIV. It requires the highest refinement of civilization and at the same time true intelligence.

The classic ideal itself was vague: inevitably so, derived as it was from five centuries of Greek and

Roman writers. The eighteenth century disregarded the originality, the keen sense of reality prevalent in the Greek epic and in Greek dramatic literature. The use of everyday material was considered vulgar, simplicity was childish, and mysticism was evidence of barbaric superstition, regardless of its artistic value.

That ardent feeling cannot be conveyed in a stilted tone, that a sensitive reaction to the sufferings and the absurdities of life cannot be forced out of its natural expression, was something beyond eighteenth-century comprehension. The nobility of expression found in the Greek poets had grown naturally out of the nobility of the thought it expressed, and alongside of the grand style one is apt to find coarseness and buffoonery. But in Voltaire's day dignity and loftiness were the qualities to be striven for, at all costs. Hence all the tedious abstractions and circumlocutions. In ancient times harmony and clearness were possible because people felt harmoniously and thought clearly. The ancient poets were not shy of the mysterious. It forbade transparency, but not clearness. Furthermore, they never hesitated to mix the ceremonial with common impudence, or lyric heights with comic caricature in the same work, be it epic, tragic or comic. In Voltaire's eyes, on the other hand, good taste decreed the absolute separation of the various types and methods of expression; their mixture by the ancients struck him as shocking and ridiculous. And as for clearness, he strove for it so energetically, even devoutly, that he involuntarily sought to simplify things that were really complex and to give superficial explanations for things that were fundamentally inexplicable. One of his firmest beliefs was that there was a basic rule and formula governing all good art.

As we know, Frederick the Great found in the *Henriade* "fiery imagination." We see in it today only an eloquence coming from intelligence or, where the foundation is a little deeper, from reason. As a matter of fact, in the eighteenth century it was reason, thanks to Voltaire's influence, which had to take the place of everything else and which, according to the fundamental conception of the time, acted as talent, genius, virtue, intellect and taste. Toward the end of the century Marie Joseph Chénier expressed this strikingly:

C'est le bon sens, la raison, qui fait tout;
Vertu, génie, esprit, talent et goût,
Qu'est-ce vertu? raison mise en pratique;
Talent? raison produit avec éclat;
Esprit? raison qui finement s'exprime.
Le goût n'est rien qu'un bon sens delicat;
Et le génie est la raison sublime.

These lines voice the psychology and ethics of Voltaire's century, and its conception of poetry.

21

In Cambrai Voltaire felt, as he wrote to Thiriot, happier than he had ever been in Paris. If this should continue, he would surely forsake his native town, unless perhaps Thiriot should vow to love him forever. This passage is one of the politenesses with which the extravagant flatterer is always rather liberal. It is certain, however, that he found his hospitable reception very pleasant. However, he went on to Brussels, largely because he was anxious to meet Jean Baptiste Rousseau.

At fifty-one this exiled poet was bored with his exile. A marvelously complex genius, he had an unusual technical gift for verse, a rare ability to find the right expression. Yet he was, by inclination, a malicious satirist, who found it impossible to refrain from forming his taunts and jibes into mocking, cleverly rhymed persiflage. No one was immune to his poisonous sting. No consideration of gratitude or friendship could stop him.

He offers an even sharper contrast: as a writer of odes he became more and more pious and fervent. As an epigrammatist he wrote some of the most offensive verses in the French language, and nearly all of these indecent epigrams are directed against the Church, especially against monks and nuns.

After the appearance of several of his early plays

and poems Jean Baptiste found various protectors, such as Baron de Breteuil, the father of Madame du Châtelet, and M. de Francine, director of the opera. This did not keep him from falling out with both of them at the first opportunity.

He was a regular patron of a café situated on the corner of the rue Dauphine and the rue Christine in Paris, the hostess of which was a widow by the name of Laurent. Here, literary men, painters, musicians, poets and thinkers used to meet. The writers did not fail to read their verses to each other. They were criticized and more than occasionally scoffed at, which naturally enough frequently caused anger. This café was thus the source of many amusing ballads and biting epigrams.

Apparently there was a very poor spirit of *camaraderie* in this group of wits. This is often the case with people of related talents. And it was very hard for Rousseau to restrain his venom. It was a horrible clique in which pretended friends backbit anyone guilty of success.

To a sneering couplet from Rousseau, the poet Danchet replied with an epigram whose first four lines are not without barbs:

> Fils ingrat, cœur perfide,
> Esprit infecté,
> Ennemi timide,
> Ami redouté.

Voltaire, in his *Vie de J. B. Rousseau* (1738), asserts that Rousseau wrote no less than seventy-two epigrams on the habitués of this café. Of course, the number means nothing, but surely the unrestrained, satirical, malicious habit of thought means a great deal.

Just at this time (1701) Rousseau found a new and influential protector in the Duke de Noailles, and had the satisfaction of seeing his play *La Ceinture Magique* presented for the Duchess de Bourgogne, with many prominent men, even royal princes, filling the cast.

But it was his odes rather than his plays that brought him fame. His success in this field did not come easily nor at once. He entered a contest with Antoine de la Motte-Houdart, the author of the then admired tragedy *Inès de Castro,* when, in the year 1707, the French Academy offered a prize for the best ode on *The Glory of the King.* La Motte was given all the votes.

Rousseau answered with his usual weapons. He wrote verses on the Abbé Bignon, although he had secured Rousseau his place in *l'Academie des inscriptions et belles lettres,* and even on the Duke de Noailles, because on the strength of the Duke's influence he had expected an election to the Académie Française, but La Motte was accepted, while Rousseau was not considered.

Beside himself with resentment, Rousseau wrote an extraordinarily sneering poem against La Motte and all his friends who frequented the café. In it he attacked the Captain of the Guard, La Faye (who got physical revenge) as well as Boindu, the Abbé de Bragelongue, Crébillon, and finally a man of exceptionally coarse nature, the mathematician, Joseph Saurin, who in his youth had been a Calvinist in Lausanne and had become a Catholic in France. Saurin was an energetic, plain-spoken man. He had a habit of telling people to their faces exactly what he thought of them, and therefore did not have many friends.

Saurin was the one who caused Rousseau's banishment from the café. In order to get revenge, the poet concocted the strange scheme of accusing Saurin of being the author of the offensive poem which libeled his friends and himself.

Rousseau's scheme was not so foolish as it seemed: he argued that in searching among the papers of a man like Saurin, who had changed his religion, the authorities would find, not the poem, but probably enough incriminating evidence of other kinds to send him to prison for a considerable time.

Rousseau, therefore, bribed a wretched cobbler's apprentice to testify that Saurin had secretly requested him to let his libellous poem get in the hands of those it attacked. He himself fell prostrate before the wife of the Minister of War, Madame de

Voisin, and begged her protection against the slanderer, Saurin. She wrote on the same day to Le Comte, Chief Justice of the Criminal Court, and Saurin was arrested at once (September, 1710).

Although the victim of this trick had few personal friends, he now suddenly got all of Rousseau's enemies on his side. And their number certainly was large. Fontenelle, who had been insulted by Rousseau, appeared in prison and offered Saurin his purse. Everyone came to his assistance and presented petitions for him. All that had to be considered was the rank absurdity of the accusation that Saurin was the author of a pamphlet which abused Saurin. After two months he was released and given permission to bring action against Rousseau at criminal law.

For Rousseau there was nothing left but to flee. The sentence of the Parliament decreed exile for life, because he "had composed and disseminated foul and libellous verses, and thereafter had employed fradulent means to obtain evidence for the false accusation against Saurin."

First he went to Switzerland, where Count de Luc took care of him, until he offended his son and had to leave the house. Then he went to Vienna and there Prince Eugene cared for him. From Vienna he had moved on to Brussels hoping that the Marquis de Prie, who was Commander in the Netherlands, would give him some sort of position. Lord Cadogan, who was then in The Hague took him to England and got subscribers for his works. But after his return to Brussels he forfeited the favor of his protector. In his unfortunate bent for satire he helped Count de Bonneval compose a libellous poem against Prince Eugene, and thereby lost the pension which the Prince had granted him.

These were the qualities of the man whom Voltaire was so anxious to meet: undoubtedly a talented lyricist and maliciously witty satirist, but by no means a perfect gentleman or an agreeable companion. As Voltaire himself was a rather exacting person, with a similar inclination to ruthless satire, it cannot be surprising, that the harmony between the older and the younger poets was not long-lived.

At the beginning all went well. Even the fact that the first Rousseau heard about Voltaire concerned a disturbance the young man created in church during Mass, did not influence him unfavorably. We have a letter Rousseau wrote to a friend (September 22, 1722), in which he speaks very warmly of his fellow-poet:

"Monsieur de Voltaire has spent eleven days here, during which we have scarcely been apart. I was delighted to meet a young man who justifies such high hopes. He was so kind as to entrust to me his poem (the *Henriade*) for five or six days. I can assure you it does its author high honor. Our nation needs a work like this: the economy is admirable, and the verses are perfect except for a few weak places, the faults of which, however, he admitted to me. I have not found anything in it which can justly be criticized."

It was Voltaire's intention to have the *Henriade* printed in The Hague; he had ample grounds for fearing that its publication would be forbidden in France, and when he arrived at The Hague he took preliminary steps. At that time Holland was regarded as a refuge of literature, an asylum for free thought.

He liked The Hague exceedingly, especially when the sun shone. Holland won his heart at first sight. He enjoyed its fields and meadows, its green trees and canals, which constitute an earthly paradise extending from The Hague to Amsterdam. Amsterdam, then Europe's treasure-house, inspired him with great respect. A thousand ships were in the harbor, and among the five hundred thousand inhabitants he came across not one idler, not one fop, not one pauper, not one snob. Like Holberg, he admired the spirit of the people. He saw the Prime Minister of the Republic go on foot, unescorted by lackeys, in the midst of the crowd. In Holland nobody thought of stopping what he was doing to watch the Prince pass. On every hand Voltaire encountered simplicity and industry. He had another new experience: he, who all through life never ceased bemoaning his poor health, felt strong and fit in Holland.

The next meeting with Rousseau turned their friendship into bitter, rankling hostility, that lasted as long as they both lived. They were both so irritable that a trifle could sever the friendship, and both so belligerent and vengeful that each tried to outdo the other in vituperation. From the moment of their falling out they never tired of hurling the foulest and most abusive sneers.

To give an idea of Rousseau's aggressiveness, the following verses from his pen, directed against Voltaire, may be cited:

> Petit rimeur antichrétien,
> On reconnaît dans tes ouvrages
> Ton caractère et non le mien,
> Ma principale faute, hélas je m'en souviens,
> Vint d'un cœur qui, séduit par tes patelinages
> Crut trouver un ami dans un parfait vaurien,
>   Charme des fous, horreur des sages . . .
> Mais je ne me reproche rien
> Que d'avoir sali quelques pages
> D'un nom aussi vil que le tien.

It is incredible how often in his works Rousseau went out of his way to abuse Voltaire, parry his attacks, belittle his poetry, and expose him to ridicule and contempt.

As early as 1731 Voltaire expressed his scorn of Rousseau in his *Le Temple du Gôut*. And his scorn becomes more and more withering.

Take, for instance, the vitriolic poem *La Crepinade* (1736); or read in the first edition of the *Ode on Ingratitude* to the Duke de Richelieu (also 1736) the verses on Rousseau:

> Dis nous, Rousseau, quel premier crime
> Entraîna tes pas dans l'abîme
> Où j'ai vu Saurin te plonger?
> Ah, ce fut l'oubli des services;
> Tu fus ingrat, et tous les vices
> Vinrent en foule t'assiéger.

One should look up the attacks on Rousseau: in *Mémoire du Sieur de Voltaire* (1739), in *Mémoire sur la Satire* (same year), the detailed *Life of Rousseau,* the *Epistle of Defamation* (to Madame du Châtelet, 1735), which begins:

> Ce vieux rimeur; couvert d'ignominies,
> Organe impur de tant de calomnies;

where Rousseau, as in the fifty-fourth rhymed letter on Newton's philosophy, is told over and over that he has red hair; the essay *Sur le Sieur Rousseau* (1736); and the epigram of January, 1736; which makes the point that if Rousseau is still alive, it is only his desire to defame that keeps him so:

> S'il est vrai qu'encore il respire,
> Car il est mort quant à l'esprit;
> S'il est vrai que Rousseau vit,
> C'est de seul plaisir de médire;

and two more epigrams, 118 and 120, both of which are embittered and scornful; the first is the better:

> Rousseau, sujet au camouflet,
> Fut autrefois chassé, dit on,
> Du théâtre à coups de sifflet,
> De Paris à coups de bâton;
> Chez les Germains chacun sait comme
> Il s'est garanti du fagot;
> Il a fait enfin de dévot,
> Ne pouvant faire l'honnête homme.

As far as can be seen—neither gives any full account of the first quarrel—the original cause of hostility was so trivial that only literati could have made it the ground for such a lasting hatred.

Rousseau had read Voltaire his *Jugement de Pluton,* a vigorous satire on the Parliament of Paris, which had sentenced him. Voltaire, who found the satire too rude and brutal, said: "Master, that was no work of our great and good Rousseau." Thereupon they went for a drive around the town, at which Voltaire jocularly said: "Now get even with me! Now take revenge!" And he read him the letter to Madame de Rupelmonde. Rousseau, who had been converted while in exile and formally belonged to the pious, maintains that his anger was so aroused by the terrible insults to religion, even to the Saviour Himself, that he interrupted the reader with the words: "I don't understand how you can read such contemptible lines to me." Nevertheless, both poets visited the theater together. After the theater they talked about Rousseau's *Ode to Posterity,* which the latter had read to Voltaire, and, when they parted, Voltaire closed that evening's discussion with: "You know, master, that is an ode that will never reach its address." After that, the two seem never to have spoken to each other.

This *Ode à la Postérité* deserves our attention. It gives us a good idea of Jean Baptiste's style when he had flights of fancy. The first stanza reads:

> Déesse des Héros qu'adorent en idée
> Tant d'illustres Amans dont l'ardeur hazardée
> Ne consacre qu'a Toi ses vœux et ses efforts;
> Toi, qu'ils ne verront point, que nul n'a jamais vue
> Et dont pour les Vivans la faveur suspendue
> Ne s'accorde qu'aux Morts.

The poet makes a bid for posterity's admiration, by calling attention to all he had to overcome during his life. A few stanzas will give a sufficient idea of the lyric style employed before Voltaire's time:

> Le Ciel, qui me créa sous le plus dur auspice
> Me donna pour tout bien l'amour de la justice,
> Un génie ennemi de tout art suborneur,
> Une pauvreté fière, une mâle franchise,
> Instruite à détester toute fortune acquise
> Au dépens de l'honneur.

It is enlightening to find that Rousseau dared boast of his strict sense of honor and of his masculine frankness. He furthermore explains how his many virtues have won him the wicked envy of scores:

> C'est cet amour du vrai, ce zèle antipathique
> Contre tout faux brillant, tout éclat sophistique
> Où l'orgueil frauduleux va chercher ses atours.
> Qui lui seule suscita cette foule perverse
> D'ennemis forcenés, dont la rage traverse
> Le repos de mes jours.

It is regrettable that Voltaire was so cruel and petty that it was impossible for him to leave Rousseau alone. In 1738 he is still able to write the lengthy *Life of Jean Baptiste Rousseau,* the authorship of which he tries to conceal. He dwells again and again on the fact that Rousseau's father had been a shoemaker, and he accuses the son of being ashamed of and disowning his father. He charges him—perhaps in good faith—with the authorship of the *Moïsiade,* which actually had been written by Lourdet. With rankling hatred he enumerates every libellous poem, in order to humiliate Rousseau, regardless of the fact that the latter, at the beginning of the year, had suffered a stroke which robbed him of his reason and of the use of his limbs. Voltaire fondly imagined that he disguised himself by now and then speaking of Voltaire (very warmly) as of a stranger. But he is known in the dark as soon as he opens his lips.

Strangely enough, the fourth volume of Rousseau's works closes with a letter of Voltaire to the publisher, M. Seguy. The letter is dated September 29, 1741, and was written in Brussels where Rousseau had died March 17th of the same year. Rather naïvely the publisher had asked Voltaire to subscribe to the collected works of the late poet "who had been his friend."

Voltaire answered that he would gladly subscribe although unfortunately he was one of the truest enemies of the deceased. He claimed this enmity was a great sorrow to him. He had always thought that writers should have brotherly feelings for each other. Were they not sufficiently persecuted? Did they have to add to each other's misery? It seems as though fate, in bringing him to the city where the famous and unfortunate Rousseau had ended his life, had wished to bring about a reconciliation; but the illness to which Rousseau succumbed had robbed Voltaire of the consolation for which both of them had yearned.

Words! Words! Words!

22

In March, 1724, Voltaire's tragedy *Marianne* was played at the *Comédie Française,* but had no success. It was pleasantly received when it was offered in printed form, and two piracies appeared before Voltaire put his own edition on the market; but on the stage it did not go, and the poet was self-critical enough to admit that its failure was deserved. The same year he went with the Duke de Richelieu to the fashionable baths at Forges, where the two friends kept house together. The failure had exhausted Voltaire somewhat and his health as usual worried him. The waters did him much good, and after a short time he felt well. Later, however, he was debilitated by the treatment, and Richelieu, who had been appointed Ambassador to Vienna, urged him to accompany him there. Voltaire wished to let Thiriot go in his stead, but Thiriot was too lazy to care about his future.

In Forges, Voltaire lived among prominent people, saw daily the Duchess de Béthune-Sully, the Princess de Guise, later mother-in-law of the Duke de Richelieu, and the Marquise de Prie. For a month Forges became Paris, and it was in Forges that he won the true friendship of the Marquise de Prie; and that meant something. At that moment she was France's real Regent.

The Duchess de Berri had died in May, 1719. December 2, 1723, the Regent had expired suddenly and Duke Henri de Bourbon at once became Prime Minister of the young King. Madame de Prie in turn, controlled the Duke de Bourbon by her gayety and her firm will. For financial adviser she had chosen Voltaire's protector, Pâris-Duverney.

Before she left Forges for Fontainebleau, she ordered her majordomo to prepare an apartment for Voltaire to occupy in the autumn. In letters to Madame de Bernières he affected indifference: but in reality he was now at the consummation of his wishes.

The young King, who, during his entire life was celebrated and adored like an idol, even by Voltaire, is the gloomiest figure in French history: handsome, elegant, not stupid, but apathetic, heartless, without sense of duty, ice-cold, surfeited. At the age of fourteen Louis XV looked eighteen and physically mature.

He was surrounded by pages each more perverted
than the other. There was the young Epernon, son
of the Count de Toulouse; he was the clinging vine
type; there was the young Duke de Gesvres (nephew
of the handsome Cardinal de Rohan), who loved
dainty embroidery; there was the young Duke de
Trémouille, first gentleman of the bed chamber, who,
in 1724, was discovered to have made the King his
Ganymede. At the age of sixteen he dominated the
King in every respect. Without shame he appeared as
the rival of Mademoiselle de Charolais, the sister of
the Duke de Bourbon, who had tried in vain to make
a conquest of the King. Gesvres, jealous of La Trémouille, revealed to the Duke de Bourbon the behavior of the young Court.

It was not easy to offer actual interference. There
were too many who openly professed their abhorrence of women, among them the Minister Maurepas
and the Abbé Fleury, the former tutor of the King,
who was indispensable to him.

The mildest measures were taken; the Duke de
Trémouille was forced to marry. He yielded, but for
eight years did not live with his wife. It was of importance to arouse the King's appetite for women. The
best thing was to get him married as soon as possible.
A list was made of seventeen princesses who might
be suitable; among them was an English, a Portu-
guese, a Danish, a Prussian, a Russian, one from
Modena, one from Saxony—one from Eisenach, one
from Lorraine, all young—some too young—only a
few Roman Catholic, although the religion, of course,
was of the highest importance.

Without any great deliberation the Duke de Bourbon and Madame de Prie decided in favor of the
Duke's sister, the lovely twenty-one-year-old Princess
de Vermandois, a sane and healthy girl who was
being educated in a convent near Paris. The Duke
wrote an extensive memorandum, in which she was
preferred to all the other young ladies.

It was important for the Marquise de Prie, whose
future depended on it, to ascertain how easily the
young Princess would let herself be used as a tool,
and how much gratitude she could be expected to

show the one to whom she owed her advancement. So, she resolved to get acquainted with the young lady. She went to the convent where the Princess was staying, was introduced to her under an assumed name, and set to work carefully, letting the Princess first suspect, then clearly see the high position she was meant to assume. The young girl was too proud to show joy. Madame de Prie, in order to get an idea of the young lady's attitude, asked her opinion of Madame de Prie. The Princess responded vehemently that she loathed that malicious creature: that she pitied her brother because of his daily contact with the most universally abhorred woman in France. The Marquise left the reception room of the convent with these words: "You may be sure that you'll never become Queen!"

To the Duke, however, she was clever enough to praise the beauty of his gifted sister; she left it to Pâris-Duverney to find reasons to show this marriage as not desirable. Pâris-Duverney was nervous lest Mademoiselle de Vermandois destroy his influence as well as that of his protectress. He told the Duke that Fleury, who, as beloved tutor of the young King, was very powerful, did not approve of the marriage, and should it be pressed would surely try to prejudice the King against the Duke; aside from that, his sister, as Queen, would most probably blindly obey her mother, the old Duchess, thus making the Duke dependent upon the dowager.

Another princess was sought, one of less independent character whose gratitude could be relied upon. She was found in Maria, twenty-one-year-old daughter of Stanislaw Leszczynska.

Stanislaw was King only in name, since August the Strong had dispossessed him after his short reign in Poland. Stanislaw had not only lost his kingdom; his estates, too, had been taken away from him except a pension granted by Charles XII. He now lived like a pauper with wife and daughter in Weissenburg in Alsace, associating only with a few officers of the garrison and a few priests. All his efforts to find a marriage for his daughter somewhat in accordance with her rank, had come to naught. Naturally, he received the letter telling him that his Maria had been chosen to become Queen of France, with astonishment and delight. Two physicians sent from Paris found the young girl to be healthy and a virgin, and on May 27, 1725, the young King publicly declared his wish to marry the Princess Maria Leszczynska. Her dowry was so meager that Madame de Prie had to bring chemises for her. On August 15, the Duc d'Orléans, acting as proxy for the King, was married to the Princess in Strassburg. Here Madame de Prie won Maria over entirely. On September fifth the marriage was celebrated at Versailles with great pomp. As is well known, Louis XV to everyone's surprise, was sensually in love with his not too comely and very pious wife, who, too, treated him very warmly. But about a year later a political event caused this relationship to cool.

On August 27, Voltaire journeyed to Fontainebleau. "My address is in care of Madame de Prie," he wrote to Thiriot. The little comedy *L'Indiscret* (about a young man who loses the favor of his beloved because he had been so indiscreet as to boast of her) was dedicated to the Marquise, thus:

> Vous qui possédez la beauté
> Sans être vaine ni coquette,
> Et l'extrême vivacité
> Sans être jamais indiscrète;
> Vous à qui donnèrent les dieux
> Tant de lumières naturelles,
> Un esprit juste, gracieux,
> Solide dans le sérieux
> Et charmant dans les bagatelles,
> Souffrez qu'on présente à vos yeux
> D'aventure d'un téméraire
> Qui, pour s'être vanté de plaire,
> Perdit ce qu'il aimait le mieux.

> Si l'héroïne de la pièce,
> De Prie, eut votre beauté,
> On excuserait la faiblesse
> Qu'il eut de s'être un peu vanté
> Quel amant ne serait tenté
> De parler de telle maîtresse
> Par un excès de vanité
> Ou par un excès de tendresse!

Those familiar with Voltaire's works will remember a fantasy presented the previous year at the Villa Bélébat near Fontainebleau. The occasion was the marriage of the Marquise de Livry to the Master of the Hunt, the jovial good-for-nothing M. de Mauconseil. The piece was probably not written by Voltaire alone.

President Hénault and others helped him. Of everything he wrote it most nearly resembles Bellmann, and none of his works is so like Watteau.

Bélébat was situated in the parish of Courdimanche. The priest was an ass, a glutton, a soak, an imbecile and a poet; he was a perfect character, therefore, for the central rôle, which was played by Voltaire. He is represented drunk, making his last will and confessing his sins in a song with the refrain *Confiteor*. Our interest in *La Fête de Bélébat* lies in the fact that after the singing of the chorus:

> Que de tous côtés on entende
> Le bon nom de Voltaire et qu'il soit célèbre etc.

the Marquise de Prie crowns Voltaire with laurel, as she sings a short song which gives him credit for all the pleasure of the performance. Later in the play, when the chorus sings the praises of the Marquise, Voltaire appears in his own character, and, addressing the gorgeous lady, tells her that, though he is honored by her wreath, a kiss from her lips would be better:

> Vous connaissez Alain, ce poète fameux,
> Qui s'endormit un jour au palais de la reine:
> Il en reçut un baiser amoureux;
> Mais il dormait et la faveur fut vaine.
> Vous me pourriez payer d'un prix plus doux,
>   Et si votre bouche vermeille
> Doit quelque chose aux vers que je chante pour vous
>   N'attendez pas que je sommeille.

The young Queen pleased everyone by her gentleness, her simplicity, modesty, and politeness. She was properly grateful to the Duke de Bourbon for having made her Queen of France, but she was especially delighted with the flattery and loving attentions of the Marquise de Prie, who constantly came to her rooms to see what she was doing, to offer her services, to advise the Queen or even dictate her letters.

Voltaire, therefore, had reason to hope that he, too, would soon be favored by the Queen. He wrote to Madame de Bernières that he would not be so indiscreet as to be introduced to the Queen during these hectic, unsettled days; he preferred to wait until the crowd had dispersed and Her Majesty had sufficiently found herself in her new surroundings. Then he would arrange to have *Œdipe* or *Marianne* played before her, and would dedicate one of his new plays to her. She had sent word that she would be pleased to have him do this. The King and Queen of Poland (August the Strong was not recognized at Versailles) had asked him to read them the *Henriade,* which the Queen of France, too, had heard highly spoken of. But he was in no hurry.

Soon he was introduced to the Queen and had reason to be pleased. On October 17, 1725, he writes to Thiriot: "She cried over *Marianne,* she smiled when she heard *L'Indiscret.* She often talks to me. She calls me *mon pauvre Voltaire."* Rivals appear on the scene: other poets, like Didier, petitioning for an annual pension. The Duke de Montmart, keeper of the Queen's privy purse, gives Didier his answer: "If you must be a poet, be a poet like Voltaire." And the Queen grants Voltaire, without his asking, a yearly sum of fifteen hundred livres from her civil list. He sees this as the first step toward the realization of his most cherished dream: to be a personage of standing and importance at Court. "I am on good terms with the second Prime Minister (a curious expression) Duverney. I may count upon Madame de Prie's friendship. I don't complain any more of life at Court; I am beginning to have reasonable hope of being able to help my friends now and then." (Letter of November 13, 1725, to Madame de Bernières.)

He seems to have nearly grasped all a young man of even his unusual abilities could dream of at that time.

At the age of thirty-one, he is regarded as the foremost poet of France; a splendid career is open to him as a courtier. He has a yearly pension from the King, another from the Queen. He has the good-will and active protection of the woman who through the Prime Minister and "the second Prime Minister" exerts a powerful influence on the government, and whose hold on the Queen is incontestable because the Queen is indebted to her for her own position. His early ambition in literature has been gratified. But now there opens before him the prospect of the rich fulfillment of another dream—political ambition, which he had silently, and for long vainly, fostered. He feels that he is no less intelligent than the abbés, bishops and cardinals, who have ruled France before and during his lifetime, and he believes in the sovereignty of intellect. He begins to see a golden future and his attitude takes on a composure that reveals his self-confidence.

High in favor, brilliant, talented, energetic, he stands at the first glorious climax of his life.

The crash was sudden.

23

Pâris-Duverney met with no success. He had tried to impose a general tax, not exempting the clergy or nobility, of one-fiftieth of the entire income, but popular resentment vetoed the plan unconditionally. The parliaments and provincial towns returned a most emphatic "No!" The farmers brandished their hay-forks; they were plagued with enough taxes already. A real storm of hatred, however, against him as well as against his protectress, Madame de Prie, was let loose because of his decree canceling the pensions granted by Louis XIV and reducing drastically those granted under the regency. The anger of the Court was so hot that neither Pâris-Duverney nor Madame de Prie dared appear in Versailles.

In their distress they could not even look for support from the Queen: for the King had begun to lose interest in her. The brief intoxication had worn off, and Maria Leszczynska, destitute of coquetry or any other charm that could enable her to recapture the wandering affections of her spouse, ruined her cause by her childish oddities, such as her fear of ghosts, her senseless coolness, her wanting to have somebody always around to hold her hand when she was frightened by anything, and her disgusting habit of getting up at night and running around the bedroom to look for her little pet dog.

Sadly, Madame de Prie watched the union grow cold. In her antipathy to the King's tutor, old Fleury, the bishop de Fréjus, she laid all the blame on his influence. It was plain that he disliked Maria Leszczynska. And with the gradual weakening of the Queen's hold upon the King, the questionable companions of his youth—the little Duke des Gesvres and all the rest—began to come back and form a close circle about him. Both Minister Maurepas and Bishop Hercule de Fleury were woman haters and kept a close watch on the young King's intimate friendships.

As there was no place in Versailles where such misogynists could meet, they had their club in Paris, in the house of a nobleman from Lorraine, Paul Edouard Deschauffours. He was a genial man of good family, who had lost his fortune and now tried to win it back by making his house a meeting-place for the abnormal.

The attitude of the authorities to them was uncertain. The tribunal had, indeed, the right to burn at the stake anyone convicted of sodomy, but was indulgent to those who were considered too great to be affected by such measures. In March, 1724, a muleherd had been burned at the stake in the Place de Grève. In December of the same year a new case of that kind came into court. It concerned the Abbé François Guyot Desfontaines, a man of some literary consequence. He had studied at the Jesuit college and taught there for fifteen years, and had written odes as well as criticisms. Among the latter was a book of *Literary Paradoxes* in which he satirized La Motte with especial viciousness. He was the editor of the *Journal des Savants,* which had not appeared for seven months previous to his arrest. He had made a piracy of Voltaire's still unpublished *La Ligue* (*Henriade*) and had the impudence to insert a couplet against La Motte in the fifth canto:

En dépit des Pradons, des Perrauts, des Houdarts
On verra le bon goût fleurir de toutes parts.

The first time he got off; but in April, 1725, he was
arrested and this time the accusations brought
against him by two chimney-sweeps would almost
certainly have sent him to the stake.

Apparently he cannot have had many protectors,
since in his extremity he approached a man to whom
he had been introduced only two weeks before. He
appealed to Voltaire for help. And with that innate
humanity which was the key-note of Voltaire's character, he got up from a sick-bed to ride to Fontainebleau and ask Fleury and Madame de Prie, then still
omnipotent, to issue a pardon to the poor wretch who
meant nothing to him, indeed whom he hardly knew.
He saved Desfontaine's life, and thus, as is well
known, succored a snake who became for the next
twenty years his spiteful, tireless enemy.

Voltaire's action was the more noble, in that in his
first poetic work he had argued in favor of the normal
sexual relation, as opposed to homosexuality.

Now the influential clique of these abnormals attacked Voltaire's protectress, the Marquise de Prie,
and the Duke de Bourbon. It was this crowd that persuaded the King to cast off the Queen, and thus prevented Bourbon and Madame de Prie from exerting
any influence on the Monarch.

The Duke as well as Madame de Prie knew very
well that in Fleury they had an adversary who as
royal tutor had influence over the King, and he would
surely be the last person to stimulate the King's interest in his wife. So they decided to destroy him. How
pitifully small was their knowledge of mankind!
Using the Queen for their tool they only succeeded
in making the King dislike her more than ever. Apparently the Duke never suspected that the King
really hated him and that the seemingly cold young
man simply could not live without Fleury.

One day the Duke de Bourbon requested the Queen
to get him a private audience with the King (that
meant: a meeting at which Fleury was not present).
Under some pretext Louis XV was called to the

Queen. She wanted to withdraw, but the Duke asked her to stay and hear what he had to say. He began to read a letter from Cardinal de Polignac in Rome, which was nothing but a lengthy indictment of Fleury. The King was bored. When the Duke wished to continue the King gave unmistakable signs of impatience. The Duke, hurt, wished to know: was His Majesty displeased with him? His Majesty said yes, he was. Was His Majesty unfavorably inclined toward him? —Yes.—Was the Bishop de Fréjus the only one to enjoy his confidence?—Yes.—And when the Duke fell upon his knees the King pushed him back and left the room in anger, mainly at the Queen, who had enticed him into this trap.

Meanwhile Fleury, wishing to see the King, had been confronted by doors locked by the order of the Duke. After waiting several hours to be admitted, he departed for Issy. In a temper, the King had locked himself into his rooms, and when the Duke de Montmart saw how things were going, he procured a decree ordering the Duke de Bourbon to bring the King his tutor at once. Deeply humiliated, the Duke had to obey.

If he and Madame de Prie were to rise again, a great blow must be struck. The whole cabal that met at Deschauffours', including a senator, two bishops (Saint-Agnan and La Fare), and several other highly placed gentlemen, would have to be intimidated and ridiculed, but the main thing was to make ridiculous the set, whose vices everyone knew but nobody called by name.

Just then occurred an event which for a moment caused the scale to dip in Madame de Prie's favor and gave her fresh courage.

Madame de Tencin had the misfortune to have one of her lovers commit suicide. This was very awkward. The lady had a thrifty habit of accepting cash presents from her admirers, not from one at a time but from so many as to make quite a nice thing of it. Bolingbroke was one of her victims, until his eyes were opened. One, the senator La Fresnaye, was driven to frenzy by the number of rivals his mistress encouraged. On top of this came the loss of his for-

tune. He went to the rooms where she lived as sister
and wife of the Archbishop de Tencin—the same
rooms in which these two had hatched the scheme to
get Fleury a cardinal's hat—and shot himself in her
presence. He left a will, full of terrifying revelations
concerning Madame de Tencin, of her way of living
and of collecting a fortune.

It was very embarrassing: What should be done
with the corpse? Instead of reporting to the police
and having the body removed, Madame de Tencin
hurriedly notified her friends, the President and the
Procurator of the Great Tribunal, and these high
officials had the body put in quicklime so they could
render a verdict of death from apoplexy. The Great
Tribunal considered the matter settled. The Tribunal
of the Châtelet, however, was not content with this
explanation. It ordered the lady arrested and brought
to the Châtelet. But Fleury and Maurepas, in Versailles, did not cease their efforts until Madame de
Tencin was freed from strict confinement and given
temporary lodging in the Bastille.

Nevertheless, it was a great defeat for Fleury and
the other enemies of Madame de Prie. Fleury even
spoke of retiring. On April 20, 1726, Madame de Prie
wrote to the Duke de Richelieu: "Everything is all
right again. I am more at ease." At that time the police commissioner was Réné Hénault, the same of
whom Voltaire had once asked what was done with
people who forged *lettres de cachet*. He answered:
"They are hanged."—"And anyhow that's something,
until the same can be done with those who sign the
genuine," answered Voltaire.

Hénault owed his position, indeed, his career, to
Madame de Prie, and she counted upon him as a tool.
Were he faithful and courageous he could take up
the battle against her enemies in Versailles. She
counted even more upon her satirist, her young poet
friend, who in his very first composition (*Anti-Giton*)
had revealed himself as a dangerous opponent to the
Mignons: recently in his *Festival Play in Bélébat*
addressed to Madame de Prie, he proved himself no
less keen an enemy of the Catholic clergy.

But, Hénault proved too weak. He was satisfied to

get hold of M. de Deschauffours and to let a hundred guilty escape. On the day of his conviction Deschauffours was burned at the stake. Consequently this nobleman was of no use as a witness for the State.

As for Voltaire, before Madame de Prie could make use of him his fangs were drawn. Hénault himself put the poet *hors de combat* by sending him to the Bastille.

It was all over with Madame de Prie; she became sick, emaciated, even ugly. One day Fleury made the suave suggestion to the Duke, that it would be possible to put in order the difficult conditions at Court, if Madame de Prie and Pâris-Duverney "would go to the country."

When she disregarded this warning and remained in Versailles her enemies made short work of her. One day the King rode to Rambouillet to hunt, and the same evening granted the Duke an interview. The King seemed friendly enough; but the Duke had scarcely departed, when he was handed a *lettre de cachet,* which exiled him to Chantilly, forbade him to hunt, which he loved, and drove him to complete despair. Madame de Prie was ordered to take up her domicile in Courbépine, in Normandy, where she raged in hurt pride for some time and then committed suicide by poison. Pâris-Duverney was taken to the Bastille, where he was kept for eighteen months. After his release he was persecuted with a foolish judicial action that had no result.

24

Voltaire also suffered from the overthrow of his protectors. The man who had made up his mind to humiliate him and get him out of the way, was a degenerate without ability or virtue, a man of a great family, who was known to be a coward and who lived on usury.

It was in December, 1725, that one evening at the Opera the Chevalier de Rohan-Chabot called to him in a very offensive manner: "Monsieur de Voltaire,

Monsieur Arouet, what is your name?"—According to several witnesses, the poet answered: "I don't drag a long name after me; but I do know how to bring honor upon the name I have."—Other witnesses report the famous retort: "My name begins with me; yours ends with you." The last is more credible, as he made use of almost the same phrase in *Rome Sauvée,* where he has Cicero respond to Cataline:

> Mon nom commence en moi. De votre honneur jaloux,
> Tremblez que votre nom finisse dans vous!

Several days later Voltaire and the Chevalier again came face to face in the Théâtre Français, in the loge of Adrienne Lecouvreur. Rohan repeated his insolent question, whereupon Voltaire referred him to his answer of the night at the Opera. Rohan raised his stick, remarking that he would continue this conversation with a thrashing. When in reply Voltaire put his hand on his hilt, Adrienne Lecouvreur feigned a fainting spell, which for the time being ended the quarrel.

On February 4, Voltaire lunched at the house of Duke de Sully, where, according to the expression used in the memoires of President Hénault, "he was regarded as a son of the house." A servant notified him that someone waited to see him at the gate of the palace. He went down stairs. A coach stood at the gate. Two men met him and asked him to mount the step. He did so believing that whoever wanted to talk to him was seated inside the coach. But scarcely had he obeyed the request when he was seized and a shower of blows rained upon his shoulders. Six lackeys stood around him. From a second coach standing at a short distance the Chevalier de Rohan directed the attack, crying out among other commands: "Don't hit him on the head; that part of him may produce something good yet." And the crowd which had gathered to watch the beating was touched by this evidence of solicitude: "Oh, what a good man!" was its cry.

When Voltaire succeeded in freeing himself, he returned at once to Sully's dining-room and asked the assistance of his host for a guest whose mistreatment and humiliation must be shared by the one at whose table he had just eaten.

Here, however, he underwent the first cruel disappointment which was in store for him in his intercourse with people above him in birth. With unworthy and outrageous caution the Duke refused to interfere in a matter which he considered was none of his business.

Ten years of friendship were forgotten in that moment, in which, humiliated and misused, Voltaire stood before the Duke. Forgotten was the glory Voltaire had shed upon the name of Sully in the *Henriade*, by making an ancestor the inseparable friend of Henry IV. Deeply hurt, Voltaire replaced Sully in the poem by Duplessis-Mornay.

The Duke was not anxious to antagonize a family so powerful as the Rohan. Added to this—in spite of all the show of democracy which the aristocracy liked to make by inviting poets and writers to their tables —was the old contempt of the high born for the middle classes. To teach them to keep their proper distance, it would do no harm to remind them from time to time of the difference in station.

Recollect how helpless Molière was in his time. Even in England the Earl of Rochester instructed his negro servant to thrash Dryden in punishment for a satire which offended him. Among the most aristocratic of Voltaire's intimate friends there were not a few like the Prince de Conti and the Abbé Caumartin who had only pleasantly mocking remarks to make on this incident such as: "What should become of the rest of us if poets had no backs!"

From Sully's palace Voltaire hurried to the Opera where he was certain to meet Madame de Prie. He told her what had happened, received vivid sympathy and the promise that she would do what she could for him at Versailles. However, when it got that far the standing of the Duke de Bourbon proved too shaky and uncertain to permit him to challenge the Rohan family. Therefore, nothing was done. The poor victim of the thrashing tried to be unconcerned and continue his usual intercourse with his friends. As formerly he showed himself at Court and around town. But nobody gave him sympathy and those upon whom he had counted turned away from him.

With his cool head and his hot temper Voltaire firmly resolved to get revenge. From morning to night he practiced fencing. He fenced with soldiers of the Guard. All his connection was with fighters and boxers. Again and again he challenged Rohan, but he was constantly watched by the police who wished to keep him from attacking a member of such an illustrious family.

A letter of the Police Commissioner to the Chief of the Criminal Police reads:

"Monsieur, His Royal Highness (Bourbon) has been informed that M. le Chevalier de Rohan is going out today and since he might plan a new attack on the Sieur de Voltaire, or the latter might commit some ill-considered action, it is the wish of His Royal Highness that you have the Sieur de Voltaire watched to prevent any consequence of a possible meeting."

A note of the Police Commissioner made on the basis of a report says:

"From reliable sources comes the information that the Sieur de Voltaire has the intention of insulting M. le Chevalier de Rohan without delay and in a sensational manner. Within the last six weeks he has repeatedly changed his residence, even his district, and it is known that at present he is staying with a certain Leynault, a fencing master in the rue Saint-Martin, where he keeps very bad company. It is said that he is friendly with soldiers of the Guard and that various bullies visit him. But regardless of how much of this is true or false, it is certain that he continues to harbor evil intentions and just as certain that he has summoned one of his relatives from the provinces to be his second. This relative, better balanced than M. de Voltaire, would like to calm him; but apparently this is not possible. M. de Voltaire is more excited and furious than ever in his behavior as well as in his remarks. All these reports make it seem to the Police Commissioner advisable, perhaps this very night, to carry out the King's order concerning the Sieur de Voltaire. He regards it as his duty to prevent a breach of the peace of which he has been informed in advance."

One evening at last, Voltaire succeeded in finding Rohan in the loge of Adrienne Lecouvreur and said to him: "If your latest money-squeezing affair has not made you forget your insult to me, I hope that you will meet me man to man."

The Chevalier accepted the challenge for the next day and chose nine o'clock as the time, the Porte Saint-Martin as the place. However, he informed his family who at once took steps with the Duke de Bourbon to prevent the duel.

This action, unworthy of a nobleman, or of any man of honor inspired a few comments from the Marshal de Villars. He writes:

"On account of a fall which had impeded his movements, Rohan was not skilful with the sword. He took the measure of having Voltaire chastised by his lackeys in broad daylight. Instead of turning to the Courts, the latter thought it nobler to seek revenge with the sword. It is said that he sought satisfaction ambitiously and recklessly. The Cardinal de Rohan therefore requested the Duke to have Voltaire taken to the Bastille; the order was given and executed, and the unfortunate poet on top of his thrashing was arrested. The public, always ready to criticize, in this instance found rightly that both parties were at fault: Voltaire in insulting the Chevalier de Rohan; the latter by committing a crime which warranted the death penalty—he had a French citizen thrashed. The government itself was at fault in failing to punish an act generally considered criminal, and in sending the aggrieved party to the Bastille to quiet the aggressor."

It is astonishing that among all Voltaire's friends and protectors the Marshal is the only one to regard Rohan's behavior as absolutely culpable. Even he has enough aristocratic prejudice to consider Voltaire also in the wrong in answering Rohan so sharply. And it is noteworthy that Villars here uses the word citizen to signify one who was considered inferior. This was sixty years before the revolution.

Voltaire was arrested on the night of April 18, 1726,

and taken to the Bastille. The police report says that
he had two pocket pistols on his person. His family,
Hénault maintains, was quite satisfied with this action, which prevented the young man from committing a fresh offense and which saved his relatives
from any consequences. The Jansenist Armand,
Voltaire's elder brother, apparently could not get
over the fact that his family should have made
an enemy of the family whose motto was: *Roi ne
puys, Duc ne daygne, Rohan suys.*

However the persons involved were thoroughly
conscious of committing a wrong, which they excused as a necessity. This can be seen from a letter
which was sent by Hénault to Condé, the Governor
of the Bastille:

"You have failed to report to me either Voltaire's
or Madame de Tencin's incarceration in the Bastille,
although I myself signed the orders in virtue of which
they were taken there . . . the Sieur de Voltaire possesses a genius which demands consideration. His
Royal Highness has asked me to inform you that it
is the King's intention to grant him every concession
and liberty which does not jeopardize his safe de-
tention."

Apparently the authorities did not want to deny a
family, at whose head was the *Grand Aumônier of
France,* a trifle like the arrest of a private citizen. On
the other hand, everything was done to soften the
penalty. Voltaire was in the Bastille, side by side
with Madame de Tencin, whose beauty had in him an
eager admirer, whose nephew, the Comte d'Argental,
was his most intimate friend. As soon as he was released, Voltaire informed D'Argental that his greatest
sorrow during his stay in the Bastille was that she,
too, was made to suffer the same penalty. "We were,"
he wrote to Madame de Feriol (Madame de Tencin's
sister) "like Pyramus and Thisbe. It was but a wall
that separated us; but we did not kiss, as they did,
through a cleft in the wall."

He dined at the table of the Governor and was
permitted to receive the visits of his friends. He felt
hurt that several whom he asked to come, such as
Thiriot, Madame de Bernières, and Madame du Def-

fand, stayed away; but Hénault had interfered and
the permission was limited to five or six persons,
whose names were approved by him.

From prison Voltaire wrote to the Minister of Justice:

"The Sieur de Voltaire most respectfully brings to
your knowledge that he was murderously assaulted
by the brave Chevalier de Rohan with the assistance
of six bandits behind whom he himself very courageously took his stand. The Sieur de Voltaire has since
continuously sought for an opportunity to re-estab-
lish, not his own, but the Chevalier's honor, which
proved to be too difficult. Admittedly Voltaire went
to Versailles, but it is not true that he pushed his pur-
suit to the home of Cardinal de Rohan. He can easily
prove the contrary, and offers to spend his whole
life in the Bastille if he be not correct on this point.
He requests the privilege of dining with the Governor
and of receiving visitors. Still more urgently he asks
permission for immediate departure for England.
Should anybody question his departure an officer
could escort him to Calais."

On May second, Condé received the order to release
Voltaire on condition that he go in exile to England.
Condé was to accompany him as far as Calais and
see him embark and leave the harbor.

Voltaire on his journey was to pass through Paris.
Hastily he wrote to his friend, Madame de Bernières,
asking her to lend him her coach which Condé would
return to her. He also asked her to come with Thiriot
and Madame du Deffand to tell him good-bye.

On May fifth he reached Calais where he had to
wait four or five days for a boat. When he reached
England, he did not at once find himself contented.

But his exile was destined to be highly profitable
to his further development, and what had been meant
as a penalty, became an inestimable benefit.

IV

ENGLAND

1

IT WAS a perfect day in May, under a clear and
cloudless sky, when Voltaire landed in England; a
mild west wind blew over the banks of the Thames,
whose fresh green delighted the eye of the exiled
poet. As far as he could see the river was covered
by merchant vessels all sails reefed in a salute to the
King who was being rowed downstream in a gilded
barge led by other boats with musicians, and followed
by thousands of little boats. The rowers of the royal
barge were dressed like French pages of an earlier
day in white puffy trousers and short jackets with
little silver tabs on the shoulders.

Thus in his first glimpse he got an impression of the
fresh life and the conservative, typically British, re-
tention of ancient costumes.

At the same time he could see the thousands of
people on the banks, on foot or on horseback, eagerly
watching the horse-racing and athletic contests.

He reached London the same evening where he attended a party of ladies and gentlemen of the highest
circles, and spent the night at Lord Bolingbroke's in
Pall-Mall. To these people he described his impressions of the forenoon: the Olympian pageant, the
throng of elegant young men and women he had seen
dashing over the commons to see the horse-races, the
pedestrians, the knots of well-dressed gentlemen and
of pretty, simply clad young girls whose look of
healthy contentment had been a joy to look upon.
The ladies explained to him that the people who
mattered took no part in these vulgar amusements;
the young dandies who had attended the races like

men-about-town were nothing more than students
and apprentices on hired horses, and the pretty young
ladies in cotton dresses on foot or on horseback were
nothing but chambermaids and country lasses out in
their Sunday best.

Thus his first evening gave him some notion of the
class distinctions in England. At the same time, however, he realized that the British lower class was not
at all oppressed, on the contrary, was very content.

Bolingbroke, ever since he had negotiated the
Treaty of Utrecht, was a great man in France. In the
Paris Opera everybody stood up when he entered.
Though he had not regained his political influence in
England, he was pardoned, after his complete break
with the Pretender, and now he divided his time between his mansion in London and his estate in Dawley, Middlesex, which he preferred. Dawley took the
place of his French manor, *La Source*, which he was
about to give up.

Before Voltaire's arrival Bolingbroke could not
overcome a certain doubt (as is shown by his letters)
as to how Voltaire would keep his promise to dedicate the *Henriade* to him and as to what he would
say about him in the dedication. He wisely assumed
that the poet had forgotten his promise. This was the
case, for, this work, undergoing constant revision—
had in the course of time been intended for various
protectors, like the blue purse in Musset's *Un Caprice*,
which Madame de Blainville had crocheted so slowly
that it had been intended for no less than three persons.—Several years later, however, Voltaire in-
scribed to Bolingbroke the tragedy *Brutus*, written
from impressions of England; and the dedication was
not couched in the conventional few words but in his
Discours sur la Tragédie, in which he shows the loyal
devotion to which his Lordship was justly entitled.

This was not the first time that he did public homage to Bolingbroke. The first occasion was the letter
to Dr. Gervasi, after Bolingbroke had sat beside Voltaire's sick-bed:

> Et toi, cher Bolingbroke, héros qui d'Apollon
> As reçu plus d'une couronne,
> Qui réunis en ta personne

L'eloquence de Cicéron,
L'intrépidité de Caton,
L'esprit de Mécénas, l'agrément de Pétrone
Et la science de Varron,
Bolingbroke, à ma gloire il faut que je publie
Que tes soins, pendant le cours
De ma triste maladie,
Ont daigné marquer mes jours
Par le tendre intérêt que tu prends à ma vie.

Bolingbroke was widely enough acquainted with the English poets to introduce Voltaire to the important ones. He got along well with them, except when knowledge of the English language was essential. He called the triumvirs of England's Parnassus—Pope, Swift and Gay—by their first names. Voltaire could have had no better introduction.

2

He was not limited to Bolingbroke's Tory circle. He had, in France, met many important Englishmen, such as Lord Stair, the English ambassador to Paris, Bishop Atterbury, who lived in exile in France; and a rich and gifted merchant, Everard Falkener, who soon was to take an almost brotherly interest in him.

Typical of the customs of the times is the fact that Voltaire came to England, supplied with letters of recommendation from members of the same government which had condemned him to exile. The ministers apparently were a little ashamed of having had to expel a man not because of any wrong he had committed, but because of a wrong he had suffered.

The French Foreign Minister, Monsieur de Morville, asked Horatio Walpole, brother of the Prime Minister Sir Robert Walpole, and Stair's successor as English ambassador to France, to do everything possible for Voltaire while he was in England. Horatio Walpole wrote to the Duke of Newcastle:

"I hope that you will excuse my commending to you—at the urgent request of Monsieur de Morville —Monsieur de Voltaire, a poet of great talent who has recently come to England to get out a subscription edition of an excellent poetic work, called *Henri IV*.

Although he was imprisoned in the Bastille, it was not because of any state matter but because of a personal quarrel with a private person, and I therefore hope that Your Excellency will give your support by recommending the subscription."

Likewise he wrote a letter to Bubb Dodington, Lord Melcombe, highly respected as a patron of literature, but of doubtful reputation as a politician. It commences like the letter to the Duke of Newcastle. Then it continues:

"Monsieur de Morville who in the furtherance of literature and learning, is France's Mæcenas or still better France's Dodington, has asked me to use my influence among my friends in support of the subscription. For this reason as well as because of the merits of this man I believe you to be the best person to approach; and at the same time I must confess that I am glad to make this the excuse for reopening a correspondence with you."

Bubb Dodington's poor reputation as politician came from the fact that in spite of his buying votes and of other dishonest campaigning, he did not succeed in being elected to Parliament. In private life he was clever and witty, a great defender of the intellectuals. For three months Voltaire lived in his Eastbury house, and later always recalled him gratefully as a very rich and active man, talented and courageous. Later he introduced Thiriot to him, recommending him gracefully by saying that before he had sent Dodington his *History of Charles XII*, now, however, he sent him something far better.

In Eastbury Voltaire met Edward Young, later well known as a didactic poet. Voltaire became his friend. This was before Young became a mystic. He had not yet written his *Night Thoughts*, which Voltaire later called "a confused mixture of bombast and obscure trivialities." After an unpromising youth he had gained some respect as a lyric poet and dramatist, but still tried to increase his reputation by flattering famous personages. At any rate he was an unusually brilliant conversationalist.

In Eastbury Voltaire also met James Thomson, the popular author of the *Seasons* who gave him the impression "of great genius and great simplicity." In his *Autumn* Thomson refers to Eastbury:

> Oh, lose me in the green delightful walks
> Of Dodington, thy seat, serene and plain,
> Where simple Nature reigns.

Voltaire, from the beginning was accepted by the Prime Minister, Robert Walpole, by the Duke of Newcastle, by the widow of the Duke of Marlborough, and by the Court of the King as well as that of the Prince and Princess of Wales.

To George I he had six years previously paid his respects, by sending him, in 1718, his *Œdipe*. He accompanied it by verses whose flattery nowadays seems absurd. The poem begins:

> Toi que la France admire autant que l'Angleterre,
> Qui de l'Europe en feu balances les destins;
> Toi qui chéris la paix dans le sein de la guerre
>   Et qui n'es armé du tonnerre
>   Que pour le bonheur des humains.

The King ordered Lord Stair to present him with a watch, and Voltaire had the watch sent to his father to impress upon him that his son received presents from the King of England.

3

Shortly after his arrival in England Voltaire had the misfortune to run short of cash. He had taken with him to London a letter of credit for twenty thousand francs on a Jewish banker by the name of Acosta; but as he did not need the money at once he postponed its presentation. When he finally went to the bank he was told that Acosta had become bankrupt the day before. He could give him a few gold pieces only. If the story is true that King George I, hearing of this misfortune, sent the poet one hundred pounds, the sum was very welcome. For he had not yet received any payments under his father's will, and by his exile he had lost the pensions granted him by the King and Queen of France.

This lack of funds hampered him considerably at the beginning of his stay. The custom of the time required the guest to give large tips to the servants and so it was difficult for him to accept any invitations. When he was invited a second time to Lord Chesterfield's, he declined; the meal would have been too expensive for him. In February, 1727, he asks Thiriot to locate the people who owe him money.

Thanks to his recommendations Voltaire was favorably received by the Prime Minister, in spite of his friendly connections with Bolingbroke and the latter's Tory circle. Robert Walpole was interested in politics, not in literature; his wife, however, showed a lively interest in the poet, and so did his young son who was still at Eton, the Horace Walpole who was later to become famous in France, especially as the object of the enthusiastic adoration of the blind Madame du Deffand.

In a letter to her son Lady Walpole described the visit of the famous Frenchman to her house. This visit was excitedly talked of between him and his school comrades, and even forty years later, in a letter to Voltaire, Horace Walpole showed what an impression this event made upon him. He wrote:

"Your glory has not been unknown to me since, but I remember that, young as I was, I regarded it as the greatest honor to our house that you lunched with my mother that day, although I was still at school and was not so fortunate as to see you. My father was at that period in a position which might have blinded other eyes than mine."

At first Voltaire could talk with French speaking people only. Although in his early youth he had learned to read a little English and had English books brought to him during his stay in the Bastille, he was unable to express himself in understandable English. His first visit at Pope's country estate at Twickenham therefore turned into a comic fiasco: Voltaire's English proved to be entirely unintelligible and Pope could not speak a word of French and even read it with great difficulty. Much later, when Voltaire not only read English but wrote it fluently, he still was unable to overcome the difficulties of pronunciation. In the preface to a little book which he published in English at the end of 1727 he confesses that he still could not pronounce English: that he had learned it as one would learn Latin and Greek, that it was as hard for him to understand the spoken language as it would be for us to understand the pronunciation of the people of antiquity, if we could hear them.

Ultimately his ear did get used to the sound, his tongue to the pronunciation. His acquaintance with Colley Ciber gave Voltaire the opportunity to visit Drury Lane Theatre. Chetwood, who had been there as prompter for twenty years, used to furnish him each evening with a copy of the play. Voltaire took it to his seat so he could follow the performance. Within four or five months he learned to write the language, though not with exactness. As a matter of fact, even his French was weak in this respect. At that time spelling was not considered important. Voltaire spelled even proper names incorrectly, now one way, now another. (Thus he always spells Law as Lass.) After several more months he understood conversations he overheard, and was able to express himself fluently.

This knowledge was a great help once, when he was taking a walk in the streets of London. After the numerous wars between England and France a Frenchman was far from a popular figure on the streets of London, and some toughs who could not get used to this foreign looking character called after him and were about to throw stones at him. To prevent their attack, he stopped and mounted a milestone and from that eminence delivered a harangue: "Brave Englishmen! Am I not unfortunate enough in not having been born among you?" He was such a success that the mob that had insulted him crowded around him and wanted to carry him to his home, so delighted were they that a foreigner had spoken to them in such excellent English.

The letters Voltaire wrote from London to Thiriot were written in English, just to annoy the censors who opened them. From remarks of his contemporaries we can see that every time he wanted to confide anything to Madame du Châtelet in the presence of others, he used English. As late as 1764 he spoke fluently to visitors in Ferney and recited by heart selections from Dryden. In the last year of his life he spoke English with Franklin.

In London he even got into the habit of working in the native language. He began his *Brutus* thus, and in his dedication to Bolingbroke he explains that he had grown so used to thinking in English that after his return to France it was rather difficult for him to think in French.

What is still more striking, he wrote the *Civil War in France* as well as the *Essai sur la Poésie Epique* in English, not French. When it seemed to him of importance to publish the latter in French he could not bring himself to translate it, but—with little knowledge of human nature—entrusted the task to the scoundrel Desfontaines, who had pirated and abused the *Henriade*. Desfontaines knew so little English that he translated the word *cake* by *Cacus* (giant).

Voltaire seems for a while to have become entirely reconciled to the fact that his exile would last a very long time. The influence of the Rohan family was not likely to diminish.

In his very interesting and unusually instructive *Advice to a Journalist* [1] (1737) Voltaire winds up his dissertation with the question what language the well-equipped French journalist should master. His answer is worth noting: "A good journalist must know English and Italian; for many works of genius were written in these two languages and genius can scarcely ever be translated." German was not included. Even much later, Frederick the Great spoke French and wrote all his works in French. In England, too, at that time French was the official language at Court. The German born George I could not speak English. Voltaire during the first half year of his stay in London was limited to circles where French was spoken.

One of these was the home of Bolingbroke. The

---

[1] *Journalist* in the meaning of the time was a contributor to journals; an essayist; a critic.

mistress of the house was a Frenchwoman, the former Madame de Villette. By her own account, after
all the years she had lived with Bolingbroke she knew
the meaning of "very warm" and "very cold"; but
further than this her knowledge of the English language did not go. Hence the entire conversation in
this house, as far as the lady of the house entered into
it, was French. Chiefly French also was the erudition
of the master of the house.

The circle which first attracted Voltaire was the
clique of French fugitives which met in the Rainbow-
Coffeehouse, in Marylebone. Several of the clique
welcomed Voltaire; others—like Saint-Hyacinthe—
persecuted him from the first with petty criticism
and later became his enemies.

Voltaire at once recognized that, if he wished to
derive any benefit from his stay in this foreign country, he must learn its language thoroughly. About the
middle of the next century another eminent Frenchman, Victor Hugo, spent twenty years on British soil
without learning English. Such was not the nature of
the passionately inquisitive Voltaire.

4

Voltaire was not the sort of man to submit to his
fate. From the beginning he sought companionship,
except when he wanted to work. But when he was
alone he was consumed with furious anger at the
ridicule he had suffered without getting any satisfaction. He had been punished with exile for his efforts
to defend his honor.

He could stand it no longer; it became his obsession, and after a stay of several months in England he
secretly returned to France to seek and punish his
mocker.

In vain however he sought his enemy. It seemed, as
he later wrote, as if Rohan were warned by the instinct of a coward. The search was fruitless, and fear
of renewed arrest and incarceration forced Voltaire
to return to London.

The letter he wrote on August 12, 1726, to Thiriot (he does not reveal from where, but certainly it was from the French coast) exhibits an unusual access of ill-humor. He feels as though uprooted from his native country; his hopes are destroyed, his future appears devoid of a ray of light.

In this letter he speaks of his short journey to Paris: Thiriot could probably imagine that, as he had not visited even him he had not visited anybody. He had hunted one man only but had not found him, and now he is about to make a headlong departure:

"Now it has happened, my dear Thiriot. The great probability is that I shall never see you again in all my life. I am still undecided whether to go to London. I know that England is a country where the fine arts are respected and appreciated, where although a distinction is drawn between classes, no distinction is drawn between men but that which is based on their merits. It is a country where one can think freely and keenly without having to fear slavery. If I were to follow my inclination I should settle there, with the purpose of learning to think. But I don't know whether my little fortune so severely reduced by travel-expenses, my increasingly poor health and my taste for perfect solitude will permit me to throw myself into the noise of Whitehall and London. I have excellent recommendations and I would have a warm welcome in England. I have not yet made up my mind to undertake the journey. There are only two things I have to settle in my entire life: the first is to risk it honorably as soon as I can; the second is to end it in the solitude which is in keeping with my misfortunes and my experience of mankind."

He goes on to say that he does not mind having to give up the pensions formerly granted to him by the King and Queen; that his only sorrow was that he could not transfer them to his friend, Thiriot. It would be a consolation to him in his solitude to be able to think that once more he could do something for his friend; but it was his fate to be unfortunate in every respect; the greatest pleasure an honest man could have—that of bringing joy to his friends —was denied to him.

What irony of fate! How superfluous was this worry of being unable to transfer his income to Thiriot! Soon enough the latter was to transfer Voltaire's income to his own account without asking or thanking him!

From Thiriot his thoughts turn to another friend, the last, the only one he wanted to see in Paris the day before his departure from France. Since then he had not heard from her. He does not know what Madame de Bernières thinks of him. And he cites a few verses, making a small alteration, from Racine's *Mithridate* (act II, scene IV):

> Prendrait elle le soin de rassurer mon cœur
> Contre la defiance attachée au malheur?

All his life he will cherish her friendship for him, and maintain his for her. He wishes her health and wealth, much pleasure and many friends "such as yourself, my dear Thiriot. . . . Speak to her sometimes of me!"

He was indebted to her in many respects. How active and energetic she had been when, in 1724, they were engaged in having *La Ligue* printed secretly in Rouen. How kind and solicitous she had been to him, when she gave him—and to avoid any evil gossip, Thiriot as well—shelter in her own house.

Nevertheless she was not one whose feelings can remain unchanged after a separation, and she was just as unlikely to stand up for anyone when it was not to her advantage. Not even over the unjust fate of her most intimate and dearest friend could she feel indignation.

Again what irony of fate! How superfluous was Voltaire's worry lest Madame de Bernières should miss a friend.

The first letter she sends to him in England informs him that she honestly had to confess, she had been to the Opera with the Chevalier de Rohan.

Voltaire, in his lengthy and affectionate answer (October 16, 1726), very mildly asks her to think of him once in a while so that, when he should see her again some day, he could find in her heart a sympathy which "at least would resemble friendship." He re-

marks very truly that most women know no middle-
ground between passion and indifference. He would
like so much to be able to hope for simple friendship.
"I can forgive you for having been to the Opera with
Chevalier de Rohan if you feel a little shame for it."

After this the correspondence seems to have stag-
nated. Madame de Bernières, after a period of mutu-
ual misunderstanding, separated from the President.
She became a widow in 1734, and immediately
married a man named Prudhomme, an officer of the
garde du corps; she died in 1757. She was thirty-four
years old when she became Voltaire's best friend,
and four years later, though still his friend, she went
to the theater with the man who had him thrashed.

About the same time a great sorrow came to Voltaire. He received the news of the death of his only
sister. How profoundly this loss affected him is
shown in his letter to an old friend of the Arouet
family, Mademoiselle de Bessières.

5

Voltaire met the most generous hospitality at the
home of the rich London merchant Falkener, whose
luxurious country estate "Wandsworth" was entirely
at his disposal. It was here that he devoted his time
to the study of English, and that he later wrote in
English the first act of his *Brutus* and his two essays
in the same language.

Ballantyne has pointed out the passionate love of
liberty expressed in this English-French *Brutus* and
the many allusions to the situation between England and France as well as to Voltaire's own fate.
In the two following verses Greece stands for England; Ionia, France;

> La Grèce entière est libre et la molle Ionie
> Sous un joug odieux languit assujettie.

It is of his own unjust arrest that he speaks in these
words:

> Arrêter un Romain sur de simples soupçons,
> C'est agir en tyrans.

And apparently he was thinking of the submission of the French to the tyranny of King and Church when in *Brutus* he says:

> Escloves de leur rois, et même de leurs prêtres,
> Les Toscans semblent nés pour servir sous des maîtres.

In his essay on epic poetry which was written in English, a fiery love of freedom is revealed. Voltaire's forceful English style proclaims:

> Liberty of thought is the life of the soul. . . . It is a great misfortune that there are so few French imitators of our neighbours, the English. We have been obliged to adopt their physical science, to imitate their financial system, to build our ships on their plan; when shall we imitate them in the noble liberty of allowing the mind to take all the flight of which it is capable?

His illness and depression made the visit in the little village a few miles out of London highly desirable. He therefore retained a deep gratitude for Falkener; he was delighted when his host, who had acquired his fortune by the sale of Eastern silks and fabrics, was appointed ambassador to Constantinople —a contrast to French practice. And in 1732, Voltaire dedicated to him a work half in prose, half in poetry, the tragedy he loved best, *Zaïre*.

Falkener was a man of good education, interested in art and literature, with a knowledge of ancient languages and a hobby for collecting antiques. In the dedication of his *Zaïre* Voltaire calls him his "fellow-countryman in literature." In a letter to Voltaire Falkener wrote: "I live here just as when you left me, neither merrier nor sadder, neither richer nor poorer; I am enjoying excellent health as well as everything that makes life comfortable; I am not in love, I covet nothing, I aspire to nobody's position and I envy nobody: and as long as this keeps up I shall surely call myself a truly happy man."

Falkener, after having been Ambassador at Constantinople, became private secretary to the Duke of Cumberland, the King's second son. He followed the Duke to war and was present at the defeat at Fon-

tenoy; in 1746 he accompanied him to Scotland,
where the battle of Culloden suppressed the rebellion. Later he became postmaster-general and held
this position until his death.

6

The *Daily Journal* of January 27, 1727, contained
the following note:
"Last week the Sieur de Voltaire, the famous
French poet in exile, was presented to His Majesty,
who received him with favor. It is said that the French
government dropped him a hint that it would be unwise to publish his poem *La Ligue*. It has been prosecuted in court by the Cardinal de Bissy because of its
eulogies of Queen Marie's attitude in religious matters, and its numerous thrusts at the abuse of the
Pope's power and the corruption of the confessional."
Voltaire was presented at the Court of St. James'
to the man whom nine years previously he had called
a Hero, whose subjects he had likened to Melpomene's sons. He saw the King five months before his
death. But he did not lose by his death, as he had been
warmly recommended to King George II and Queen
Caroline, who were crowned in June, 1727.
Among those close to the Queen, when she was still
Princess of Wales, was a very unassuming lady, Hen-
rietta Howard, later Countess of Suffolk. The former
Madame de Villette, now Lady Bolingbroke, wrote to
her in her most flattering French (with abominable
spelling, without accents or apostrophies, with two
words instead of one) an unqualified recommendation for Voltaire, meant for the Princess of Wales:
"No one has a finer understanding or a fuller appreciation of a great and deserving intellect than yourself. Please grant your protection to this, the sole
French poet we now possess, and be so kind as to
deliver to Her Royal Highness the enclosed copy of
his recent tragedy, which he has taken the liberty of
inscribing for her."
Voltaire had yet another protectress at the new
Court in the person of another favorite of the royal
pair, Mrs. Clayton, afterward Lady Sundon. He never

forgot his indebtedness. From France he later wrote to her: "I wish, for the honor of Versailles, for the progress of virtue and of literature, that we might have here a few ladies like you. You see that my wishes are infinite. But infinite, too, is the respect and gratitude with which I, Madame, call myself your devoted and obedient servant." The irritable little tyrant George II never accustomed the ladies of his Court to such courtesy.

Queen Caroline's friend, Lord Hervey, was also a friend of Voltaire: he had visited the poet in Paris. This pleasant man traveled and wrote poetry, a sample of which is found translated in Voltaire's *Lettres philosophiques*. Hervey had an attractive wife, who before her marriage had been the inspiration of many, as the incomparable Molly Lepell. Several verses, which Voltaire addressed to her in his best English, reveal that she made a serious impression upon him. She is probably the only Englishwoman of whom this can be said. The verses read:

> Hervey, would you know the passion
>   You have kindled in my breast?
> Trifling is the inclination
>   That by words can be express'd.
> In my silence see the lover;
>   True love is by silence known,
> In my eyes you'll best discover
>   All the power of your own.

This means well; but Voltaire's French verses are preferable.

7

Not long after his arrival Voltaire started to pay his visits to the writers and scholars of England.

Among the dramatists he called on was Congreve whom he greatly admired and spoke of as England's Molière. He found him weak and ill, not far from death. Voltaire was disappointed that Congreve spoke contemptuously of his own writings, wished to be thought of only as a gentleman, and regarded his literary activity as dilettantism. Voltaire has only to criticize in Congreve's plays: that they are too few.

He says they "are all excellent and follow strictly the rules of the theater." What Voltaire likes especially is that the villains express themselves in a decently intelligible manner.

England's second dramatist, William Wycherley, Voltaire could not visit. He was dead. But Voltaire paid him great respect and found that *The Country Wife,* though not a school for good manners, was an education in wit and good comic effects. He even went so far as to declare *The Plain Dealer* the wittiest of all plays ancient or modern. This play was based on Wycherley's impression of Molière's *Le Misanthrope,* and as a poetic work it is far behind Molière. On the stage, however, it has more vitality and Voltaire elaborated it in his own play *La Prude* (1740). *La Prude* is a painstaking work, but its satire was so sharp that it could not be performed publicly. It was played only once (1727) in a private performance at the castle of the Duchess de Maine, in Sceaux, where Voltaire recited the rhymed prologue.

Samuel Johnson, though still a youngster at the time of Voltaire's stay in London, published a collection of spiteful and untrue anecdotes about him, and persecuted Voltaire with inexhaustible bitterness.

Voltaire's first visit to Pope was a failure, but later the two met at the home of Bolingbroke and in Twickenham, at the home of Bubb Dodington.

There were not a few similarities between Pope and Voltaire. Both were physically weak. But, while Pope's physical frailty was the almost helpless infirmity of a hunchback, Voltaire's weakness was something Herculean. In his letters he insists on his broken-down health. In spite of it all he lived to eighty-three.

There was a certain resemblance in the poetry of the two; they wrote a didactic and at the same time satiric verse that is extinct in the present day. Voltaire had a passionate admiration for the poetry of Pope as well as for that of Gay. What he admired in Pope was the influence of Boileau. Voltaire preferred Pope's *Essay on Criticism* to Boileau's *L'art Poétique,* and Pope's *Rape of the Lock* to Boileau's *Le Lutrin.*

Pope and he had exchanged compliments before they were able to converse together. Bolingbroke had sent a copy of *La Ligue* to Pope, who replied with warm praise of what he understood of it—certainly not a great deal. Voltaire sent Pope his expression of deep sympathy, when he heard Pope had cut his hand in a fall from his coach, the hand that had written so magnificently of the stolen lock of hair, of criticism, which had put Homer in English dress.

As early as October, 1726, Voltaire wrote to a friend in Paris:

"Never have I met such a pleasing imagination, such bewitching charm, such variety, so much quickness and so cultured a knowledge of the world combined, as in this little figure."

As late as the year 1756 he confesses to Thiriot: "I surely do not write as good verses as Pope."

Sir John Denham, in his poem on Coopers-Hill, apostrophized the river Thames in this wise:

O could I flow like Thee, and make thy Stream
My great Example, as it is my Theme;
Though deep, yet clear; though gentle yet not dull;
Strong without rage, without o'erflowing full.

Voltaire applied these lines to Pope's poetry, addressing him thus:

Que votre poésie, et forte et naturelle,
Ne soit de la Tamise une image fidèle;
Soyez profond, mais clair; soyez doux, sans lenteur;
Plein, sans vous déborder; rapide, sans fureur.

Voltaire found Pope's crystal poem the *Essay on Man* of great poetic value, though later, as his optimism wore off, he saw in it false ideas of a happy life.

After the earthquake in Lisbon he recognized that Pope had done nothing more than restate Shaftesbury's *Characteristics* and Leibnitz' *Théodicée*. The optimism began to anger him. He wrote that Universal Love was the name given the instinct of animals to eat each other. He aimed *Candide* as much against Pope as against Leibnitz.

Somewhere he says: "Those who go about preaching the rightness of things-as-they-are are charlatans.

Shaftesbury, who brought this nonsense into fashion was himself a very unfortunate man. I saw Bolingbroke a victim of grief and fury, I found even Pope, whom Shaftesbury inspired to put this silly lie into verse, more pitiful than anyone I know, physically malformed, spiritually exhausted, constantly ill, always a burden to himself, and hounded until his last hour by a hundred enemies." And elsewhere: "My poor Pope, my poor hunchback, who told you that God could not have created you without a hump! . . . As for myself, I suffer, and I confess it."

Later Voltaire induced Madame du Châtelet to correspond with Pope, and she writes: "He always speaks of you with infinite respect."

A far deeper impression was made on Voltaire by Jonathan Swift who, in April, 1727, arrived from Ireland for a half-year's sojourn in England. Voltaire met him at Dawley and at Twickenham and spent three months with him in Petersborough. If Voltaire's *Discours en Vers sur l'Homme,* which began to come out in 1734, forms a parallel to Pope's *Essay on Man* (1733), there is no doubt that Voltaire's *Micromégas* would never have been written, had not Swift published *Gulliver's Travels* the year Voltaire came to England. Except for the end, which he disliked, Voltaire admired this work tremendously.

Swift was as much influenced by French literature as Voltaire by English. He took the idea of his first famous satire *Tale of a Tub* (1704) from Fontenelle's *History of Mero and Enegu* (which means: of Rome and Geneva), which in the same way makes fun of the differences of the various Christian faiths. Swift was also influenced by Boccaccio's tale of the three rings, which Lessing long afterward elaborated in his *Nathan der Weise.*

As can be seen, in the later part of his life Voltaire stood nearer Swift's pessimism than Pope's optimism. But during his stay in England he was more disposed to Pope's view in spite of the depression to which at times he was subject.

All the passionate refutation of Pascal which was to conclude the *Lettres philosophiques* and which according to Voltaire himself was written in Wandsworth, is a fight against misanthropy. It was written with the premise than man is neither so bad nor so unhappy as Pascal makes him out.

Voltaire says that Falkener's letter reached him as he was about to begin his refutation of Pascal. He particularly states that the letter came from a friend in a foreign country. Hence this must have been written in France. No matter when the letter was written, in 1728 or in 1729, its tone is distinctly optimistic: "You wonder why God has made man so wretched. Why not wonder instead that he hasn't made him still more limited, still more ignorant, and still more wretched?"—And strangely enough this passage is almost word for word the same as one in Pope's *Essay on Man* (1733):

> Presumptuous man! the reason wouldst thou find,
> Why formed so weak, so little and so blind?
> First, if thou canst, the harder reason guess.
> Why form'd no weaker, blinder and no less?

Both poets speak of life in general. But usually Voltaire devotes himself to comparisons between England and France. During his extensive contacts with England's great men and with English middle class families he continued to think of the English as behind the French in moral *finesse*—this in spite of his enthusiasm for the British national virtues. England was great in the art of thinking, France in that of pleasing.

And though he associated with England's wealthy class, he found their way of life comparatively frugal. He believes that "in Parisian middle-class homes there is five hundred times as much silverware as in those of London." The dwellings in Paris were better, the furniture better, the service better, the food better. There are thirty different religions in England, but only one kind of sauce. More poultry and game are consumed in Paris in one evening than in a week in England. Paris burns a thousand times as many wax candles. For, except at Court or in Court circles in England, only tallow candles are used.

On the whole, he finds the English cruder and rougher than the French. They do not understand fine speech; nor are they interested in good, soft music. As they drink mixed drinks and eat over seasoned food, they crave drums and trumpets. And he summarizes his opinion in the oft-repeated comparison of the English people and English beer: on top foam, at the bottom yeast; and what is in the middle is excellent.

8

The greatest of all Englishmen Voltaire was not able to see. Isaac Newton was soon to die. He died on March 20, 1727, eighty-five years old. With astonishment and enthusiasm Voltaire, who had been beaten by ducal lackeys and exiled to England, watched Newton's coffin carried to Westminster Abbey, followed by dukes and earls.

He saw science honored by men whose position and wealth were princely. He saw clearly that Roman Catholicism in France was not only arresting the development of literature, but choking civilization and that Protestantism could not be professed even by the very great. He understood what it meant that this England, which had decapitated one king and deposed another, had overthrown the ecclesiastical power and permitted full freedom to thought, speech, and literature.

He, who in France had dreamed in vain of a diplomatic career, was astounded to see how England honored her scientists and men of letters. Newton as well as Locke had been rewarded with profitable government posts. Addison had been a secretary of state and was buried in Westminster Abbey; Prior and Gay held important positions as ambassadors. Voltaire, by paying his respects at Versailles, had received a few thousand francs in pensions, which he now had lost, whereas in England minor figures like Hughes, Rowe, Ambrose Philips and Congreve had profitable sinecures.

He saw that art was as highly esteemed as science, even that art which French prejudice despised, the art of acting. The greatest dramatic artist France ever

had, Molière, had been excluded from the French
Academy, and had to be buried at night. Even this
would have been denied him except that his widow
had the good sense to scatter the Parisian mob by
throwing a large sum of money in its midst.

Newton was buried March, 1727. Three years later
the famous actress Anne Oldfield was buried, also in
Westminster Abbey, and with almost as much ceremony and honor as Newton.

England observed a national memorial day for
Shakespeare; France had none for Molière.

The difference that struck Voltaire most forcibly,
however, was this: He had left a country where the
gag was the government's constant and most effective
tool, and he had come to a country where the gag
was not known. Here every writer, from Swift down,
could attack the policy of the ministry with a satiric
ferociousness that in France would have sent him to
jail for life. Here nothing was done to him. The
strange thing was that this freedom of speech could
be reconciled with order and quiet.

Apparently his countrymen did not desire liberty.
They held fast to every antiquated system and thus
hindered as much as possible the growth of new ideas.
Aristotle's doctrine persisted in France longer than
in any other country. Descartes, who attempted to
think without prejudice and without preconceived
ideas, was forced to live for twenty years in Holland;
even so, his philosophy was denounced and forbidden in Italy in 1643, in Holland in 1656. As late as
1693, when England had advanced so far beyond
Descartes that Newton's principles were freely developed at Oxford, at Cambridge and in London, the
Cartesian teachings were regarded in France as so
dangerous to the Commonwealth, that the Royal
Council prohibited them in the Sorbonne. When the
Cartesian physics finally took root in France (after
the clergy discovered that its laws were "spiritual-
istic"), they became the sacred dogma, and the gag
was tied on in their favor.

Voltaire was soon made to feel this when he tried
to publish, in France, what he had learned in England from Newton and Locke. The censor wouldn't

pass what he had written until he altered Locke so much that the doctrine was completely obscured. Truth had to be smuggled into France like a dangerous outlaw; in England it was free-born and openly acknowledged.

France was the incubator of metaphysical systems. In England metaphysical speculation was abandoned in favor of progress on the basis of experience. The French tried a short-cut to the origin of the universe and of the intellect and endeavored to derive the entire nature of life from first principles. The English scientists never began with abstract ideas, but with accurately observed phenomena from which moderately and carefully they would progress to the unknown principles and try to recognize them if possible by logical deduction.

Of course, England, too, had noted metaphysicists. There were some among Newton's pupils. England had at least one who has a place in history: Berkeley (later Bishop) who denied the reality of the material world. Voltaire met Berkeley; the circumstances of the meeting, however, are not known. Voltaire seems to have had a favorable impression, for he calls him one "whose desire to work for the best of mankind has grown into a passion."

Nevertheless, a letter Voltaire wrote to his Quaker friend, Andrew Pitt, proves that he did not accept the arguments of Berkeley's *Alciphron,* published shortly after Voltaire left England. He acknowledged its ingenuity, but could not be persuaded by it.

Berkeley repelled him as Descartes had.

Although Descartes set out analytically and critically, he soon lost himself in speculation unsupported by fact. Newton's method on the other hand, had been to confine himself at the beginning to the earth, and to apply what he observed to the universe outside of the earth. Then he investigated whether the conclusions would square with observations. Why should gravity not exist on the other planets as well? Why should the motion of the moon not be taken for a falling motion? And could it not be gravity that kept the moon in its orbit? Wasn't it even possible that all matter exercised a similar attraction, that it was gravity that conducted the movements of the heavenly bodies and kept together the universe?

In Locke, it was the new presentation of the problem of perception which captivated Voltaire. That ideas are not inborn, but derive from external or internal experiences and are the transformation of sensory impressions or of reflexes, was a doctrine which appealed to him by its apparent simplicity and clearness. He remained its exponent all his life. That Locke's doctrine contains a contradiction in assuming the passivity of the mind at the reception of the impulse and yet postulating its activity at the derivation of the idea does not seem to have impressed Voltaire. In spite of his skepticism with regard to inborn ideas, he continued to maintain the irrevocability of not a few fundamental ideas which, he insisted, were accepted by all people and all nations.

Thus it was that he accepted without question Locke's proof of the existence of God: the world must have a first cause. A truth of which we are persuaded intuitively, leads from the world to the Creator, just as we deduce the watchmaker from the watch. What does not really exist, cannot create reality. The introduction of God into his speculation helps Voltaire as well as Locke over various philosophical difficulties. If one asks whence comes the ability of the mind itself to perceive the truth, the answer is that God could have given this characteristic to matter.

The really overwhelming scientific lesson Voltaire took back with him from England, however, was taught him by Newton's discoveries. As early as 1726 Voltaire met Doctor Samuel Clarke, one of Newton's ablest disciples, who listened patiently to the questions of the intelligent Frenchman and taught him the new doctrines.

Samuel Clarke (1675-1729) was about twenty years older than Voltaire but with the same versatile gifts and the same highly critical inquisitiveness. He was one of the first to understand Sir Isaac's "sublime discoveries"—as he called them—and was one of the most active in the dissemination of Newton's philosophy. First attracted by mathematics, he later studied

Hebrew and became a clergyman. Queen Anne appointed him her personal chaplain and made him prebendary of St. James, Westminster. His clerical career, however, was rudely interrupted when, in 1714, his book *Scripture Doctrine of the Trinity* was charged with heresy. As a freethinker he could not remain a priest. After Newton's death he was offered his office of Master of the Mint but he refused.

Clarke seems to have been a pleasant, honest and moderate man, who viewed life and religion with the eyes of a strict Newtonian. He gave Voltaire his views, and Voltaire's belief in Descartes' *Principles of Philosophy* was at an end, but not his respect and admiration for Descartes. In the fourteenth epistle of his *Lettres philosophiques* he speaks of him with all esteem. Naturally, he does not compare Descartes' importance in the intellectual growth of mankind with that of Newton.

From Newton's niece, Mrs. Conduit, and her husband, he heard various vivid features and anecdotes of the life of the great man.

For instance, Mrs. Conduit related that Newton at the age of twenty had begun to read Descartes, and beside each passage which seemed to him incorrect had written the word "error" in the margin. Finally he had to fill the margins of the pages so full of "error" that he threw the book away disgusted.

Mrs. Conduit told Voltaire another anecdote, which in the form given by Voltaire is repeated in every modern biography of the great scholar: the one of the falling apple, which inspired him with the idea of the law of gravitation as a principle of the universe.

9

Voltaire was almost as deeply impressed by the differences between France and England in social and political conditions as he was by the progress of philosophy and science in England. That the British could devote particular attention to these conditions was, as he recognized, mainly due to the fact that they wasted no time in metaphysical debates.

The farmer in France was a beast of burden, liable to taxation at the whim of others. At that time La Bruyère's famous description (*Les Caractères,* Chapter XI) of the hardships he had to endure still held true:

"It is always a shock to me to witness man's inhumanity to man. One sees human animals, male and female, distributed over the country, black and sunburned, bound to the soil, in which they dig and toil with unconquerable stubbornness. If they straighten up they show human features and are people. At night they retire into their caves, where they live on black bread, water and roots. They save others the trouble of sowing, plowing and harvesting, and hence they should not be in desperate want of the bread which they have sowed.

"The provincial aristocrat, of no use to his country, to his family or to himself, who often has not even a roof above his head, nor decent clothing nor any virtues, nevertheless repeats ten times a day that he is noble, mocks at the President of the Parliament as bourgeois and is forever fussing with his documents and titles which he wouldn't exchange for the position of chancellor."

In England he captured that impression of quiet luxury he received earlier in Holland. Here there were no poll taxes specially for the farmer. Clergy and nobility were not exempt. The farmer did not wear wooden shoes, he ate white bread, was decently clothed and did not risk crushing taxation, if he enlarged his farm or covered his roof with tiles. Voltaire found a large number of country gentlemen with a yearly income of five or six hundred pounds, who didn't find it below their dignity to till their own land and who never thought, as did every Frenchman, as soon as he owned a bit of land, of moving from the country to the city.

He discovered that the nobility in this country formed no closed caste, but the great merchant whose trade was of advantage to England and the whole world, was awarded a title, while nobility's younger sons were trained in middle-class activities.

So it seems plain that the exile which was pronounced as punishment, actually afforded the young writer a wealth of knowledge and understanding which he probably would never have reached without it.

His mortifying beating by the lackeys of a nobleman became of advantage to him in still another way. He, whose entire social intercourse in France was with men and women who had all the privileges, would never without exile have become conscious of the wrongs to which they were exposed who did not belong by birth to the nobility. Having been educated with aristocrats, the respect they showed his talent in daily association, the homage they paid his genius in daily life, had for many years blinded him to the insolence and prejudice that underlay their pretense of recognizing his equality. Only when the smooth surface, on which he had glided with confidence, cracked and let him plunge into the cold water beneath, did he recognize the real structure of French society.

10

Burke has drawn attention to the fact that during the two generations that came between Louis XIV's death and the outbreak of the Revolution there was scarcely one prominent Frenchman who had not either visited England or learned English. Among the other notables who crossed the Channel and were introduced into English society were: Buffon, Helvétius, Lafayette, Montesquieu, Maupertuis, Rousseau, Roland and Madame Roland.

None of these except Voltaire took the trouble to seek and master the learning of England.

His later works prove that he continued the study of English literature after his return to French soil. The fourth act of *Mahomet* (performed for the first time in 1742) was influenced by George Lillo's drama *George Barwell or the Merchant of London* (1731); the well-known twentieth chapter of *Zadig*, by *The Hermit*, a work of the unimportant English poet, Thomas Parnell, a fact over which Fréron made a great to-do.

Strangely enough Voltaire seems to have over-looked Daniel Defoe's masterpiece *Robinson Crusoe,* which appeared in the year 1719. At any rate he has, as far as I know, never mentioned either the author or the character.

On the other hand, he read an older, very difficult and abstruse English poet, and esteemed him highly: Samuel Butler, the author of the mock-heroic poem *Hudibrae,* and a contemporary of Milton. *Hudibrae,* which deals with the civil war at the time of Crom-well, is as detailed as it is witty. Voltaire took four hundred lines from this work and condensed them to about eighty, very clever and amusing. Among his comments on this work, there is one that proves how high his critical genius could place him as a judge of art. He compares *Hudibrae* with the French *Satire Ménippée* as well as with the Spanish *Don Quixote.* "*Hudibrae* has the advantage over both of the others, of being written in verse; it also has the further advantage, of being written with wit. The *Satire Ménippée* does not even approach it. But thanks to this same wit, the author of *Hudibrae* has made his work far inferior to *Don Quixote.* Taste, simplicity, the art of inventing and narrating delightful adven-tures with gusto, the art of being sparing with dry argument, is far more valuable than any wit. That is why *Don Quixote* is read by all nations, and *Hudi-brae* by the English only."

Voltaire read Shakespeare, and foreign as Shake-speare's style and technique were to all the ideas of dramatic poetry with which Voltaire had grown up and from which he could free himself only to a lim-ited extent, he was amazed at the magnificence of this genius. He resolved to impart to his countrymen the riches of this mine.

He recognized Milton sufficiently to state, in his essay on epic poetry, that Milton had contributed as much to England's honor as Newton. At the time of his arrival in England, Milton's daughter was still living; although he found no occasion to be intro-duced to her, he met many who had known her very well and heard from them all there was of first-hand tradition about the great poet.

In his English *Essay on Epic Poetry* Voltaire says that Milton got his idea of *Paradise Lost* from an Italian comedy, *Adamo,* written by an actor, Andreino, which in his youth he had seen in Florence. This statement was declared by critics, as politely as possible, to be absurd. Voltaire answered that he had the authority of friends of Deborah Milton not only for this, but also for the fact that Milton originally conceived the idea, not as an epic, but as a tragedy, of which he wrote one and one-half acts.

One day when Voltaire was dining with Dodington, in spite of all due respect to Milton, he called the episode on Sin and Death in *Paradise Lost* boring and repulsive; whereupon the poet Young, comparing Voltaire's own lean face with the face of Milton's *Death,* improvised the following lines:

> You are so witty, profligate and thin,
> At once we think thee Milton, Death and Sin.

It is certain that Voltaire's admiration for Milton did not extend to his allegories. Nevertheless, his admiration was deep and warm. He says that Milton got from the Italian comedy inspiration for the "noblest work ever created by human imagination." And even the comedy was witnessed twenty years before he began *Paradise Lost.* While in educated French circles jokes were made about the serpent, the devil, Adam's rib, and the bite of the apple, Milton's imagination had been able to draw from this material treasures of which nobody had dreamed. Milton described the history of creation without bombast, told of female curiosity interestingly, brought probability and reasonableness into supernatural occurrences. The fundamentally sterile theme became a thing of awe under Milton's pen. Voltaire admires the conversation between Adam and the angel, the keen delineation of Satan's spiteful, invincible, and crafty character; also the sureness Milton shows in the part where he dares to describe God himself and lets him speak. God, says Voltaire, has been pictured as an almighty tyrant: always by the pagans, often by Jews and not seldom by Christians.

Milton's God, on the other hand, is a creator, a father, and a judge.

What Voltaire remarks on particularly is the purely human content of the poem. Here, love between man and woman is not, as in other religious works, accounted a vice, but a virtue. The characters are naked but honorable. With chaste hand the poet removes the veil which usually conceals the joys of love. Here we have tenderness and warmth without frivolity. The poet has imagined himself in the state of innocence in which Adam and Eve lived for a short time.

Voltaire complains that the Duke of Buckingham, in his *Art of Poetry*, preferred Spenser to Milton, and that Dryden compared him sometimes with the greatest poets of antiquity, Homer and Virgil, then again with the worst French poets, such as Chapelain and Lemoine. He is glad of the justice which Addison, "the best critic and greatest writer of his time," accords Milton.

Voltaire did not wish to withhold his praise or his criticism. Yet he did not wish to offend the English in their national pride. He therefore selected the device of emphasizing the difference of national tastes in England and France, and picturing what a French critic would have to say against *Paradise Lost*.

Such a critic would object to those passages in which the poet speaks in his own name, now about himself and about his blindness, now about his theme and its superiority to that of the *Iliad*. Voltaire, however, for his part, finds in such a comparison a very excusable human weakness. On the other hand he strongly emphasizes how shocking an idea like the summoning of a devil's parliament, this pandemonium, would be to the cultured Frenchman. He disapproves of this Hall of Parliament with its Doric columns and its gilded vaulting. Death, Sin and Chaos, leave him cold. And he formulates a doctrine as to what allegories should be: short, unconstrained, and noble. Apparently he is of the opinion that his own allegories in the *Henriade* achieve this perfection. It seems to him a clever conceit to have Sin posted at the doorway to Hell, able to open the gates but unable to close them again; for, this is clear allegory. On the other hand, it seems to him absurd to have Satan and Death engage in combat, and prepare to wrestle. Against the rational aspect of the poem he had no objections; but the picture ought to be perfectly clear.

Addison admired the war in Milton's *Paradise.* Voltaire (rightly) cannot share this admiration. It should be allowed several pages at most, but never two books. To French readers it sounds rather odd when the angels bombard their enemies with mountains, complete with forests and rivers. Voltaire disapproves of the heavenly artillery, and he has a perfect right to. What purpose do these cannons serve? They cannot hurt their invulnerable and immortal targets. They can only remove the demons from their position. It's like a game of nine-pins.

As can be seen, this criticism, written originally in English for Englishmen, is kind and gentle. In later years, Voltaire gradually became less admiring of Milton. Fundamentally, Milton's subject repelled him, and when George Gray, in 1770, turned out a parody on Milton and sent it to Ferney, Voltaire answered that he always thought the story was well suited to humorous elaboration. In his verses on the epic poets, Milton does not fare so well. After mentioning Homer, Virgil, and Tasso, Voltaire says:

> Milton, plus sublime qu'eux tous,
> A des beautés moins agréables;
> Il semble chanter pour les fous,
> Pour les anges et pour les diables.

In the twenty-fifth chapter of *Candide* he lets Pococurante ridicule Milton and call him a barbarian who wrote a ten-book commentary on the first chapter of Genesis. While Moses describes the Almighty as creating the earth by his word, in Milton's work He takes a big compass from a cupboard in Heaven to draw up a ground-plan. The marriage of Sin and Death is horrible. Candide is sad over this criticism: "He thinks something of Milton." But obviously not too much; and Voltaire with him.

As was to be expected of a Frenchman educated in

the classical tradition, Voltaire from the beginning gave great importance to Addison. He calls him the first Englishman to write a logical play, and one whose style is elegant, through and through. Addison's *Cato* is recognized by Voltaire as a masterpiece of diction and metrical nicety. He even goes so far as to call *Cato* the grandest figure that ever trod any stage. On the other hand, he regrets that the other characters of the play are unimportant; also that the coldness of the love intrigue spoils the effect of the tragedy. The highest praise from Voltaire's lips, however, is that he finds Addison comparable to Racine in infallible elegance.

11

The superiority of Shakespeare's imagination seems to have impressed him more than Addison's reasoning. It inspired him and awakened an urge for imitation. If it did not appeal to him unconditionally, this was due to the fact that the prejudices of his country and age made him look down upon Shakespeare as at one who ignored the rules of unity of time and place, who did not hesitate to mix the burlesque with the solemn. This was "bad taste," and automatically excluded him from the ranks of the great.

In the *Letters on England* which he prepared during his stay there and later elaborated, he says of Shakespeare:

"The English, like the Spaniards, had a theater when the French had nothing but a hovel. Shakespeare, who is called England's Corneille, blossomed at about the time of Lope de Vega. He created the theater. He had a strong, terrible, natural and inspired genius, without either the slightest notion of good taste or the least knowledge of the dramatic conventions. . . . The virtues of this poet have been the ruin of the English theater. There are such splendid scenes, such magnificent and such terrifying passages in his monstrous farces called tragedies, that these plays are always performed with great

success. The original and titanic ideas of this poet
are still sublime after two centuries. Nearly all modern writers have copied them. . . . Nobody considers
that he should not be imitated, and the misfortune
of his imitators is that their model is regarded as
incomparable.

"In the very moving play *Othello* a man chokes his
wife to death on the stage—and after being strangled,
the poor girl exclaims that she dies innocent. In
Hamlet the grave-diggers dig a grave, and at this
grisly labor they drink, sing songs, and joke about a
skull they uncover, as people of their sort actually
do."

Voltaire, as a sample of the best in Shakespeare,
translates the soliloquy *To be or not to be.* He turns
it into a rhymed verse.

The reader of today who is inclined to see in this
criticism a proof of Voltaire's personal, or at least
French, lack of taste, should, to be just, consider that
this was not only the French, but also the English
conception of the time. The prominent and intelligent Englishmen whom Voltaire met in London used
about the same expressions and had a lower estimate
of Shakespeare probably than Voltaire. Nor did the
English public show better discernment.

Pope got up an edition of Shakespeare's works.
Although only seven hundred and fifty copies were
printed, the price had to be reduced considerably,
before the edition was subscribed. As a young man,
Addison wrote verses on England's greatest poets;
but Shakespeare's name was not among them. Swift
was so ignorant of Shakespeare that he thought the
Wife of Bath from Chaucer's *Canterbury Tales* was
a Shakespearean character, and in his works Shakespeare's name is mentioned but once. When a leading English publisher commissioned Samuel Johnson
to prepare an edition of the works of English poets, it
was thought obvious that English poetry commenced
with Cowley. Hence the *Lives of the English Poets*
contains no biography of Shakespeare. Charles
James Fox remarked to the painter Sir Joshua Rey-
nolds that in his opinion Shakespeare's greatness

would have been more assured had he not written his *Hamlet.*

Five years after Voltaire's arrival in England, the English dramatist and anti-critic Charles Gildon put out his book entitled *The Laws of Poetry,* in which he called Hamlet's famous soliloquy unnecessary to the play, ridiculed the soliloquy of the Bastard Falconbridge, and summarized his criticism in the words: "In the entire works of Shakespeare there is not one monologue for which there is any natural or reasonable excuse."

From Voltaire's *Discours sur la Tragédie* (the dedication of *Brutus*) it can be seen that in Bolingbroke's opinion there was no such thing as a good English tragedy. Th. Rymer, in *A Short View of Tragedy* (1693), says disapprovingly: "With Shakespeare one cannot speak of rules or of anything regular." Other contemporaries held the same opinion. Rowe wrote: "He lived, guided only by a sort of a natural light, and entirely unfamiliar with any rules of art." Dennis says: "In Shakespeare's works one finds faulty poetic art and an absolute ignorance of its rules." Pope remarked that it had to be admitted that, critically regarded, Shakespeare was just as repulsive at some times as he was inspired at others; he offers the most liberal selection of illustrations of both the good and the bad.

The eighteenth century in all countries believed thoroughly in rule, and was completely persuaded of the infallibility of its own taste, to which it universally gave the name of "good taste."

12

Lanson has compiled from two newspapers of the time, the *Daily Post* and the *Daily Journal,* a list of the plays given at three English theaters, Drury Lane, Lincoln's Inn Field and Haymarket, which Voltaire had occasion to attend during his stay in England. Of Shakespeare's dramas he could, in 1726, have seen *Othello, Hamlet, Macbeth, King Lear, Henry IV, First Part, The Merry Wives of Windsor, Richard III,*

Henry VIII, Julius Cæsar, in 1727 the same plays, and in addition *Measure for Measure, The Tempest, The Merchant of Venice, Henry IV, Second Part,* and in 1728 and 1729 the same plays.

This does not tell us which plays he actually did see. If we turn to Voltaire's own writings, he seems to know only *Julius Cæsar, Hamlet, Othello, King Lear,* and *Richard III.* Until 1755, he did not know *Romeo and Juliet.* This is proved by a letter to Garrick from a French dramatist who read aloud long passages of this drama to Voltaire. Voltaire at first laughed at the enthusiasm of his French visitor, then was stirred by what he heard, called it beautiful, poignant, natural —and then asked to have the play read him from the beginning to the end. After which he jestingly remarked that, had the British not taken so many French ships and had they not behaved like such pirates, he would have been nicer to the founder of the English theater. In his *Discours* to Bolingbroke, one can clearly distinguish the things in Shakespeare that at first displeased him.

He takes up *Julius Cæsar.* The vivid scene in the market place, in which Brutus and Antony clash, has a powerful effect on him. But it offends his French prejudice that artisans, carpenters and shoemakers should appear on the same stage with a Brutus and a Cassius. The portrayal of jealousy in *Othello* is vividly interesting; but it seems too horrible and ridiculous to have Desdemona strangled on the stage and then give her a speech to make afterward. In the same way, while Hamlet's soliloquies excite his admiration, he is horrified that grave-diggers are permitted to appear in a tragedy. Such grossness can only be explained by the fact that Shakespeare lived in a barbaric age when the custom of keeping court fools had accustomed eminent men to hear the comic mixed with the dignified. The noblemen of that day had not got beyond the stage of hiring "jesters" to say rude and dull things to them. The jesters returned as the English stage clowns, in disregard of the fundamental law of good scenic art which requires a strict separation of the high from the low, of the noble from the vulgar. In such an unenlightened age even

Shakespeare was unenlightened. It is sufficiently revealing that he did not even know Latin.

What he lacked, therefore, was that he did not live in a civilized age. At Addison's time he would have become the perfect poet.

In following years, Voltaire often tries to inject the French dramatic style with some of the Shakespearean vigor. Under Shakespeare's influence, he began, in 1731, to write his *La Mort de César,* which he believed was written according to "English taste." In *Zaïre* he imitated Shakespeare's *Othello* (and Racine's *Mithridate*); he employs the Ghost from *Hamlet* in his *Semiramis.* But with the passing of years and the growing enthusiasm for Shakespeare at the expense of the classical taste in England, and soon also in France, Voltaire became more and more annoyed because everybody overlooked the preposterousness of the English dramatist being a poet for the higher civilized world, which knew Aristotle's rules and demanded their observance. Like Tolstoi a century and a half later he found Shakespeare's pathos bombastic.

From about 1760—when he noticed that what he had said against Shakespeare was being used against Voltaire—he employed abuse to express his feelings. Finally he became purely nationalistic in his fundamental æsthetic concepts. He believed—as he wrote to Horace Walpole—that tragedy as well as comedy in Paris stood high above the dramatic art of ancient Athens. He considered English drama was like English pudding, something nobody could relish except the English themselves.

It pained him that the traditions of the times of Louis XIV were forgotten by the younger generation. When he said to Diderot that Shakespeare was a Gothic colossus whom nobody could seriously compare to the Apollo of the Belvedere, the younger Frenchman replied that, of course Shakespeare was only such a colossus as St. Christopher in Notre Dame; but that the greatest men could stand or walk between his legs.

Then Voltaire lost all restraint. He called Shakespeare a "drunken savage," gifted it is true, with a

talent for fantasy, but whose plays could please only
in England and Canada. Such an outburst does not
sound well to modern ears; but it certainly was
greeted with enthusiasm by the French Academy of
1776, which was of precisely the same opinion. And if
one read Voltaire's objections to the monologue of
the porter in *Macbeth* (which Schiller omitted in the
translation for his theater) and to the coarse epithets
of *Othello* (which are omitted at modern product-
ions) one notices that Voltaire's estimate of Shakespeare is not very different from Goethe's.

In his essay *Shakespeare als Theaterdichter* (1826)
the twenty-seven-year-old Goethe has about the same
opinion as the eighty-two-year-old Voltaire. He insists on the necessity of revamping *Romeo and Juliet*
as well as *Macbeth* for the theater in Weimar. He defends Schröder's omission of the entire first scene
from his acting version of *King Lear,* "because it
shows Lear as so unreasonable that one can not blame
his two bad daughters."

It was the unfortunate temper with which Voltaire,
as an old man, wrote his criticism of Shakespeare,
that has hurt him. What he meant would have easily
been excused, had he said it in a less abusive manner.

13

Although Voltaire had the foresight, in his *Lettres
Philosophiques,* not to mention the theological disputes which were rife in England at the time, they
occupied a great deal of his attention. A fierce battle
had broken out for and against revealed Christianity,
as well as for and against deism.

He had no need to come to England to learn about
free thought.

Before he was born there were freethinkers in
Paris: some forgotten, as Mesnault, Méré, Debarraux,
but also some who today have worldwide fame—as
Molière, La Fontaine, Boileau.

As today it is suggested that the story of Christ's
Passion and the teachings of Christianity were in
existence long before Jesus, so Voltairianism existed

in France long before Voltaire. He took it over almost like an inheritance from more moderate predecessors.

On French soil he had prominent scientific fore-
runners in Pierre Bayle and in Fontenelle. Carefully
and shyly, but unequivocally, the idea of tolerance
was expressed in Bayle's excellent and cleverly arranged *Pensées Diverses sur la Comète.* He was quite
outspoken in his *Commentaire Philosophique sur le
Compelle Intrare,* his fight against the zealots who
wanted to force conversions. From the *Project de
Dictionnaire* Voltaire took some good passages for his
Jeannot et Collin, and from the article *Asyndicus* in
the *Dictionnaire* he got his story *Cosi Sancta.* Most
probably it was from Bayle that he borrowed the idea
for his *Dictionnaire Philosophique.* According to
Bayle, religion annihilates all natural ideas of justice
to such an extent "that one is rendered incapable of
distinguishing good deeds from bad." It "seems to
rob us of what little sense Nature gave us in the first
place."

Bayle's attitude was that of a skeptic. His ever-
ready genuflections to the Faith, his constant humble
avowal of the miserable weakness of his poor reason
compared to the sturdiness of the Faith, are full
of irony. At times he seems to become very outspoken, as in the little Essay *Ce que c'est que la
France Toute Catholique Sous le Règne de Louis le
Grand.* His reason for writing this was the Revocation
of the edict of Nantes. It expresses indignation over
the persecution of the Protestants by the infamous
dragonnades. Still more anger does it express over
the hypocrisy with which this action was everywhere
described as mild.

His satire does not appeal, like Voltaire's, to the
great reading public. It might perhaps have taken
him up, had he not been forced to become a fugitive
and to write anonymously. He says that the world is
bad; therefore it was part of God's immutable plan
that it be unhappy as well as ridiculous. But as God
acts only out of infinite wisdom, He punishes the
world in the quickest and most expedient way. Were
it His object to make man miserable and ridiculous,

there could be no more effective method than to keep the Roman Church in a position of the highest possible respect and power.

As we have seen, Voltaire had close relations with Fontenelle. Fontenelle's *Histoire des Oracles* brings a few home truths to the attention of his readers. The "oracles" are used as a symbol. The belief in their supernatural nature in his book correspond to Bayle's belief in the supernatural character of comets. He shows that the Christians of antiquity thought the oracles were the works of demons, and that they were wrong in simply denying their veracity. Numbers of pagan philosophers had denied the divinity of oracles: for oracles "and more than that, religions," had originated in an attempt to give an explanation for some natural phenomenon, such as the vapor rising out of a hole in the earth. The dignity of the oracles and the comfort of the priests both required that the utterances come from caves. Reflected from a vault, the voice sounded bigger, more terrifying.

In the *Préface de l'Histoire de l'Academie des Sciences*, Fontenelle had outlined the experimental method, and ever since 1721 Voltaire kept in touch with him. At that period Fontenelle's support of the Cartesian "vortex" doctrine struck him as absolutely impossible, maddening.

The *Lettres Philosophiques*, which gave Voltaire's impressions of his stay in England, are supposedly letters he wrote to Thiriot from London in 1734. It is characteristic that he carefully omitted all mention of the theologic-philosophical quarrels in English literature and the press. It was not until 1767 that he discussed English freethinkers in his *Lettre sur les Auteurs Anglais.*

The introduction to one of his earliest works contains a few references to British piety, but it is only the sect of the Quakers that he mentions with interest and respect. He had made the acquaintance of an English Quaker, Andrew Pitt, who for thirty years had been a linen draper and then had retired from business and settled in a comfortable house on the outskirts of London. In spite of his advanced age when Voltaire met him, he was vigorous and healthy, because he had never indulged in passions or dissipation. He had never been ill. When he died in 1736, an English newspaper said of him that he had many virtues and not a single vice. He was one of the preachers and controversialists of the sect, and was somewhat indignant at the vein in which Voltaire wrote about the Quakers; but from 1728 was in friendly correspondence with him.

From him Voltaire received a strong impression of true piety and firm character and the same contempt for all hocus-pocus that Voltaire felt so strongly.

14

As long as he lived in England he did not find time to write about the Quakers. He was especially busy with his old poetic work *La Ligue,* the first sketch of which became on English soil *La Henriade.* This sketch was considerably improved, and Voltaire showed again that he was grateful for reasonable criticism no matter whence it came.

A Greek by the name of Dadiky, who was interpreter to the King of England, chanced to read the first proof of the poem, in a printing shop. He called upon its author and told him: "I am from Homer's country. He did not start his works with ingenious and puzzling ideas."

This referred to the opening lines of the *Henriade:*

> Je chante les combats et ce roi généreux,
> Qui força les Français à devenir heureux.

"Who forced the French to become happy" seemed obscure to the Greek, so these lines were replaced by the simple and dignified opening in its final and permanent form:

> Je chante ce héros qui régna sur la France
> Et par droit de conquête, et par droit de naissance,
> Qui par des longues malheurs apprit à gouverner,
> Calma les factions, sut vaincre et pardonner.

It was Voltaire's intention to publish a new edition of the composition on which he had worked so long, and add to it his completely revised dissertation on poetry.

As he tells in his *Commentaire Historique,* he found certain similarities between Henry IV and himself. At least both looked to England for help:

> Je ne dois pas être plus fortuné
> Que le héros célèbre sur ma vielle:
> Il fut proscrit, persécuté, damné
> Par les devots et leur douce séquelle:
> En Angleterre il trouva du secours,
> J'en vais chercher . . .

He got the help he sought. King George I, and the Princess of Wales, who soon afterward became Queen, gave him their patronage. The Princess had noble interests; it was she who helped Milton's daughter, as soon as she was informed of her poverty; it was she who intervened between Clarke and Leibnitz. She favored the work of the French poet, and procured for him what he called an "immense subscription." The members of the Court and all the first names of England were on the list; as far as that goes, it perhaps could have been called immense. According to our ideas, it was not especially long; there were 344 names.

Voltaire left no stone unturned in his efforts to increase the number of subscriptions. He asked Swift to use his influence in Ireland to procure some there.

In England, the Earl of Oxford supported the subscription. In Ireland the Lord-Lieutenant, Lord Carteret, a warm friend of literature did the same. The Lord-Lieutenant went so far as to permit Voltaire to open a little book shop in the Palace of the Viceroy, where his composition was distributed.

To show his gratitude for the support of the English Royal House he dedicated his work to the Queen. In the dedication he says: "It was the fate of Henry IV to be protected by Queens. He enjoyed the support of the famous Elizabeth who was the glory of her generation and an example to princes. Where can a better protector for his memory be found than she in whom Elizabeth is reincarnated!" This sentence too occurs: "Supported by the spirit in which this poem is written, I am taking the liberty of offering it to the noble consort of the King who is almost unique in enjoying the inestimable glory of reigning over a free nation, of the King who wishes that his power consist in being loved, his praise in being just." George II sent the poet four hundred pounds and granted him admission to his private suppers. As a friend of Queen Caroline, the Queen of Prussia sent him a medallion with the portrait of the English Queen.

It was rather droll that Voltaire dedicated his composition to a Protestant Queen. A composition in which he, out of compulsory piety, is so Catholic. In France the poem was pronounced heretical because it did not say enough that was bad about the despised Protestants; in England it really cut a queer figure with its feigned Papism. But this was overlooked in admiration. According to Voltaire's statement the great sale of the work on English soil laid the foundation for his wealth. The first foundation, however, was laid long before, and it is an exaggeration when later on Voltaire writes that the French edition had cost him everything that the English had made.

The large quarto edition which appeared in England at a price of three guineas, was published by two honest booksellers in London, and was quickly sold out. Three subsequent cheaper editions were exhausted in three weeks. Voltaire's receipts were a hundred and fifty thousand francs.

Thiriot had been requested to arrange for a subscription edition in France. He had collected the money from eighty subscribers when Voltaire received a letter from him with the strange information that the entire sum had been stolen from his house while he was at Mass. Of course, the dissolute rascal Thiriot, who always was in straits, had appropriated the money.

Although Voltaire was not deceived for a moment by the pretended theft, he was too well bred and too good a friend not to accept the statement. He answered simply: "This adventure, my dear friend, may spoil your going to Mass; but it shall not keep me from loving you always and thanking you for all the trouble you had." Many years later (December 3, 1744) he wrote to Destouches: "He has frequently offered to make good this loss; but it would have ruined him, and I should be unworthy of the name of a writer, if I would not rather forfeit one hundred louis d'ors than embarrass a friend."

The general feeling at that time was that Voltaire had given French literature what it had long lacked, and what so many other literatures possessed: a national epic. According to the ideas of the eighteenth century the *Henriade* was a work of the very first importance. However, when in 1837 the manuscript of the *Chanson de Roland* was found at Oxford, the real national epic of France was found. Taillefer sang this as he led the Norman knights to the assault at Hastings. It is simple and great and heroic.

15

The letters from England and on England which Voltaire wrote to Thiriot between the years 1727 and 1729, and elaborated up to the year 1731, were to French intellectual life of the eighteenth century much as Madame de Staël's *De l'Allemagne* was to that of 1810. These letters revealed to the French what England was at the beginning of the eighteenth century, as Madame de Staël's work described German character and intellectual life at the beginning of the nineteenth century. As is well known, the prohibition of the Napoleonic police made the publishing of *De l'Allemagne* difficult. How trifling this difficulty was in comparison to those that Voltaire had to meet almost a century before, when he wished to publish his *Lettres Philosophiques!*

He did not dare to say in French what seemed to him worth saying about England's government and literature; and it did no real good to tone down the passages which were shocking in France, but in England were regarded as boringly self-evident.

When in 1733 Thiriot visited London, Voltaire

begged his friend to stay and live with him in a free country.

The letters made their first appearance in the English language under the title: *Letters Concerning the English Nation. By Mr. de Voltaire.* Thiriot contributed a preface which was revised by Voltaire. The book was a great success. Voltaire writes: "The philosophical, critical, poetic, heretical and diabolic letters have sold in London with great success. But the English are damned heretics, every one of them, willing to approve of a devil's work. I am very much afraid that the Gallic Church will not be at all enthusiastic about the book."

When the letters were published in France the following year, the clergy demanded their suppression. The doom of the book was sealed. It was condemned by the Parliament as a menace to the religious and civil order of society, and was publicly burned by the executioner.

Voltaire had done his best to cut out any improper remarks. The thirteenth letter, entitled "Sur M. Locke," which carefully describes Locke's opinion of the relation between body and mind, has been preserved to us in its original form which Voltaire later corrected. The thoughts, in the original, are much keener and clearer, the style is more vivid, the discussion is more illuminating. The original is witty and eloquent. The letter in the book is frequently dull and colorless.

Voltaire dared to mention the Anti-Trinitarians and to hint—that Newton did not believe in the Trinity. Newton had left a manuscript attacking the doctrine as contradictory to the Bible. But Voltaire avoids any discussion of the English deists, and it certainly cannot be regarded as an attack on religion when he says ironically:

"That inexplicable figure which is neither of the clergy nor of the laity, that species which in France is called 'the abbé,' is entirely unknown in England; the priests over here are all self-contained and scholarly. When the English learn that in France there are young men who are known for their excesses, who became prelates through female influence, who openly carry on love affairs, who delight in writing amorous verses and giving elaborate suppers every evening, but who at the same time call upon the Holy Ghost and impudently style themselves successors of the Apostles—when the English learn this, they thank God for being Protestant. But of course they are nothing but wretched heretics who should be burned and sent packing to the Devil, as master François Rabelais says. That's why I don't intrude in their affairs."

No modern man would regard it as traducing religion when Voltaire says that on the London Stock Exchange, Jews, Mohammedans and Christians meet as if they had a common religion and that the only ungodliness they recognize is the filing of a claim of bankruptcy.

Apparently the book was more dangerous in a political way. It must have awakened dissatisfaction with political and social conditions in France. The French must have been ashamed, at the beginning of Louis XV's reign, to read words like these: "The English nation is the only one which has regulated the King's power by opposition, and has succeeded in attaining the reasonable form of government under which the ruler has unlimited power to do good, but finds his hands tied if he wishes to do wrong, where the lords are great without being overbearing, and have no vassals, where the people take part in the government without bringing about confusion."

Voltaire shows how this form of government originated, tells of Magna Charta, and how little liberty this granted the people, who, nevertheless, found it a great step in advance. He describes the growing importance of the House of Commons until its power exceeded that of the House of Lords.

Then follows a tribute to the British merchant marine: the respect it commands, the important part it plays in the power of the nation. Voltaire describes how Prince Eugene was able to drive Louis XIV's victorious army from Savoy because the London merchants loaned the Prince fifty million francs at a few days' notice. That is why the English merchant feels as proud as did the Roman citizen of antiquity. Voltaire says there is a constant temptation to draw a contrast between English conditions and French as regards the contempt which any provincial nobleman had for a French merchant who, no matter how active and rich, has no social position.

The next letter recommends vaccination, states that the Circassians knew this procedure long ago, that Lady Mary Wortley-Montague introduced it in England and that Queen Caroline, when Princess of Wales, had it tried on four criminals sentenced to death, who were pardoned when the experiment proved to be harmless.

16

Voltaire introduces the various remarks he has to make on English philosophy and natural science, with a short but striking portrayal of Sir Francis Bacon. He says of Bacon: "He did not know Nature, but all the ways which led to her." And he draws attention to the astonishing passage in the *Novum Organum* in which Bacon, long before Newton, described and demanded an investigation of the attraction between the earth and heavy bodies, between the moon and the sea, and between the planets. Bacon said an experiment should be made whether a clock (one run by weights) would go faster on top of a mountain than at the bottom of a cave; for, if the pull of the weights were reduced on the mountain and increased in the cave, it is apparent that the earth has a real force of attraction.

In the letter on Descartes and Newton Voltaire tries to be just to the former and explain his nature and genius in such a way that the French national feeling should not feel too hurt by the obvious inferiority of his doctrine to Newton's. Special emphasis is laid on Descartes' service in searching out the past; his mistakes are pointed out without any belittling comments: "Even though he did not pay with good coin, it was his great merit to warn against bad coin."

Newton's discoveries are described enthusiastically. Voltaire knows that, in 1665, the great scholar put aside his calculations because, while he knew exactly the time required for the moon to revolve around the earth, he had only Pilote's inaccurate figures for the earth's radius, so that his result was about one-seventh too small. Seventeen years later, in 1682, Newton chanced upon the degree system of measurement developed by the Frenchman Picard. This permitted him to determine the size of the earth much more accurately than heretofore and so he resumed his calculations of 1663. With the new figures for the earth's radius he saw that his calculations would check, and the sublime discovery was made. Voltaire does not fail to stress the honor Picard's measurements have brought to France, in contributing their share to make possible the greatest forward stride in the history of science.

After expounding Newton's astronomical studies, Voltaire's interest in which Maupertuis had probably awakened, he proceeds to the explanation of Newton's theory of optics as opposed to Descartes'. He shows how Newton's prisms demonstrated the truth of the theory that light is a combination of colored rays which united make white.

He does not forget to draw attention to Newton's importance as the inventor of integral and differential calculus, and recalls his contest with Leibnitz in this subject; but here he turns to Fontenelle for assistance in making the mathematics comprehensible. Finally comes a discussion of Newton's efforts to find a more accurate definition of chronology, in one part of which the great scholar points out the incorrect identification of the average length of a king's reign with the thirty years of a generation; a reign averages twenty years; and in another part he shows how it is possible to date the history of antiquity with a greater degree of exactitude by means of astronomical dates. It is true, Newton regards the expedition of the Argonauts as a historical fact, and tries seriously to ascertain how many years elapsed between it and the first Peloponnesian War. Then Newton, who had been forced to abandon his original vocation to theology, furnishes a commentary upon Revelations "in order," says Voltaire, "to console mankind for his otherwise too great superiority over them."

In the passage in which Voltaire describes how Cardinal de Polignac charged Newton with atheism, he cannot suppress a deep sigh. "Let one imagine how Newton, Locke, Clarke, Leibnitz would be persecuted in France, or imprisoned in Rome, or burned in Lisbon. What is one to think of human reason? That it was born in this century in England?"

17

To the letters on England Voltaire has added a section which is in but loose connection with the work but well within its spirit: refutations of selected thoughts of Pascal. These probably were not written at a sitting, but were jotted down at occasional and repeated perusals of Pascal in the years 1728 to 1733.

The attacks of Voltaire upon Pascal had at all times outraged the pious. An intellect of universally acknowledged greatness was impudently attacked by another intellect for which even its adorers did not claim this quality. Nevertheless, wherever Voltaire opposed his own sane and clear judgment to the paradoxes born of Pascal's dogma ridden, tortured mind, Voltaire is right. Though theologians may find depth in Pascal's contemplations, a thinker will find them merely deeply moving. Their interest does not depend upon their truth but upon their emotion.

One point, however, fascinates the attentive reader here more than even the debate between the pessimist Pascal, and the optimist Voltaire; this is the conflict into which Voltaire enters with his own opinion of twenty years later. In his advancing years he expressed himself no less pessimistically than Pascal in his *Pensées*.

The pessimism is, however, fundamentally different. Pascal's is that of a sickly, melancholy nature, which clings to a belief in revealed religion and to dogmas. Mankind for Pascal is an indefinable mystery, which cannot be understood except with the aid of the dogma of Original Sin, which is a mystery itself. Voltaire replies that the incomprehensible is not explainable by something still more incomprehensible; and although man is a complex phenomenon, he is not a puzzle without an answer. That he is subject to change is no more curious than that a dog at times caresses, at other times bites, or that a hen at first cares for its chicks and later abandons them.

Pascal tries to make mankind afraid of itself; Voltaire tries to induce self-confidence. He queries: "Am I to despair because I cannot see God's face nor understand the mysteries of the Trinity? I might just as well despair because I have not four feet and two wings." He tries to hold a middle course between futile dissatisfaction and foolish contentment. "It is the idea of a fanatic to see man as a poor criminal awaiting execution. It is the dream of a spoiled debauchee to regard the world as a place for pleasure, a paradise. In my opinion it is sensible to believe that the earth, and the people and animals in it are what they should be according to the dictates of Providence." As can be seen, Voltaire uses here the expression "dictates of Providence" where one would expect him to use the word Nature. He is a deist, but he is careful.

Voltaire opposes his view of life to Pascal's aphorisms, in which man's continuing to struggle is explained by his inherent wretchedness and misery, which he can endure only when he does not have to think of his tortures. Voltaire maintained his opinion all through life, even when his content was supplanted by the bitterest pessimism. This is it: Man is not made for self-analysis. Anybody practicing it becomes an idiot. Man is made for action. It is as natural and inevitable for man to act as for fire to ascend, or for a stone to fall. Voltaire furnishes here a clear view of his own character.

To Pascal's melancholy preoccupation with Original Sin he opposed not only his urge to activity but also his soothing belief in Providence. Later—after the earthquake in Lisbon—when this belief in Providence was shaken, his confidence in his theories gradually disappeared. But this was not enough to induce him to go over to the doctrine he had fought so sturdily, the doctrine of Original Sin. He discarded the belief in Providence. He never discarded his belief in action as the purpose of life.

In his study of the important questions of life, Voltaire, like Pascal, came at various times in touch with the æsthetic, in which he was as much interested as in metaphysics and theology.

Pascal sneered at the phrase "poetic beauty." He insisted that nobody knew what it meant; that nevertheless it was conventional to apply it to certain curious things, like "golden age," "fateful laurels," "glittering stars"—really an absurd jargon. One knows, he writes, the aims of geometry and medicine; but no one knows the aim of poetry. Voltaire retorted that Pascal showed very little taste to believe that any one would call expressions like those mentioned poetically beautiful; and besides that, the aims of poetry are perfectly clear.

A modern reader should pay attention to this; for it is, in a few words, Voltaire's poetic creed: "The aim of the art of poetry is to paint impressively, clearly, subtly and harmoniously. Poetry is harmonious eloquence."

One can say without exaggeration that these words are the æsthetic principle of the eighteenth century.

18

We saw how Voltaire's residence with Baron Görtz led his thoughts to a King who, scarcely twelve years older than himself, could easily fascinate the poet by his unusual virtues and shocking peculiarities. This was Charles XII.

Voltaire had never let the King out of his mind. He gathered in England most of the material for his Charles XII and made his rough notes in English. Some of these are preserved in the Bibliothèque Nationale in Paris.

As was his habit, Voltaire eagerly consulted every one who could give him useful information for his work. Bolingbroke, as former Minister of State, was of considerable help. Likewise Jeffrey, who had been English Ambassador to Charles during his long stay in Turkey. In 1727, the Duchess of Marlborough gave him valuable information concerning details of the conversation between the Duke and Charles, in Old Ranstadt in 1707, when the allies wished to find out what rôle Sweden intended to play in the war. Voltaire mentions the Duchess as the source of his information. He tells us how in his camp at Old Ranstadt the King received deputations from nearly every sovereign of Christendom. Some asked him to relinquish his German territory, others would have liked him to turn his army against the German Empire. One rumor sprang up, that he was going to unite with France against Austria. Among the envoys was, representing Queen Anne of England, the Duke of Marlborough, who had never besieged a city without occupying it, never fought a battle without winning it. Likewise, he was the craftiest of courtiers and diplomats, one who had got the better of France as much by his cleverness as by his army. Fagel, the Secretary of the States-General, said that, every time the Dutch government resolved to resist his wishes, he came before them in person, talked French—a language which he spoke very poorly—and persuaded all of them. Voltaire says that Bolingbroke vouches for the truth of this.

Marlborough knew that Charles was angry with the Emperor of Austria and that the French had secretly tried to win him over, a serious state of affairs which might easily lead to a defeat for the allied powers. In the year 1700, it is true, Charles had given his word not to interfere in the war between the English and Louis XIV, but Marlborough did not believe that a Sovereign would feel bound if his promise conflicted with his interests. He therefore resolved to undertake the journey to sound the King on Sweden's intentions.

Voltaire writes:

"Mr. Fabrice, who was with Charles XII at that time, assured me that the Duke of Marlborough did not approach the Prime Minister Count Piper, but secretly sought out Baron Görtz whom the King had begun to trust just as much. He even arrived at the King's quarters in Görtz's coach which brought about

a certain coolness between Chancellor Piper and the
Duke. When he and the English Minister Robinson
were introduced he addressed the King in French
and told him that he would be happy to learn under
the King's banners what he lacked in the art of war.
The King answered this without any compliment, apparently unaware that it was Marlborough who
spoke. I happen to know that the King thought the
great man's clothing too elegant, his appearance too
refined for him to be a warrior. The conversation was
slow, as the King spoke Swedish and Robinson had
to serve as interpreter. Marlborough never made the
mistake of submitting a proposal before the time was
ripe, and through long practice he was expert at
judging a man's mind from his look. He studied the
King attentively. While speaking to him about wars in
general he thought he detected a real dislike of France
and a scarcely concealed delight at the operations
of the allies. At the mention of the Czar, he caught
a flash in the King's eyes, although the conversation
was very quiet. He noticed a map of Russia on a table.
That was all he needed to conclude that Charles' real
intention and ambition was to seize the throne of
Russia as he had annexed Poland. . . . Satisfied that
he had seen through Charles XII, he made him no
offer."

This Fabrice was a Swedish baron, born in Holstein, deeply indebted to Görtz, who had sent him to
Charles. During the many years Charles spent in Turkey he was thoroughly in his confidence. In Bender
the King had him read Racine aloud. Charles' favorite of Racine's plays was *Mithridate,* because of the
bravery and tolerance of its main character. Fabrice
was a brave, wide-awake spirit. In Bender it was he
who warned the King, who could scarcely be convinced, that the Sultan was thinking of forcing his
departure. Fabrice induced the Turks not to use force.
He loaned twenty-four thousand thalers to Charles
who was as careless about money as about everything
else. He tried to release the Swedish prisoners in Turkey. He was with Charles in Demotica, where he says
money was so scarce that he forgot whether it was
round or square. And he rode beside the King's coach,

when the latter was taken to Timurtasch by the Turks.

Fabrice had been First Gentleman of the Bed Chamber to George I when the latter was Elector of Hanover, and the King retained his liking for him. He sat in George's coach on the last journey to Osnabrück, when the King died in the coach from a stroke. In 1727 he returned to England with the King's jewels and other valuables.

It is not known how Voltaire met Fabrice, whether at George II's court or through Lord Chesterfield who was his intimate friend. In the preface to his *History of Charles XII* (1748) he says that he used the memoirs of Fabrice, Villelongue, Poniatowski and Fierville; in his *Commentaire Historique* (1776) he says that he wrote his *History of Charles XII* with the help of Fabrice who—after the battle of Poltava—had lived with the King for seven years. Later Voltaire had a talk with King Stanislaw, studied *Adlerfelt's Military Journal,* and sought every bit of information he could come across.

The work was written during the years 1727 and 1728, and was complete in its main features at the time of Voltaire's return to France, in March, 1729. It was, of course, revised and expanded when it was published two years later. Voltaire also altered it whenever unfavorable criticism, mostly very trifling (that of Nordberg and La Mortrayes) made trouble which his enemies could use.

19

Voltaire's *History of Charles XII* has maintained its standing as a portrait of an unusual man, done by a master, although the accuracy of the biography has been surpassed by Swedish writers. At its publication it awakened Europe's interest in Sweden, as Shakespeare's *Hamlet* did in Denmark.

Characteristically Voltaire begins by dramatically opposing two persons: Charles XII and Peter the Great. Peter was taken up at once, for however great the author's interest in the magnificently formed character and the remarkable fortunes of the Swedish King, his real hero is not Charles, but Peter. Not the martial and stiff-necked Peter who brought misfortune upon his country, but the Sovereign, who in spite of his brutal pleasures, in spite of the crudeness of his morals and the cruelty of his revenge, was an educator, a civilizer, the conqueror of a barbaric system of many centuries, one who introduced handicraft, arts, and science to a stubborn but talented nation.

With the clearness which is Voltaire's fundamental virtue as an historian, he begins by putting Polish society and the Polish people side by side with the Swedish and the Russian. Thus he paints in a strong background for August the Strong and Stanislaw Leszczynska, as well as for Charles XII and Peter the Great.

Voltaire did not know Swedish, but even had he known that language, it would scarcely have given him any material that would have helped him in picturing Charles XII. Was he not the pioneer biographer? It was not until 1740 that the immense folio published by Joran A. Nordberg, the King's chaplain, appeared in Stockholm. This was a collection of material on the King, assembled by a pedantic cleric. He with smug complacency criticizes his predecessors, especially, of course, the outstanding one, Voltaire, at whom, in his preface, he sneers thus: "His clever pen and his style deserve praise; but he is a prize liar."

He makes much of every petty detail which he believes to be incorrect. These inaccuracies really amount to nothing: Voltaire called one of Charles XII's servants Frederic, while this was not his real name. In speaking of the siege of Thorn, he mentions that Liesven wore a red gallooned uniform; the uniform was gallooned, but not red. He says that before the battle of Poltava the King called Count Rehnschöld into his tent for advice; actually all the generals were in that tent, not to give advice, but to take orders. He says that during a battle one of the horses that pulled the King's coach was shot, and that four grenadiers carried the King upon their lances; as a matter of fact they were not grenadiers but guards, and they carried the King's litter not upon their lances but upon their shoulders. Now and then, Voltaire reproduced certain documents in part only, as for instance the letter which the King ordered Augustus to write to Stanislaw to congratulate him on his accession to the throne.

All these minor defects of which Nordberg complains were corrected by Voltaire, when he saw the criticism was justified. The work went into one edition after another; the last contains none of these mistakes.

Nordberg's work was soon translated and Voltaire learned the criticisms. In 1744, he replied to his opponent's accusation of lying. His letter is a little masterpiece, demonstrating the superiority of intelligence and politeness to boorish rudeness, the superiority of wit to pedantry. The letter closes with this amusing thrust:

"A historian has many obligations. Permit me to remind you of two which are of some importance: not to slander and not to bore. I can forgive you the first because your work reaches only an insignificant public. But I cannot forgive you the second since I was compelled to read your work. Otherwise I remain, as far as I can, your devoted and obedient servant."

20

Voltaire made his work a psychological study and an entertaining story. He also furnishes a description of the geographical and political background. But the inferiority of his sources, the imperfect facilities for historical research, especially into contemporary events, finally the nature of his abilities, his taste for the dramatically fascinating, are the reasons why his work is less authoritative than that of modern Swedish scholars, such as the two Carlssons.

There are various important data which he carelessly neglects at the very beginning. An instance of minor importance is Charles' ardent absolutism in refusing, in defiance of the constitution, to take the

oath upon his coronation. Of major importance is the
fact that Denmark did not declare war on Sweden
without provocation; in time of peace Charles had
sent his troops to Holstein (then Danish territory)
to support his brother-in-law, Duke Charles Frederick, against the Danish King.

Voltaire had no means of verifying his information
as to dates and figures. He believed that at Narva
King Charles defeated 80,000 Russians; probably the
number was only 40,000. At any rate, it was glorious
enough for the Swedes to be victors at the odds of one
to five, if not—as was long believed—one to ten.

Just as unfamiliar is he with the details needed to
make the description of a battle fascinating. Thus
compared to Carlsson he gives a poor account of the
battle at Kissow. It is true, in this as well as in others
of his historical writings, he overlooked details. It
was the great net sum of fundamental truth that
fascinated him.

His style is the foundation of modern history writing. It marks the beginning of interesting and entertaining histories, as opposed to the old chronicles
and dry documents. It is striking that Voltaire is
never poetic, and never wants to be. Later, he makes
fun of the slow-witted La Beaumelle, who attempted
this style of writing. Voltaire's prose has neither color
nor melody. It is clear, concise and regular. He therefore may well be considered the exponent of simple
historic truth.

His *History of Charles XII* is filled with the evidence of first hand witnesses. When he speaks of
the battle of Narva, Voltaire refers to information
he received from Axel Sparre. Giving an account of
the tragic fate of Patkul, whose extradition Charles
XII demanded of Augustus the Strong, and whom he
had impaled, notwithstanding his being Peter the
Great's Ambassador, he makes every possible excuse
for Augustus the Strong, and as his source he gives
information received from the lips of Marshal Saxe,
son of Augustus. On the Latin discourses at the first
meeting of Charles XII and Stanislaw Leszczynska,
Voltaire quotes King Stanislaw himself. He got his
information about Charles' death from the King's

Adjutant, the French Siquier, who stood next the King when he fell.

The attentive reader can easily see that Voltaire had many factors to take into consideration. Most of the main characters were still alive when he wrote. Its hero, Peter the Great, had just died. It was inevitable for a close friend of Maurice of Saxony to speak respectfully of his father. On the other hand, it was impossible not to speak warmly of August's unfortunate rival, King Stanislaw, Voltaire's own protector and the father-in-law of France's King. Voltaire's description of King Stanislaw as a young man glorifies him no more than do modern sketches; these, too, emphasize Stanislaw's winning appearance, the combination of courage and gentleness in his features, the honesty and fairness of his character. Voltaire, however, is compelled to pass over the almost wretched political and monetary dependency of the Polish King upon Charles XII. Voltaire tells of Stanislaw's sudden painful retreat from Warsaw, when August unexpectedly invaded the country, while Charles was losing time besieging Lemberg. Voltaire does not forget to tell how, during the flight of the royal family to Posen, the nurse lost track of the young Princess and the King found her in a trough in a stable. It was Maria Leszczynska, who later became Queen of France.

Notable, too, is the moderation with which Voltaire describes the generals who had to yield to Charles' or Rehnschöld's superiority in inspiring the troops. Great admiration is expressed for Schulenburg's retreat, in which by crossing the Oder, he saved his army from being cut off. Schulenburg, when this was written, was still alive, and, although advanced in years, had not retired from military life. After commanding the Saxon army, he went into the Venetian service and as a Venetian general defended Corfu so courageously against the Turks that a monument, which still stands on the island, was erected to him. In 1740, he sent Voltaire, through the French ambassador, the journal of his campaign of 1703 and 1704. Voltaire answered the seventy-nine-year-old general with a very pleasant letter, in which he does justice to Schulenburg's merits and expresses his joy that what he had written about these campaigns in his *History of Charles XII* was correct. He asks Schulenburg for further information.

As can be seen, Voltaire's *History of Charles XII* is the work of a contemporary, on the basis of the written and spoken testimony of reliable eye-witnesses. These witnesses are of various nationalities: Swedes, Poles, Germans, French, Russians, English. The first draft was written in England and was based on English sources.

It was on English soil that Voltaire became a historian.

It was on English soil that the telescope through which he observed life gave him an even longer view. England gave him the fulcrum of Archimedes outside of France, from which he could move France and the entire continent. Here he found a contrast to French conditions, which made his refined and highly cultured countrymen seem like slaves living under a religious and political yoke.

He early felt himself to be a defender of reason; he left England, a defender and knight of liberty.

Newton seemed to him the great liberator in the realm of the mind. English social, civil and literary freedom became his ideal, not, however, so far as to attract him to that side of English politics which calls for the education of the masses to understand the affairs of government and to take part in its administration. The democratic aspect of political freedom remained strange to him. But it was an ideal state of which he had scarcely dared dream in France which he found realized in England. There no one could be robbed of his freedom by arbitrary order, there no one could be punished without trial and sentence, there speech and thought were free, there all forms of religion were tolerated, there in Parliament, in literature and in the Press all views were permitted to be aired. What he said of another country, many years later, he was now saying of England:

"Liberté, liberté! ton trône est en ces lieux."

V

BATTLES AT HOME

1

IN THE middle of March, 1729, Voltaire, with the permission of the authorities, returned to France; but not to Paris. According to the custom of the time, a pardon was always limited, always conditional. A parole, a probation, was set. The returned exile was at first required to live a few miles outside of Paris, and Voltaire chose for his stay St. Germain en Laye. There he rented a few modest rooms at a wig-maker's. He wrote to his unfaithful Achates, Thiriot, told him of his arrival, and asked him for a meeting. Thiriot, who was living as a parasite in the home of a certain M. de Noce, did not fail to visit his famous and useful friend. As in Vienna eighty years later there was a man who had printed on his visiting cards *"ami de Beethoven,* Thiriot found his livelihood in his friendship with Voltaire. He was sought in society because he brought news of Voltaire or could read a letter or a poem from Voltaire.

Voltaire's request for the pensions formerly given him, one by the King and one by the Queen of France, was answered by the Cardinal de Fleury in a letter which was politely but definitely a refusal. Voltaire recognized that it was useless to expect a pension from the King. However, he still had some hope of changing the Queen's mind, and his friend Pallu, who was *maître des requêtes* and whom he approached, did obtain this pension for him. Five hundred francs he gave at once to his beloved Thiriot, and promised him six hundred more from the profits he expected from his *History of Charles XII.*

Now and then Voltaire stole into Paris, where he hid at the home of an old clerk of his father's. At last Maurepas granted his request for permission to return. He no longer thought of staying with Madame de Bernières in the rue de Beaune, but rented a modern apartment in a house of rather forbidding appearance in the rue Traversière-Saint-Honoré. He sought seclusion to avoid incurring displeasure anew. He won a large sum in the Lepelletier-Desforts lottery at about this time. This turned not only the Comptroller-General but also the Minister against him, so that again he felt unsafe and for a while thought of returning to England. He resolved to disappear from Paris. With the same friend who had accompanied him on former trips to watering-places, he went to the Plombières baths, which he revisited with the same companion the following year.

In Paris he had lived not far from the Comédie Française, then situated in what is now the *rue de l'Ancienne Comédie*. His name appeared again on the bill-boards, when *Œdipe* was revived, with the admirable Adrienne Lecouvreur as Jocasta.

The tragedy *Brutus,* which was begun in England, was now finished: a good work which suffered from the weakness of having a love story worked in to help the box-office.

When Voltaire read the play to the actors they were not enthusiastic; perhaps they disliked its republican spirit. As usual, he revised the play again and again. At its première (December, 1730) the tragedy was a tremendous hit, which, however, did not mean much as the audience of the first night consisted mainly of admirers and friends of the author. Subsequently the applause and the attendance steadily decreased. The public wanted to see love on the stage, not Roman sternness, the struggles, victories, and defeats of two tender hearts, not the rude republican customs of antiquity.

The author's reputation was injured by an accusation of plagiarism made by the envious Piron. Piron contended that the play was stolen from one of the same name staged in December, 1690, forty years before, which had been written by a Mlle. Bernard with the assistance of her friend, Fontenelle. Fontenelle himself was too noble to back this charge.

Jean Baptiste Rousseau, on the other hand, took up the charge of plagiarism and called the play "A coat turned the third time, which Voltaire offers as new." First, he says, he stole Corneille's *Œdipe,* then *Marianne* from the poet Tristan, and now Mlle. Bernard's *Brutus.* Rousseau went so far as to dig up and modernize Tristan's play and have it performed simultaneously with Voltaire's *Marianne.* The public would not have it. To Rousseau Voltaire now used the expression which Molière has applied to Trissotin Vadius in the third act of the *Femmes Savantes*:

> Allez, fripier d'écrits, impudent plagiaire!

Brutus had to be withdrawn after the fifteenth performance. The importation of the London edition of the *Henriade* was forbidden. Copies sent to France were seized at Calais. The few that were saved were smuggled into the country by using the sheets as wrapping paper for other books.

As to the *History of Charles XII,* 2600 copies of the first volume had just been printed, when the edition was confiscated. Charles's opponent, Augustus of Poland, was still alive. Not long after, however, it was found that a friendly attitude to Stanislaw could easily be reconciled with one to Augustus, as the former's daughter was Queen of France while the daughter of the latter was married to the Dauphin. The problem now was—to have the *Henriade* as well as the *History of Charles XII* printed secretly on French soil. For this purpose Voltaire chose Rouen where he had a protector in the person of a member of Parliament, Cideville, and where it seemed possible to find not only a discreet printer but also officials who would discreetly close an eye. Voltaire told his acquaintances that he was going to England, and secretly traveled to Rouen. There, to avoid notice he did not accept the hospitality offered by Cideville. At first he lived in a dirty, miserable little inn, L'Hôtel de Mantes, which in a letter to Cideville he describes:

> Arachné tapisse mes murs,
> Draps y sont courts, lits y sont durs;
> Boiteuses sont les escabelles;

Et la bouteille au cou cassé
Y soutient de jaunes chandelles
Dont le bout y fut enfoncé
Par les deux mains sempiternelles
De l'hôtesse au nez rétroussé :

He moved to the house of his publisher, Jore, who
soon became his bitter enemy. He posed as an English
tourist, spoke a mixture of English and French, read
the proofs of both books, and in the three months of
voluntary imprisonment and disguise, sketched two
tragedies, *Eriphyle* and *La Mort de César,* which
later were printed and played.

2

The theater attracted him as much as ever; but the
actress who had won not only admiration and adoration, but also respect, who had always played naturally, and not used the sing-song declamation of Racine's friend, La Champmeslé, was no more. Adrienne
Lecouvreur, the enchantress, the great tragic artist,
had passed away.

On March 15, 1730, she appeared at the Théâtre
Français as Jocasta in Voltaire's *Œdipe,* after which
she played a rôle in a lighter play, *Le Florentin.* The
next day she suffered a violent attack of dysentery.
Five days later, she died, after she had made her will
and appointed as her executor Count Feriol d'Argental, the young man whom Voltaire always calls his
"angel."

How widespread the suspicion was in Paris that
she had been poisoned is proved by a frequently
quoted letter of Mademoiselle Aïssé. Voltaire insisted
that this was an unfounded rumor. He was present at
Adrienne's last illness. She died in his arms. An
autopsy revealed that she had died of an inflammation of the lower abdomen—which does not disprove
the possibility that the inflammation had developed
naturally. The inflammation, in Voltaire's opinion,
was the result of an emetic which Adrienne had
taken, and this sounds possible.

It must be admitted that Voltaire, well knowing
the inclination of the public to regard every sudden
death as a murder, frequently opposed in his writings
the belief that historical personages had died of poison. Also, it must not be forgotten that Voltaire was
in close relations with the noble house and the lady
that public opinion pronounced guilty. She was the
Duchess de Bouillon, not the Polish Duchess of the
same name who is erroneously accused in Scribe's
and Legouvé's well-known drama *Adrienne Lecouvreur*, but the sister-in-law of the Duke de Richelieu,
Louise de Lorraine, who, in 1725, at the age of
eighteen was married to Emanuel de La Tour, Duke
de Bouillon. At various times Voltaire addressed
short poems to her. In one of these occur the lines

> Deux Bouillon tour à tour ont brillé dans le monde
> Par la beauté, le caprice et l'esprit:
> Mais la première eût crevé de dépit,
> Si, par malheur, elle eût vu la seconde.

Adrienne Lecouvreur was born in 1692—she therefore was two years older than Voltaire—and had
grown up among middle-class people in a little town
between Soissons and Rheims. In 1702 her father, a
hatter, moved to Paris and rented an apartment near
the theater. The little girl grew up with a passion for
the stage, a desire to recite verses, a craving for a
great rôle, like Eleonora Duse at the end of the nineteenth century. At fifteen, she performed, with a few
other young people who had the same taste, plays
as ambitious as Corneille's *Polyeucte*, in which she
played the main part, Pauline. A great lady, the wife
of the president Le Jay, permitted the young people
to use her salon, which was frequented by many
prominent visitors. However, the police (as early as
that!) prohibited these performances without a li-
cense. For a time the Grand Prior de Vendôme permitted Adrienne to stage dramatic performances in
Le Temple. Afterward she was taught by the actor
Le Grand, trouped with provincial companies for
several years, and in 1717, entered the Comédie
Française, playing the star rôles in Racine's and Corneille's plays and at once made a hit by the unaf-

fected way in which she acted. She did not recite her parts, she lived them. If the character was a Queen or a Princess, she dressed like one, looked like one, walked, spoke and felt like one. She gave the audience the full force of the great passions the character underwent. We have her portrait by Coyel in the rôle of Cornelia. In it she appears a dream of pain but beautiful as one whose goodness has developed into beauty. Everything about her was striking, figure, posture, face, and above all her voice which, though not very strong, varied continuously in inflection, intonation, modulation, or in sudden outbursts. She was not tall, but had a wonderful figure, slender but not thin. She carried her head erect, her mouth was well-formed, and her features could express sorrow, joy, tenderness, terror or pity.

She led the not too strict life of young actresses of the day. She had various casual love affairs, one with Voltaire, who to explain to Thiriot the deep sorrow he felt at her death, says—in verse—that such profound anguish is "excusable in a man who was her adorer, her friend, her lover and also a poet." She had two daughters, one by a high official of Strassburg, one by an officer of the Duke de Lorraine.

She was not flirtatious but honest, true and intelligent.

She is pathetic in two of her affairs, one, in which she was loved without returning the feeling, and in the other in which she loved with the most violent physical passion of her life and was both lover and sister.

3

The son of Augustus the Strong and Countess Aurora Königsmarck, Maurice of Saxony had, after a demobilization which dissolved his regiment, thrown himself into gambling and other excesses. Permission to go to France saved him from this worthless existence. At the French Court he was welcomed and in August, 1720, he was appointed Maréchal de Camp with an annual income of 10,000 livres. He immediately started negotiations for the purchase of a regiment. He had married young, but his wife, Johanna Victoria Tugendreich, by no means lived up to her name.[1] On the contrary, she led a very free life, indulged in orgies with three trumpeters, and traveled incognita in company with a page.

It was not difficult to dissolve the marriage and this was done in March, 1721. The lady, however, continued to scheme against her former husband. In a letter written in the autumn of 1721, Aurora of Königsmarck says that the Countess had given Frau Rosenacker two poisonous powders with instructions to mix them with the coffee of Maurice.

Maurice was one of three hundred bastards sired by Augustus the Strong—the only one of this large number to make himself prominent. He had inherited the physical power of his father and some of the beauty of his mother, although his bust is not that of a strikingly handsome man. He was athletic, courageous, brutal, unrestrained, the darling of the ladies— one to whom no aim is unattainable.

Two years younger than Voltaire, he was twenty-four on his arrival in France. Ladies vied for him. Adrienne Lecouvreur at once saw in him her divine affinity. From the moment she let him possess her she no longer felt free. Maurice did not feel himself bound to any woman, much less to an actress. Besides, in spite of his prowess as a soldier, it was not on the battlefield but in the boudoir that he hoped to advance himself in the world.

The throne of the Duchy of Courland was due to be vacant soon. Duke Frederick William had governed this Polish feudal state up to his death in 1711. He left a widow, Anna Ivanovna, a niece of Peter the Great. She was later Empress of Russia. As she was childless, Courland had been governed since Frederick William's death by his uncle, Duke Ferdinand, and now that that old Duke was tottering on the edge of the grave, Courland feared for its independence if it did not elect a successor in time. Maurice of Saxony, who had aspirations to the throne, became convinced that he would be a favored candidate

[1] Translator's note: Tugendreich in German means "rich in virtue."

for the heart and hand of Anna Ivanovna. As the son of the Countess Aurora Königsmarck, who was the rightful overlord of the East Sea provinces of Sweden (at this time confiscated by Russia), he had ample excuse for visiting Courland and Petersburg. Anna Ivanovna surrendered at first sight. Not only that, but her younger sister in Petersburg, the Princess Elizabeth, became her rival.

What he lacked most to achieve his ambition, was money. Aurora of Königsmarck got a loan of seven thousand thalers in Dresden on her most precious family jewels, three rare pearls. However, she was the kind of mother who wished to keep her son for herself at all costs. Far more unselfish was Adrienne Lecouvreur. It was not to her interest for her lover to succeed in Courland as Duke and husband. Nevertheless, she did not hesitate, and sent him all she could spare in cash, all she could realize by pawning her jewels: forty thousand livres.

In June, 1726, Maurice was unanimously elected Prince of Courland and heir to the throne, by the Diet of Mitau. Russia, however, would not consider for a moment an independent duchy. The Poles also feared Courland would break away from them and when Augustus realized that he could not save his crown without robbing his son he was compelled to prevent by his veto the action which would secure Maurice the right of succession in Courland. In November, 1726, the Polish Diet declared the election invalid and outlawed Maurice. When a corps of Polish dragoons advanced upon the border, Maurice, whose army numbered only about two thousand, saw himself forced to surrender Courland and, with the ducats given him by his father for traveling expenses, he returned to France.

Here he was received with open arms by the rare woman who had given him her life and kept herself for him alone.

With others she was always fearful that what was offered her as friendship would degenerate into desire. "I belong to a profession," she says in one of her letters, "in whose friendship one does not easily believe. Nevertheless, it is only friendship I wish to know, it is the only thing that flatters me and that I believe is worthy." What she felt for Maurice of Saxony was far more than friendship. In a letter dated October 23, 1728, she writes: "A person for whom I have waited three years will arrive at last tonight, to the best of my knowledge in good health. Just now a messenger has reported that his coach is broken down thirty leagues [about eighteen miles] from here. A half-covered coach has been sent, and he will be here tonight."

Adrienne Lecouvreur, who loved Maurice of Saxony, and apparently never suspected his great abilities, was not destined to live to the time of their full fruition. Only after her death did her lover become one of the most famous generals of his century. In November, 1741, he occupied Prague by a stratagem. From August till November, 1744, as Marshal of France he defended French Flanders against the allied armies with far outnumbered forces. His skillful maneuvers rendered the overwhelming number of enemy troops ineffective. He was a great military genius, vigilant and discreet; he delayed making his plans to the last moment, then was as rapid to execute as he had been slow to formulate. He grasped every situation quickly and correctly, and always provided the solution in time. Just before the battle of Fontenoy (1745), when he lay sick in Paris, Voltaire asked him how he could think of setting out in this condition. "The idea is not to remain alive, but to advance," was his answer. And he won the decisive battle of Fontenoy, which restored France's long-lost prestige.

This famous battle exhibited chivalry in full flower. A regiment of the French Guard and the regiment of Royal Scots were the first to advance. At a distance of fifty paces the English officers greeted the French by taking off their hats. The officers of the French Guard returned the salutation. The English Commander, Lord Charles Hay, called: "Fire, gentlemen of the French Guard!" Count d'Auteroche, Lieutenant of the Grenadiers, answered in a loud voice: "We do not wish to fire first; do you fire first, gentlemen of the English Guard."

Voltaire, who—so characteristically—did not take it amiss that Maurice had supplanted him in Adrienne's affections, glorified him and ridiculed his jealous detractors in the following verses:

> Ce héros que nos yeux aiment à contempler
> A frappé d'un seul coup l'envie et Angleterre,
> Il force l'histoire à parler,
> Et les courtisans à se taire.

A thing Maurice accomplished that Adrienne Lecouvreur was to live to see, was an experiment which shows us how far ahead of his time he was in imagination and invention, even apart from military matters. In 1729 he constructed a boat which could move without oars or sails and was expected to make the run from Rouen to Paris in twenty-four hours. When the vessel proved unable to stem the current, he was the object of public ridicule. He had obtained letters of approval from two members of the Academy of Sciences and a grant of monopoly for his invention. He had bad luck at the trial run and his experiments cost him, who was anything but rich, thirty thousand livres. Adrienne Lecouvreur quoted her Molière, whose works, of course, she knew by heart: "What the devil was he doing on that galley!" As late as 1768 Voltaire himself thought this experiment simply absurd. He is content to add politely that the Marshal later redeemed his naval errors by undertaking the most complicated war maneuvers on land.

As to his genius as a commander, Frederick the Great has given unquestionable testimony. In one of his letters to Voltaire (July 25, 1749) he says: "Here I saw France's hero, that Saxon, that Turenne from the century of Louis XIV. My conversations with him were an education to me, not in French, but in the art of war. The Marshal could give lessons to any general in Europe."

4

Adrienne Lecouvreur's infatuation with Marshal Saxe was at its height when the young Count d'Argental fell passionately in love with her and begged her not to let him pine for her in vain. Free from coquetry as she was, she wrote him:

"Is it possible that a highly gifted man like yourself could have so little self-control? What do you think you can attain except embarrassing difficulties, or worse? I am ashamed of having to quarrel with you as you inspire me with so much pity; but you force me to it. Please be reasonable and ask the one whom you send to torture me to let me breathe again for a little while. During the last four days he has scarcely given me time to do so. The very next time we chance to meet I shall clearly explain to you the impropriety of your behavior, and I have not the slightest doubt that you will appreciate your injustice.

"Farewell, unhappy child! You bring me to despair."

Soon thereafter Adrienne learned that d'Argental's mother, Madame de Feriol, fearing that her son might marry Adrienne, was thinking of sending him away, as far as St. Domingo. Madame de Feriol, who led no more virtuous a life than her sister, Madame de Tencin, was as conventional as frivolous—two qualities which so often go together—and in order to quiet her Adrienne resolved to go to her and to explain her relation to the young man. Being an actress, however, she was received in a manner which made any confidence out of the question. She wrote the lady this solicitous and at the same time dignified letter:

"Paris, March 22, 1721

"Madame,

Not without great depression do I hear of your anxiety, and of the precautions to which this anxiety is driving you. I can add that I have heard with great sorrow of the criticism you have expressed of my behavior. Nevertheless I write you, less for the purpose of justifying myself, than to convince you that this behavior in so far as it concerns you will in the future be exactly as you prescribe. On Tuesday I asked to speak to you for the purpose of confiding in you, and of asking your commands. The reception accorded me upset my plans, and gave me shame and sorrow.

"It is necessary, however, that you know the true nature of my feelings—if you will permit me to say something more: it is necessary that you do not refuse to listen to my sincere warning if you do not wish to risk losing your son. He is the most respectful and most honorable man I have ever met. You would admire him if he were not your own son. Once more, Madame, condescend to coöperate with me in rooting out this weakness which is upsetting you and for which, whatever you may say, you cannot blame me. Do not show him contempt or bitterness; in spite of all the tender friendship and respect I feel for him, I would rather that he hated me than that he be exposed to the least temptation to forget the consideration he owes you. You have too keen an interest in his welfare not to work for it ardently; but you cannot succeed by yourself, especially if you try to fight his inclination by authoritative commands, or by drawing an unfavorable picture of me, even if it be a true one. Doubtless this passion is a very strong one as it has persisted so long, so hopelessly, in spite of your insults to me, in spite of the travels upon which you have sent him. And yet he has not seen me during a stay of eight months in Paris, at least not in my house. He did not know whether I would admit him. I thought him cured and that was my reason for receiving him during my recent illness. As any one must understand, my friendship with him would be very pleasant, were it not for this unfortunate passion which astonishes as much as it flatters me, but which I do not wish to abuse. You fear that if he were to see me, he might forget his obligations, and you exaggerate this fear so much that you go to the length of using force. But, Madame, it is not fair to inflict so many kinds of unhappiness upon him. Do not add a new injustice to the one I show him. It were better to pardon him. Let all his hatred fall upon me and let your own goodness soothe and heal him.

"I shall write to him if you wish it; I shall never see him again if you demand it; I shall even retire to the country if you think it necessary; but do not threaten to send him to the end of the world! He can be useful to his country, a joy to his friends, an honor to his mother; it is essential, however, to direct his great gifts wisely and to give his fine qualities a chance to unfold. Forget for a while that you are his mother, if it is that which prevents you from giving him your kindness. Please do not refuse it to him. To be brief, Madame, you will sooner see me lead a retired life, or else bestow my love upon him, than to find me content to know him tortured by me and at the same time because of me."

At the time this letter was written d'Argental knew nothing of it. It touched him deeply when sixty years later at the age of eighty he found this beautiful thing among his mother's papers.

The devotion shown by Adrienne Lecouvreur is all the more moving because she was the first actress of France. Voltaire fought to raise the daughters of the stage in public opinion. Adrienne's story shows how poorly he succeeded.

5

The ladies of the aristocracy contended for the favor of Maurice of Saxony. One of the rivals of Adrienne Lecouvreur was the young Duchess de Bouillon. Apparently she followed the actress with envious eyes from her loge, for, one evening when Adrienne was playing Racine's *Phèdre,* losing her patience, she turned boldly to her rival with Phèdre's speech:

> Je suis point de ces femmes hardies
> Qui portant dans le crime une tranquille paix
> Ont su se faire un front qui ne rougit jamais.

This sounds like an insult, but it must have been a reply to some threat; otherwise the word crime means nothing.

In July, 1729, a little hunchback abbé had an interview with Adrienne, and he must have said something that made her suspect the Duchess.

His name was Siméon Bouret, and he was the eldest son of the Treasurer of Metz.

The father on account of business had to spend
the summer of 1727 in Paris and he took his seventeen-year-old son along. At Christmas, 1728, they
again came to Paris and when the father was called
back to Metz by his official duties, he left his son in
the capital to study drawing and painting, for which
he was undoubtedly gifted.

The young man lived in a rooming house, and
spent nearly all his evenings at the Théâtre Français,
as he was very fond of the drama. During his first
stay in Paris he had met a young nobleman, de
Périgord, who was greatly interested in art and
wished to become a painter. As a painter he remained mediocre. But with the little abbé he visited
the Academy of Arts, which at that time was in the
Louvre, and thus the two became comrades.

A month after his return to Paris the abbé again
met de Périgord who suggested that they visit the
fair at Saint-Germain. On the way they met a third
young man, sixteen or seventeen years old, who wore
livery and was introduced to them as the page of
the Duchess de Bouillon. On their way they stopped
to look at the display of an art dealer, and as Bouret
looked attentively at the pictures the page asked if
he knew anything about painting. He answered that
he was a painter of miniatures and the page requested him to paint his portrait. The abbé consented.

The page lived in the Hôtel de Bouillon, Quais
Malaquais, very near the rue de Marais, where Adrienne Lecouvreur had her apartment. There the very
next morning the abbé started to work on the portrait. In a week it was finished and set in a snuff box
of tortoise-shell.

6

A short time later when the comrades met in the
gateway of the Hôtel de Bouillon to visit the fair a
second time, the page informed Bouret that he had
shown the portrait to the Duchess and she thought it
well done. He then took him into the palace and introduced him to the Duchess.

She said many nice things about the portrait,

drew his attention to some faults, and asked him at once if he would not like to paint her portrait. Bouret answered it would be a great honor. He promised to return in two days. This was at the end of January or beginning of February, 1729.

The Duchess, who was then about twenty-two, was of one of the most famous families of France, the house of Guise. Her maiden name was Louise Henriette Françoise de Guise. Four years before she had become the fourth wife of the rather decrepit grand seigneur Emmanuel Théodore de la Tour d'Auvergne, Duke de Bouillon, who was nearly forty years her senior.

Bouret, who painted her portrait, describes her: very comely; rather tall than short; an oval face, rounded beneath; open forehead, black eyes, black eyebrows, dark hair; the mouth strongly turned upward, very red lips, a large mole near the right eye.

That the abbé was really introduced to the Duchess is proved by the correct description he gives of the furniture and works of art in her boudoir.

The young ladies of high nobility led a free life without risking serious disapproval; it was suspected (as reported in Paulmy's *Sottisier* and in the *Memoirs* of Maurepas) that the Duchess chose her lovers impartially, now from among the favorites of the stage, now from those of her own rank: actors and singers as well as princes, among them Quinault Dufresne of the Théâtre Français, Tribou of the Opera, Grandval who, in 1729, made his first appearance on the national stage, and was at this time the declared favorite, and the Compte de Clermont, of the royal family. Nevertheless, she developed a passion for Maurice of Saxony who was almost officially linked with Adrienne Lecouvreur. He had known her intimately; but he lost interest in the Duchess less on account of Adrienne than on account of a little opera singer, Marie Carton, who the following year accompanied him to the camp at Mühlberg.

The Duchess imagined that her advances were ignored because of the attractions of Adrienne Lecouvreur. She was quite indignant.

7

At the Duchess' request the abbé came to the Hôtel de Bouillon and finished her portrait in eight or nine sittings. During the third sitting, the Duchess, learning of Bouret's great interest in the theater, asked if he knew any actors or actresses and which he considered the greatest. He answered that he knew of none any finer than the brothers Quinault and the young ladies Lecouvreur and Duclos. Thus, he praised an actor whom the Duchess favored and an actress whom she hated.

The Duchess asked: "Do you know Mademoiselle Lecouvreur personally?"—"I know her on the stage only."—The Duchess then told him to try to make her acquaintance or to meet some close friend of hers.— "As you do not know her, you must do me the kindness of delivering to her a letter I am going to dictate."—And she dictated Bouret a letter which supposedly came from a member of the royal family, a prince of the blood. The latter contained a declaration of love to Adrienne and asked her to break off her relations with the Count de Saxe.

At the request of the Duchess, Bouret took the letter but he did not deliver it.—The next day the Duchess told him that the letter was a poor idea but that she had another one. It would not be hard for him as a portrait-painter to gain access to Adrienne Lecouvreur.—But Bouret did not think this would be so easy.—The Duchess answered that the purpose was nothing serious, only to administer to her a love-potion. Bouret, who apparently was very surprised but did not dare to give such a grand lady a refusal, promised to do his best and continued to paint. While he was thus occupied, the Duchess asked him if it was his habit to go to bed early.—"About ten or eleven o'clock."—"Very well, be tonight at the gate of the Tuileries, which leads to the Palais Royal, then I will send for you when I return from the ball."

When he arrived two masked gentlemen asked him if he were there at the request of the Duchess. They further asked him whether he would like to make money; if so his fortune was made, provided he kept a close mouth in regard to the matters confided to him. He answered he could if it did not concern an underhanded scheme.—"No," said the two, "of course not! You recall the person the Duchess discussed with you; the problem is simply to gain admission to her and give her a few pills which will inspire her with indifference to the Count de Saxe and will make her fall in love with another man." —If that were all there was to it, it ought not to be so difficult.—Bouret was then led to the Duchess who was in tears and was sitting on a stone near the parapet at the Quai du Théâtre. To her companion she mentioned the name of Maurice de Saxe over and over again. The abbé could understand these words only: "I am very unhappy." She wept as though in despair. Finally she told Bouret that she was very well satisfied with him; he could continue his painting the next day.

When he arrived the following day the page was waiting for him as usual and led him to the rooms of the Duchess. While Bouret painted, Madame de Bouillon said: "You know what the two gentlemen told you yesterday. She is an unworthy woman. She must be put out of the way. It would be doing a service to the state. Besides you can be sure of a reward."

Bouret answered he would do all he could to gain admittance to Mademoiselle Lecouvreur's house. The same day and again the day following he overheard whispered conversations between the Duchess and her friends: only the name of the Count de Saxe was audible.

8

It seems that the idea of using the little cripple for criminal purposes occurred to the Duchess because of the combination of his interest in the theater and his talent as painter of miniatures, which gave him an opportunity to meet anyone and should insure him a welcome from any actress.

At first she hopes with his aid and a stupid letter to induce Adrienne to break with Maurice in the hope of an affair with a personage of even higher station. Then she realizes that this plan, which was really worthy of a schoolgirl, would lead to no result. She resorts to the simpler and cruder means of getting the abbé to deliver a few pills, the effect of which he should believe to be erotic, but which as a matter of fact would be a deadly poison.

The Duchess, therefore, does not scruple to put out of the way a woman of a class below her; she scruples still less knowing that this child of the people is an actress, a profession condemned by the Church. By and by, she let even Bouret penetrate the veil which hid her real intention. Finally she brings up the political-social consideration, that Adrienne's murder would be "a service to the state."

Strange to say, the great lady's passion gave her no insight into the affairs and reactions of him for whom she yearned in vain. Her diagnosis of Maurice's indifference was altogether wrong; she confused the noble, devoted friend with the sensual little creature who really had Maurice in her toils.

It is characteristic of the social state of the day that the Duchess had the imprudence to confide her plot to more than ten persons. In spite of her precaution of having her helpers appear in disguise and under cover of night, she was sure that whatever might happen she would be protected by her high position against the government and the police.

9

When Bouret had finished the portrait, the Duchess told him it would be best for him to stay away from her palace until he had executed the orders of the two eminent gentlemen. He would find them the same evening at nine o'clock at the entrance to the Tuileries. He met them and they asked if he were willing to carry out their scheme. He said he was. At a subsequent meeting he was asked whether he had found a chance to meet Adrienne Lecouvreur. When he answered that he had not, they told him that the matter was pressing; he ran no risk, even though what

he delivered might have a somewhat serious result.
—"But suppose she were to die from it?" he asked.
Even in that event, he had nothing to fear; a fast
coach would be in readiness to take him across the
border. Then they forbade him expressly ever to
enter the Hôtel de Bouillon or to try to speak to the
Duchess for any purpose whatsoever.

It was not really very clever. The abbé was intimidated rather than won over. There was nothing in it
for him to be used as the murder tool in a matter
which was none of his business. On the contrary, he
could be very certain of losing his peace of mind and
stood every chance of being executed for murder.

The business struck the young abbé as very weird,
and for a whole month he did not appear. But the two
disguised gentlemen had him summoned by a servant. In those days it was not advisable for a citizen
to resist two *grands seigneurs*. Again he had to listen
to the demand to keep his promise.

Honest as he was, he thought it his duty to warn
Mademoiselle Lecouvreur of the danger she was in,
and following the advice of his father-confessor he
tried to drop her a hint. Having sought her vainly at
her home he sent her an anonymous note, dated January 24, 1729, in which he asked her to be at a certain
hour on the great terrace of the Luxembourg, where
she would receive important news. To enable her to
recognize him the writer of this letter would tap
three times his abbé's hat on approaching her.

Adrienne appeared, accompanied by a man and a
woman.

Here, at last, the abbé exchanged a few words with
the actress. He told her that he felt obliged to inform
her that somebody intended to poison her. Adrienne
asked very naturally: "Is it from the Opera that the
danger is threatening me?"—"No."—"Then it must
be from the Hôtel de Bouillon!"—She told him that
she wanted to ask the advice of a competent man. If
he would come to her the next day, he would be
advised how he should behave.

On July 27, the Count de Saxe interviewed Bouret
and among other things asked him if what he said was
not a fiction. Adrienne Lecouvreur said: "This comes

from the Duchess de Bouillon." Her sure instinct for
the person from whom the danger threatened showed
keener than that of the Duchess who was doggedly
following a wrong trail. Adrienne forbade Bouret to
speak of the matter to others.

The following day as Bouret stood on the street
in front of his house, a Savoyard notified him that
two of his friends were awaiting him on the Quai de
l'Ecole. As in a melodrama, he found there the same
disguised gentlemen, muffled in their cloaks. Ordering
him to follow, they led the way to the Quai de Louvre, where they violently accused him of having told
on them, and threatened to kill him.

Bouret denied having revealed anything and said
he was willing to deliver the love-potion; just let
them give it to him. He was promised double reward, and given new instructions, absurdly mysterious. The idea, however, was apparently to give
him the full burden of responsibility. He was to go
on the next day from Pont Tournant in the direction
of the marble statue through the little alley of taxus
trees. In the second tree at the right he would find a
package of pills, most of which were harmless; but
three of them would be separately wrapped in paper,
and these he should administer to Adrienne Lecouvreur as soon as he got a chance. But first they would
like him to obtain for them a portrait of the Count
de Saxe.

Undeniably, they were asking a great deal of the
poor fellow. Under penalty of their anger and their
revenge, the eighteen-year-old little cripple, aided
only by his minor ability in miniature painting, must
quickly become intimate enough with Adrienne Lecouvreur to induce her to take pills and besides to
give him a picture of her adored friend.

This demand shows the superstition of the Duchess
and her friends; for the portrait was to be used to
bewitch the original.

On the morning of July 29, Bouret informed Adrienne and Maurice de Saxe of this. They both advised him to go to the garden of the Tuileries and
get the pills. He brought the package to them. They
found many white pills and also the three wrapped

separately. After sniffing their odor, they all became
ill. Immediately the police commissioner Hénault was
informed. But a chief of police under Louis XV was
not like Aristides, who was so just that it became necessary to ostracize him. Hénault, though he was indebted to Madame de Prie for his position, had
abandoned her as soon as the King denied his favor
to her friend, the Duke of Bourbon. Furthermore he
had put Voltaire in the Bastille as a penalty for his
mistreatment at the hands of the Chevalier de Rohan-Chabot. His justice likewise favored the Guise-
Bouillon and the Count de Clermont over a mere
actress and a little abbé. On the same evening he had
Bouret arrested and sent to the prison of Saint-Lazare, where he was kept for three months. The suspicious pills were given to a member of the Academy of
Sciences, Monsieur Joseph Geoffroy, for examination.
According to Sainte-Beuve who saw Geoffroy's report
(which later disappeared), the chemist wrote his decision in the meaningless jargon so characteristic of
the so-called science of chemistry at that time: some
of the pills appeared doubtful, but their number was
insufficient to form the basis of a reliable opinion.

10

On August 1st Bouret was questioned for the first
time. The following day the police-lieutenant Camu-
set, who had examined him, sent Hénault a report;
the dullness is undeniable but the honesty is highly
questionable. He says: "Various circumstances tend
to show that the abbé invented his entire story." It
contains the psychological observation that the abbé,
regardless of his crippled condition, was in love with
the lady in question.

Through another abbé who had been confined in
Saint-Lazare by an order of the King, Adrienne
wrote four or five letters to Bouret while he was in
jail. He answered them promptly and returned her
letters. In her first letter she requested him to retract
his statements if they were false, and promised to
obtain pardon for him if the matter were his inven-

tion. But it seems that she soon came to see that this was impossible, and through a lackey she sent him three louis d'ors, worth twenty-four francs each, one taler (six francs), two shirts, a bottle of perfume, and a few books which he returned after reading them.

Adrienne addressed a letter to the police commissioner, in which she expressed herself with dignity about the abbé: "I saw and asked him frequently to explain the affair; he answered very sensibly and honestly. Not that I do not hope he has been lying, but I have a hundred times more reason to wish he were insane, if only that it might obtain his pardon! But if he is innocent, think what it means to me that his life is in danger, and how cruel is this uncertainty. Do not consider my station or birth: look into my soul. It is honest and lies bare before you in this letter."

Meanwhile Bouret's father, the treasurer, returned from Metz to Paris to take steps for the liberation of his son. The old man was ill but he did not rest until on October 23rd, 1729, the young abbé was freed. He called on Adrienne Lecouvreur three or four times and she told him that there was a rumor that the Duchess de Bouillon had tried to have her poisoned; freedom, therefore, would still not insure his son's safety. In truth the Duchess de Bouillon gave the police commissioner a sharp reprimand for freeing Bouret.

Unhappily the treasurer fell ill in Paris and could not take his son to Metz. The result was a new Lettre de Cachet of January 23rd, 1730, and a second incarceration, this time in the prison at Fort-l'Evêque. Bouret was charged with "use of poison" and of giving false information to the famous actress Adrienne Lecouvreur.

Adrienne, who had played in *Horace* on January 21st, appeared again on February 4th (in *Electre* and *Le Florentin*), then let a whole month pass without playing, and again returned to the stage on March 5th, in *Le Malade Imaginaire,* next on the 13th in *Œdipe,* and thereafter on March 14th as well as 15th (in *Œdipe* and *Le Florentin*). That evening she made her last appearance. During or right after the performance she became violently ill with what Mademoiselle Aïssé, who was at the theater called "a dysentery, or inflammation of the intestines." After a serious crisis which took place on March 17th the physicians diagnosed it as an "intestinal hemorrhage," and on the morning of the 20th Adrienne Lecouvreur died.

Everything indicates that the Duchess, failing to give her the poison through Bouret, succeeded in some other way. It is of little weight that on her own deathbed, although she confessed many transgressions the Duchess did not admit any guilt in the death of the actress.

Nothing speaks louder for the guilt of the Duchess than that after Adrienne's death she was refused a burial and grave.

At that time one was not too particular with daughters of the stage. Courtiers and court officials dismissed or chastised actresses, just as they liked. For a mere trifle they might be sent to Fort-l'Evêque, or even to a house of correction. This was why the proud and beautiful actress, Mademoiselle Clairon, retired so young. Shortly before, under the gentle Fleury, something still worse had happened: Two very young sisters, noble Spaniards, the dancers Camargo, the elder of whom was a genius transcending her art, disappeared one day, kidnapped by a lecherous rascal, and the police refused to interfere, because he was a nobleman. When the kidnapper had enough of the two young girls, he simply sent them back to the theater, and Paris was content to laugh.

Adrienne, however, was so well liked and admired by the public that at the news of her death Paris became somewhat upset; this, however, did not prevent the priest of Saint-Sulpice, Languet, from refusing to bury her in consecrated soil. She had left a considerable legacy for the poor in her own parish and also in his. To a chaplain who went to her at her deathbed to give her the sacrament, she answered: "Don't worry! I know why you came, Monsieur l'Abbé; I did not forget your poor in my will." Then she turned to the bust of the Count of Saxony, which stood in her bedroom and quoted: "This is my world, my hope and my God."

Voilà mon univers, mon espoir et mes dieux!

The minister wrote to the police commissioner that it was not the intention of the Cardinal de Fleury to interfere in the question of ecclesiastical burial for an actress; moreover he wished to follow whatever course the Archbishop of Paris and the priest of Saint-Sulpice should deem best. "Should you," he wrote, "as it seems you will, definitely refuse to grant the permission, the body must be removed at night and buried with as little disturbance as possible." It was exactly the same answer as that of Louis XIV, when the actor Baron went to St. Germain to inform the King of Molière's death. Louis said he could not assert his authority over the head of the Archbishop of Paris, but would request the prelate to "avoid scandal."

A Christian burial, therefore, was out of question. After nightfall the body was taken, by order of the police commissioner, from the house in the rue des Marais-Saint-Germain 21 (the house where Racine had lived, later occupied by the actress Clairon) in an old hack, and buried by two porters in a desolate lot.

As mentioned above, Adrienne named young d'Argental as her executor. It was considered unusual greatness of soul that he, a member of Parliament, did not refuse. All he actually had to do was to divide her estate between her two children.

11

The poor abbé was still kept in jail. He was subjected to one cross-examination after another to make him retract his earlier statements; but he stood firm and always described the occurrences the same way.

On May 18, 1730, Père de Couvrigny, a Jesuit who was father-confessor to the prisoners in the Bastille, and who, following instructions, had reproached

Bouret with libel, wrote to the police commissioner
that Bouret stubbornly insisted that he had libeled
nobody, and that to admit that he had, would be to
libel himself. The father-confessor concludes: "The
matter is terrible and extremely grave."

Three months later the persecuted Bouret turned
in a lengthy moving letter directly to "Monseigneur,
le lieutenant de police, dans son hotelle à Paris," and
requested protection, pity, and justice. Even if he
were to face death with its horrors, he would prefer
it to self-defamation.

No answer came, and no liberation. But we can see
that Bouret was made to understand the circumstances: without unconditional retraction of his accusation his liberation was impossible.

On August 24 the unfortunate young man sent a
retraction as complete as it was senseless. He says
he had pretended he had a secret to tell Mademoiselle Lecouvreur, in order to be admitted to her
house. He had fabricated the whole thing—the
remarks of the Duchess, the page, the disguised
men.

Four days later, on September 3, he again gave the
lie to all his earlier statements and simply begged to
be pardoned.

Probably in order to make him manageable and
to make sure that Adrienne's death was well forgotten when he received his freedom, the poor wretch
was kept in jail for twenty months. On June 3, 1731,
only twenty years old, he was discharged without any
further difficulties.

In 1759, the actor Laval wrote in his *Tableau du
Siècle* that the priest of Adrienne's parish declined to
bury her among believers, "although she had expressed a fervent wish to receive the death sacrament."

Mouval remarks that the priest, according to the
laws of that time, was justified in excommunicating
her, since she had died without having renounced the
stage—as the priest of Saint-Eustache had the right
to condemn the body of Molière.

Where he was not justified, was in his refusal to
admit her to the cemetery. Even Molière's body was

allowed in the same cemetery in which Rosimond, the actor who died in 1688 without confession, was buried. In other cemeteries the priests had assigned places for Racine's friend, the actress La Champoneslé, who died in 1698, and to the actresses Lavoy and Le Grand (1726 and 1728).

But in the case of Adrienne Lecouvreur, not only ecclesiastical burial, but any burial was refused. The body was not even put into a coffin, but at midnight was lugged into a cab like a package by two porters, accompanied only by a police guard. The police commissioner received a plain order to make impossible any investigation into the cause of the actress's death by destroying all traces. When the body was thrown into a hole and covered with quick lime, a second autopsy was rendered impossible.

The power of the persons who persecuted Adrienne Lecouvreur during her life and after her death, is shown by the fact that not even Maurice de Saxe dared rebel against the mistreatment imposed upon a friend. Only Voltaire who, in close relation with the house of Bouillon, could not or would not believe the Duchess capable of such a thing, protested again and again the way in which France treated its greatest actress after her death.

Today it seems that the lawlessness of pre-revolutionary France was summarized in Adrienne's fate. As a daughter of the middle classes she was not counted in society. As an actress she belonged to a despised profession condemned by the Church.

As the Duchess belonged to the governing caste, and as she had a member of the royal family as a lover, she could use any weapon against a woman of the middle class who was in addition an actress. Adrienne, although the first actress of France, was to the Duchess a *fille de rien*. And the Duchess remained immune to punishment, while the poor little hunchbacked abbé whom she had tried to use as her tool, was locked up almost two years, until he disappeared silently into the unknown.

What really happened remained a mystery for Voltaire, even later for Sainte-Beuve. It has not been

entirely cleared up today, but there can be no doubt
that the account given here is correct.

12

The silly, brutal attitude of the clergy toward the
defenceless body of the distinguished woman inspired what is perhaps Voltaire's finest poem, which
was later set to music by Frederick the Great. In an
earlier chapter we spoke of the homage Voltaire paid
her during her life. One more instance must be cited.
It appears in the oldest edition of *Le Temple du
Goût* (1731):

> Lecouvreur plus loin récitait
> Avec cette grâce divine
> Dont autrefois elle ajoutait
> De nouveaux charmes à Racine.

and these four lines:

> Seul de la nature elle a su le langage;
> Elle embellit son art, elle en changea les lois,
> L'esprit, le sentiment, le goût fut son partage;
> L'Amour fut dans ses yeux et parla par sa voix.

Now he wrote the great poem *La Mort de Mlle. Lecouvreur, célèbre actrice*. It begins with an eloquent
description of his anguish on viewing the dying
woman:

> Que vois-je? quel objet! Quoi! ces lèvres charmantes,
> Quoi! ces yeux d'où partaient ces flammes éloquentes,
> Éprouvent du trépas les livides horreurs! . . .
> Que vois-je? c'en est fait, je t'embrasse et tu meurs!

He describes the general sorrow over the loss and
thereafter tells how a grave was denied to one who
would have had altars erected to her in Greece:

> Que direz-vous, race future,
> Lorsque vous apprendrez la flétrissante injure
> Qu'à ces arts désolés font des hommes cruels?
> Ils privent de la sépulture
> Celle qui dans la Grece aurait eu des autels.

He points out the unworthy inconsistency in the
attitude of those who sighed for her while she was

alive and who now, after her death, treat her like a criminal:

> Quand elle était au monde, ils soupiraient pour elle;
> Je les ai vus soumis, autour d'elle empressés;
> Sitôt qu'elle n'est plus, elle est donc criminelle!
> Elle a charmé le monde et vous l'en punissez.

Thereafter he dares to glorify England at the expense of France as the country which has abolished not only tyranny but also prejudice. There, anything can be said, any real worth is respected. In London Adrienne (like Anna Oldfield) would have been allotted a grave in Westminster among heroes and bel-esprits:

> O rivale d'Athène, o Londres! heureuse terre!
> Ainsi que les tyrans vous avez vu chasser
> Les préjugés honteux qui vous livraient la guerre.
> C'est là qu'on sait tout dire et tout recompenser;
> Nul art n'est méprisé, tout succès a sa gloire.

Here Voltaire emphasizes more and more strongly the shame of France in standing outside of civilization which, re-born from Athens and Rome, reigns in London; he concludes with the bitter question as to why his fatherland was no longer the land of honors and talents:

> Des lauriers d'Apollon dans nos stériles champs
> La feuille negligée est elle donc flétrie?
> Dieux! pourquoi mon pays n'est-il plus la patrie
> Et de la gloire et des talents?

Naturally, Voltaire did not dare to have this poem printed. He read it to a few friends but refused to distribute copies of it. He was, however, unwise enough to confide a copy to the most unreliable of his friends, Thiriot, the man whose life consisted of getting Voltaire's manuscripts into his possession and making himself popular by reading them aloud to society. He found even higher favor, apparently, with admirers of the poet, by permitting them to make copies of the works—which Voltaire of course had strictly forbidden.

During his stay in Rouen Voltaire learned that his

safety was threatened because of this poem, and that
the trail led back to Thiriot. One cannot but admire
the consideration with which he writes him, the politeness with which he assumes that of course no one
possesses a copy. The letter is dated June 1:

"You will remember that about a month ago I sent
you several verses on Mlle. Lecouvreur's death, the
expression of my natural sorrow, and a perhaps too
ardent indignation over the manner of her burial.
... I am highly obliged to you for your discretion in
not giving away a copy of it. But I am told that you
were in touch with people who have betrayed you
by the aid of their good memory; the strongest parts
especially were remembered; these have been dis-
torted; they have reached the ears of the ministry
and it is not safe for me to return to France whither
my work calls me. (As can be seen for safety's sake
he makes it appear that he is not on French soil.)
I expect you, my dear Thiriot, to inform me about
the truth of these rumors and to advise me what to
do. Tell me whether you advise me to write and to
speak, or to lie low and wait for better times."

The scientific genius Condorcet, who wrote at the
outbreak of the revolution in 1789, and who was
passionately revolutionary in his sympathies (in 1794
he took poison to avoid being decapitated as a Marquis), says in his enthusiastic *Vie de Voltaire:* "Who
would believe that the elegy on Adrienne Lecouvreur
could be made the cause of such a serious persecution!" He means that it was the elegy that forced Voltaire to leave Paris. However, we know that he left
before that. Meanwhile he lay low in Rouen to wait
for the storm aroused by the eulogy to subside. Soon,
however, he perceived that the best means of disarming hatred and fanaticism would be a decisive
victory on the French stage, by which he could regain
the favor of the public. For the theater of these days
formed the only bond between the class of people
who thought, and that which in daily life did not
bother to think. And, odd as it may sound, the casu-
ally brought together crowd which forms a theater
audience fused into a unit.

13

It was a question of winning this unit for himself.
Voltaire tried to do it with the tragedy *Eriphyle,* but
it did not fulfill the purpose. Far from being discouraged by this failure, five months after his defeat
the poet had a new tragedy on the stage, written in
only twenty-two days, and with *Zaïre* he made his
greatest success, one which surpassed all expecta-
tions and all earlier triumphs by other poets.

During the preparation of these pieces he was,
however, in constant unrest. What new intrigues
might not the Rohan family hatch against him? He
could not settle again in Paris, where he felt he was
tolerated rather than entitled to stay. After he left
Rouen, persecuted by Jore who had allied himself
with Voltaire's bitter enemy Desfontaines, he sought
shelter in the house of the Duke de Guise in Arceuil.
But the fatal illness of his friend, President de Maisons, called him back again to Paris. The President
succumbed to this second attack of smallpox. His loss
was a great sorrow to Voltaire.

Restlessly, Voltaire continues to change his place
of residence. First he goes to Plombières, then to
Rouen. Next he finds a temporary home with the
Countess de Fontaine-Martel; she was an elderly lady
who had once been a beauty and now, having become
rich and a freethinker, lived in grand style opposite
the Palais Royal, where she gave Voltaire an affectionate welcome. Voltaire's friend, d'Argenson, found
her malicious and miserly. On the other hand Voltaire praises her in his verses because she carried her
years so well, never envied younger women but enjoyed the good things life had to offer her. She put
no restrictions on her own speech nor on that of
anyone who conversed with her. Voltaire praises her
soirées and her: she is worldly and happy and does
not grudge youth things she liked when young. And
in her house reigns freedom:

> Vous avez loge à l'Opéra
> Au lieu de banc à la paroisse;
> Et ce qui rend mon sort plus doux,

C'est que ma maîtresse chez vous,
La Liberté, se voit logée;
Cette liberté mitigée
A l'œil ouvert, au front serein
A la démarche dégagée.

The rehearsals of Voltaire's plays were held at the house of the Countess Fontaine-Martel. She had a little private theater. Here was held the performance of *L'Indiscret* as previously described, and here the actors of the Théâtre Français put on *Eriphyle* for the first time, moving the audience to tears. This is where Voltaire, as he puts it (in a letter of February 3, 1732), won a victory in the first skirmish, which he was compelled to relinquish in the second. His presentiment did not fail him; his success at the public theater was conditional; the audiences applauded various parts which contained attacks on princely power and on superstition, but the apparition in the fifth act was an inevitable failure in a theater where the foppish young aristocratic patrons were permitted to crowd their chairs onto the stage proper, distracting attention by their behavior and narrowing the scope of the actors.

This nuisance was not confined to the French stage. The Shakespearean theater had the same thing to cope with. In the Comédie Française on each side of the stage were four rows of cushioned benches, surrounded by a gilded rail. At extraordinary performances another row was added outside of the rail. Also the back of the stage was filled by fifty persons seated in a semicircle. Anybody will understand how ruinous this practice was to the stage effect. Sometimes the spectators could scarcely distinguish between the noblemen and the actors. A few years later (at a performance of *Athalie,* on December 18, 1738), the stage was so obstructed by benches and spectators that the performance had to be broken off.

It was thanks to Voltaire's energy and his repeated complaints, that these seating arrangements were discontinued in the year 1739.

14

When Voltaire saw that *Eriphyle* was a failure at its first production, his first effort was to restore the confidence of the actors. He requested Count de Clermont, to whom he had addressed a few verses in his *Fête de Bélébat*—a prince who as a descendant of the great Condé had considerable influence—to assemble the actors in his house and assure them of his belief in the play. In addition he wrote a new prologue to be recited by Dufresne, the favorite of the public. When this did not prove sufficient for the success of the tragedy, he recast it entirely, regardless of the complaints of the actors who had to learn their lines all over again.

But this, too, was of no avail. Voltaire made his resolution with habitual firmness. He interrupted the printing which Jore had started, took his manuscript back, stopped its publication, and used only a few lines in his tragedy *Semiramis.* A defeat meant nothing to him. He always had something in preparation —five or six irons in the fire at once; if one failed it stimulated him all the more. He could not be discouraged by the wits who met at the house of Madame de Tencin, among them Fontenelle and La Motte, who seemed so much impressed by his dramatic defeat that they seriously, and with the best intentions in the world, asked him to give up poetry for which he apparently had no talent, and to devote his great abilities to other fields where he surely would be successful.

He went to work at his rapidly outlined tragedy *Zaïre* as he had done before with *Eriphyle;* he not only altered it again and again during the rehearsals but even after the first performance he revised the lines. Dufresne, who was to play the character of Orosmane, and who was used to making playwrights dance to his own tune, lost his patience and continued at the rehearsals to speak the lines in their old form. But Voltaire was more stubborn than the actor. One day when Dufresne was giving a big dinner, he was presented with a gorgeous pie from an anonymous donor. When it was cut open there was inside a large number of partridges each of which held in its bill a little paper roll. All of these rolls contained corrected verses from *Zaïre*. The actor was compelled to submit, and the play, which had earned considerable applause at its first performance, was a great success. Voltaire had to show himself in his loge and the entire theater applauded him, in thanks for the tears he had drawn from them.

Never had he celebrated such a triumph. Of course, his opponents, as Piron and Le Bland, criticized the play: and most violently, Jean Baptiste Rousseau, although later he denied each of the silly attacks which were proven to have come from him. Rousseau, condemned the play passionately on religious grounds. He emphasized that in Corneille's *Polyeucte,* Pauline's passion is overcome by pity, whereas *Zaïre's* proves to be stronger than pity, stronger than religion. Hence the play was entirely unchristian. Two parodies on *Zaïre* were performed, *Harlequin on Parnassus,* by the Abbé Nadal, and *The Found-lings* by Romagnesi and Riccononi. But both were failures.

Zaïre, according to Voltaire's own opinion, is his love tragedy. Ladies had frequently told him that there was not enough love in his tragedies. His reply was that tragedy was not the right place for this emotion. But since they insisted upon seeing heroes and heroines in love, he was willing to make an exception and please them for once. And in the shortest time he ever took to write a play, he turned out *Zaïre.* It is to the ladies, therefore, that we are indebted for this tragedy.

Undeniably the play was the eighteenth century equivalent of the sex play of today. And not only in France: three years after its premiere in Paris, *Zaïre,* translated by the dramatist Aaron Hill, was played at the Drury Lane Theatre in London, and won thunderous applause. The rôle of Orosmane was given to an amateur of high standing, a relative of Hill's, in order to spare it the unnatural affectations of English actors. The character of Zaïre was played by an eighteen-year-old debutante, the young wife of Colley Cibber.

The Italian translation was done by no less a person than Count Carlo Gozzi, whose peculiar style was not exactly suited to the task; nevertheless, the translation was excellent and appealing. In the French original Orosmane, after being stabbed, has only one line to say. Nerestan has a final speech of three lines. In the German translation as performed by Lessing in Hamburg, in 1767, these four lines are omitted, to satisfy the impatience of the audience. Gozzi, on the other hand, prolonged this part by adding eight lines to be spoken by the dying Orosmane:

Questo mortale orror che per le vene
Tutte mi scorre, omai non é dolore,
Che basti ad appagarti, anima bella.
Feroce cor, cor dispietato, e misero,
Paga la pana del delitto orrendo!
Mane crudeli—oh Dio!—Mani che siete
Tinte del sangue di si cara donna
Voi—voi—dov'è quel ferro? etc.

As can be seen, Italian taste demanded an even stronger tragic emphasis.

15

In *Zaïre,* which Voltaire believed represented the peak of his achievement as a writer of tragedy, one gets a perfect impression of how far from reality French tragedy has grown after its century of development. It is something like the libretto of an opera, which has become absorbed by the melody. The observance of a traditional artistic convention neither would nor could escape this unreality, so long as it refused to allow itself to be influenced by any new ideas except those which could develop within the prescribed limits. It is, for example, an innovation when French characters find a place in the *dramatis personae* of *Zaïre.* Tragedy in France had never before been national. It was always concerned with Greeks, Romans, or Spaniards. It is also unprecedented that in a conflict between love and religion the weight of the argument should be thrown on the side, not of Christianity, as in *Polyeucte,* but of love. The depicting of jealous murder by a well-born character was another novelty.

Nevertheless, the play must have been a musical entertainment similar to an Italian opera. The emphasis was not on the characters—not one name has been remembered by posterity—but on the cadence and polish of each couplet; on careful balance, within each couplet, and in the structure of the tragedy as a whole, with its symmetrical contracts produced by the variation and synthesis of emotional tempo in the different scenes.

The rhymeless poetic tragedy of England, and of Germany and Denmark, was never musical to this degree. It lacks the chiming tone of rhymed verse. The pair of lovers that moved the audiences of that time so deeply, fail to move us in modern times. What we appreciate is the lesson the poet tried to teach us by the misfortunes of the lovers: namely, the irretrievable harm done by the stress upon the differences in religion. His play teaches that Paganism has its virtues, the same virtues which as a rule are called Christian; it teaches furthermore that even the best Christians destroy normal happiness by regarding the demands of their fanaticism as sacred obligations.

Othello and Desdemona are still read because Shakespeare does not try to teach us anything or improve our morals.

Even the eloquence of the play, which Voltaire's contemporaries accounted its strongest point, is repugnant to us today. It is always too gushing. Voltaire is never content simply to mention Zaïre's royal antecedents. He must use some high-flown figure every time. She always has twenty kings for ancestors; as if there had ever been twenty Christian kings, in Jerusalem!

Vous, le sang de vingt rois, esclave d'Orosmane!

Or again, Zaïre, when left alone for a moment by her confidante, cries out: "The universe doth abandon me!"

> Fatime ne vient plus. Quoi! dans ce trouble extrème
> L'Univers m'abandonne! on me laisse à moi même.

In addition, the play is afflicted with the clumsiness of the so-called classical style, the desire to use anything rather than simple expressions. For instance, in the part where Orosmane says:

> Madame, il fût un temps, où mon âme charmée
> Ecoutant sans rougir des sentiments trop chers
> Se fit une vertu de languir dans vos fers.

It is typical of this style, that, instead of the simple: "Where are you going?" he says portentously: "Où portez-vous vos pas?" and instead of "Let us go," he says: "Otons nous de ces lieux!"

But we must overlook those weaknesses in *Zaïre* which are common to all French tragedies, even the best. In the fundamental idea of the play there is something which Lessing later adopted in his *Nathan der Weise*, where Orosmane is replaced by his prototype, Saladin; and in the relation of the main character Orosmane to Zaïre, we can see something prophetic of Goethe's Thoas, another Scythian king, in his relation to Iphigenia.

16

Voltaire felt his position becoming more and more precarious. Some unknown person published his *Epistle to Urania,* which he had written ten years previously to the Marquise de Rupelmonde. In it, you remember, he discussed religion very plainly. Although the poem was anonymous, public opinion discovered its author. Not only the pious, but the conservatives as well, were furious. It was to be expected that the authorities would interfere. The chancellor d'Aguesseau asked his secretary, Langlois, what he thought about it. The answer was. "Monseigneur, Voltaire ought to be locked up somewhere out of reach of pen, paper, and ink. He is dangerous to the state." The Archbishop of Paris, M. de Vintimille, complained to the police commissioner and

Hénault summoned Voltaire to him. Voltaire, however, emphatically asserted that the Epistle was not written by him but by the deceased Abbé de Chaulieu, whom he had heard recite it frequently.

The young actress, Mademoiselle Gaussin, who played Zaïre, had given an excellent performance in an earlier rôle, as Tullie, in *Brutus*. At that time Voltaire dedicated the following humorous verses to her:

> Que le public veuille ou non veuille,
> De tous les charmes qu'il acceuille
> Les tiens sont les plus ravissants.
> Mais tu n'es encor que la feuille
> Des fruits que promet ton printemps,
> O mar Tullie, avant le temps
> Garde-toi bien qu-on ne te cueille.

It seems that the fruit mentioned here was plucked in good season, and the plucker was none other than he who expressed the fear that it might be plucked too soon.

Voltaire wrote many verses to Gaussin, among them the following on the occasion of her twentieth birthday in August, 1731:

> Le plus puissant de tous les dieux,
> Le plus aimable, le plus sage,
> Louison, c'est l'Amour dans vos yeux.
> De tous les dieux le moins volage,
> Le plus tendre et le moins trompeur,
> Louison, c'est l'Amour dans mon cœur.

His gratitude was great when Mademoiselle Gaussin made a triumph as his Zaïre. He paid homage to her in the poetic epistle (the thirty-ninth) which is woven into the dedication of the piece. The epistle begins:

> Jeune Gaussin, reçois mon tendre hommage,
> Reçois mes vers au théâtre applaudis!
> Protège-les: *Zaïre* est ton ouvrage;
> Il est à toi, puisque tu l'embellis.
> Ce sont tes yeux, ces yeux si pleins de charmes,
> Ta voix touchante, et tes sons enchanteurs,
> Qui du critique ont fait tomber les armes.

Perhaps this homage was not too exaggerated. The charm of the young actress probably helped in disarming the critics. The poem closes with a fiery out-burst:

> Heureux cent fois le mortel amoureux
> Qui, tous les jours, peut te voir et t'entendre,
> Que tu reçois avec un souris tendre,
> Qui voit son sort écrit dans tes beaux yeux,
> Qui, pénétré de leur feu qu'il adore
> A tes genoux oubliant l'univers,
> Parle d'amour, et t'en reparle encore!
> Et malheureux qui n'en parle qu'en vers!

When the performances of *Zaïre* were interrupted for some time because of an illness of Mademoiselle Gaussin, Voltaire had it played at the house of Madame Fontaine-Martel; several times he himself played the rôle of Lusignan (as he often did later). He played the part with such fire and verve that it seemed to some spectators a bit too virile and active for a man who was supposed to have been imprisoned for twenty years.

But apparently Voltaire preferred an excess of vividness, although in general he abhorred ranting on the stage.

Once he was coaching a young actress, and thinking her too phlegmatic he explained to her how in his opinion the rôle should be played. She answered: "One would have to have the devil in one's body to play that way." "Yes," he responded, "that's exactly what one must have."

On another occasion a beginner irritated him by her constant gesticulations; he tied a band around her right arm and standing in the wings he held the other end of the band in his hand to force her to a quieter rendition. At first she subdued her motions; but when she finally got warmed up to her part she threw up her arm so passionately that the band broke.—"Excuse me!" she said, "I know that was wrong."

"On the contrary, on the contrary!" he exclaimed. "That is just as it should be. I hoped you would break the band. When the gesture comes from the heart, then it is right."

17

In January, 1733, Voltaire's hostess, the epicurean philosopher in female dress, the Countess Martel, fell fatally ill, and Voltaire had the difficult assignment of telling her of her approaching end. She would have neither priest nor sacrament. But characteristically of the spirit of the time, Voltaire thought himself bound to see that she should not pass away without being on good terms with the Church. He wished this for himself, too. So he brought a priest to her. Afterwards, with his habitual lack of feeling, he gave a burlesque account of how the Countess, under pressure, submitted to the last ceremony.

About this time appeared a well-known poetic composition *Le Temple du Goût,* a true production of the eighteenth century, written partly in verse, partly in prose. In it he discussed the writers of Louis XIV's and his own time very flippantly, but in general so truly that posterity has concurred in his estimate. In some cases, as in that of J. B. Rousseau, he criticized with a punishing wit sharpened by the ideas of the exiled poet. The work has about the same value that Boileau's *L'Art Poétique* had for the previous period.

It caused a furore. People were shocked that Voltaire dared criticize such great writers as Rabelais or Bayle. On the other hand, contemporary writers who were praised in this work, like Count de Caylus, indignantly demanded from Voltaire that he omit their names; they were noblemen who wished to be regarded as dilettantes only, not as writers.

Voltaire's polite answer to Caylus read: "I must say that I prefer the pleasure of obeying you to the pleasure of glorifying you." Whereupon Caylus answers like a true aristocrat: "Again I thank you for your politeness; it reaches its height in the event that I do not find my name in the new edition."

The storm that came up over this little work was the fiercest that Voltaire had had to weather so far. The whole reading world became worked up over it.

Parodies of it appeared in the small theaters which correspond to the modern revues.

The puppet theater gave the signal for the attack. Its play is rather broad: Polichinel is ill. He is advised by a physician to let himself be flogged in order to raise a perspiration. But this treatment had been tried without success. Another physician advises a purgative; a Temple of the Taste (*Le Temple du Goût*) is brought onto the stage, and it turns out to be a night-stool. The joke, however, proved too coarse, and the play was ordered withdrawn.

Next, the Italian theater went to work. In the skit played there, Voltaire was taken off in a square-cut English suit which, to emphasize his supposed stinginess, was of cotton, not of wool. He behaved like a complete fool, expressed himself very stupidly and without the slightest notion of good critical judgment. Thus he was supposed to represent bad taste as opposed to good.

References of contemporaries prove that some of them were pained by such a silly attack on a highly esteemed writer. Voltaire joked about it. He wrote to Thiriot that since Socrates had had to be content to be brought onto the stage by Aristophanes, it was not up to him to complain about the Romagnesi's satire.

After the death of Madame de Martel, Voltaire continued to live at her house for some time. In May, 1733, he moved to a house in the rue du Long Pont, the property of a rich corn merchant, whom he had met at the home of one of his father's clerks. As he believed the corn business profitable he let Demoulin speculate for him, and not without success.

The street on which the house stood was narrow and unattractive, but Voltaire installed himself as comfortably as possible and invited young and old friends for dinner. Shortly after he had settled in these quarters he saw for the first time the lady who was to fill the next seventeen years of his life. Voltaire knew the Duchess de Saint-Pierre; he knew her friend, the intelligent and brave Louis de Brancas, Count de Forclaquier, son of the marshal. They visited him occasionally. One day the Duchess brought along her intimate friend the Marquise du Châtelet, and this trio came one evening for dinner, a modest, impromptu feast of chicken fricassée, which was followed by excellent champagne. That occasion inspired the following short verse:

> Ciel! que j'entendrais s'écrier
> Marianne, ma cuisinière,
> Si la duchesse de Saint-Pierre,
> Du Châtelet et Forcalquier
> Venaient souper dans ma tanière.

This is the beginning of the friendship between Voltaire and the Marquise du Châtelet, who shortly thereafter made possible for Voltaire many quiet and fertile years of work. At first it was a passionate love affair, but in the course of time it changed into a spiritual relationship, in which the man found self-content and calm while the woman suffered from Voltaire's frequent journeys and his negligence. She wanted something more than platonic affection.

18

Gabrielle Emilie Le Tonnellier de Breteuil was born on December 17th, 1706. When she met Voltaire, in the early summer of 1733, he was thirty-eight years old and she was twenty-six. She was only eighteen when she was married to the Marquis Florent Claude du Châtelet-Lemont who was descended from an old family of Lorraine. He allowed himself to be entirely under her thumb. He was a typical gentleman and officer of that time. The couple had a son and a daughter, and beyond that they did not bother each other.

Voltaire had seen Emilie at her father's as a little girl. One of the writers who belonged to the little court of the Duchess of Maine, in Sceaux, a witty man by the name of Dumas d'Aigueberre, brought them together again.

As a mere child she had learned Latin and Italian; at the age of fifteen she began to translate Vergil, and she was early attracted by mathematics. But regardless of her considerable talents she was first of all a woman, and a very passionate one at that. When her

husband early ceased to pay her attentions, she surrendered to temptation and began a love affair with
the Marquis de Guébriant. When Guébriant before
long cooled off she attempted to commit suicide. This
remained no secret; and the rhymesters of the time
made their jokes about it. Maurepas discussed it in
detail in his memoirs. Later, she had the brief adventure already related with the Duke of Richelieu.

We have several portraits of her and it is not hard
to visualize her as she was when Voltaire met her for
the second time. She seems quite handsome in the
portraits by Nattier and Latour and Marie Anne Loir,
although these were painted at an advanced age. She
had peculiarly sympathetic features. She was never a
beauty. Tall and slender, she had a distinguished
head, a large nose, a very nicely formed mouth, a
strong chin expressing will power, big, appealing
eyes, clear and green as the sea, surmounted by heavy
eyebrows. The entire face seemed to be dominated by
the forehead which was high and thoughtful. Her
long, black hair was curled like a child's, and pinned
up in the back; the bust was voluptuous but firm. According to the amiable Madame du Deffand, her arms
and legs were a little too sturdy. She spoke fluently
and rapidly but in society she knew how to express
herself so naïvely that nobody could suspect her scientific knowledge.

19

When she allied herself with Voltaire she was still
very emotional; her intellect was just developing.
What she knew about the fine arts and science, was
mainly music; she had a good voice, liked to sing
and was familiar with the operas. As a rule, she preferred the lighter, soothing music to the heavier. But
when she attended a private rehearsal of *Samson,* the
libretto of which was written by Voltaire at the request of the composer Rameau, Madame du Châtelet
seemed to be won entirely by the queer old composer.
"My gratitude," she writes, "is as great as the pleasure
I enjoyed, and that means a great deal. I was espe-

cially delighted with the overture, the dance and the violin melodies. The third and fifth acts are admirable." Shortly before the premiere, however, the performance of the opera was prohibited under the pretense that the theme was biblical, although the Italian theater was permitted to produce a *Samson,* in which Harlequin appeared as Samson's servant and had a row with a turkey.

Thus, Voltaire's growing musical ambition was nipped in the bud. He wanted to demonstrate that he could instill new life into opera by cutting down the tedious recitals and replacing them with arias, which blended the French taste with the Italian, and gave the ballet a rich ceremonial appearance. But it is psychologically interesting to read his text and see how he visualized the old biblical story.

In his opera he allowed no speaking—all singing, and the hero was not given a confidante. The audience should not have to endure a constant repetition of French feminine endings so annoying to the ear. The absurdities in the story must be eliminated. One should not expect Rameau to "distribute Samson's jawbone of an ass in notes of sixteenths." No bees should be found in the carcass of the dead lion, for bees do not swarm in dead flesh. Finally, Delilah must not be the unworthy character of the Bible and she must not distract attention from the hero. The main feature should be, not his amorousness, but his heroism.

20

One of the most appealing sides of Voltaire's character was his constant readiness, the moment he had a little money, to help the many young people who turned to him for help. It is astonishing that he, who had such early, bitter lessons in the ingratitude of his fellow men, was so ready to give these strange people access to his person and to his house. It seems as though no unpleasant experience could change the inborn nobility of his nature.

At about this time an obscure young abbé, named Michael Linant, who wrote verses, insinuated himself into Voltaire's favor. Voltaire not only supported him, but also introduced him to his friends. First Voltaire hoped to get Madame de Martel to take him in: Linant could live just as Voltaire did, make himself useful and be rewarded for it. But Madame de Martel did not want to have anything to do with the new protégé. At Voltaire's hearty recommendation she had already taken care of Thiriot, whom she gave an annual allowance of twelve hundred francs, in return for which, of course, he did nothing. She was shy of Voltaire's latest protégé. The poet recommended him still more warmly to Cideville in Rouen: "Linant's verses are as graphic and colorful as they are harmonious. True, as a poet he has too many ideas and too great a poetic passion; but these are the faults of youth, which will be eliminated by time, and in conversation he is far softer-spoken than in his verses."

Cideville treated Linant as if he were his own son. Nevertheless, Voltaire did not let the young man out of sight, he recommended him to the Duchess of Maine as a reader, begging Madame du Deffand for the sake of her pleasure and the pleasure of the Duchess, to secure the position for this very promising young abbé.

But the Duchess stood firm; she had no desire to have Linant near her. This was not surprising; he lisped, stammered, and was very near-sighted; besides that he was cock-sure and obstinate. "What shall I do with him?" Voltaire, in 1732, writes to Cideville. "He can't be a secretary, as he cannot write legibly, and I very much fear that he has the amiable quality of laziness, which is no small vice in a man who has to make a career. Couldn't Cideville secure him a position with the Archbishop of Rouen?"

In the following year (May 29, 1733) Voltaire again writes to Cideville about Linant: "If the abbé wants to return to Paris, I will rent him a room somewhere near here; then he can eat his lunches and suppers with me." The abbé didn't have to be asked twice. He arrived posthaste. Voltaire had absolutely no use for him. He already had a secretary, a certain Céran, who read the Latin poets aloud to him and copied his verses, carelessly and badly. As Voltaire himself had no time to entertain Linant outside of mealtimes, and as the somewhat simple Céran did not seem sufficient company for the abbé, he took another young man into his house, a poet named Lefèvre and Voltaire now had three poor, tragedy-writing young people to feed and support.

After some time, Linant returned to his protector Cideville, in Rouen, but soon was back again in Paris, where Voltaire gave him the outline of a tragedy on Rameses the Great, which he began to elaborate. In September, 1733, however, Voltaire had to report that Linant had left him, without having finished even one scene of the tragedy; and now he begins to have serious doubts about the future of his protégé.

With moving naïveté he writes to Cideville: "Seriously considered, it does not appear certain that Linant possesses any of the rare talents without which poetry is a miserable handiwork. It would be a real pity if he were wasting even a little genius with so much laziness. Please encourage him to work ... he had the intention of becoming a teacher, but knows scarcely any Latin. If you like him, my dear Cideville, do not spoil him with too much praise, but induce him to learn to do something."

To Linant himself Voltaire writes a brief poem urging him to diligence. It says that idleness may be a virtue in the rich or in those who have a life full of work behind them; but with the poor it always is a vice, and anyone who is as ambitious as Linant should make himself a bed of laurels before he thinks of lying down.

> Courtisans de la gloire, écrivains ou guerriers,
> Le sommeil est permis, mais c'est sur des lauriers.

On December 27 of the same year, Linant informs his protector that he "has renounced the theater," and now Voltaire is forced to relinquish his high hopes of the abbé. But he does not abandon him for all that. When Linant has offended a prominent lady, the Countess Neuville, by an impudent love-letter, Voltaire makes excuses for him, even writes a little poem on the occasion, addressed to the Countess, in which we find the following lines:

Il est difficile de taire
Ce qu'on sent au fond de son cœur;
L'exprimer est une autre affaire,
Il ne faut pas parler, si l'on n'est sûr de plaire,
Souvent l'on est fat, en montrant trop d'ardeur.

In the year 1736, he let Linant have the profits from his play *L'Enfant prodigue*. In the summer of 1735, he gave him—much as Madame du Châtelet opposed it—a position as teacher for her son. But Linant had scarcely arrived when, unmindful of the respect he owed the mistress of the house, he sent a letter to her from an estate in the vicinity, which he had visited uninvited; he concluded it rudely with the following words: "The tediousness in Cirey is of all tediousnesses the greatest." He showed this letter to his hosts who promptly urged Madame du Châtelet to dismiss him. Out of pure goodness of heart, Voltaire let the culprit stay and even spared him reproaches.

Linant proceeded to play the superior. To Voltaire's anger he never spoke of his benefactor in Rouen as "Monsieur de Cideville" but as "dear Cideville." When Madame du Châtelet wished to dismiss him for this, Voltaire pleaded with her, that Linant was just a boy, he was twenty-seven, without much knowledge of the world; that he would die of starvation if he were driven out, lazy and ignorant as he was; and that, after all, he knew enough Latin to give instruction in it, "at least to learn it at the same time with his pupil." At any rate, he could guide his pupil's method of thought.

Meanwhile, Linant asked Voltaire's protection and shelter for his sister; she, too, might live in Cirey. When Madame du Châtelet demurred, Voltaire succeeded in securing her a position as governess for Madame de Richelieu's child. Unfortunately the child did not live long, and Voltaire again pressed his friend to overcome her prejudice, and take the girl in. And he did this in spite of the fact that he had good reason to suspect that Mademoiselle Linant, who was just as haughty as her brother, felt she was too good to enter the service of Madame du Châtelet.

Linant, finally, had started to do some work, and as Voltaire jokingly writes, it looked as though in about fourteen years the young man would finish the fifth act of a tragedy. But brother and sister behaved so arrogantly that Madame du Châtelet found it "absolutely necessary" to dismiss them both.

Regardless of all this, Voltaire continued to let Linant have indirectly (through the publisher Prault) small sums of money, with repeated expressions of sorrow that the young man did not want to assure his future by decent behavior, when it would have been so easy for him. "His pupil," he writes, "would surely have pensioned him even after his schooling was over; there is honesty and ambition in the Châtelet family. Whoever has educated a du Châtelet lives in the house in comfort until his death." (Letter of December 23, 1737.) On November 28, 1750, Voltaire reports Linant's pitiful end: "He died of poverty brought on by his own laziness."

We have seen how impatient Voltaire's temperament could be. But in this as well as in hundreds of other such cases we see him as the most indulgent man in the history of the world.

21

The success of *Zaïre* encouraged the poet to write a new tragedy. In February, 1733, he wrote to Thiriot about his latest work *Adélaide du Guesclin:* "The theme is French and is my invention throughout, and I have filled it as full as I could with love, jealousy, excitement, decency, honesty and greatness of soul."

As famous as *Zaïre* and as unknown as *Adélaide* have become, *Adélaide,* in spite of its romantic foundation, is quite as effective as *Zaïre.*

Adélaide is a tragedy such as Oehlenschläger liked to write a century later, a tragedy in which as in a stained glass picture, personalities are depicted in great, simple sketches, with clear outlines, each expressing a few emotions that are pure because they are uncomplicated, and hence are easily got over from the stage.

Madame du Châtelet, as well as Louis de Richelieu, appear to have been enchanted by *Adélaide du Guesclin*. A letter from the former to the Duke reads in part: "I am delighted that you are pleased with Adélaide. The play moved me. I find it tender, noble, well-written; the fifth act is especially delightful. It probably will not be played soon; for the poor little actress Dufresne is desperately ill; she has sent back her rôle."

As we can see, the chivalric-heroic tone of the tragedy did not fail to have its effect on Voltaire's friend, although her inclination was more to mathematics and the natural sciences, and she did not enjoy poetry very much.

The poet's friends awaited the first performance with high hopes. It was given on January 18. They failed to take into consideration, however, that his recently published work *Le Temple du Goût* had caused great embitterment. The play was hissed from the first act on. The hissing doubled in the second act when the Duc de Nemours, arm in sling, appeared on the stage. Finally the play was drowned in laughter. At the end of the play when Vendome asks: "Are you content, Coucy?" a wit in the crowd answered, "Comme çi," (so-so). A tumult broke out and the words were mockingly repeated from sides of the theater.

In 1752, the tragedy was successfully taken up again, under the title *Duc de Foix*. Fearing ridicule, Voltaire weakened the play considerably in this revision. But more than thirty years after the premiere, in 1765, the actors, without the poet's permission, performed the play with its original form and title. It was received with universal and enthusiastic applause. Madame du Châtelet lived to see only the defeat, not the victory.

Voltaire tells us an anecdote about the banker Högger (Voltaire drolly spells the name Oghières) who had commissioned the composer Mouret to write a march for one of Charles XII's regiments. Mouret played the march in the presence of invited guests at the banker's home. They all found it abominable. So the composer made use of it in one of his operas, which was attended by the banker and his friends. "That is the kind of march we wanted," they said to Mouret. "Why didn't you give us one like that?"

"It is the same," Mouret responded.

22

Voltaire was requested by the Duke of Richelieu to arrange a second marriage for him. The reason for this step is unknown. Voltaire pretends that the idea was originated by him. This, however, seems incredible. He wrote to Cideville that he had handled the affair like the intrigue in a play, and that he was the witness at the wedding. The bride was Marie de Guise, of the famous family which for a long time was the first of France after the house of Valois, and which was the most dangerous rival of the royal house. Nevertheless, the bride's parents, the Duke and Duchess of Guise, led a life which was a scandal (according to President Hénault), even in this anything but straightlaced age.

The house of Guise, was of far greater consequence than the house of Richelieu. Therefore the Duke de Guise would hardly have consented to the marriage had Richelieu not waived the matter of dowry. It was Voltaire who drew up the contract. He wrote various poems on the occasion of the wedding.

As a young girl Mademoiselle de Guise had already received poetic tribute from him:

> Vous possédez fort inutilement
> Esprit, beauté, grace, vertu, franchise,
> Qu'y manque-t-il? Quelqu'un qui vous le dise
> Et quelque ami dont on dise autant.

During the weeks preceding Richelieu's wedding he wrote a brief poem to her, which seems to be inspired by her courage in entering into such a risky alliance; in pretty verse it gives her a bit of prosaic, but practical advice. The end reads:

Vos doux appas auront la gloire
De finir l'amoureuse histoire
De ce volage Richelieu!
Ne vous aimez pas trop, c'est moi qui vous en prie
C'est le plus sûr moyen de vous aimer toujours;
Il vaut mieux être amis tout le temps de la vie
Que d'être amants quelques jours.

According to her contemporaries, Mademoiselle
de Guise had lovely eyes, but otherwise was not
especially good-looking; it seems that she had the
bad habit of talking about herself a great deal and no
less about her father. Considering her father's reputation—he was said to have tried to help his luck at
cards—this was rather ill-chosen. Hence the following polite, but astonishingly bold admonition to the
young lady from Voltaire:

Plus mon œil étonné vous suit et vous observe,
Et plus vous ravissez mes esprits éperdus;
Avec les yeux noirs de Vénus
Vous avez l'esprit de Minerve,
Mais Minerve et Vénus ont reçu des avis;
Il faut bien que je vous en donne
Ne parlez désormais de vous qu'à vos amis
Et de votre père à personne.

Still more characteristic of the free language of
that time in erotic matters is the epithalamion Voltaire sends to the Duchess. One can see from this
poem that Richelieu's past was too well known to
remain concealed; at the same time one is struck with
how lightly and humorously his indiscretions are
treated, compared with the severe criticism to which
the bride's father was subjected. The poem begins:

Un prêtre, un oui, trois mots latin,
A jamais fixent vos destins;
Et le célébrant d'un village,
Dans la chapelle de Monjeu,
Très chrétiennement vous engage
A coucher avec Richelieu,
Avec Richelieu, ce volage,
Qui va jurer par ce saint nœud
D'être toujours, fidèle et sage.
Nous nous en défions un peu;
Et vos grande yeux noirs, pleins de feu,
Nous rassurent bien davantage
Que les serments qu'il fait à Dieu.
Mais vous, Madame la duchesse,
Quand vous reviendrez à Paris

Songez vous combien de maris
Viendront se plaindre à votre Altesse?
Ces nombreux cocus qu'il a faits
Ont mis en vous leur espérance;
Ils diront, voyant vos atraits:
"Dieux! quel plaisir que la vengeance!"

The wedding introduced with such merry and frivolous words was, however, shortly after the celebration, the cause of a sad occurrence. Certain of the Guise family were highly incensed by the marriage: a descendant of the House of Lorraine had lowered herself to marry a Richelieu. (They were positive that his father's name was not Richelieu, but Vignerod.) Soon after the wedding the Duke joined the army and there he met his wife's cousins, Prince de Lixin and his brother, Prince de Pons. Both had refused to sign the marriage contract, this was the cause of a quarrel between Richelieu and Lixin, which was followed by a challenge. In the duel the Prince de Lixin was killed while Richelieu received an injury which was believed at first to be fatal, but which soon healed.

23

A month before this event, Voltaire met an unexpected misfortune. The wedding had taken place in April at the castle of Monjeu. On May 8, a letter from the minister ordered an officer at Dijon, Monsieur de la Briffe, to arrest the Sieur de Voltaire at Monjeu, "provided that he was still there," and to have him brought to Château Auxonne. Voltaire had a tip from Maupertuis, and got a letter from d'Argental, advising him to flee at once. Consequently he was not to be found in Monjeu. As far as was known, he had gone to Lorraine (which did not become French until more than a generation later) to try the baths there. The intendant, therefore, returned the royal order as impossible of execution.

The letters on England had annoyed the government. The English edition had a good sale. The London publisher had stipulated that a French edition must not appear too soon, and Thiriot had agreed in

Voltaire's name. Meanwhile the publisher, Jore, was holding the manuscript and Voltaire was afraid he might break the contract. Although the work was already printed, Jore had promised to withhold it. He, too, would have been sure to be put in the Bastille, had he published the book and had it become known that it was he who had printed it.

Jore's father had been in jail three times—a year and a half each time, in 1697, 1698 and 1712—because he had sold books which attacked the Church and the State. In 1731 his son received a *Lettre de cachet,* because he had printed Abbé Desfontaines' ironic preface to an account of the trial of Père Girard and the respectable Cadière. Jore and Desfontaines would both have been thrown into the Bastille, had not Voltaire used his influence to save them.

The authorities learned that an edition of the *Lettres Philosophiques* was in preparation in Rouen, and a detective was sent there. Voltaire upon learning of this wrote Jore and requested him to hide the whole edition at the house of Voltaire's friend, Formont, and to see to it that not a copy could be found. For six months all partners had kept silent. Then suddenly, in the midst of the wedding ceremonies, Voltaire was informed that the *Lettres Philosophiques* were being sold in Paris. Jore, at once sent to the Bastille, blurted out that Voltaire was the author and that the edition was hidden at the house of Monsieur de Formont. The authorities were outraged at the book, and when sentence was imposed, it prescribed that the work "being scandalous, and offensive to religion, good morals and the respect owed to the State, should be burned by the executioner, at the foot of the great stairway." This was done.

The orthodox pamphlets published against the work, charged Voltaire with defamation and degradation of his own people, Abbé Gouget asserted that Voltaire had glorified the barbarous Shakespeare, while he did not even mention the name of the French poet, Grévin: "Jacques Grévin, who died in 1750 at the early age of twenty-nine years, would perhaps have succeeded as well as Shakespeare, had not death cut him off in his prime."

As we saw, the author had been hunted with a warrant even before sentence had been passed upon the work. He had quickly disappeared, and Madame du Châtelet, who had remained, lonely and desperate, in Monjeu, wrote in her distress to Richelieu who had just left for the army, of course in such a way as to leave Voltaire's real place of refuge secret.

"You know that my friendship for you affords me the greatest comfort and consolation in my misfortune. I have met with possibly the worst misfortune. My friend Voltaire—you know my feelings for him— is probably at Château Osonne (Auxonne) near Dijon. He had just left us a few days ago to try the baths in Plombières, which his health has long demanded, when a messenger from Monsieur de la Briffe brought me a *Lettre de cachet* ordering him to Osonne until further notice. The messenger was told that he was in Plombières; I do not doubt that he will shortly receive the King's order and that he will obey. There is nothing else to do, if it cannot be avoided. I simply can't describe how I suffer. I cannot summon the courage to face the definite knowledge that my friend, with his poor health, is in a prison where he surely will die of shame if not of illness. I shall neither have word from him nor be able to send him any information. . . . Oh, under what ironic circumstances did I receive your letter! You envy me the good fortune of being with one in whose company it is so delightful to live. You would be right had this been so. I spent ten days here with him and Madame de Richelieu; I do not think life has ever been more pleasant for me. I lost him when I most strongly felt the happiness of possessing him, and how I have lost him!"

In reality Voltaire had fled to Lorraine. When, however, he heard the rumor that his friend, Richelieu, was fatally wounded, he forsook all consideration of safety, and set out for the army.

24

The cause of the war was that Stanislaw, who, in 1733, was elected King of Poland for the second time, was driven out by the Emperor Charles VII who, in alliance with Russia, set August III on the throne. A French army marched to the Rhine and encamped near Philippsburg facing Prince Eugene. The result of this campaign was that Stanislaw gave up Poland, but received Lorraine instead, on the condition that after his death it was to be annexed to France.

Voltaire's arrival at the camp was wildly celebrated. Men outdid one another to honor and entertain him. The highest nobles, the seventeen-year-old Prince of Conti, the counts de Charolais and de Clermont, all members of the royal family, all relatives of the great Condé, received him with distinction.

Conti one day saved Voltaire's life, when the latter was mistaken for a spy by soldiers of the Prince's regiment.

The Duke of Richelieu—who had fully recovered his health—was not of a Spartan nature. Although only a colonel in rank, he had in camp for his own use sixty-two baggage-mules, thirty horses, and a swarm of servants. At that time he still fitted the description Voltaire had given of him in his epistle to Pallu,

> Alcibiade qu'à la cour
> Nous vîmes briller tour-à-tour
> Par ses grâces, par son courage,
> Gai, généreux, tendre, volage,
> Et séducteur comme l'Amour
> Dont il fut le brilant image.

One might be led to think from this that Richelieu was not cut out to be a soldier. His later life, however, shows how gifted he was as a commander. Thus, in 1743, trying to remedy the defeat at Dettingen, he showed no little bravery. Two years later, at Fontenoy—he had meanwhile been promoted to major-general and adjutant to the King—it was largely his advice that brought about the victorious outcome of the battle. When the English column resisted all attacks, Richelieu, covered with dust, rode over to the King and begged him to fire four cannon into the enemy, while the troop *"La maison du roi"* and others should attack on both flanks. He personally transmitted the order for this charge. After the battle was won, the King said to him: "I will never forget the important service you rendered today."

When in 1747 Genoa rebelled against its Austrian oppressors and the English blockaded the port so that the inhabitants were short of food, money and amunition, Richelieu was sent to the relief of the city. On a small boat he sailed right through the English fleet, received fresh troops from France and Spain, drove back the enemy in several battles and made the coast line safe. Out of gratitude the Genoese erected a monument to him in their city. On this occasion, Voltaire sent him an epistle, which commences:

> Je la verrai cette statue
> Que Gêne élève justement
> Au héros qui l'a défendue.
> Votre grand-oncle, moins brillant
> Vit sa gloire moins étendue.
> Il serait jaloux à la vue
> De cet unique monument.

Richelieu's reputation grew so great that the pretender to the English throne, Charles Edward, when he was ready to embark from France to invade England, requested and obtained Richelieu to command his forces. The venture, however, proved to be impracticable.

In the year 1756, Richelieu accomplished a feat that was really great. With about twenty battalions transported on French ships, he conquered the island of Minorca by defeating the English fleet and storming the citadel of Port-Mahon, which was considered almost as impregnable as Gibraltar. Thirty years had been spent in building its fortifications. He (as well as Voltaire) tried to save the life of Admiral Byng. Byng had done his best, but nevertheless was brought before a court-martial in London and shot. Richelieu, finally, just before Rossbach, conquered the English army under the Duke of Cumberland at the mouth of the Elbe river, forcing the latter to surrender. For these deeds Voltaire glorified his friend in prose and verse. One should note Epistles 92 and 94. In the first are the words:

> Mais je médite un gros ouvrage
> Pour le vainqueur de Port Mahon.
> Je veux peindre à ma nation
> Ce jour d'éternelle mémoire.

The second begins with the warm assertion that Richelieu has always been his hero and that he had foreseen his glory:

> Depuis plus que quarante ans
> Vous avez été mon héros;
> J'ai présagé vos destinées.
> Ainsi quand Achille à Scyros
> Paraissait se livrer en proie
> Aux jeux, aux amours, au repos,
> Il devait un jour sur les flots
> Apporter la flamme devant Troie.

They had been friends since their youth, and Voltaire had loved Richelieu all his life. He had an unquestioning faith which Richelieu often abused.

On the whole, Richelieu remained faithful to Voltaire, did him many a service, accepted many services from him, borrowed large sums of money and honestly esteemed his genius; but he felt under no more obligation than the easiness of his temperament and the insensibility of his nature admitted. On the other hand, Voltaire was an exacting friend.

It is certain that Richelieu dropped his friend's interests very quickly when Court politics made it seem inadvisable to support him—for instance, when Voltaire sought admission to the French Academy.

Everything about Richelieu betrays the typical *grand seigneur* of the eighteenth century. Very aptly he is glorified in Diderot's *Les bijoux indiscrets* (1747) as Selim, the clever and powerful grand-vizier of a sultan who represents Louis XV. His mind was narrow and his heart dry; he was a cynic but an elegant one, who combined an invariable politeness to women with a scorn that was the outgrowth of their shallowness as well as his own. He was not ashamed to serve as go between for the woman he thought the right one for the King. He could not see what more shame there was in offering the sovereign a nice woman than a handsome vase or a precious jewel. His cynicism included an insuperable skepticism, a superior irony; with this irony, however, he combined the reckless courage of the ancient Frankish warrior.

He had the self-confidence of the successful gambler, but added to it a tact of which he was master. And he had inherited or acquired some of the great cardinal's gift of persuasive speech. Finally—he was glittering, radiant with the splendor of all the lovely, eminent ladies who had loved and embraced him. All felt that they wanted to serve him, observed and speculated for his advantage, and from them he learned to guess, to observe and to feel. He adopted feminine intuition and added womanly diplomacy to his manly courage.

He and Voltaire remained loyal to each other all their lives. They never quarreled for more than a few days, and even then often neither of them was to blame. When, in 1748, Richelieu was ordered by the French Academy to compliment the King upon the peace of Aix-la-Chapelle, he asked Voltaire to write a short speech for him. Voltaire did so, but could not refrain from showing the charming little composition to Madame du Châtelet. At that moment the Marquise de Boufflers came to see her and in her enthusiasm copied the speech. Consequently, upon Richelieu's arrival at Court to deliver his speech, the courtiers recited to him parts of it before it was delivered. In his rage he would not hand the King the *Eloge de Louis XV,* which he had brought, but sent the package without a word back to the poet. For he believed Voltaire had intentionally imparted to others that he, not Richelieu, was the author of the speech.

Among Voltaire's epistles there is a very amusing one which originated in the camp at Philippsburg (Epitre 45). Here he reveals for the first time the satirical view of war, which in his case, of course, does not exclude admiration for courage and bravery. It is the epistle which begins with a description of the hardships of war and of the thunder of the cannons which can be heard at the camp:

> C'est ici que l'on dort sans lit
> Et qu'on prend ses repas sur terre;
> Je vois et j'entends l'atmosphère
> Qui s'embrase et qui retentit
> De cent décharges de tonnerre.

Then he pokes fun at the 50,000 Alexanders at four sous a day, who here, covered with dirt and laurels, fight for the idea called honor. He extols their bravery and finishes his hymn thus: "True, it is a glorious thing to taunt death and Prince Eugene, but oh! what a price you pay for your heroic glamour! All this while your wives and mistresses back in Paris are fitting horns to your heads."

> O nation brillante et vaine!
> Illustres fous, peuple charmant,
> Que la Gloire à son char enchaîne,
> Il est beau d'affronter gaiment
> Le trépas et le prince Eugène.
> Mais hélas! quel sera le prix
> De vos héroiques prouesses!
> Vous serez cocus dans Paris
> Par vos femmes et vos maîtresses.

Voltaire was naïve enough to believe that the authorities would not take offense at this little military escapade. But in that he was wrong. The authorities had it in for him. Soon even he appreciated that he could no longer remain in France, and when the *Lettres Philosophiques* came out, he seriously considered joining Thiriot in London. But he felt a bond which restrained him. In a letter of the end of June, 1734, he expresses this, though not too clearly: "As long as I am loved so warmly by several persons in France, it is impossible for me to seek refuge in another country. Where friendship is, there is one's fatherland." The Marquise du Châtelet, for her part, wrote sadly:

"A hundred dangerous remarks are attributed to him. The minister was glad to seize on this pretext. I am firmly persuaded they plan to ruin him. They speak of exile; I no longer know what to believe. But I know this, that were I in his place, I should have gone to London or to the Hague long ago. I confess to you that all this depresses me greatly. I cannot get used to the thought of living without him, or of losing him forever. This thought would entirely poison my life."

After one month of restless wandering, Voltaire for the first time settled in Cirey, the manor of the Châtelet family; it was situated on the border between Champagne and Lorraine and thus enabled him to keep one foot in France, the other outside of France, and at the first warning he could easily get to safety.

Cirey was situated—we should say ideally, but in that day it was considered dismally out-of-the-way—in a lovely grass-grown valley between two ranges of high hills covered with forests. It was remote only in so far as one could with a few steps reach the border by going past Saint-Dizier into the little realm of the Duke of Lorraine.

Here was safety and quiet in which to work. Here, a little paradise could be created for two lovers who at the same time were two ardent fellow students. Here was the refuge for the half-willing, half-unwilling exile.

VI

LOUIS XV

1

CONSIDERING Voltaire's refuge in Cirey, our first feeling is one of astonishment, that such an isolation should have been necessary in a state whose King, Louis XIV, had staked his honor to be his country's, even Europe's, Mæcenas, and had become famous for it. He not only made architecture, sculpture, and painting arts of the Court, but also surrounded himself with the best wits of the time, and appreciated the works of Racine, Boileau and Molière.

The duty of maintaining this tradition should have been very dear to Louis XV. Actually there was nothing farther from his thoughts. One day, someone dared to propose to the King the possibility of attracting the writers and scholars of the epoch to the Court, as Frederick the Great was doing in such a brilliant manner. Louis protested: "This is not the custom in France, and since there are far more wits and great men here, than there are in Prussia, I would have to have a very long table to assemble them all." Then he began counting on his fingers: "Maupertuis, Fontenelle, La Motte, Voltaire, Piron, Destouches, Montesquieu, Cardinal de Polignac." "Your Majesty has forgotten d'Alembert and Clairaut," said a courtier. "And Crébillon," the King continued, "and La Chaussée!"—"And the younger Crébillon!" somebody remarked, "he is said to be more likeable than his father; and, too, there is Abbé Prevost, and Abbé Olivet."—"Well," answered the King, "all this must have lunched or dined here in the past twenty-five years!"—"All this" was the King's name for France's famous men.

How foreign must literature have been to Louis XV

in his earlier years, if he spoke that way at a riper
age, in the days of Madame Pompadour! It certainly
was his least care; he left it to others to keep it within
its proper bounds.

Even though his relations with the Queen were no
longer as warm as at first, the connection between
them was not severed until the Queen, either from
bigotry or from fear of infection which one of her
ladies had talked her into, withdrew from the King.
From that time the entire Court was curious to find
out to what temptation the King would succumb. His
first gentleman-in-waiting—Bachélier, an influential
man, who knew that his influence would increase if
he could make the King dependent upon his discretion—eagerly arranged an assignation between the
King and a certain lady of the Court who showed herself inclined to assume the duties which the Queen
had dropped.

Madame Louise Julie de Mailly-Nesle was the first
of five sisters to whom the King, either in turn or at
the same time, made love. They occupied his time
and his thoughts from 1733 until December, 1744,
when the last of them, the one of whom he was most
deeply enamoured, suddenly died.

During these twelve years, in which Frederick the
Great, who was about the same age as Louis XV
(born 1712; Louis 1710), was maturing with hard
study and hard knocks into a genius, forceful of will,
and performing the first great deeds of his life, Louis
XV passed his days and nights in love affairs with
these five sisters.

2

The Maillys were a family with a military reputation that went back to the eleventh century. The
present Marquis de Nesle, father of Mademoiselle de
Nesle, could look back upon a distinguished line of
ancestors; but he himself was distinguished only for
his debts and his excesses. He had started with a
yearly income of 250,000 livres, and spent everything,
so that he finally eked out a miserable existence by
perpetrating frauds.

His eldest daughter, Madame de Mailly (born in 1710) had been married in 1726 to her own cousin, and soon thereafter she had a liaison with a Monsieur de Puisieux. The Court broke that up by appointing Puisieux French ambassador to Naples. Madame de Mailly was a brunette with fiery black eyes, a thin, oval face with a piquant expression, warm cheeks, a ravishing figure, with the proud grace of a bacchante. She was always beautifully dressed and half undressed, famous for her legs which were called the most shapely at Court. She was really in love with her own beauty. She never went to bed without dressing her hair and adorning herself with all her diamonds.

She burned with desire for the King, and found him "darling, like Cupid" and attracted his attention by means of her uncle, the Duke of Richelieu; she left it to Bachélier to arrange their first meeting and to work upon the King who in his youth was always shy and diffident, until the connection was made. Louis XV was, like so many degenerates, in the bottom of his soul filled with a desolate melancholy, so that at times he did not want to see anybody. He had no ambition for anything.

In spite of her coquettish appearance Madame de Mailly was a tender and loving woman who was genuinely devoted to her King. Her love was disinterested—an unheard-of thing for a royal favorite. She was not after a title, or money, or possessions. She was the most comfortable mistress a comfort-loving king could have wished. Her only weakness was her fondness for champagne; even as late as the year 1738 she drank through whole nights with the King. On June 26 of this year he went to bed at six o'clock in the morning (having first heard Mass, to be sure). On July 3 he got up from the table at five in the morning, played checkers for an hour, heard Mass, went to bed and did not get up until five o'clock in the afternoon.

Being parsimonious by nature he kept his mistress short of funds and allowed her to feel all the humiliations of dependency. In the beginning he gave her a handful of gold pieces several times, then nothing;

Bachélier, who happened to witness her embarrassment over the threats of her creditors, interested himself in the matter and persuaded the treasurer Chauvelin, who was anxious for the favorite's good-will, to take care of her expenses at certain night parties by means of the secret funds of the Ministry of the Exterior. Chauvelin, however, lost his place in 1737, and the Court made fun of Madame de Mailly's patched underwear.

Added to these hardships came the fact that with her twenty-eight years she was, according to the ideas of that time, an old woman, far too old for the King. Her own husband said to everyone who cared to listen to him, that he could not understand what the King found in his wife—she was not even young and was outshone by countless young women in Versailles. These remarks, repeated to the King on all sides, were a deep hurt to his vanity, and made him still harder on his mistress. One night, hearing through the fireplace of his bedroom two of the husbands of her sisters gossiping about the bad taste of the sovereign and about Louise's ugliness, he became so furious that he called down to them through the chimney: "Will you shut up, Flavacourt!"

Meanwhile Madame de Mailly took part in all ceremonies at the side of the King as before; on the rides to the various castles she always sat in his coach. Various ladies tried to flatter her, in order to get positions of honor at the Court. There was the Princess de Charlis, who wanted to have her lover, Vauréal, the Archbishop of Varennes, obtain the succession of Fleury. Likewise there was Madame d'Estrées, who gave the favorite the advice and hints which she received from her lover, Cardinal de Rohan. For a moment these ladies had the poor woman persuaded to demand that the King treat her as *maîtresse en titre,* make her a duchess, etc.; but the King returned answer that the scandals of Louis XIV's time were not going to be repeated; that never in his reign should bastards conceived in double adultery be allowed the same rank as princes of the blood. As can be seen, the King had his code of honor.

Madame de Mailly, who had a daily opportunity to feel the hostile attitude of Cardinal de Fleury, committed the indiscretion of mimicking the aged cardinal and making fun of his nightly carousals and his senile lusts. She reproached the King with being afraid of the old priest. One night she arrogantly asked the King who was by no means anxious to drop Fleury: "When are you going to think of discharging your old teacher?"

3

The favorite was unhappy. She had been more tranquil as long as she could conceal her relations with the King; but after five years the affair had become known, and she counted very little on the courage of the King to defend her against the Cardinal's attacks. The only friend in Court whom she thought she could trust was Bachélier, and it was he who had advised her never to trust anybody at Court.

At about that time, behind convent walls where supposedly the mind was occupied only by pious thoughts and romantic dreams, sat a young girl. It was the younger sister of Madame de Mailly, who sat and dreamed ambitious dreams, planned clear schemes whereby she could win the King's heart, overthrow the Cardinal, and dominate the Court. Daily she wrote to her sister, implored her to take her in, appealed to her goodness, displayed her sentiment, her childish grace, her tenderness, and her wit, surely not without the hope that her sister would show one or the other of her ingratiating letters to His Majesty, and that the King might become interested in the yearning young prisoner confined to the cloister.

Louise de Mailly needed a confidante from her immediate family, and Félicité de Nesle had always been her favorite sister. So she granted Félicité's wish. The young girl arrived and never left her sister's side, accompanying her on all her visits and showing her a more than sisterly devotion. Thus the name Félicité was constantly on Madame de Mailly's lips and before long she was admitted to the most intimate circle of Louis XV. From May, 1739, on, she lived in the palace with her sister; in June she began to be present at the King's suppers.

Félicité de Nesle was a brunette. She had a long neck and a more youthful but no less attractive figure than her elder sister. Her features were harder, without any trace of goodness or tenderness which was so characteristic of her sister. But she was far more talented and she based her confidence on that. She was lively and wilful, at times so full of wanton ideas that, even though sober, she gave the impression that she had drunk too freely; she affected naïveté when it seemed to make an impression, or flaming coquetry when she thought that was called for, and with it all was so witty, so roguish, and so entertaining that she soon was indispensable to the King, who thought her the most amusing child he had ever met. Soon he went so far as to dine with her constantly; she accompanied him on all his little journeys to Compiègne, to Fontainebleau, etc. He began to tease Madame de Mailly with the virtues of Félicité and contrasted them with her own faults. He even began to quarrel with her over trifles, to make himself unpleasant to her until one day he remarked significantly that he felt as deeply for her sister as for her.

The open interest which the King showed in the young girl, and the necessity which thereby arose to have her married, brought Félicité de Nesle many splendid offers. The Princess de Charolais decided the matter by having the Archbishop of Paris, who wished to become a cardinal, ask for the hand of the young lady for his relative, Monsieur de Luc, who was to take the name of Vintimille at the wedding. In September, 1739, Madame de Mailly notified her friends of the wedding; the King gave the bride a dowry of 200,000 livres, promised her a position as maid-of-honor to the Crown Princess, an income of 6,000 livres, besides an apartment in Versailles. He arrived from his country seat, la Meutte, at the moment when bride and bridegroom were about to retire, and did the bridegroom an honor he had never given anyone, "handed him the shirt." Soulavie, who wrote the memoirs of Marshal Richelieu, and who assumes that the King's relations with Mademoiselle de Nesle began in June, 1739, insists that the King and bridegroom changed places that night, so that Monsieur de Vintimille spent the night in la Meutte. This, however, is scarcely probable, as the couple lived for some time as husband and wife.

Madame de Mailly agreed to everything; she loved the King unselfishly. Madame de Vintimille, absolutely sure of her power over Louis, did not hesitate to leave her sister near him. While the latter had suffered for a long time from the tiresome, even humiliating influence of the Princess de Charolais, Madame de Vintimille got rid of the lady in the twinkling of an eye; all she did was to draw the King's attention to the Princess' efforts to make her lover, Vauréal, Minister of the Exterior, and the Princess fell into disgrace.

After the death of the Duke of Grammont, Count de Grammont asked the two sisters, with both of whom he was intimate, for a recommendation to the position then vacant, that of Colonel of the regiment of Béarn and Navarre. The presentation of the list of applicants by the Cardinal had so far been a pure formality; the Cardinal himself always made the choice. This time the King at once arbitrarily appointed Grammont to the vacant position. It was not so much a personal interest in Count de Grammont which prompted Madame de Vintimille, as her desire to get the King accustomed to independence of His Eminence.

But Madame de Vintimille also desired to engage in politics and to this end she used her sister as a willing tool. The two brothers Belle-Isle were close friends of Madame de Mailly. Grandsons of the great financial swindler, Fouquet, they had to suffer from this relationship for a long time. The elder brother, later Duke and Marshal, the more able though the more delicate, was a keen politician, quick at repartee and very eloquent. He showed the two sisters that the foreign policy of old Fleury was timid and unwise. War should be declared against Austria and Austria should be divided. It would be quite simple: France would find dependable allies in Prussia, in

Piedmont, and in the elector of Bavaria, for whom France could secure the imperial crown.

Madame de Vintimille wished to reawaken and satisfy the national pride. For that she needed a hero and thought she had found him in the person of the elder Belle-Isle. Belle-Isle was as shallow as he was eloquent.

In vain old Fleury emphasized the obligations France had assumed, the loan she had received, the prospect of acquiring Lorraine, and the King's pledge. All this meant little to the sisters. Madame de Vintimille readily got the King's consent, and war was declared. She had Belle-Isle appointed ambassador to Frankfort, so that he could conduct the election of the emperor, and Charles VII was elected. But things went otherwise than she had hoped, partly because Belle-Isle did not get all the troops he had requested, partly because everything went wrong. France met only defeats, and the eighty-nine-year-old Fleury had to make humiliating advances to Maria Theresa to reëstablish the peace.

In the later editions of his *Précis du Siècle de Louis XV* Voltaire omitted the passage in which he at first openly said that the Cardinal wished to prevent the war, but that the brothers Belle-Isle, supported by a lady in great power at the moment, had resolved to change Europe's physiognomy.

For a moment, it seemed that the brothers had a bright outlook. Marshal Belle-Isle appeared and was treated in Frankfort more like one of the most powerful electors than the French ambassador. It was probably then that he dazzled Bernstorff and became his idol; his pretty wife played a part. But in Bohemia and in Bavaria, the French armies crumbled to pieces. In December, 1742, Belle-Isle saved only about 13,000 men from the occupation of Prague.

By that time, however, his protectress had been dead more than a year.

4

After the death of the Princess de Conti, the King purchased her fine country seat Choisi, on the Seine;

it was famous for its terrace overlooking the river, and for the eight marble statues in its garden, which had been carved at the order of Fouquet in imitation of ancient sculpture.

The King gave this château to his favorite as a residence. It was furnished with the most beautiful mirrors, and sculpture, and equipped with discreet corridors and secret doors. It was situated at the foot of a hill, protected from the wind, near the forest of Sénart. The King himself supervised the decoration, had trees planted in the garden and had others removed for the sake of the view. Here, Félicité de Vintimille kept the King away from the atmosphere of the Court; never was he in Versailles more than one whole day in a week; he saw the Cardinal for a quarter of an hour during a week. And here the energetic young woman tried to teach her King to have a will of his own, to make him keep an eye on domestic affairs, to enable him by this introductory schooling to keep a watchful eye on affairs of state. For Félicité it meant a step in this direction when the King dismissed a cup-bearer who stole his champagne. She even tried to free him from the guardianship of Bachélier, and dared to ask him: "Sire, are you going to tell this, too, to your valet?"

It was her intention to overthrow the Cardinal and to supplant his régime by another which would be more sensible and energetic. She induced the King to work, to become interested in current affairs. For herself she had independent mental interests, poor as French soil was for these. Her correspondence with Madame du Deffand reveals an enthusiasm for the wit of this lady, and the intellectual life she represented, which is surprising in so calculating a young person. She is enamored of Madame du Deffand's letters. She is "transposed into a dream world" when she gets one, and longs to get acquainted with her circle: "You speak to me of Madame du Châtelet. I am dying to see her. Now that you describe her to me, I am bound to know her as she is. I am grateful to you for telling me what you think; it is a pleasure to me to have your guidance. I will try to meet her and then the King of Prussia shall be the theme of our conversation, if she will do me the honor of listening to me; for I am afraid that she will find me stupid."

Madame de Vintimille was in the eighth month of her pregnancy when she was seized with a fever, for which the physicians of that time could recommend nothing but blood-letting—three times a day. As it was absolutely essential that the King go to Versailles, he left her in Óhoisi, in the company of her sister, two noblemen and the Duke d'Ayen (who, according to her husband and d'Argenson, was her second-string lover); he asked Madame de Mailly during the three days of his necessary stay in Versailles, to keep him posted four times daily and by express messengers, as to the patient's condition.

Upon his return the King told her that he was going to give her the residence the Duke and Duchess of Fleury had occupied until then. She hoped to feel strong enough to take possession of the apartment the following week. But the fever would not abate. Her mood was sometimes irritable, sometimes deeply melancholy.

She arrived in Versailles with a great following of friends and admirers, and the King dined every night in her room.

On September first she gave birth to a son. On the eighth she was suddenly taken with so severe a pain that she thought she had been poisoned. The next morning she died. The body was opened by physicians, poorly stitched up again, left naked in the bedroom, where anyone could enter. As no dead body was permitted to remain in a royal palace, it was removed to the corner of a coach-house where it remained until it did not present a human appearance, while the face still had the distortion of her death spasm. The mob of Versailles mocked the poor body with that contempt which it often shows for illicit love, and which it showed for all Louis XV's mistresses.

5

The shock of this sudden death, and the indignities heaped upon the helpless corpse, induced the King to

see in the occurrence a penalty for his sins, proof of
an avenging God. He feared Divine retribution; he
cowered at the thought of Hell; surely when he died
it would open its jaws to swallow him. At first it was
in vain that Madame de Mailly assured him that Hell
was a nursery-tale. He wept a great deal, constantly
had the word religion on his lips, and tried to live
with Madame de Mailly as brother and sister. He did
not succeed. As the good and tender comforter she
was, Louise de Mailly now held a new attraction for
him. He was moved by the tears she shed at the death
of her sister. He resolved to keep her near him always, and for that purpose he had an apartment
furnished in Versailles, right above his little gallery,
under the pretense of preparing new quarters for the
Count de Meuse.

Here the King and his favorite led the strangest
existence, a life of remorse and desire, of tears seasoned with kisses. Some days he fasted, as a sort of
atonement for the nightly indulgences; when embrac-
ing Madame de Mailly, he had death and burial constantly on his lips, while she wept with him.

Every evening his grief was more assuaged and his
respect for Louise de Mailly increased. She had
learned from her younger sister to be independent.
She continued the political schemes of the deceased.
The Cardinal detested Belle-Isle and spoke so contemptuously of him that, on his return from Germany, where it is true he had accomplished but little,
the Marshal was received with extreme coldness, not
only by the Cardinal, but also by the King and the
courtiers. He protested and proffered his resignation. But Madame de Mailly did not give in, she
used her influence in every possible place, and succeeded in changing the King's mind so completely
that in May, 1743, he raised Belle-Isle to the rank
of Duke.

Louise de Mailly had a big heart; she spared herself no pains to help those whom she liked; it was
painful to her to see anyone insulted by the silence
the King nearly always kept, and she astonished the
entire Court by inducing the King to speak a few

words to those to whom he so far had been cold. And
Madame de Mailly rejoiced over everyone who was
content with his King.

However, while her better side was developing this
way and her star was apparently in the ascendant,
the King began to tire of her tête-à-têtes. He was
bored with this woman whom he had scorned once
before, and who became visibly older day by day.

But he had not sufficient energy to tear himself
away and, as was his habit, he showed his weariness
only by malicious digs. It was about that time that
the smartest and shrewdest courtier of the epoch induced the final break with England.

While Madame de Mailly was under the influence
of the Princess de Charolais, the latter had constantly
warned her of the Duke of Richelieu. The few times
he was invited for supper he made a deep impression
upon His Majesty, partly by his wit, partly by reputation as a successful gallant. The Princess de Charolais whose love he had accepted some time ago, and
then scorned, again accepted and then completely
forgotten, harbored a deep hatred for him because he
had held her favor so lightly. She succeeded in persuading Madame de Mailly that no one of the King's
associates could become more dangerous to her than
this man who had made inconstancy his principle
and faithlessness his obligation. Madame de Mailly,
therefore, showed an icy coolness from the beginning,
which it cost him a considerable effort to thaw and
which for a long time stood in the way of his ambition. Now, returning to Court, he had a bitter prejudice against the favorite. He was firmly resolved to
secure for the King another and younger mistress
who would be absolutely devoted to the Duke, and
with whom he could work in harmony.

6

Madame de Mailly had a younger sister, Marie-
Anne de Mailly-Nesle, who in 1734, at the age of
seventeen, had been married to the Marquis de la
Tournelle, a pious nobleman who lived on his estate.

This estate had become very valuable, thanks to a canal engineered by the great Vauban.

Probably because de la Tournelle's young wife was bored in the country, he obtained a commission as a lieutenant-colonel in Condé's infantry regiment, through the influence of Madame de Mailly. At the first meeting with the young Marquise the King could not refrain from exclaiming: "Mon Dieu, how beautiful she is!" Her portrait, done by Nattier in 1740, brought fame to the painter and at the same time gave her the reputation of being the most beautiful lady in Versailles.

Marie-Anne's appearance at Court put the Cardinal in a state of the highest perturbation. He could cope with Madame de Mailly whose aim was to reign over the King's heart; but he feared the political influence Madame de la Tournelle might wield. The memoirs of the Duchess of Brancas give us a glimpse of this. The Duchess was an intimate friend of Richelieu, and Fleury all but cross-examined her to find out whether or not Richelieu was planning to put Madame de la Tournelle in the place of her sister. She denied any knowledge of it.

Richelieu was thinking of nothing else.

Madame de Mazarin, the aunt of the sisters, on her deathbed put Madame de la Tournelle and Madame de Flavacourt under the guardianship of Madame de Mailly. By her death the office of a lady-in-waiting to the Queen became vacant. Madame de la Tournelle applied for it, and her eldest sister supported her application. As was his habit, the Cardinal delayed a long time before mentioning the matter to the King; then he handed the King a list of the applicants, on which he had placed the name of Madame de la Tournelle last. The King took a pencil, wrote Madame de la Tournelle's name at the top of the list, and said: "The Queen is informed and will award the place to this lady." The Cardinal and the Minister Maurepas, wishing to prevent this appointment if possible, pointed out that Madame de Villars had been promised the appointment long before. But as that lady absolutely declined to enter a contest with the house of Nesle, the plan had to be dropped.

Young as Madame de la Tournelle was, she had three love-affairs behind her: one with Monsieur de la Trémoille, another with Monsieur de Soubise, and a third with the young Duke d'Agénois, for whom she still retained tender feelings. But her ambition was stronger than any erotic passion. The King fell head over heels in love with her, and had the Duke d'Agénois' letters opened by the police. One day he showed her a few letters which could not fail to lower the Duke in her esteem. The handsome young man, according to the carefully prepared plan of his uncle, Richelieu—who was also the uncle of the Nesle sisters—had been sent on an official journey to Languedoc. There, as the letters revealed, in the solitude of provincial life he had been responsive to a certain young lady's advances. The King put the letters of the faithful Agénois, as he called him, on the table before Madame de la Tournelle, exclaiming: "Ah! le beau billet qu'a la Châtre, voilà ce que m'envoie la poste!" The first half of this remark is a quotation: Ninon had given la Châtre at his request a written assurance of her fidelity. One day, during a tête-à-tête with one of his successors, she recalled la Châtre's certificate of fidelity and laughingly exclaimed: "Le beau billet," etc.

Madame de la Tournelle's appointment as lady-in-waiting did not necessarily make the position of her sister at Court impossible. But Richelieu and his party, in which Madame de Tencin was very active, were interested in depriving Madame de Mailly of her influential position to make it easier to remove her from Versailles forever. They played upon her credulity and allayed her suspicions; Madame de la Tournelle herself, as well as Madame de Flavacourt, assured her of the sisterly affection and absolutely unquestionable gratitude of the new favorite. The sisters appealed to her goodness, to her desire to do what the King would like best. If she would resign her position she could be sure of the King's infinite gratitude, she could retain his undying affection for a mistress who had shown herself equal to a sacrifice that proved the nobility of her soul.

They succeeded in persuading the poor, credulous

woman so completely that in a letter to Cardinal
Fleury, the contents of which Richelieu and Madame
de la Tournelle had talked over beforehand with the
King, she renounced her position in favor of her sister, Madame de Flavacourt.

On September 20, 1742, the Court heard news:
Madame de la Tournelle had succeeded Madame de
Mazarin as lady-in-waiting to the Queen, and Madame
de Mailly resigned her position, income and all, and
without any compensation, in favor of Madame de
Flavacourt.

Doubtless, Madame de Mailly had hoped that her
sacrifice would mean so much to the King that she
would not have to go away, that she would be allowed to live on in the palace near him.

7

The King, who had never known the least resistance from a woman, was surprised and annoyed by
Madame de la Tournelle's calm reserve and her negative attitude. He wrote; she did not answer; he wrote
again, and again received no answer. He was used
to seeing women led before him like deer at the
battues. At first he thought of favoring some one else.
But this time he was caught. His impatience did no
good. After every attempt to revolt he had to return,
an ever more and more abject adorer. He felt consumed by unsatisfied desire. But Madame de la Tournelle was firmly resolved to make herself indispensable. She did not want to run the risk of being
thrown aside, as her sister was now—by her own
machinations. She treated the King about as Anne
Boleyn, after the dismissal of her sister Mary Carey
—had treated the King of England.

It can easily be understood what the elder sister
suffered as witness of all these erotic skirmishes. She
dined and supped alone with the King as usual; but
the meals were extremely dismal. The King was
either silent, or else made some remark that made
her cry. Nevertheless she fancied she had won back
Louis' favor. One day, however, he shattered her

illusions by telling her that he was madly in love with Madame de la Tournelle, that although he so far had not possessed her, he hoped to do so soon, and that therefore he could not love another any longer.

Deeply humiliated, but with the feeling that she never could do without her beloved, Madame de Mailly, kneeling, promised to be content with everything if she only were permitted to stay. The King replied unfeelingly that she must leave the palace that very day. She dragged herself after him, fell at his feet, and begged for a postponement, just a short postponement. If she were allowed to stay she would keep this new passion of his secret from his subjects. If they were to hear of it, it might decrease their respect. Moved, Louis consented, but permitted her to stay that one night only, and complained to Richelieu of that. Richelieu promised to arrange everything. He went to Madame de Mailly, made it plain to her how little she was considering her dignity if she clung to the King and the palace. He offered to accompany her to Paris if she wanted him to. She answered: "I shall make this sacrifice, though it kill me; I will go to Paris tonight."

We can read the letters Madame de la Tournelle wrote to her uncle Richelieu, after she had succeeded in driving away her sister. Her attitude is absolutely hard. She uses the most vulgar expressions: *"Sûrement Meuse vous aura mandé la peine que j'ai eue à faire déguerpir madame de Mailly."*

She describes how she still put the King off. As often as he expected to reach the goal of his desires, he saw himself disappointed.

"He has informed you that the matter between us was all arranged; in a letter of this morning he asks me to explain that this is an error; for he does not want you to think more happened than really did. It is true: at the time he wrote he imagined that it would happen that same night. But I have put certain obstacles in the way, for which I am not at all sorry."

She states her conditions. She wishes to be *maîtresse déclarée*, as Madame de Montespan had been under Louis XIV. She does not want a modest apartment like Madame de Mailly, but a palace where she can receive the King "in a way worthy of him." Furthermore, she wants a country estate, an allowance of fifty thousand livres a month, diamonds worth five hundred thousand livres, the right to draw money from the state treasury, if necessary, and finally the title of duchess, acknowledged by Parliament. In case she should become pregnant, her condition should not be kept a secret and the child should be pronounced legitimate.

The King, always afraid of expenses, afraid of public opinion, afraid to make any decision at all, shied at these demands. But the favorite would make no compromise, affected indifference, spoke of returning to the Duke d'Agénois, insisting that the intercepted letters meant nothing more than a passing fancy, not real infidelity. At the same time she goaded the King's passion by clever coquetry.

The public was persuaded that she had capitulated long ago. She received through the mail all the scurrilous ballads which were sung in Paris about her and the King. Most of these verses can scarcely be quoted. We may cite one which merely says this: If the mob dares be shocked to see three sisters relieve each other, the Archbishop de Tencin would undoubtedly absolve their sins:

> Si la canaille ose crier
> De voir trois sœurs se relayer,
> Au grand Tencin envoyez la,
> Alléluia.

Apparently amused, Madame de la Tournelle herself sang this song to her guests.

Long before she gave the King any right over her person, he as well as she, had to stand all kinds of persecution. The Cardinal severely upbraided his former pupil, and showed him intercepted letters from Parisians, stating that: "The King is no longer loved as much as before." He appealed to his religious emotions, threatened him with God's ire. All in vain. Then the Cardinal saw the necessity of inducing Maurepas to let loose the flood of mocking ditties which he and his circle had manufactured;

they whistled about Madame de la Tournelle's ears like bullets. But nothing could move her, nor was there anything to make an impression upon the King, who was madly in love.

For a long time she let him languish in vain and scratch timidly at her door. He was not admitted until she felt perfectly sure of her power over him. The peace and cheerfulness which, in December, 1742, appeared on the bewildered face of the monarch was sufficient proof to the courtiers that Æneas and Dido had found each other in the grotto. From now on, Louis XV behaved like one in a giddy ecstasy. The affairs of France interested him even less than before. He has no room in his thoughts for the siege of Prague, nor for the defeats in Bavaria, nor for the state of his army. He rushed through the meetings of the Privy Council; he feasted on fine food and good wines. When his mistress wrote to her uncle, he added a wanton postscript of the kind that can be written, but not printed. Neither victories nor defeats mattered to him compared to the fact that Richelieu had sent trout from the Lake of Geneva, or an especially slimy anecdote.

Then, at the beginning of the year 1743, the ninety-year-old Cardinal de Fleury died, and the King, finally released from all guardianship, breathed freely. The favorite had moved to Versailles, and she gave the King what he needed: quiet. She could lie the whole day long on the chaise-longue, wrapped in thought, and nothing would bring her out of it.

One day she noticed that the King was ill-humored toward her. She could not imagine the cause. But she showed no curiosity. The reason for his ill-humor was that he had opened a letter from Richelieu to her which prescribed a plan for the favorite's conduct, hour by hour. Soon she noticed that Louis was becoming very self-conscious in his attitude toward her, and also that he was adopting a hostile view of the ambitious hopes of Richelieu. She said not a word about it, but refused to appear at the dinner-table, had her meals brought in from a restaurant—and that in the Palace of Versailles!—and refused the King's visits, as long as she was not in surroundings worthy of his and her own positions. While she maintained this attitude, she showed an excellent knowledge of human nature, by humoring the King's desire to appear impenetrable. She was clever enough to feel him out and never to say anything derogatory about one he valued, nor fall out with anyone to whose company he was used. She kept a friendly attitude toward the Noailles family although they stuck faithfully to Madame de Mailly.

The King remained deeply in love. He gave Madame de la Tournelle the petname of "Princess" and was constantly in her and her sister's company. Madame de Flavacourt, to whom he was very partial, was given the petname of Poulette. She was unusually beautiful, cultivated a reserved manner, and answered every importunate compliment with an amazed, almost frightened expression.

The King liked the fourth sister still better, the recently married Duchesse de Lauraguais, a malicious gossip. Her appearance alone was enough to break up the boredom of the Court; being merry herself, she spread a contagious merriment about her. She had not the regal beauty of her sister but she was pretty and popular; not slender, but stout, with that lively, bursting health more typical of a woman of the middle class than of a duchess. Her sensuality was not of the inaccessible but of the broad kind. One day when she was chattering roguishly and wantonly, which smoothed every wrinkle from the King's brow, he fell into her open arms and forgot himself in her warm embrace. When she presided, the suppers were jollier than ever before. The King did not refrain from petty intimacies in the presence of company and soon it was rumored at Court that the King and the Duchesse de Lauraguais had found each other in a common caprice. One can easily imagine that all kinds of comments were made about the entrance of the fourth sister into the lists. This fourth, however, was not ambitious. A comfortable armchair, in which she could take it easy and talk scandal about her neighbor, was all she asked of life.

8

Marie-Anne was too proud and too clever to up-
braid either the King or her sister for these incidents.
She gave no sign of having noticed or heard anything
about it. But this new incident had an unexpected
effect upon her feelings. She began to fall in love with
the King, and after some time she realized to her
own surprise that she actually loved him. At the same
moment she felt the passion in herself, it increased in
the King. Marie-Anne took full possession of him,
gave free play to all her whims. She provoked him,
vexed him, resisted him, denied him admission to
her room and her embraces, and won him back by
showing him in a thousand different ways her beauty,
whose charm could not be rivaled by the grosser
attractions of her sister.

Nattier painted her a shining figure of Strength,
with a tiger-skin around her shoulders and a cuirass
over the fine, full breast: a young body with splendid,
rippling white skin, with a shining forehead and a
bewitching look in her big blue eyes, and with the
smile of a child on her moist lips; her expression is
at once passionate and tender.

The Minister Maurepas was the nucleus of the
opposition to the favorite, and his envious old wife
set all kinds of obstacles in the way of her advancement. But the King had no desire save to comply with
all of Marie-Anne's wishes.

On the banks of the Indre river was the duchy of
Châteauroux, whose fields brought an annual income
of 85,000 livres. Some time back the King had bought
it from his relative, the Count de Clermont, who had
to pay debts. It was given for life to Madame de la
Tournelle, who became Duchess of Châteauroux. As
duchesses were entitled to a seat of honor in the
Queen's Court, every new duchess was presented to
her. This time the presentation took on a ceremonial
air. There were eight ladies present, five of whom
were sitting; among these the Duchess of Lauraguais.
When the Duchess of Châteauroux stepped from the
King's chambers to take her place before the Queen,

Maria Leszczinska said to her: "Madame, I congratulate you upon the favor bestowed upon you by the King."

The patent of nobility, which Maurepas was compelled to make out, reads in part:

"Because of these reasons, and because Our dear and much beloved cousin, Marie-Anne de Mailly, widow of the Sieur Marquis de la Tournelle, is descended from one of the greatest and most famous houses of Our Kingdom, because she is related to Our House and to the oldest of Europe; further, because her ancestors have done great and important services to Our Crown for several centuries, because she herself is attached to the Queen, Our dear Wife, as lady-in-waiting, and because to these excellences she adds all the virtues and worthy qualities of mind and heart, which have brought her universal respect and esteem, We have found it fitting to bestow upon her by letters patent of October 21st ult. the duchy and peerage of Châteauroux in Berry, with all lands and all appurtenances . . ."

As a duchess, Marie-Anne had reached her immediate goal. To fortify her position, her uncle Richelieu worked with untiring zeal, in alliance with that genius of intrigue, Madame de Tencin. This lady was formerly a nun who had three pregnancies. Through her brother the Cardinal she obtained a papal letter releasing her from her vows and giving her the title of canoness. Richelieu had made her acquaintance when she came to Paris from Grenoble to give birth in secret to d'Alembert, and then abandon the child entirely. She sought recognition as his mother after d'Alembert became famous, but her son repudiated her. She developed into a politician who appreciated the value of men of letters in politics, and cultivated them assiduously. With her remarkably clever and adaptable brain she was able to talk from any point of view, according to her company. We have seen how highly Voltaire esteemed her. She had not only a sane mind, but one that was overfull of sanity, the result of a life unusually full of experience.

Madame de Tencin lived for her brother only. And Richelieu, she thought, was the only one who could make her brother minister. She, therefore, attached herself to him, arranged his financial affairs, supervised his son's education, spied for him at Court and in town smoothed the way for him to the Queen, warned him of every threatening danger, warned him against giving way to old grudges, or to sudden impulses, kept her ears alert for his advantage, and informed him of any impending development such as the growing influence of the Bishop of Mirepoix over the King, which was so disastrous to Voltaire's application for membership in the Academy. It was she who pointed out to Richelieu how stupid it was to protect such a wicked person as Voltaire, just out of pure friendship and admiration for the Duchess of Châteauroux.

She was attached to Richelieu because of their mutual interests only. She distributed her favors impartially among a considerable number of friends; she had a passion only for her brother. She defended her relations with him by recalling the case of another brother and sister, the Duchess of Grammont and the Duke of Choiseul.

It was Madame de Tencin who first had the inspiration to make the Duchess of Châteauroux a political personality, an idea soon taken up by the favorite. Thus, without any hatred on her part, she crossed Voltaire's efforts, the great political problem that Amelot, the Minister of Foreign Affairs, had laid on him. For a long time Amelot had hoped to make use of the friendship between Voltaire and the King of Prussia.

9

Very rarely in the history of the world has there been a friendship between a sovereign and a creative artist that gained fame for both.

In ancient times, Aristotle was Alexander's teacher, and Alexander sent him material for study from his campaigns. But he had no influence upon the philosopher.

Cæsar and Cicero were acquaintances. Cicero was Cæsar's political enemy, nevertheless Cæsar paid homage to him as a literary figure and answered his attacks with chivalrous politeness; but neither was Cæsar indebted to Cicero for mental enrichment, nor Cicero to Cæsar.

In a later century the friendship between Goethe and Charles Augustus lasted from the early youth of both until the Prince's death. Goethe's friendship with the Duke of Weimar brought him an assured position, which in turn brought him many invaluable experiences. But he got no ideas from his prince. Charles Augustus was no genius, in spite of his great qualities.

More recently, there is the connection between Richard Wagner and Louis II. Wagner was indebted to King Louis for wealth and the leisure for work; but mentally the King exerted no influence upon the composer.

The friendship of Voltaire and Frederick the Great is unique. It was not perfectly harmonious. For the first fifteen years it was enthusiastic; then it was undermined and broke down under Voltaire's lack of restraint and Frederick's resentment. Later, the breach was healed and so remained.

This relationship shows the spirit of the eighteenth century. The king and the poet belonged to different worlds, even though they spoke the same language. Writer and king had genius, and they influenced one another.

When, in August, 1736, Voltaire received the first letter from Frederick, Crown Prince of Prussia, he was nearly forty-two years old. The writer of the letter was twenty-four. Voltaire was an international celebrity, and the most famous writer of the epoch. Frederick was a young prince, known only for what he had suffered.

He had suffered for his talents as Voltaire had for his wit and revolutionary leanings. Both had been victims of the brutality of the age and of the arbitrary power of the government.

Frederick's father, whom Carlyle has idealized, was in spite of his great abilities as an organizer, stubborn and hot-tempered, in spite of his sense of justice, rough and cruel. He had prescribed a plan for his son's education, omitting everything unessential, such as Latin and literature. He hated anything foreign; if he permitted French it was because German at that time was scarcely regarded as a language. He liked to thrash his subjects personally on the street, when they had aroused his dissatisfaction by anything.

Because Frederick as a boy indulged in forbidden studies, made debts and showed no interest in military parades, his father wanted him to renounce the throne. When he refused, his father treated him with cruelty and sneered at him for a coward for putting up with it. In 1730, Frederick tried to flee to England. But an intercepted letter to his friend Katte betrayed the plan to the King. Again the Prince was cruelly maltreated and then tried before a court-martial, intended by his father to sentence him to death. Such was the style of the time. Twelve years before Peter the Great had his son flogged to death, and himself administered some of the lashes. As the Prussian court-martial was not blindly obedient, the King had to be content with having his son sent to Küstrin for imprisonment.

At the age of seventeen, Frederick had a love affair with the daughter of a teacher in Potsdam. He used to accompany her on the flute while she played the clavichord. The King had her led round the Potsdamer Platz and publicly whipped before the eyes of the Prince.

In Küstrin, Frederick's friend Katte, because he was an accomplice in the plan to flee, was decapitated under the Prince's window, so close that Frederick could give him his hand in farewell.

10

In his first letters Frederick approaches Voltaire with deep devotion and gratitude: Voltaire's works (he says) convey a wealth of spirit. At every re-reading they appear new. He is so great that by the sheer force of his personality he decides the issue as to whether ancient or modern literature is the

better. There is nobody in Europe who cannot learn
from Voltaire. He hopes Voltaire will not find him
unworthy of his instruction, unimportant as he is;
for what does high birth amount to beside genius!

Voltaire, surprised by such an ovation from the
son of a King, answers gladly from Cirey: So there
actually was an heir to a throne, who could appreciate his ideas! A man like Frederick should be able
to establish the golden age in his empire and rise
above royal dignity to humanity.

Frederick answers: Is it possible that the same Voltaire to whom our hands build altars and statues, is
thrust aside in his fatherland! This is a paradox, a
puzzle. Voltaire has no fault but that of being superior to other people. If Frederick should ever get to
France, his first question would be: Where is Monsieur de Voltaire? King, Court, Paris, Versailles,
women, amusements—none of these things would
make his journey worth while.

They share constant allusions to classical antiquity.
Frederick calls Voltaire Apollo or Socrates, while
Voltaire calls Frederick Trajan or Titus. He com-
bines Vergil's talents with the virtues of Augustus.

Frederick explains in rhyme: The verse in which
you mention my name will bring me immortality.
Without you the name would get no more than a
place on the genealogical table.

The young Prince was in the habit of writing
French verses every day. Now he sent them to Voltaire to be returned corrected. For a foreigner he had
an admirable command of French; but his artistic
culture was not high enough to enable him to realize
the absurdity of hoping to be a lyric poet in another
language than his own; he was still less aware that
although he was an excellent speaker he was not a
poet at all. In the odes, by which, as Voltaire says in
his letters, "His Royal Highness condescended to
embellish French poetry," he gives "amitié" four syl-
lables, instead of three, "carrière" three instead of
four, and "tête" rhymes with "trompette." His spelling was outrageous.

The delivery of these letters was so slow that Frederick considered it incomprehensibly fast, when a

letter of April 17 reached him on May 9. Two virile intellects are revealed in them. It is not surprising that Voltaire appears to be superior to the young man at the beginning. But a year and a half later there occurs a case of conflicting opinions in which Frederick proves to be the more unprejudiced and logical thinker. This was the discussion of Wolff's conclusions on the question of free will.

Voltaire's letters are less outstanding for his wit, which became so famous, than for clearness, logic, and a charm which is the charm of strength.

From the first, the Prince wished to make the personal acquaintance of Voltaire. But the latter felt tied to Cirey and its mistress:

"I would regard it a priceless piece of luck to pay my respects to Your Royal Highness. One travels to Rome to see churches, paintings, ruins and bas-reliefs. A Prince like yourself deserves a far longer journey; he is a far greater rarity. But I cannot abuse the friendship of the one whom I have to thank for the hospitable refuge where I now am, by forsaking it to make this excursion. You doubtless think like Julian, that great man so unjustly maligned, that friends should always be preferred to kings."

Frederick sends presents: a cane with a gold knob, carved with a head of Socrates; his own portrait, which he ordered the moment Voltaire expressed a desire to own it; a valuable writing stand, accompanied by verses, to the Marquise du Châtelet. From Rheinsberg he sends his friend, Monsieur de Kaiserling, to Cirey, to pay the Prince's respects to the goddess of the town; he told his friend that this enchantress possessed all the gifts of the mind, and spent her time in searching for the truth. In reality Frederick could not abide her, as she stood in the way of his wishes: "Please tell Madame Marquise du Châtelet that she is the only one to whom I should be content to leave Monsieur de Voltaire, for she alone is worthy of possessing him."

Madame du Châtelet pointed out that the Prince so cruelly treated by his father, was not King as yet, and therefore not his own master. "When he becomes

King, we shall both go and visit him." This plan was never carried out.

In the year 1736, Voltaire succeeded in procuring for his protégé Thiriot the position of correspondent to the Prussian Crown Prince. Thiriot scrupulously sent all Parisian news of the day, including all malicious and spiteful pamphlets directed against Voltaire. When Madame du Châtelet learned of this, she could not refrain from writing the Crown Prince an angry letter to warn him of this pretended friend of Voltaire, who aroused her deep mistrust.

11

On May 31, 1740, Frederick became King. At last he was free to entertain anybody and to see Voltaire. This delighted him, busy as he was right after his accession. He made his debut as a true pupil of Voltaire: he abolished torture, and did away with the cruel poaching laws. He disbanded the Palace guard of giants, which his father had recruited, shanghaied or purchased at a high price. He recalled Wolff who had been expelled from Germany, and made him a Professor in the University at Halle.

The first meeting of the two men is agreed upon. Frederick is to see those clever hands, those clear eyes, kiss those eloquent lips:

> Je baiserai cent fois cette bouche, éloquente
> Dans le sérieux et le badin,
> Dont la voix, folâtre et touchante,
> Va du cothurne au brodequin
> Toujours enchanteresse et toujours plus charmante.

Voltaire was in the Netherlands, busy publishing Frederick's book *Anti-Machiavelli,* in which strictly honest politics were defended. The King did not live up to his book which was meant as an attack on the French minister, Cardinal Fleury.

Voltaire asks the King to bring drops along for him, as he surely would faint from joy. Frederick writes: "It will be the most wonderful day of my life; I believe I shall die from it."

Frederick was stricken with chills; the place of meeting had to be changed, and Voltaire had to travel to him.

At Moyland Castle, near Cleves, he was led through several empty halls to a bare room, where on a bed, covered with a riding coat, lay a little man. It was Frederick. The fever was cured by his emotion. From the eleventh to the fourteenth of September the two great men were together for the first time. One might have anticipated a little disappointment on Frederick's part. But a week later he writes to Jordan:

"So, I have seen this Voltaire, whom I was so anxious to know. I was suffering from chills and fever and my soul was as affected, as my body was weakened. But with people of his type one must not be ill; one has to feel even better than normal. He has the eloquence of Cicero, the gentleness of Pliny, and the wisdom of Agrippa. He unites the virtues of the three greatest men of ancient times. (Frederick knew no more about classical antiquity, than to think of Cicero, Pliny and Agrippa as its three greatest men.) His mind is at work continuously. Each drop of ink from his pen is a spark of his spirit. . . . Madame du Châtelet is to be envied his possession."

At various times, but always in vain, Voltaire had tried to win membership in the French Academy. He tried especially hard in 1732. He did not get even half of the votes. A member of the Academy, entirely forgotten today, who at the age of twenty-seven was permanent secretary at *l'Academie des inscriptions et belles-lettres*, Claude Gros de Boze, declared on that occasion that beyond question Voltaire could never become a member. Foreign countries were already of a different opinion. D'Alembert tells of an Academy member who traveled in Germany and informed the sovereign that Voltaire had no seat in the French Academy, and received the answer: "Who then *is* in it?"

When the death of Cardinal de Fleury created a vacancy, Voltaire applied ambitiously for the seat, wrote all kinds of letters, in which he insisted that he was a good Catholic, that he did not know what these *Lettres Philosophiques* were, that people ascribed to him. He denied that he had ever published a book of that title—an attitude which was not at all in accordance with Frederick's taste. But it was well known that nobody was admitted to the Academy who was a Jansenist or a freethinker. The first Voltaire could deny without difficulty; but the latter was less easy to disprove.

However, it seemed self-evident that he ought to be in the French Academy. King Louis gave his consent, apparently at the instance of Madame de Châteauroux who, in turn, was influenced by Richelieu. But he could withdraw this consent, and this was to be brought about by means of intrigues.

In his *Memoires pour servir à l'histoire de M. de Voltaire,* he himself tells bitterly the course of that affair, in the following words:

"An old ass by the name of Boyer, the Dauphin's tutor, a former Theatine, later Bishop of Mirepoix, took it upon himself to support the caprice of Monsieur Maurepas. To this Boyer the King left all matters concerning the clergy. This matter he construed as one which belonged to ecclesiastical discipline. He explained to the King that it was blasphemy for a man like myself to succeed a cardinal. I knew that Maurepas was behind it all. I went to see the minister and told him: 'A seat in the Academy is not an important honor, but it is nevertheless distressing to be excluded from it, after one had been proposed. You are opposing Madame de Châteauroux, who is loved by the King, and the Maréchal de Richelieu, who guides her. What connection is there, I ask you, between your quarrels and a seat in the French Academy? I implore you to answer me frankly. In case Madame de Châteauroux should prove to be more influential than the Bishop of Mirepoix, would you still resist me?' He thought for a moment, then he said: 'Yes, I shall destroy you.' "

True, the King had given Voltaire his consent; but Richelieu was induced by Madame de Tencin to change his mind, and the wind, therefore, shifted. The Bishop of Bayeux, a gracious prelate whose nearest claim to literary prestige was the fact that he had charge of a little provincial academy in the city of Caen, was urged to apply for the vacant seat; he was elected unanimously on March 22, 1742.

As one can imagine, Voltaire was highly incensed, and so was Frederick. He wrote: "To be sure, I am not surprised that Voltaire should lose out before a court composed of nothing but Midases equipped with the crooks and mitres of a bishop and the ears of a jackass. Learn to despise a nation that disregards real worth . . . and come to a country where you are invited and where there is no bigotry."

This was not the only defeat Voltaire suffered in these days. Crébillon, senior, the censor, having aspirations himself in the field of tragedy, had prohibited the performance of *Mahomet*, and now, in 1743, he also forbade the performance of the play *La Mort de César*, as Voltaire says, "because Brutus should not have killed César, and in that he is incontestably right, for no one should kill anybody." (Nevertheless, the play was performed several months later, perhaps through the efforts of Madame du Châtelet.)

But this last prohibition matured Voltaire's desire to leave the field of battle. Many years before (in August, 1735) pupils of the Collège d'Harcourt had performed the innocuous play *La Mort de César*. And King Frederick had it performed. Voltaire writes to Cideville: "As he has bestowed upon me the compliment of producing *Julius César* at one of his country-seats, it is only natural that to please him I am leaving these West Goths who cannot see their way to performing the play in France."

It became an idée fixé with Frederick to have Voltaire with him daily. Hearing of the annoyances Voltaire had to suffer on French soil, he wrote jubilantly to his friend Jordan: "I believe Voltaire will now leave France for ever." And later, in June, 1743, he wrote these verses:

> Paris et la belle Emilie
> A la fin ont pourtant eu tort;
> Boyer avec l'Académie
> Ont, malgré sa palinodie,
> De Voltaire fixé le sort.
> Berlin, quoi qu'il puisse nous dire,
> A bien prendre, est son pis-aller.

Mais qu'importe? Il nous fera rire
Lorsque nous l'entendrons parler
De Maurepas et de Boyer
Plein du venin de la satire.

Madame du Châtelet was very sad when Voltaire departed; she always suffered from his absence; but this time she was especially fearful of the temptations which the King of Prussia would offer him. On June 28, 1743, she writes to d'Argental:

"He has gone to Holland, whence he will probably proceed to Prussia. This is the basis of all my fears. For the King of Prussia is for me a very dangerous rival. I am enormously grieved, and although I feel that he is doing a certain wrong—for, in his place I would not have gone—my innermost feeling is one of anxiety. I have remained here in the hope of making possible the production of *César* and thus hastening his return; I doubt, however, that I shall succeed, and in that case I shall depart for Brussels, where he has promised to meet me."

12

As badly as Voltaire was treated, his prestige gained by the friendship and open admiration of the King of Prussia. For the old days were gone, when the France of Louis XIV dominated Europe by the threat of its commanders and armies. A number of defeats like that at Dettingen had made France's armies a laughing-stock in Europe, and French politics became a standing joke.

Outside of France, Louis the Much-Beloved was simply disregarded; on the other hand, everybody's attention was focused upon the King of Prussia. Each of the powers was trying to win him over; the British made efforts to keep alive his dislike of France.

For France, which had proved unable either to hold its former allies or to win new ones, it would have meant a great advantage to attain an alliance with this King whose name was a byword for beneficent power. He was Voltaire's hero, but in turn Voltaire was his idol. It, therefore, seemed to be worth while trying to make use of the poet as secret diplomat.

Voltaire had always cherished the hope of winning the Prussian King for France. One can see that from the answer which Frederick sent him from Potsdam on August 20, 1743:

"The description you give of France is painted in pretty colors. But, say whatever you like, an army that runs away for three years in succession and is defeated everywhere it shows its face, is certainly not a troop of Cæsars or Alexanders."

The Ministry in France, then, resolved to make use of Voltaire's contact with Frederick. Count d'Argenson was always favorable to Voltaire, and Richelieu was even more active in furthering the matter. Madame de Châteauroux was easily won over, and through her the King. At the same time that the clerical party was celebrating its triumph over Voltaire, he was leaving Paris with secret instructions from the Foreign Minister, Amelot. His object was to make clear to Frederick the danger that threatened him from Austria, which had recently attacked France, and to induce him, if possible, to come to the aid of France by sending one hundred thousand men to Silesia. Voltaire says of this in his *Memoirs*:

"Some pretext was necessary. For that I took my quarrel with the former Bishop of Mirepoix. The King gave his consent. So I wrote to the King of Prussia that I could no longer endure the persecutions of the Theatine, and that I wished to find refuge with a philosophical King, in order to escape the chicaneries of a dull pious bishop. As this prelate always signs his name *anc. évèq. de Mirepoix* (instead of ancien évèque), we made great sport of changing the *anc.* to *âne.*

"The King of Prussia, who never lets a chance go by to take a crack at monks and court prelates, answered with a deluge of jokes about the jackass Mirepoix, and told me to come ahead. I arranged that the Minister would read every letter and every answer (Voltaire apparently has no feeling that he is abusing Frederick's friendship or that he is demeaning himself to a sort of espionage). The Bishop was informed.

He complained to Louis XV that I, as he said, made him out before foreign courts as a block-head. The King answered that this was a matter agreed upon, that he should not worry about."

As a reward Voltaire made the condition that his cousin Marchand should become army purveyor of food and uniforms. Of course, he received his share, such as the brothers Pâris had already given him from the large contracts for food which he procured for them. When, later on, the Minister d'Argenson wished to give the office to a certain Monsieur de Vallat, Madame du Châtelet wrote in Voltaire's absence (August 28, 1743) to Count d'Argenson and adjusted the matter.

Voltaire at first went to The Hague, where he lived in the palace of the King of Prussia. Count von Podewils, the Prussian Ambassador in Holland, was his host. This count, young, handsome, and loved by a young woman who was the wife of an influential official of the States-General, received from his mistress copies of the secret agreements of all states hostile to France. Voltaire had them copied and directed them to the French Foreign Ministry. Thus he was able to give exact information about military expenses and strength of troops of the Dutch Republic—matters which nobody in France knew. To please Madame du Châtelet and to flatter her discretion, he sent all letters and packages through her hands.

Voltaire wrote to Frederick, who had formed a very poor opinion of the French after the battle at Dettingen: "It does not seem that the French were lacking courage. Two hundred and fifty musketeers broke through five English squares, and yielded only when dying; the greater number of dead and injured noblemen gives indubitable proof of bravery. What couldn't this nation do, if commanded by a Prince like you!"

Nevertheless, the King was not persuaded of the military virtues of the French army.

It would have been helpful to Voltaire's plans had he been able to turn the King of Prussia against Holland and bring about dissention with the States-Gen-

eral, which were secretly transporting munitions
through Prussian territory; but here he met the
most stubborn resistance on the part of the Prussian
Ambassador. For, in the event of a break with Holland, he would have been called home at once from
The Hague, and at no price would Count von Podewils leave his beloved. Upon such circumstances was
the fate of an empire dependent.

Voltaire had not the slightest scruple about opening Frederick's letters before people for whom they
certainly were not intended. Frederick, on the other
hand, from pure love and admiration, had no more
hesitation about misusing Voltaire's letters.

Frederick wrote to the Prussian Ambassador to
Versailles, Count de Rottembourg: "Enclosed I am
sending you part of a letter from Voltaire, which I
ask you to get into the hands of the Bishop de Mirepoix in some secret way, without involving yourself
or me in the matter. My intention is to cause Voltaire
to break with France, so that there would be nothing
left for him to do but to come to us."

Both parties were too clever to be fooled. Voltaire
was not long in discovering that Frederick had delivered him to his enemy. Frederick wrote to Count
de Rottembourg on October 14: "Voltaire has, I don't
know how, found out the little trick which we have
played upon him, and is very cross about it; he will
get over it, I trust."

Voltaire wrote to the Minister Amelot:

"He wrote me several letters about the man whom
we were using as our pretext (the Bishop de Mirepoix) and I addressed some to him, which were written with the same frankness. In his notes as well as
in mine there are several daring verses, which cannot hurt a King but can hurt a private person. He
presumed that, if I were to have a serious quarrel
with the man who was the butt of these jokes, I
should be forced to accept his invitation, which so
far I have declined, to come and live in the Prussian Court. But I swear to you that I would rather
live in a Swiss town than enjoy the favor of a King
who is liable to mix friendship with treason."

In reality the time was still remote when Voltaire

would prefer Ferney to a stay in Berlin, and Voltaire's grudge was really not deep. He was quite happy in Frederick's company.

13

From August 30 until October 12, Voltaire stayed in Berlin.

Frederick pretended he could see no possibility of an alliance between Versailles and Potsdam: He has, he says, no confidence. He knows what the French ambassador in Mainz has proposed: Peace with the Queen of Hungary, reëstablishment of the Emperor and compensation at Prussia's expense.—Voltaire answers that this was a rumor spread by Austria in order to prevent an alliance of the two powers. "Weren't you misrepresented in the same way last May? Was it not written to Holland that you were proposing an alliance with the Queen of Hungary against France?"—"I swear to you," replies Frederick (but, writes Voltaire, "with averted eyes") "that nothing is further from the truth."—"Very well, Sire, but why not simply make an alliance with France and the Emperor against the common enemy who hates and slanders us both with the same passion? What other ally can you get except France?"

To make his decision, Frederick had, as he said, to assure himself first of the coöperation of several of the princes of the Empire; so he set out for Bayreuth, accompanied by Voltaire. Before the departure the negotiations between the poet and the King were continued, sometimes on the same sheet of paper which passed from room to room in the castle. A curious example is the sheet of September, which Voltaire in October sent to the Foreign Ministry. It contains nine detailed questions and nine sharp answers mostly in the negative. One can see from these answers, that Frederick had been advised to be on his guard; somebody has informed him that under the mask of friendship he had been cherishing a spy at his bosom. That "somebody" was probably the French ambassador in Berlin, Monsieur de Valori himself, whom Voltaire, of course, was supposed to support, but whom he gave no place in his schemes. Here are a few of the questions and answers:

(Voltaire)

Is it not clear that the party of peace will infallibly be the victor in Holland? . . . Is it not clear that France shows strength and prudence?

Would you not bring immortal glory upon yourself by simply proclaiming yourself the protector of the Empire? Is it not to your highest interest to prevent the English from setting up your enemy, the grand-duke, as head of the Holy Roman Empire?

Anyone who has talked for as much as one quarter of an hour with the Duke of Aremberg, to Count von Harrach, Lord Stair, with anyone from Austria, has heard them say that they are burning to invade Silesia. Have you, then, Sire, another ally than France?

Whichever part Your Majesty may take, will you honor me with your confidence as one who desires to spend his days at your court? May I have the distinction of accompanying you to Bayreuth? I must know in time, however, in order to prepare myself for the journey. . . .

If Your Majesty . . . will make me the bearer of some pleasant information to my court, I implore you to give me this order.

(Frederick)

I admire France's prudence; but may God save me from imitating it!

France is more interested than Prussia in preventing that; and, my dear Voltaire, on this point your information is faulty. The Emperor cannot be elected without the unanimous vote of the princess, and so, as you can see, the election still depends on me.

Let them come; they shall have a warm reception:
    On les y recevra, biribi
    A la façon de Barbari
        Mon ami.

If you wish to come to Bayreuth, I shall be glad to see you there, provided that the journey will not injure your health. It is, therefore, up to you to make the preparations you think best.

I am not in communication with France; I have nothing to hope nor to fear from it. If you wish, I will write a compliment to Louis XV which will contain not one true word. But, politically, we have nothing in common,

(Voltaire)	(Frederick)
	and it is not up to me to speak first. When I am asked something, there is still time to answer. . . .
Do what you will, I love Your Majesty with my whole heart. V.	I love you with my whole heart; I respect you; I shall do everything to get possession of you, barring actions that would make me ridiculous and be prejudicial to my interests and be out of keeping with my honor. . . . The French monarchy is a strong body without soul or nerve. F.

Voltaire had only introduced the problem to sound out the feeling of the King of Prussia. It is obvious that he had not full power to form an alliance. According to its phrasing, Frederick's answer contained only a mocking rejection of the alliance plans. If, however, his words are studied more minutely, it can be seen that what he wants most is, not to take the first formal step himself, but to receive an offer that would serve as the basis of a discussion. In the contrary event he would make himself "ridiculous." It could therefore be seen in advance that the negotiations which Voltaire had started by his near relationship to the King, could without difficulty be pursued by a personage who was at the source of power —a personage such as the Duchess de Châteauroux.

14

At his earlier stay in Rheinsberg, while Frederick was Crown Prince, Voltaire had made the acquaintance of Frederick's sister, the Margravine of Bayreuth, and had received a most favorable impression of this bright, highly gifted lady.

In thanks for a little gift she had sent him he had written her on December 26, 1741: "I shall never cease, Madame, to look back with longing on the days when I had the honor of paying my respects to you

in quiet Rheinsberg. The goodness with which the
Margrave flattered me is ever in my mind, and what
I wish is, just once more in my life, to partake of
the same honor."

In Bayreuth, then, he was welcomed as an old
friend. The Margravine Frederica Wilhelmina, whose
memoirs inform us of her father's cruelty and of her
own sad youth, had had built a little one-story castle
about a half mile out of the city. It was called the
Hermitage. Its rooms were marble, even the concert-
hall was of white and green marble with a frieze, on
which the most beautiful ladies of that age were portrayed. Her bedroom was panelled with rare Japanese woods. From the windows one could overlook
romantically planned gardens. The mistress of the
house was not romantic but she honored Voltaire and
sat up at night to copy from his manuscript of *La
Pucelle*. During the fortnight Voltaire was there,
there were fêtes arranged in his honor; operas were
sung and comedies played, hunts were planned and
suppers arranged.

Before the poet's return to Berlin, Frederick, within the short time of four days, had a pretty hall in his
castle transformed into a theater in order to play in it
an opera Voltaire wished to hear. Princes and Princesses from the vicinity assembled and Voltaire was
idolized and pampered by all of them. Frederick's
young sister, the charming Ulrike Eleonore, later the
mother of Gustave III of Sweden, began a real flirta-
tion with him. He was not backward in playing his
part, either, as can be seen from the free language of
the following delightful humorous rhymes:

> Souvent un peu de vérité
> Se mêle au plus grossier mensonge.
> Cette nuit dans l'erreur d'un songe
> Au rang des rois j'étais monté;
> Je vous aimais, princesse, et j'osais vous le dire,
> Les dieux à mon réveil ne m'ont pas tout ôté;
>   Je n'ai perdu que mon empire.

That the Princess was not offended by the boldness
of the poet is best shown by her attempt to put her
answer into verse, a reward at the execution of
which her brother most certainly helped her. She

writes that when Voltaire is in Berlin, his only thought is of his Emily and thus Ulrike becomes by illusion his queen of beauty. Doubtless he, too, felt the difference between himself and Emily, on one hand, and the Princess on the other:

> Au haut de 'Hélicon vous vous placez vous-même:
> Moi, je dois tout à mes aïeux,
> Tel est l'arrêt du sort suprême.
> Le hasard fait les rois, la vertu fait les dieux.

Voltaire never lost sight of Ulrike Eleonore. One of his sweetest and most meditative poems is the one he addressed to her when she was Princess of Sweden. It points out the stupidity of those who trifle away their time in playing. The poem ends with the classic verse:

> S'occuper c'est savoir jouir:
> L'oisiveté pèse et tourmente.
> L'âme est un feu qu'il faut nourrir
> Et qui s'éteint s'il ne s'augmente.

While the poems to the Princess show Voltaire at his best as an elegant epigrammatist, there is a poem he wrote to Frederick in those same days which reveals the future Voltaire, the champion of the forsaken, the neglected, the pitiable—one of the many poems which do credit to his great heart.

In the prison of Spandau there was an old nobleman from Franche-Comté, a man over six feet tall, whom Frederick William I had kidnapped because of his height. He had been promised a position as chamberlain, but the King's mania made him a simple guard. The poor conscript tried to desert, but was caught and taken before the King. He was foolish enough to tell him to his face that he was sorry he had not killed such a tyrant. His nose and ears were cut off, he was made to run the gantlet thirty-six times, and then was sent to Spandau to trundle a wheel-barrow.

Frederick refused to let his own mother intercede for this prisoner. Voltaire addressed to him the poem which starts:

Génie universel, âme sensible et ferme,
Grand homme, il est sous vous des malheureux mortels;
Mais quand à ses vertus on n'a point mis de terme,
On en met aux tourments des plus grands criminels.

So Frederick, who was gracious, but not sentimental, allowed the old man to be taken to a hospital, with a pension of five sous a day. When the time came for them to part, the King said to Voltaire: "Choose yourself an apartment or a house, decide what necessities and what luxuries you want in your life; state your conditions in such a way that you will be made happy by the fulfillment of them, and leave the rest to me."

The parting was not without emotion on both sides. Voltaire's resentment at the harmless and really flattering "betrayal," and Frederick's discomfort in suspecting he was being spied upon, were forgotten.

Voltaire went to Brunswick, where the Duke gave him a hearty reception, and then to Brussels, where Madame du Châtelet awaited him impatiently and with open arms.

15

Madame de Tencin made every effort to win Prussia's recognition of the political importance of Madame de Châteauroux. According to her plan, the Duchess was to take Voltaire's place in Frederick the Great's confidence. The King was to be persuaded that the Duchess's influence was not only greater than Voltaire's, but that it was decisive in France.

Frederick in his *Histoire de mon temps* (Vol. 3, chap. 4) says that he decided in 1743 not to use his ambassador at the French Court, the Baron de Chambrier; instead he wished to send Count de Rottembourg, a noble gentleman, who, in 1740, had gone from French into Prussian service. He was more adaptable and active, and besides was related to all the prominent personages of that Court: "So Count de Rottembourg went to Versailles. His introduction was taken care of by Richelieu and the Duchess de Châteauroux."

Rottembourg carried a letter addressed to Riche-

lieu, in Frederick's own handwriting, telling him—
what Frederick knew—that, if Louis XV were engaged in the occupation of Flanders in the next year,
Prince Charles would cross the Rhine and invade
Alsace. The only way to prevent this attempt at conquest, was for Frederick himself to invade Bohemia.
He offered France an armed alliance, but on the condition that none of the present French Ministers were
to be informed of this treaty which His Prussian
Majesty desired to conclude between the two Kings,
with Richelieu as the third party.

At once a council was held, attended by the King,
the Duchess, and Richelieu. As the latter felt that he
lacked the diplomatic knowledge essential to draw
up such a treaty, he advised Louis to consult also
Marshal de Noailles and Cardinal de Tencin. The
King of Prussia gave his consent, and from then on
Count de Rottembourg worked with the Duchess de
Châteauroux.

Frederick the Great had been clever enough to prepare the lady for this collaboration by a flattering letter; he asked her opinion as to how his envoy could
best introduce the matter to the King of France.

In June the treaty of alliance between Prussia and
France was signed. Madame de Châteauroux had
toiled to bring it about; what motivated her, however,
was, less that she recognized the advantage of an alliance with the great Frederick, than that by agreeing
with his dislike and distrust of Amelot she could
strike Maurepas. For in Maurepas she saw, with good
reason, the personal enemy who had started the
whole series of scurrilous ditties about her!

Proudly she received the following letter:

> "*Potsdam,* May 12, 1744.
>
> "Madame,
> "It is very flattering for me, to be partly indebted to you
> for the inclination of the King of France, to tie between
> us the permanent bond of an everlasting alliance. The re-
> spect I have always had for you blends with my gratitude.
> In a word, Madame, I am persuaded that the King of France
> will never have to regret the step he has taken, and that
> this alliance will be of mutual advantage to both nations.

It is too bad that Prussia must ignore the debt of gratitude
which it owes to you; in my heart, however, this feeling
will remain deeply. I ask you to always be sure of this.

"Madame, your very devoted friend

"FREDERICK."

The Duchess answered with the following note:

"Sire,
"I am very happy that I may flatter myself as having contributed to the connection which I have established between
you and the King. I am properly sensible to the proofs of
the goodness which Your Majesty bestows upon me. I wish
very deeply to find frequent occasion to prove my gratitude
and the deep respect with which I have the honor to be

"Your Majesty's devoted and obedient servant

"MAILLY, DUCHESSE DE CHÂTEAUROUX."

16

Madame de Tencin had thought out a rôle for the
Duchess de Châteauroux, which the latter took up
eagerly. She was to be what Agnes Sorel had been to
Charles VII—the mistress who made a man and a
hero of a dull and listless king. She was to induce
Louis XV to take command of his army.

The Duchess was now so sure of his favor that she
could dare to displease him. She stirred the King's
will, talked to him seriously, conversed with him
about governmental affairs, about war and peace,
and reminded him of his responsibilities, until he put
his hand to his spinning head and cried: "You are
killing me!"—"That is all the better, Sire, a king
should celebrate his re-birth!"

The ambitious woman saw just one problem before
her: to buckle on the King's armor and set him at
the head of his troops, for the honor of his crown,
and for the salvation of his people. She wished to
appear as the better queen, as the rightful one; she
wanted to smother the jeers under public rejoicing
over victories which, as anybody could see, had been
inspired by the Duchess of Châteauroux.

So Louis resolved to go to the army and the favorite was no less firmly resolved to follow him, if any way possible. She wrote at once to the commander-in-chief, Marshal de Noailles, and expressed her wish; she flattered him cleverly, and told him that the King was coming to the army; would it not be possible for her sister and herself to accompany the King—at least to follow him at a certain distance, so that they could get daily news of him? She informed him that she had asked the King's permission to write this letter, so the Marshal would not think that she was acting arbitrarily.

It was not easy for the old gentleman to answer; but it was as clear as day to him that the whole effect upon the population and upon the troops of having the King in their midst would be lost if his mistress were to accompany him. And the old soldier took courage and bravely risked the Royal disgrace by his answer: He did not believe it would be possible for the Duchess and her sister to follow the King to the army; she herself, of course, appreciates the difficulties, as she mentioned that she wished to settle in a town behind the frontier. It is true, that in the reign of the late King the Queen had undertaken such journeys and had remained with her attendants at a suitable distance; but he could not find a single precedent in favor of such a thing, and he could not refrain from remarking that it was essential for the King's as well as for her own sake, to name some sensible reason that would justify this step to public opinion. "You can see by my frankness, Madame, that I am speaking more as a true friend, than as courtier."

The Duchess answered at once with politeness and irony: She must immediately thank the Marshal for his letter, which was absolutely sensible and prudent; but she suffered from the colic, and for that illness the baths at Plombières were wonderful; she was in bad need of the cure.

Many who (like Minister Maurepas) wished for the King's departure for the army, hoped by that to separate him from the favorite, and so were opposed to her accompanying him. The popularity, which the

King's resolution had suddenly won him, gave **Madame** de Châteauroux food for thought. It would be unwise to overplay her cards. After the King had ordered the Queen, in spite of her begging, to remain in Versailles, he had to give the same order to the Duchess. Richelieu consoled her by telling her that Louis, being a man of strong habit, could not do without her long.

Meanwhile the whole month of May passed, and he did not call her. From one of her letters to Richelieu we can see that she was not only embarrassed by this, but also was very excited by something else she had found out: namely, that the King was in secret correspondence with her sister, Madame de Flavacourt, and that the latter was writing to him under a covering address. Letters in her handwriting were going to the valet Lebel.

A few days before his departure, the King had ogled Madame de Flavacourt, who had become more beautiful than the Duchess. His action was so open that it caught the Queen's attention; she had spoken to the young lady about it and asked if she were anything to the King. Madame de Flavacourt answered that the King's person had no special attraction for her; but she trembled lest she might be sent away from Court and have to live with her husband again.

17

The Duchess de Châteauroux, who knew from her own experience that one sister could supplant another and that the King's desire easily changed from one to another, felt it was of vital importance for her to get in personal touch with King Louis. She had shared his favor without anxiety with her sister Lauraguais. But this sister was not a beauty—just wanton and entirely devoted to her, and she was certainly not scheming to bring her down and to take her place. Madame de Flavacourt, on the other hand, was constantly entertaining members of the opponent's camp, and even enjoyed the confidence of the Queen.

In order to keep up appearances, it was essential

that one of the ladies-in-waiting of the Duchess set the example by departing first. The Duchess succeeded in persuading one of the Princesses of the royal family, the Duchess of Chartres; she departed for the army on the excuse that her husband had fallen from his horse. Thus, a precedent was furnished. Then Richelieu wrote to his niece that she could come, even without the King's order. He said that he would take all the responsibility. As soon as the sisters had said good-bye to the Queen (without mentioning, however, that they were going to Flanders) and had set out upon the journey, Richelieu informed the King of it; he spoke, in jesting and obscure hints, of a journey of the blind and disobedient Amor who surely deserved to be forgiven if only the blindfold had been removed from his eyes.

The ladies met the King in Lille where a building had been set aside for them, which was in direct connection with the royal quarters. They as well as Richelieu had tried their best to avoid any sensation, but the scandal in the little pious Flemish town grew to great dimensions. That the King no longer took his meals publicly, but dined with his mistress in the private chambers of the house next door, aroused more than the anger of the pious. In the camp the soldiers sang one ribald verse after another; even the Swiss Guard before the King's tent joined in singing the lines:

> Ah madame Enroux!
> Je deviendrai fou
> Si je ne vous baise.

While other soldiers serenaded under the windows of the Duchess without disguising the name:

> Belle Châteauroux!
> Je deviendrai fou,
> Si je ne vous baise.

In Paris, in the provinces, in the army, soon the only topic of conversation was the odd way in which the King was waging war. His living with the favorite in Lille was on everybody's lips.

The necessity for a temporary separation arose. The

King went off to the siege of Ypres and nine days
later the city was taken. This quick surrender was
greatly enjoyed by the Duchess, and after visiting
several Flemish towns, the King again met her in
Dunkerque.

But she would not leave him again, not even when
the disquieting news came that Prince Charles had
crossed the Rhine, and the King was forced to come
to the aid of Alsace. Madame de Châteauroux followed him from town to town. Saint-Omer, Béthune,
Arras, Péronne, La Fère, Laon, Reims, Chalons, Ver-
dun became excited witnesses of their attachment.
When the King (in the deepest incognito) went in
and out of the Duchess's quarters, he could hear a
chorus of mocking exclamations of leering enthusiasm: Long live the King! Long live the King!—And
hastily he disappeared in some garden.

In Reims some unknown illness forced the Duchess
to take to her bed. The physicians described her complaint as a sudden outbreak of fever; the courtiers
saw in it an outbreak of remorse; the Duchess was
persuaded that she had been given poison. Some
ascribed the fever to her excitement at hearing that
her former lover, the Duke of Agénois, had been
fatally wounded.

The King postponed his departure from Reims one
day, and then went to Metz where after a rapid re-
covery the Duchess caught up with him. Disregarding
the curiosity of which they were the center, the King
had a wooden bridge built between his quarters and
the Duchess's; it was done with spectacular haste and
deafening hammering in the abbey St. Arnould. Four
streets were unwisely closed to the public while the
connecting bridge was put up. The population of
Metz was much incensed.

18

Suddenly—just when the King was celebrating his
reunion with the lovable sisters—after a day spent
with inspections of the fortress—after an evening in
which many toasts had been drunk to the new ally,

the King of Prussia—after a night in which Richelieu had locked the King up with both sisters, Louis fell seriously ill.

The physicians hastened to employ the customary treatments: letting of blood, emetics, purgatives. But nothing soothed the King's headache, nothing reduced his fever, and on August 12 a physician, who had been called from Metz, declared that he could not answer for the patient's life.

The two sisters and Richelieu were the only ones at the sickbed; they admitted neither Princes of the Blood nor any high official of the Crown, except perhaps to hear Mass and then to retire immediately. The seriousness of the case was concealed as much as possible; everyone was excluded from the consultation of physicians except those whose devotion could be counted upon absolutely.

In the antechamber were the Duke de Bouillon, the Duke de Rochefoucauld, and members of the royal family, like the Count de Clermont. None of these would speak to anyone of the party of the favorite. Finally, the Count de Clermont forced his way in, approached the King's bed devotedly, but courageously, and said he absolutely could not believe that it was the King's intention to refuse the Princes of the Blood the satisfaction of assuring themselves of his improved health. They did not want to be obtrusive, but would retire immediately.

The King asked Clermont to stay, but he did not do so. However, the ice was broken. And now negotiations commenced between the Princes and Dukes who hated Madame de Châteauroux, and the Bishop of Soissons, Fitz-James, and his confessor Pérusseau, who hated her no less.

The Duchess guessed the object of these negotiations and wanted to know if it was the intention of the priests to withhold Extreme Unction unless she were driven away. The religious fears of the King had returned during his illness. He had a hallucination that the smoke of a piece of burning paper was the smoke of the flames of Hell.

She had Pérusseau summoned and asked him point-blank whether it was their intention to drive her away. But although she and Richelieu both cross-questioned the Jesuit for hours, it was impossible to induce him to give an honest answer. At first he entrenched himself behind a pretended ignorance of the circumstances. Personally he put no evil interpretation upon the relations between the King and the Duchess. Even when she impatiently interrupted him with an open confession, he declared he was unable to say anything in advance. It all depended upon the nature of the royal confession.

On August 12, the Bishop of Soissons entered the room of the King before Mass, spoke to him about his condition and the duties it imposed. That evening Louis said coldly to the Duchess: "We shall perhaps be forced to separate."

The King's fears and anxiety increased; according to the physicians' opinion he had not more than two days to live. He lived, however, thirty-one years more. On August 13, the door leading from the royal bedchamber into that of the sisters was opened a little, and Fitz-James spoke through the crack of the door: "Ladies, the King orders you to withdraw at once."

Later, when the Bishop was about to give the King the Holy Sacrament, he learned that the sisters had not yet left Metz. He refused the Sacrament to the patient. Our Lord's Body could not be given as long as the concubines stayed within the city walls.

No sooner had the sisters fled in their coach, behind drawn curtains, surrounded by a mob which insulted them and would gladly have stoned them, than Louis received the Sacrament.

On the fourteenth the King was to receive the Extreme Unction. But as Fitz-James had been told that the sisters were staying only a few miles from Metz, the holy ceremony was postponed until they had received the royal order to continue their journey.

But the patient rallied, and by the middle of September he had completely recovered.

Meanwhile the two ladies had continued their journey. Wherever they went they were received with abuse. At every change of horses the Duchess de Châteauroux had to hide. Outside every city, out-

side every little village she had to get out, take some
by-path, and wait for her coach, never, however,
without hearing the howls of the mob demanding her
head.

Finally, she entered Paris unobserved. The population there, in a silly fit of deification of the King,
fearful and with tears coursing down their faces,
kneeled in the churches and prayed for the Well-
Beloved. An illness, which really was not at all dangerous, sufficed to earn the King the name of *Louis
le Bien-Aimé.*

19

The news the Duchess received at her home in
Paris, that the King had become reconciled with the
Queen, made her desperate. She had no reason for
this. Richelieu, who had gone to the army, sent the
King a memorandum in which he referred to the
King's illness and demonstrated what abuses the enemies of the Duchess had committed on the strength
of the King's debilitated condition and his religious
remorse during his illness; if the truth were known,
this crowd was so interested in its own, selfish ambitions that it would have preferred to see a fatal outcome of the illness.

The King had gone to visit his father-in-law Stanislaw for a few days in Lunéville, where his sadness
and absent-mindedness attracted everybody's attention. In reality he was thinking only of his lost friend.
He was weary of the war. He didn't care for military
glory, if only he could have an evening of pleasure
soon; the moment the surrender of Freiburg was
signed, he hurried to Paris.

He arrived there in the evening of November 13,
heard the Te Deum in Notre Dame, attended a feast
in the city hall and was taken through the streets of
Paris in a carriage to see the illumination. But
promptly on the night of the fourteenth he left the
Tuileries, accompanied by Richelieu only, crossed
the Pont-Royal and knocked at the door of the
Duchess, in the rue du Bac.

She was so overcome at seeing him that she was

able to stammer only: "How you have treated us!"
The King begged her to return to Versailles. She
agreed to go for a few hours the next day, incognita.
Officially, she would not return before she had been
given full satisfaction and taken public revenge.

She began by demanding heads; all those who had
driven her from Metz were to pay for it with their
lives. Louis had the greatest difficulty in dissuading
her of this absurd demand. However, deep in his
own heart, he too hated those men.

Monsieur de Balleroy, because he was believed to
be the author of the sermon delivered by the Bishop
of Soissons against the Duchess de Châteauroux after
he had given the King Extreme Unction, and Bishop
Fitz-James, as well as Pérusseau, La Rochefoucauld,
and the Duke of Bouillon, were exiled or deprived of
the royal favor. The Duchess wanted to have the
Princes of the Blood punished in the same way, but
this was not possible. Finally she demanded the dismissal of her bitterest opponent, the Minister Maurepas. As the King could not do without him she had
to be content with his humiliation in being made personally to deliver the King's letter inviting her to return to Versailles, and reinstating her in her honors.
These negotiations took up eleven full days.

When Maurepas arrived in the rue du Bac he was
informed that the Duchess was not at home. When
he mentioned his name, he was told a second time
that she was not in. When he declared that he came
from the King, the door was finally opened to him. He
found the Duchess in bed; she looked at him for a
long time without saying anything, even without
greeting him. Then she read the King's note, and answered it orally, professing her devotion to the King;
but to all the Minister's assurances of devotion she returned only an ironic smile.

The Duchess was indeed bedridden, when Maurepas called. She had a little fever. At night her temperature went up. The following night her condition
grew worse. On the third day it was so alarming that
the Duchess made her last will, appointing her sister
sole heir. She confessed to a priest, became reconciled with her sister de Flavacourt, and finally re-

ceived the Sacrament from a priest of Saint-Sulpice.

From December 1 on the patient suffered terrible pains, violent cramps, and in delirium constantly murmured the word poison and the name Maurepas.

The Duchess de Châteauroux died, at the age of twenty-seven, on December 8, 1744.

The autopsy showed no indications of poison; but who knows whether the physicians knew their business and whether they were honest.

The excitement and the emotional crises through which she had passed within the last months seem at any rate to have lowered the young woman's physical resistance.

In April, 1745, the King dined in private with Madame d'Etioles in Versailles, and on May 6 of the same year the apartment of the Duchess de Châteauroux in the Palace was newly decorated to suit the taste of the other lady. On September 14, 1745, ten months after the death of the Duchess, she was introduced to the Queen as the Marquise de Pompadour.

VII

THE MARQUISE DU CHÂTELET

1

In 1734, when Voltaire sought refuge in Cirey, it
was almost uninhabitable. He had to engage masons,
carpenters and cabinet-makers. The chateau was just
about falling in ruins, and as the owners were not
wealthy, nothing had been done to check the decay,
especially since the owner was in garrison most of
the time and the mistress usually stayed either in
Lunéville or in Paris.

After a year's work, we see Madame du Châtelet
still occupied with the workmen. Even four years
later, when Madame de Graffigny visited Cirey, not
much more than Emily's and Voltaire's living quarters had been comfortably furnished and decorated,
while the rest of the house was lacking in comforts,
even in cleanliness; the guest rooms were large uninhabitable places, impossible to fortify against wind
and weather.

Voltaire was given a wing to himself. His entrance
was by the main stairway. How his residence was ultimately decorated and furnished, we can see from
Madame de Graffigny's enthusiastic description. A
little foyer, a small study hung with red velvet tap-
estry and containing a velvet settle with gold trim-
mings. (Odd taste!) His bedroom had few tapestries
but much panel-work hung with good paintings.
There were mirrors, corner-cupboards, porcelain
vases, a grandfather's clock decorated with Oriental
figures, an open case containing a silver service, the
rarest silver-work, all the superfluities that were so
essential to Voltaire, and such cleanliness that one
could kiss the floor. In the adjacent hall, on glazed
pedestals, stood two little statues, a Venus and a

Hercules. Opposite them were two cupboards, one with books, the other with physical instruments; between them against the wall was an excellent stove. In front of this on a high pedestal was a Cupid shooting his arrow, and below it Voltaire's famous inscription:

Qui que tu sois, voici ton maître;
Il l'est, le fut, ou le doit être.

This Cupid was later set in a niche. In addition there were tables, desks, clocks—in fact, as the little lady from the provinces adds naïvely: "You may believe it, there is nothing lacking." Just the same, there was only a sofa and no fauteuil; the armchairs were comfortable but not luxurious; one can feel, she says, that the ruling factors here are ease and comfort, not wealthy display. In the middle, a door leads into the garden, as though into a neat grotto. In the gallery the large portrait of Frederick the Great as Crown Prince occupies the place of honor. In a bowl lay twelve rings set with carved stones and two diamond rings.

Voltaire's rooms, however, were not comparable to those of the mistress of the house. The woodwork of her bedroom was light-yellow, with pale-blue stripes. This coloring was so dominant that everything, even the basket in which her dog slept, was light-yellow and light-blue: the woodwork of the chairs, the work-table, the corner-cupboards, and the desk. Her bedspread was of blue moiré. A large door of bevelled glass led into the library. Here were paintings by Paul Veronese. From the bedroom one went into a little boudoir which, as Madame de Graffigny says, was so lovely that at entering it one felt tempted to fall upon one's knees. It had a painting on the ceiling done by the popular French painter Martin and each section of the panelling was filled with a picture by Watteau. A single large window permitted a view of the terrace and delightful natural scenery. An alcove divided the room and led into a "divine" clothes-closet, with marble floor and fine engravings. All the linen, including the muslin curtains, was tastefully embroidered. On every hand stood and lay fifteen to twenty tobacco cases of enameled gold

studded with gems, Jaspe watches, with diamonds,
enameled ash trays, boxes, and bowls of rings and
watch charms.

The visitor was astonished; she knew that the
Châtelet family was not wealthy. But she did not
consider that Voltaire wherever he went, even on a
brief visit, brought a stream of gold. After a visit of
fifteen years he had with him a flood of gold.

2

During the time Voltaire used Cirey as his head-
quarters, he was by no means a steady resident there,
but on the contrary led the most restless life. Madame
du Châtelet had remained in Paris and did her best
to soothe the government and dispose the leaders in
Voltaire's favor. On June 22 he writes to Monsieur de
Condamine:

"You will soon meet Madame du Châtelet. The
friendship with which she honors me was not forgotten on this occasion. Her intellect is worthy of yours
and that of Monsieur de Maupertuis, and her heart
is worthy of her intellect. She renders services of
friendship with the same ardent zeal with which she
studies languages and geometry, and after doing one
all kinds of favors, she thinks that she has done nothing, just as she belittles her intellectual attainments.
Be very good to her, you and Monsieur de Maupertuis, and let us be her adorers for our entire lives.
The Court does not deserve a woman like her, for all
of its courtiers are not like you. Please tell her how
deeply I am touched by her goodness. It is a long
while since I have heard from her; but for all that,
I am no less gratefully devoted to her."

In July Madame du Châtelet writes from Paris (to
some unknown friend) that she is sorry that Voltaire's affair is in bad shape. It seems that the treasurer was appeased; he merely demanded that Voltaire deny ever having written that "unfortunate
Book" (on England); in that case he promised to
retract his *Lettre de cachet;* on the other hand, the
ministry seems more irritated than ever before.

Otherwise the Marquise du Châtelet wasted no time
with cares and worries; she saw a great deal of the
two families Richelieu and Saint Pierre; she dili-
gently studied English—for she had to do that to
keep up with her lover—and, finally, she interested
herself deeply in mathematics and physics. She had
made the acquaintance of Maupertuis. He had become her teacher and friend. He taught her geometry
and physics; he introduced her to Newton's studies.
Still a young man, only thirty-six, he knew how to
make the most difficult things easily comprehensible,
to take the thorns out of study. At the same time she
cultivated the acquaintance of young Clairaut, one
of the best mathematicians of the time, who, though
only twenty-one, had been a member of the Academy
of Sciences for three years. Already he had several
discoveries in geometry and higher mathematics to
his credit. All her life the "respectable Emily" was in
communication with these two. Both visited the
couple at Cirey.

Maupertuis' abundance of knowledge, sense and
courtesy inspired Madame du Châtelet to real enthusiasm. We have her letters to him. They reveal not
only gratitude and devotion, but also a desire to see
him as often as possible. If she hoped in vain for his
visit, she cannot suppress complaints and reproaches.
He, alone or with Clairaut, was always welcome at
her supper-table. What she feels for him is probably
purely an intellectual attachment, but with women
the borderline between this and a physical passion
is as a rule rather indefinite. She wants to become
worthy of his instruction; she fears to betray this or
that bit of ignorance and thus to forfeit his good
opinion. In his company she experiences the pleasure
of seeing the truth in its most attractive form.

Her soul and senses are too occupied with Voltaire to let this enthusiasm for Maupertuis become
anything more than admiration. From the letters
one gets the impression that her constant mention
of Voltaire was irksome to him. For, when she writes
him from Cirey at the end of October, 1734, she introduces her news of Voltaire with the excuse that
this time it had been Maupertuis who mentioned him

first, and so she was compelled to answer. In the letter to Condamine quoted above Voltaire praises the Marquise, but it seems that for some time he has not heard from her; but it is just as surprising that Emily, after tearing herself away from Paris and arriving at Cirey to continue setting the castle in order, found him no longer there. He had gone to Brussels. In her letter to Maupertuis she says he had become a hypochondriac. But there is further evidence that a serious quarrel had started between them. Probably the Marquise's enthusiasm for Maupertuis got on Voltaire's nerves, which would explain the mockery with which eight years later he attacks his former friend and companion.

One should give careful attention to the wording of a letter sent by Voltaire from Holland to his most intimate friend, Count d'Argental. Apparently he is only irritated because Madame du Châtelet had searched for him everywhere. But why did he force her to do so?

"For a whole month I had no word from your friend [not our friend]; but I was merely sorry, without being angry, without thinking myself betrayed. Still less did I raise a hue and cry over all Germany. I confess that I am very peeved about the measures she took. She did more harm than you might think; but then there are no faults one cannot like if the heart is involved. I have the same reasons to forgive, that somebody else had to misbehave. You, my dear angel, would do a great wrong in condemning me without a hearing."

He found his Emily again in Cirey, and the reconciliation was hearty and complete. She was busy doing over the house, "putting in windows where he had put doors, changing stairways into chimneys, planting linden trees where he had intended elms; she worked as though endowed with the hands of a fairy, and furnished Cirey on nothing," as Voltaire tells it. The Marquise had hoped to have Voltaire go to Paris with her, to hear the Midnight Mass, which even to-day is such a popular event in that city; but Voltaire did not dare to leave Cirey. During his flight he had written his well-known tragedy *Alzire,* which Emily was to submit for d'Argental's judgment. In Paris she sent Maupertuis the following note in which the spelling of proper names as usual breaks up the serenity of the modern perusal.

"Paris, Friday, Christmas night 1734.
"I would rather still be in Cirey and know that you were still in Basle, than to see as little of you as I do. I want to celebrate Eloïse's birth with you [Eloïse should be Elohim, God, hence Jesus]. See that you come tonight and drink his health with me and Clerau [Clairaut]. I shall expect you between eight and nine, and then we shall go together to Midnight Mass and listen to the Christmas psalms accompanied by organ music; from there I shall take you home; I am counting on this, unless Mademoiselle de Lagni vetoes it."

It seems that Voltaire's jealousy was not altogether unreasonable.

3

In his solitude in Cirey he spent his time in study and partly in elaborating the first eight cantos of the poem which his contemporaries admired more than anything else he wrote, and which has injured his reputation with posterity more than anything he wrote.

The origin of *La Pucelle* goes back to 1730, when during a dinner at Richelieu's house, the conversation turned to the poet Chapelain whose glory was great, but whose poem on the Maid of Orléans struck the contemporaries of Louis XV as merely comical.

Under Louis XIV Jeanne d'Arc had been glorified for the sake of the Kingship. Respect for the unimportant Charles VII kept her memory alive. Chapelain's *La Pucelle* dates from the year 1656. In spite of the title, Jeanne is not the central character of the work. The hero is the Bastard of Orléans, because he was the ancestor of Chapelain's patron, the Duke of Longueville, to whom the poem was dedicated.

Chapelain's *La Pucelle* is an epic in Alexandrines,

with Vergilian similes and mythological trappings in
the form of God, Satan and the angels. There is not
one correct verse, nor one really living line in the
whole work. Chapelain found his admirers among
the fine ladies (like the elegant Madame de la Suze)
whom Molière satirized in *Les Précieuses ridicules.*

Toward the end of the work Chapelain is faced
with the problem of reconciling the disgrace of his
hero and saint with the goodness of God and His
plans. He succeeds. He has the "Uncreated" God high
above Heaven in a special sort of loge to which He is
accustomed to retire to meditate on the fate of the
Universe. With its three equal sides this incomprehensible loge forms a unique triangle—an altogether
admirable triangle—and from this secret coign of
vantage the unknown Mystery (the poet explains
rather confusingly) fails to distinguish the contents
from the container:

> Plus haut que tous les Cieux une Loge secrette
> Sert à l'Estre incréé de profonde retraitte,
> Quand par ses soins vaillans et ses pensers couverts
> Il veut délibérer du Sort de l'Univers.
> De trois cotés égaux la Loge inconcevable
> Forme un Triangle unique en tout sens admirable,
> Et d'un lieu si secret le mystère inconnu
> Confound le contenat avec le contenu.

God finds the English haughty and self-possessed,
and Charles VII hard-hearted. His strict, impartial
justice therefore resolves to sacrifice Jeanne to punish the others—in reality rather doubtful justice. The
Uncreated Being, as He is called, is a heavenly King,
surrounded like Louis XIV by a Court. The Blessed
Courtiers follow the cruel trials of the inconquerable
girl, and pray for the Maid. But the King of Heaven
turns a deaf ear to the petitions of His Court. Only
later, when He sees Jeanne's pious submission and
recognizes that she is grieving only over King
Charles' misfortune, not her own, He relents and per-
mits the heavenly Court to lighten the Maid's suffering from the torments with which Hell scourges her in
her prison, by giving her concerts which numb her
pain and drive away her fears.

As Aristotle taught that woman is a blunder of

Nature, that ceased halfway in the intention of creating a man, with Chapelain even Jeanne became subordinate as a mere woman. Dunois is the hero, Jeanne nothing more than the grace by which God was pleased to strengthen the hero's arm. The preface explains that the entire composition is an allegory: France in this case means the human soul in its battle with itself; King Charles is the Will, which, although naturally inclined to the good, can easily be misled into evil if it has the appearance of good; the English and the Bourguignons are Excesses of Ire; Amaury and Agnes are examples of Sensual Desire, Dunois is Virtue, Tanneguy is Understanding, and La Pucelle, as said before, is Divine Grace personified, who, though all strength of Soul is broken down, strengthens the Will, keeps up the Understanding, unites with Virtue, conquers Instinct, and thus in the end brings Peace.

The poem, mostly boring, becomes burlesque in places, as the passage where Jeanne, in a cave of Compiègne forest, takes her sustenance from "acorns and grief" for a month.

The dreadful puns are helpful in achieving the air of solemnity for which the poet is striving:

> Sur elle l'Anglais tonne et tonne à grands éclats;
> Mais pour tonner sur elle, il ne l'étonne pas.

Some parts of Voltaire's work can be appreciated only if one knows the original of which they are a parody; for instance, in the droll lines:

> Jeanne étonné, ouvrant un large bec,
> Crut quelque temps que l'on lui parlait grec,
> La grâce agit, cette augustine grâce
> Dans son esprit porte un jour efficace.

Fun is made of the wonderful transformations of Jeanne's mind in Chapelain's poem.

4

The sublime aspect of Jeanne d'Arc, that is familiar to the modern world for the last century and a half,

had not been brought to light in Voltaire's day.
Jeanne's contemporaries had done everything possible to disgrace and besmirch her, before they
burned her on the pyre. They were, however, convinced that God spoke to man through virgins. But
one had to differentiate between false and true
prophetesses. And first of all one had to ascertain
that the virgin really was a virgin. Hence, immediately upon her arrival in Chinon, Jeanne was carefully examined by matrons. Hence again the
six-weeks examination to which she had to submit
in Poitiers, attended by midwives, proven virgins,
widows and wives. Among these women was the
Queen of Sicily and Jerusalem, the Duchess of Anjou, Lady Jeanne de Preuilly, the fifty-seven-year-
old wife of Monsieur de Gaucourt, governor of
Orléans, and the eighteen-year-old wife of the
Messire Robert le Maçon, Jeanne de Mortemer.

For Jeanne d'Arc's contemporaries virginity had
a special power. For the devil never had dealings with
a virgin. This explains the thrice-repeated examination of Jeanne by the English when she languished in
her prison, that outrageous examination which, although performed by women, the Regent of England,
the Duke of Bedford, was not ashamed to watch
through a hole in the prison wall. When this last
examination again gave the prisoner a favorable verdict, an attempt was made to dishonor her by rape
and thus to make admission easier for the devil.

In the eyes of their immediate posterity neither
Jeanne d'Arc nor Dunois was of sufficient importance to furnish the material for an epic composition. On the other hand, France's fanatic and superstitious clergy had made capital of Jeanne as a
miracle-girl. This led those who were repelled by
such superstition to scoff at the buxom country
tavern-lass, who, at the age of twenty-seven, was
called a virginal saint.

That Jeanne was only eighteen years old and had
never been a bar maid, was not known in Voltaire's
time.

The scoffers never thought, either, of the historic
Jeanne but of the legend hatched up in the vestry

rooms and polished into a clerical propaganda figure by a bad poet. How far Voltaire, too, was from trying to attack her historic aspect, is shown best by the description he gives of her in his *Essai sur les mœurs*. Here he writes:

"These victories, won by a young girl through an apparent miracle, the unction of the King, which showed her to be a saint, soon recovered the kingdom for Charles and drove out the foreigners. The instrument of these miracles, however, Jeanne d'Arc herself, was injured and captured while defending Compiègne. A man like the Black Prince would have honored and esteemed her courage; the Regent Bedford thought it necessary to dishonor her in order to strengthen the English position.

"She had pretended to work wonders [Voltaire in the spirit of his time naïvely believes Jeanne was consciously lying]; Bedford pretended to believe her a witch.

"The University of Paris started an inquisition, accusing Jeanne d'Arc of heresy and magic. The University believed what Bedford wished or if it did not, was guilty of detestable cowardice. This heroine, who was worthy of the miracle she pretended to have performed, was sentenced in Rouen by Cauchon, Bishop of Beauvais, with five other French bishops and an English bishop, aided by a Dominican monk, the representative of the Inquisition, and by the doctors of the University. She was stamped as a superstitious prophetess of the devil, slanderess of God and His saints, etc. As such she was condemned to life imprisonment on bread and water. . . .

"When she was accused of wearing men's clothes—an attire which was purposely left to her at her trial [and which she had worn at night to ward off the soldiers who attacked her]—her judges, who did not even have jurisdiction over her as a prisoner of war, pronounced her guilty of relapsing into heresy. They burned at the stake this heroine who had been the savior of their King, to whom, had she lived in our day, men would have erected altars. Charles VII later on restored her memory, although it was already made immortal by her martyrdom."

These forcible words prove that Voltaire knew well the worth of Jeanne d'Arc and what a disgrace her fate was to mankind.

One day in the year 1730 the guests at Richelieu's table expressed their conviction that Voltaire was far better equipped to treat the theme than Chapelain had been. Voltaire answered that nothing seemed to him less suited for epic treatment than the story of a bar-maid who left her tap-room to die at the stake. The story in his opinion should be told in a mock-heroic vein, in the style of *Orlando Furioso* by Ariosto. Richelieu asked him to try it; the others present joined in the request and Voltaire was amenable to persuasion. With his gift of improvization he quickly wrote some of the lines and read them to the company, winning enthusiastic applause. He promised his audience and himself that before long he would go on with the work. In his retirement in Cirey he elaborated four cantos, and thenceforward the work became his dearest pastime, his favorite sin, his secret vice, the greatest daring of his life, which might expose him to all kinds of dangers; his admirers (of both sexes) were dying to see it, and when they did they were paralyzed with delight. Voltaire's *La Pucelle* became a shibboleth, a byword, a touchstone. Those who knew something of it were initiated, were fellow-conspirators of the freethinking opposition.

5

To understand the importance ascribed to the satire by its contemporaries one must consider that "the supernatural," which no longer affects the enlightened world, at that time obtruded itself upon even those who were so intelligent that of their own accord they would never have given it a thought.

It was not until this period that the population began to throw off the grossest superstition. For instance, people had just begun to doubt the authenticity of Magdalene's and Lazarus' dwelling in Provence, to doubt the existence of saints like Saint Marguerite, whose voice spoke to Jeanne d'Arc; finally they began to question the fake miracles and relics. In 1702 an enlightened priest, the Bishop of Chalôns-sur-Marne, Gaston Louis de Noailles, threw away a relic, worshipped for centuries as the navel of Jesus Christ. Everybody in Chalôns grumbled. Royal and Parliamentary officials protested and called attention to the fact that Christ's clothing was preserved in Argenteuil and in Treves, his cloak at Turin and at Laon, one of the nails of his cross in St. Denis, etc. But the clamor of the credulous mob rebounded from the Bishop's firmness.

At that time the Devil was talked of as much as during the sixteenth and seventeenth centuries. In the hope of meeting him somewhere and asking his counsel prominent ladies in scanty attire met with all kinds of strange adventures. Deacon Pâris, mentioned before, threw the faithful into convulsions while working his miracles.

Toulon, too, had its miracle: An old Jesuit by the name of Girard, who disciplined his pupil, the pretty Mademoiselle Cadière, by frequent gentle chastisements, declared, in 1731, that this treatment had glorified the features and figure of his interesting penitent to such an extent that her hands and feet showed traces of the nails of the Saviour, blood had dropped from the wounds, also from those caused by the crown of thorns on the forehead. The monk was believed, or at least he appeared to be. Nobody dared to investigate the matter.

Then to the general astonishment it developed that the chastisements had been fertilizing. Old and ugly as Girard was, one morning it was disclosed that the pretty Cadière was pregnant, and not she alone but a number of the other penitents of the Abbé: shop-girls, working-girls, and ladies.

Now the Jansenists insisted that Girard, who was a Jesuit, was the Devil himself; whereupon the Jesuits retorted that the Devil had possessed Mademoiselle Cadière, who had obviously bewitched Girard. Provence was divided into two parties; but as the clergy had the upper hand the supporters of the King in the Parliament of Aix proposed to have Mademoiselle Cadière hanged.—A sort of justice that aroused the greater part of the population and gave rise to numerous assemblies of protest.

Now Girard had the brilliant idea of getting all of his pregnant penitents out of the way into convents. He could trust the discretion of the nuns. The Convent of Ollioules, where he took Mademoiselle Cadière, bore an evil reputation; the Abbess led a free life; the wealthy inmates of the convent were served by monks; the poorer nuns found consolation in passionate friendship for each other.

The Bishop of Toulon at first took the part of Mademoiselle Cadière; but intimidated by the Jesuits, who hinted at certain weak spots in his own conduct, he was persuaded to join them.

The trial was a scandal. The judges threatened all the witnesses appearing against Girard with torture; the two representatives sent to Toulon by the Parliament of Paris fraternized with the Jesuits. But the simple defence of the young woman in court appeared so truthful and made Girard seem so guilty that the case was brought before the Parliament in Aix, where all society took the side of the Jesuit brother. He declared with calm effrontery that he had done no more than to obey the rules of the religious mystic. That he as her confessor had locked himself up with his penitent and chastised her, as was his right and duty; what was being called indecent was essential to break down her worldly pride.

The verdict of this trial was to hang la Cadière in the square of the Dominican Convent in Toulon. But all the people of the lower classes thronged to the prison and called: "Don't worry, miss, we are here!"

Then a sudden change took place in the Parliament. The Jansenists declared that Girard deserved the stake; that he was a sorcerer, possessed of the Devil. When (in October, 1731) the verdict was announced, twelve votes were for condemning Girard to death, twelve were for setting him free. The vote of the president decided and Girard was dismissed.

Voltaire regarded the trial humorously. Hence, in the second canto of *La Pucelle,* these verses about the God Morpheus:

Aux cris du moine il monte en son char noir,
Par deux hiboux traîné; dans la nuit sombre.
Dans l'air il glisse, et doucement fend l'ombre.
Les yeux fermés, il arrive en bâillant,
Se met sur jeanne, et tâtonne, et s'étend;
Et secouant son pavot narcotique,
Lui souffle au sein vapeur soporifique,
Tel on nous dit que le moine Girard,
En confessant la gentille Cadière,
Insinuait de son souffle paillard
De diabloteaux une ample fourmilière.

Voltaire does not dwell upon the outrageousness given the affair by the courts nor upon the vulgarity and hypocrisy of the monk; what amuses him is the assertion of the Jansenists that the Devil was involved, that the case could not be explained in a natural way, that Girard must be a sorcerer. With sarcasm he swears that Girard himself, his accusers and defenders, his opponents and protectors, his witnesses and judges, were all far from being sorcerers.

Venez, venez, mon beau père Girard
Vous méritez un long article à part,
Vous voilà donc, mon confesseur de fille,
Tendre dévot qui prêchez à la grille,
Que dîtes-vous des pénitents appas
De ce tendron converti dans vos bras?
J'estime fort cette douce aventure,
Tout est humain, Girard, en votre fait;
Ce n'est pas là pécher contre nature.
Que de dévots en ont encor plus fait!
Mais, mon ami, je ne m'attendais guère
De voir entrer le diable en cette affaire.
Girard, Girard, tous vos accusateurs,
Jacobin, carme, et feseur d'écriture,
Juges, témoins, ennemis, protecteurs,
Aucun de vous n'est sorcier, je vous jure.

6

La Pucelle was a joke written by Voltaire for his own amusement and that of a few of his intimate friends. At first it was not his intention that it should be a work for the public. He had qualms about every canto he finished, and refused a copy even to persons whom he could trust. In 1737 Frederick the Great asked in vain for a copy. Six years later the Prussian King came into the possession of a few cantos, but had to promise to keep them inaccessible even to his intimate circle. The rest was kept by Madame du Châtelet at Cirey under seven seals.

But all these precautions were of no avail. Treacherous secretaries made copies which to Voltaire's sorrow came into circulation.

On September 2, 1735, at four o'clock in the morning, he was informed that several cantos were in circulation in Paris. He wrote at once asking for further information, made it plain that the matter was of extreme importance, and he prepared to flee. When it turned out that only a few copies existed and that these represented only a small part of the work, he forgot his fears. But later the number of copies increased, their contents became more complete, and it seemed especially dangerous that whoever had made the copies had filled in the gaps with the clumsiest obscenities.

It was just this, however, that gave Voltaire the idea of the means by which he could save himself. He had entirely new manuscripts made, filled so full of nonsense and bad verses that nobody could believe him the author of such coarse and stupid jokes.

The insipidity of single parts and the imperfection of the technique, however, were by no means followed by a decrease in the demand; the manuscripts were fought for.

In the year 1754, twenty-four years after he had begun the composition he learned, to his despair, that a printing was planned. In 1755 an edition appeared which was quickly followed by others. Then d'Alembert advised him to publish an edition himself. For a long time he could not make up his mind to do so. Finally, in 1762, he published the work.

From a modern standpoint it appears probable that the author was induced to withhold the work for a whole generation because of its many indecent parts. But one would be mistaken in believing that Voltaire himself found the composition indecent. The eighteenth century conception of what was fit for polite ears was different from that of the twentieth century. Most of the eminent ladies of that time read—and even wrote—without being in the least ashamed, things which would offend or embarrass a well-bred woman of today. All writers of that time mentioned the obscene more or less frankly—not only wags like Piron or Gresset, or the younger Crebillon, but even the most sedate like Montesquieu (in his *Lettres Persanes*), and the most exalted like Diderot (in *Les Bijoux Indiscrets*).

No, what Voltaire feared was an accusation of sacrilege and scoffing at the saints, although in reality he had only poked fun at a dull superstition. He says himself that the reproaches uttered against him because of his ridicule of superstition proved how necessary and useful his work was. The desire with which it was sought on all sides was a sign of the bad foundation beneath the dogmatic creed of that time. Even in the cloisters *La Pucelle* was read with enthusiasm.

7

When Voltaire visited Frederick in 1750 he presented the King with a copy of the part of *La Pucelle* then finished, but he dismissed his secretary Tinois when he discovered that the latter had stolen a copy for Frederick's brother, Prince Henry.

We find that the Duke de La Vallière purchased a copy for fifty louis d'or. In 1755 Voltaire approached d'Héméry, the police commissioner of Paris, with a request that he prevent the printing of copies. But in June, 1755, he himself sent a hand-written copy to the Marquise de Pompadour, which, however, did not contain the mocking lines about the Marquis, which Voltaire had interwoven for his own pleasure in the second canto:

> Telle plutôt cette heureuse grisette
> Que la nature ainsi que l'art forma
> Pour le bordel ou bien pour l'opéra,
> Qu'une maman avisée et discrète
> Au noble lit d'un fermier éleva,
> Et que l'Amour, d'une main plus adrète,
> Sous un monarque entre deux draps plaça,
> Sa vive allure est un vrai port de reine,
> Ses yeux fripon s'arment de majesté,
> Sa voix a pris le ton de souveraine,
> Et sur son rang son esprit s'est monté.

These are verses which he would have done better to omit, he who had known Madame de Pompadour in her youth, who had enjoyed her benefactions, who had written verses in her honor and who liked to tell her flattering things. If she had read lines like those above, the friendship would, of course, have been finished.

Anyone who in his youth has read *La Pucelle* and who has been surprised by the curiosity and indignation the work aroused at the beginning of the nineteenth century, is apt to again be surprised, if he rereads it how innocuous this composition really is. In our day it appears obsolete, largely because the things it attacks were destroyed by Voltaire himself, and because it is so interlarded with contemporary allusions that, like most literary satires, it cannot be understood without commentaries.

The only thing about the poem that shocks us today is the apparently heartless and tasteless burlesque of Jeanne. Even so, the burlesque was intended to be merely of the superstition which had crystallized around Jeanne d'Arc, as pebbles, dirt and seaweed form a solid mass around the shell containing a pearl.

In its original form, the work dealt with entirely other matters than Jeanne. Read the first cantos and note how he pokes fun at the Black Arts, which were then believed in. St. Denis rides his sunbeam, Jeanne her jackass. The Franciscan monk, Grisbourdon, enchants the mule-driver into a mule and rides it.

There is not a little humor, when, in the second canto, Baudricour accuses the King of forgetting France's distress in his love for Agnes Sorel, and when the knight announces to him that a different woman, who by virtue of her virginity possesses magic power, will come to his aid and will drive the English from the country. The only question which King Charles finds important enough to put to Jeanne is about her virginity:

> Donc, se tournant vers la fière beauté,
> Le roi lui dit, d'un ton de majesté
> Qui confondrait tout autre fille qu'elle:
> "Jeanne, écoutez: Jeanne, êtes-vous pucelle?"

Not only humorous but in keeping with the absurdity of the historic fact, is Jeanne's answer:

> Jeanne lui dit: "O grand sire, ordonnez
> Que médécins, lunettes sur le nez,
> Matrones, clercs, pédants, apothecaires,
> Viennent sonder ces féminins mystères;
> Et si quelqu'un se connaît à cela,
> Qu'il trousse Jeanne et qu'il regarde là."

Very drolly conceived is the answer by which Jeanne convinces the King of her miraculous mission:

> A sa réponse et sage et mesurée
> Le roi vit bien qu'elle était inspirée.
> "Or sus, dit-il, dites moi en savez tant,
> Fille de bien, dites moi dans l'instant
> Ce que j'ai fait cette nuit à ma belle?
> Mais parlez net!"—"Rien du tout," dit-elle.
> Le roi surpris soudain s'agenouilla,
> Cria tout haut: "Miracle!" et se signa.

The third canto satirized the stupidity of contemporary mankind. Stupidity is described as a Queen (La Sottise) ruling over a great empire filled with all the horrors for which she was responsible: the pyre which consumed Urbain Grandier; the other upon which Marie de Medici's lady-in-waiting, Eleonore Galigai was burned as a witch; the edict issued under Louis XIII prohibiting under penalty of the galleys the teaching of any philosophy other than that of Aristotle, or the sale of any emetic.

In the first part the ridicule centers about the miraculous effects of Jeanne's virginity and about all that is done, on the one hand, to end that sublime condition, and on the other, to preserve it undefiled. The effect is uproarious when the stupid monk cries out to the English: "Tremble, she is a virgin!"

> Elle est pucelle, Anglais, frémissez tous;
> C'est Saint Denis qui l'arme contre vous.

In the fifth canto the arrival of the monk Grisbourdon in Hell gives occasion for a merry description of the life led by the Devil and his vassals, a description reminiscent neither of Dante's *Inferno* nor Milton's *Paradise Lost*.

In the final revision of the work Voltaire found it
necessary for the sake of his safety to eliminate a
great part, which is now found as appendix matter
in some editions. According to the original outline
(in the edition of 1756), Voltaire's Hell housed the
great missionary Emperor Constantine because of his
crimes, as well as Saint Louis of France because of
the slaughter of the Saracens, and because of his
asceticism and his self-tortures. Its roll call boasted
not only saints, but also revered reformers like Luther and Calvin. While Luther did not interest the
poet especially, and is only mentioned in passing,
Calvin is damned as the evil-eyed, stony-hearted,
jealous fanatic who sent poor Servet to the stake;
Voltaire also treats Calvin's city, fanatic Geneva,
which he knew very well, with deep contempt.

This is not the only section that Voltaire found it
necessary to tone down, and the alterations were
never as witty or as effective as the lines that they
supplanted. The same is true in the twentieth canto
where the jackass kneels before Jeanne's bed and
announces his astonishing age: for it is Balaam's
ass from Canaan, who enjoys eternal youth, but has
to live for a thousand years in celibacy. Then follows
a passage which was absolutely in violation of the
laws of the time concerning blasphemy: it is that in
which the ass declares himself the one on whose back
Jesus made his entry into Jerusalem.

> Je vis couler, content de mon état,
> Plus de mille ans dans ce doux célibat.
> Bientôt il plut au maître du tonnerre,
> Au créateur du ciel et de la terre,
> Pour racheter le genre humain captif
> De se faire homme et, ce qui pis est, Juif.
> Joseph Panther et la brune Marie
> Sans le savoir fit cet œuvre pie.

This earlier version of the ass's story is far funnier
than the way the final text gives it:

> C'était un point de sa réligion
> Que sur un âne il entrât dans Sion;
> Cet âne était prédit par Isaïe
> Ezéchiel, Baruch et Jérémie.
> C'était un cas important dans la loi;
> O Jeanne d'Arc! cet âne, c'était moi.

However, this winds up with a very ugly fantasy, and Voltaire was right in removing this portion and preventing its publication, as far as possible.

Whoever reads *La Pucelle* today should note the introductory stanzas of the cantos. They are gay and usually contain some joke or confession from Voltaire's own life. Thus the introduction to the seventh makes reference to Voltaire's bitter experience in his youth with Mademoiselle de Livry and his friend, and at the same time he calls it unworthy to hate and to persecute the girl who has thrown one one.

Several of the conceits which have very little to do with the theme are extremely witty. When Dunois, in the course of his journey arrives at the Castle of Glory, Voltaire describes Fama as an old chattering goddess, who would like to win everybody to herself: She has two trumpets; one she puts to her lips and glorifies heroic deeds; the other she puts behind her and through it announces the names of the literary lice which make their livelihood as parasites of great persons. Then follows a list of Voltaire's literary enemies: Guyot, Fréron, la Beaumelle, and Nonnotte, whose acquaintance we have not yet made.

The work as a whole appears today not only unpoetic but hardly funny. Its indecencies, which revolt us when they pollute a figure like that of Jeanne d'Arc, are no more entertaining when applied to Charles VII's mistress, Agnes Sorel. And all in all indecency for its own sake is no longer amusing. Where the work is meant to be most daring, it becomes unreadable. What was once poetry for princes, is now scarcely poetry for servants.

It is dangerous for a great spirit to have satisfied his contemporaries to too great a degree. Voltaire did this as a serious epic poet in his *Henriade*, as a mockepic poet in *La Pucelle*.

Both works are obsolete today. They have fulfilled their purpose, have fired their ammunition. Now we look upon them as one would regard two mortars of obsolete design in an arsenal.

8

An extraordinary number of the things Voltaire said about Madame du Châtelet are on record; his remembered conversation, his letters, his published works, verse as well as prose, abound with admiration of her and devotion to her. Rarely has a writer immortalized his mistress as Voltaire has the Marquise. One has to go back to Dante, Petrarch and Boccaccio to find such constant and devoted praise of one woman; they, however, call the lady only by her first name, make her unreal, and praise her in such a way as to make her recognition by strangers impossible. One must go still further back, to the troubadours of Provençe of the twelfth century, to find this particular adoration, the expression of a love in which the intellectual element prevails. Voltaire was far from being a troubadour; but his deification of Emily has something about it which comes directly from the Provençal lyricists.

He is to be seen purely as a lover only in the earliest poems of the year 1734. One of the most deep-felt is the forty-seventh epistle to Urania.

Here are a few verses:

> Je vous adore, ô ma chère Uranie!
> Pourquoi si tard m'avez vous enflammé?
> Qu'ai-je donc fait des beaux jours de ma vie?
> Ils sont perdus; je n'avais point aimé.
> Je n'ai vécu que du jour, où ton âme
> M'a pénetré de sa divine flamme;
> Que de ce jour où, livré tout à toi,
> Le monde entier a disparu pour moi.
> Ah quel bonheur de te voir, de t'entendre!
> Que ton esprit a de force et d'appas!
> Dieux! que ton plaisirs je goûte dans tes bras!
> Trop fortuné, j'aime ce que j'admire.

None of his former feelings for women were comparable in any way with this one which conquered Voltaire both deeply and permanently. He had become so much a creature of the mind that no woman could fascinate him seriously without fascinating him mentally. Emily was a *"philosophe"* i.e., she was above prejudices to which the mob subscribed; this was why Voltaire could feel that they were on a common intellectual plane. But Emily was in addition an independent thinker, an indefatigable worker, and, what was of even greater importance, her inclinations made her the perfect complement of Voltaire. What filled his life, poetry and history, was for her of secondary interest. The things that attracted her, mathematics and physics, were sciences in which he interested himself seriously during the time they lived together. They had in common the desire to formulate a philosophy of life. He tried to deduce a metaphysical system somewhat after Newton's method in astronomy; she was more attracted by the kind of metaphysics developed by Leibnitz. Later, however, Newton became common territory, and Newton's adoration became the vestibule of the temple in which they met.

As said before, Madame du Châtelet's first introduction to the study of Newton, with Maupertuis as teacher, aroused some ill-humor on the part of her friend. It seemed to him (perhaps for the first and last time in his life) that he had been surpassed in brilliance in the eyes of the one whom he was most anxious to impress. The fortieth epistle bears witness of this. In it are these lines:

> Vous renoncez aux étincelles,
> Aux feux follets de mes écrits,
> Pour des lumières immortelles;
> Et le sublime Maupertuis
> Vient éclipser mes bagatelles.
> Je n'en suis fâché ni surpris.

But such passing ill-humor did not affect the attachment Voltaire felt. This was so deep that ten years after Emily's death, when he began to write down his memories, he commenced with a description of her character, his relations with her and their living together at Cirey, which was mentally so fruitful. He did not forget her passionate love of clothes, and he mentioned this as early as 1733 in a letter to the Abbé de Sade, in a short jesting verse:

> Cette belle âme est une étoffe
> Qu'elle brode en mille façons;
> Son esprit est très philosophe,
> Et son cœur aime les pompons.

He tells us how Madame du Châtelet did the castle entirely over, as soon as they had resolved to retire there; he tells about assembling an important physical apparatus, and how scholars visited them to philosophize with them in their solitude. He mentions the famous physicist König, who was a professor in The Hague and the librarian of the Princess of Orania and who lived at Cirey two years. He names Maupertuis who, he says, is jealous of him, and hence hostile.

He reports that he taught Madame du Châtelet English and that in three months she had as good a mastery of that language as he; thereafter they read together Locke, Newton and Pope. No less quickly she learned Italian; they read together all of Tasso and Ariosto. When Frederick the Great's friend, Algarotti, came to Cirey, where he finished his *Newtonianismo per le Dame,* she was so familiar with his language that she was able to offer in Italian many valuable suggestions.

In their secluded life she and Voltaire tried not only to round out their general knowledge, but also to keep in touch with everything that was going on in the intellectual world. Madame du Châtelet studied Leibnitz and developed part of his system in her well-written book *Institutions de Physique.* She wrote simply, clearly, firmly and gracefully.

By and by, Voltaire says, she discarded Leibnitz' ideas abandoning metaphysics altogether in favor of the discoveries of Newton. She translated his entire "Principia" into French, and after having strengthened her knowledge further she added to this difficult work a commentary which was edited by Clairaut.

9

Voltaire's description—written for publication—of Madame du Châtelet's studies and scientific production, gives an account of various complicating and embarrassing circumstances following the publication of her book on the doctrines of Leibnitz.

At first, under the influence of Voltaire as well as of Maupertuis, she had adopted Newton and the general principles of exact scientific reasoning; later, during König's two-year sojourn at Cirey, she was converted by him to Leibnitz' monadology. She appears in her book *Institutions de Physique* a convinced disciple of Leibnitz. Although Voltaire was far from being able to follow her belief in monads, differences over one point or another in philosophy could not disturb their mutual regard.

In her book Madame du Châtelet, had ventured in a very polite way to disagree with the views of Monsieur de Mairan, *Secrétaire perpétuel* at the Royal Academy of Sciences, on the question of the standard of measurement of moving energy—at the same time expressing the hope that Monsieur de Mairan would regard her objections as evidence of the esteem which she felt for his work. Monsieur de Mairan (she says) had mentioned everything that could be said in favor of a wrong premise. This wrong premise was his rejection of the principle of the conservation of energy. This fallacy was also subscribed to by Voltaire in his essay *Doutes sur la mesure des forces vives et sur leur nature,* which, mentions neither Monsieur de Mairan, nor Madame du Châtelet.

Monsieur de Mairan defended his views in an open letter and was wrong, as Voltaire was. His tone was unnecessarily belligerent, and by his remark, that his opponent probably had not read nor understood his treatise, he gave rise to a rumor that Madame du Châtelet was not the real author of her book.

The *Institutions de Physique* had been written during König's stay at Cirey, and Madame du Châtelet in her honesty was really trying to give him all the honor that was due him for the book, all the more because during her and Voltaire's last journey to Paris, on which König accompanied them, a quarrel had arisen between the physicist and herself. The cause is unknown, but the matter was so embarrassing to the Marquise that she did not speak of it to Voltaire.

In a letter to Maupertuis, who had recommended König to her (September 12, 1740), she asks his advice before the publication of her book: "Please tell me whether you think that what I said about König in

the preface is sufficient, or if the publisher's announcement should say something more about him. I
told the truth in both places; you could see from the
concessions I made you, that I have not the art of
disguising it, not even if it were unfavorable to me."

König, who ten years later was to interfere in Voltaire's life in an unforeseen manner, was a Swiss from
Berne who had been expelled from his home for the
follies of his youth. Maupertuis had sent him to
Madame du Châtelet in Cirey, as a teacher and helper
for her geometrical studies. König himself related
how one day she told him impatiently that what he
was teaching her in mathematics were obvious things
that she already knew. Thereupon he had answered
that she was right; but there were other things far
more important than mathematics, and no less enlightening—namely metaphysics. Voltaire's friend began to laugh, but König insisted that he could easily
prove them to her, if she would only pay him the
necessary attention.

After the break between them he told his friends
that to each lesson at Cirey he had brought along a
syllabus of the point he wanted to prove; he had explained it, had proved it and asked the Marquise if
she acknowledged it. As soon as she had said yes,
he handed her the paper to sign. And this pack of
signed papers, he insisted, was the foundation of the
Marquise's *Introduction métaphysique*. She had done
nothing but put his ideas into form and style; the
work itself was his.

Such remarks of König were apparently carried to
Mairan, as he expressed himself so sarcastically. The
Marquise, very angry, wrote a splendid reply, highly
sarcastic, which brought the laughter and sympathies
of the literary world to her side (*Réponse de Madame
la marquise du Châtelet à la lettre que M. de Mairan
lui a écrite le 18 fevrier 1741 sur la question des forces
vives*). This reply appeared one month after the attack.

She wrote to d'Argental:

"Mairan is now rather put out, which is very
natural. He had to be, because he was wrong and has
dragged personal matters into a purely literary differ-

ence. I was not the one who began the petty spitefulnesses. The *Institutions* is very careful to be polite to him and make every excuse for his absurdities; but his replies have been full of offensive remarks about me and completely devoid of arguments that might defend his position. Could I ever retort too sharply to his accusation, that I had neither read nor understood him, and that I had plagiarized the main features of my book?"

Voltaire, whose ideas agreed with Mairan's, while his heart was with the pretty and angry Emily, tried his best to straighten out the disagreement between her and Mairan, as well as that between her and Maupertuis. He wrote to Mairan that it was impossible for him to regard the break between him and the Marquise seriously. "I flatter myself that your little skirmish with Madame du Châtelet will serve to increase the esteem and friendship you feel for each other." To Maupertuis, who to Emily's bitter disappointment had taken the part of König, he wrote in the same conciliatory spirit. For Maupertuis, without any exact information about what had happened, gave her to understand that she was shamefully wrong in a matter in which she believed she was behaving very generously. Voltaire sent word to the scholar so admired by Emily: "Write her. A man is always in the right with a woman even when he is wrong. You will retain her friendship; she still respects you." Voltaire, however, had to write twice before the stubborn Maupertuis gave in. But then the Marquise answered heartily:

"I don't do things by halves, either in love or in reconciliation; I have given you back my heart and I count upon the steadfastness of yours. I have not concealed my sorrow over the rift in our friendship, and now I am not trying to hide my joy that we have got over it. You have taught me how painful it is to have to complain of a person whom one would like to love and whom one cannot help respecting."

Sifting this quarrel about scientific views and personal feelings, one comes to the question of the scope, the strength, the originality of Madame du Châtelet's talent for mathematics and science. Voltaire never calls her less than a genius, and this apparently not because of love for her, but out of honest and profound admiration.

Devotion to science gave stability and firmness to Madame du Châtelet's personality—a devotion, strong enough to induce her to forsake social triumphs and to spend her days and nights at her studies. Work was a necessity and a joy for her. She overcame the greatest difficulties. She delved into Newton, and understood him so well that she translated him. Though a disciple of Newton, she showed enough independence to assert herself concerning the theory of the conservation of energy in favor of Leibnitz' departure from Descartes, although Newton at the end of his chapter on optics had accepted Descartes' conclusion. She was therefore able to give a clear presentation of the ideas of the philosophers and mathematicians. Beyond that her capacities were doubtless limited, as female talent generally is, in the field of science.

At the end of the nineteenth century Sonja Kowalewska's mathematical talent, which some called genius, caused a sensation similar to the case of Emily du Châtelet in the middle of the eighteenth century. For her research work Sonja Kowalewska received an honorary degree from the Academy, which Madame du Châtelet did not. Nevertheless Sonja Kowalewska, even as a professor of mathematics in Stockholm, remained the pupil of the great mathematician Weierstrass in Berlin. If he gave her a problem to solve she showed ability and sagacity in her answer. On her own initiative she accomplished nothing.

In the same way Emily du Châtelet astounded people with her capacity, amazing for a woman, for solving the most abstruse mathematical and physical problems. But she was a pupil of Maupertuis as well as of König, of Clairaut as well as of her intimate friend Voltaire. And it is doubtful that any one of these men, despite all admiration for her aptness, ever felt inferior to her.

10

Voltaire is the only one who speaks as if she had led him to the study of sciences, and who again and again called her a prodigy scarcely even mentioning her name without attributing to her genius.

Tu m'appelles à toi, vaste et puissant génie,
Minerve de la France, immortelle Emilie,
Je m'éveille à ta voix, je marche à ta clarté.

However, the term "genius" was more liberally used at that time than now, when it is understood to mean the most outstanding intellects of mankind. In the eighteenth century the word was a medal to be pinned on the chest of any talented person.

Not always, however, does Voltaire sing of his Emily with such chaste formality. If one studies the great number of longer and shorter poems to his beloved, one finds many, especially in the early years of their relationship, in which admiration is mixed with a warm eroticism.

In the 48th Epistle he says: "Let him who will, my dear Urania, teach you to measure the earth, to read the sky and to lay before your genius problems for your eager eyes to master. My system is Ovid's, love is my theme and the soul of my verses."

Whatever he writes, to whomever he writes, he likes to weave into his verses a tribute to the mistress of Cirey.

In a poem to a young woman of Rouen, who in conjunction with Cideville has addressed to him an intelligent letter, and whose first name chances to be Emily, he praises Nature for producing two perfect creatures and giving them both the same name:

Je vois que la nature a fait
Parmi ses œuvres infinies
Deux fois un ouvrage parfait,
Elle a formé deux Emilies.

To the inquiry of Frederick of Prussia, as to what
life was like at Cirey, he answers in polite verses
that his friend and he tried to "follow your Highness'
lead" and pattern themselves after Epicurus, cherishing all the arts and adoring Nature. But they follow their master at a great distance. The proportion
between him and themselves is as if the God of day
were to send a ray into a dark room and thus by his
pure light give them the miniature picture of a
majestic landscape.

> Jardins, il faut que je vous fuie,
> Trop d'art me révolte et m'ennuie.
> J'aime mieux ces vastes forêts;
> La nature, libre et hardie,
> Irrégulière dans ses traits
> S'accorde avec ma fantaisie.

This poem, by the way, contains one of those sudden quirks, not at all uncommon in Voltaire, in
which he—long before Jean Jacques—glorifies wild
nature at the expense of all art and self-conscious
landscape gardening:
Out of dozens of little poems to Emily, let us ex-
amine a few. Most of them are humorous, but not
once, even in jest, is his adoration, or at least his
flattery forgotten. The following lines, from the first
year of their acquaintance, are significant:

> L'esprit sublime et la délicatesse,
> L'oubli charmant de sa propre beauté,
> L'amitié tendre et l'amour emporté
> Sont les attraits de ma belle maîtresse.

Nicest of all is the following motto Voltaire composed for Madame du Châtelet:

> Du repos, des riens, de l'étude,
> Peu de livres, point d'ennuyeux,
> Un ami dans la solitude,
> Voilà mon sort; il est heureux.

"Happiness" is his constant refrain in the letters
and verses of all these years: Cirey is an Eden; happiness is in Cirey. For instance read this impromptu,
written one moonlight night in the garden:

Astre brillant, favorable aux amants!
Porte ici tous les traits de ta douce lumière:
Tu ne peux éclairer, dans ta vaste carrière,
Deux cœurs plus amoureux, plus tendres, plus constants.

In little poems the concentration of which would delight a Japanese, Voltaire succeeded in combining sincerity and wit. They are works of art, like those gems of ancient Greece and Rome which reproduce accurately and delicately the likeness of a woman or a man, on the surface of a semi-precious stone no larger than a finger nail. These two epigrams are deliberately paired. The first accompanied a ring into which his portrait was engraved:

Barier grave ces traits déslinés pour vos veux;
Avec quelque plaisir daignez les reconnaître!
Les vôtres dans mon cœur furent gravés bien mieux,
Mais ce fut par un plus grand maître.

On receiving her portrait he answered, varying his expression:

Traits charmants, image vivante
Du tendre et cher objet de ma brûlante ardeur!
L'image que l'amour a gravé dans mon cœur
Est mille fois plus ressemblante.

Voltaire does not hesitate to abase himself to call himself a step-child of Nature, in comparison to her who has every gift the gods can bestow; but when she loves him the balance is reëstablished:

Esprit, raison, beaux yeux, charmant visage,
Fleur de santé, doux loisir, jours sereins,
Vous avez tout, c'est là votre portage.
Moi, je parais un être infortuné,
De la nature enfant abandonné,
Et n'avoir rien semble mon apanage:
Mais vous m'aimez, les dieux m'ont tout donné.

Fully persuaded of his happiness, above the door into his hall he had engraved the words:

Asile des beaux arts, solitude où mon cœur
Est toujours demeuré dans une paix profonde,
C'est vous qui donnez le bonheur
Qui promettait en vain le monde.

He jeopardized his good fortune several times by journey and thoughtlessnesses. His nature demanded more variety than Emily's.

11

The dedication to *Alzire* begins thus:
"Madame.

"What a poor tribute to you is a poetic work like this, that lives only for a time, whose value is fixed by the transitory favor of the public, and which then vanishes into the darkness of oblivion.

"What is a trifling romance written in verse, to you, who can read treatises on geometry as easily as others read novels; to you, who found in Locke, the wise teacher of mankind, her own feelings and the expression of her own ideas; to a lady who is at the same time a model of Beauty and a champion of Truth!"

But—Voltaire goes on—the genius is greatest who does not disdain any of the fine arts; happiest is the spirit, which enjoys the niceties of Cicero and Bossuet, of Vergil and Tasso, after having found enlightenment in Clarke and Newton. And such is her genius.

There was a time—he continues—when in France women believed they were acting contrary to the nature of their sex by seeking to acquire knowledge. The ridicule which great men like Boileau and Molière heaped upon learned ladies, seems a barbaric prejudice. Boileau wrote a satire ridiculing a lady because she understood astronomy. It would have been better had he understood it himself. She, who stands so high in scientific attainment, has at the same time an appreciation of every sort of poetry; thus she pays as great a compliment to literature as Queen Christine and the Duchess of Maine did by loving it as one of the greatest of the fine arts.

Alzire was performed for the first time in January, 1736, and had a great success. The play was given twenty consecutive times, which was an unusual run; it earned more than 53,000 livres, a sum which Voltaire, to show his gratitude to the actors turned over to them, as he did the royalties from subsequent performances.

It seems to have interested the French deeply that

the scene of the play was laid in America, whose
natives had never before been seen on a French
stage. It was Voltaire's aim, as in *Zaïre*, to arouse disgust with cruelty and fanaticism and he could not
have found a better subject than the Spanish in-
vasions in America. The atrocities committed in 1517
by Cortez in Mexico, and in 1525 by Pizarro in Peru,
were well chosen to show the barbarity and intolerance of the Christian conquerors.

12

The first few years at Cirey were highly satisfactory and happy ones for both parties. Now and then,
however, there was a cloud. The reason was to be
looked for partly in Voltaire's fears of sentence to
prison, partly in his restlessness, which called for
change and adventure.

The main cause of his journeys, however, was the
persecution to which his compositions were subject.
Looked at with the eyes of an enlightened posterity,
they were as a rule very innocent; at the time, they
offered excellent excuse for government interference.

Le Mondain, one of Voltaire's most popular compositions, was written in the year 1736, immediately
after the great success of *Alzire*. Nowhere is he more
reminiscent of Horace and Ovid; one can even say
that the entire poem has for text these verses from
Ovid's *Ars amatoria:*

> Prisca juvent alios! ego me nunc denique natum
> Gratulor. Hæc ætas moribus apta meis.

Le Mondain mocks those who praise the old times,
the golden age, in which people went around naked
and ate acorns. Voltaire is frank to admit he likes
his own era, even though it is called the iron age; it
is an age of new comforts and cleanliness, new demands and new joys, unknown to his barbaric ancestors:

> O le bon temps que ce siècle de fer!
> Le superflu, chose très nécessaire,
> A réuni l'un et l'autre hémisphère.

Adam and Eve had long, dirty nails, unkempt hair, no knives and forks and no good bed. They knew no sanitation, and without cleanliness even the happiest love is not love but an instinct to be ashamed of:

> Sans propreté l'amour le plus heureux
> N'est plus amour, c'est un besoin honteux.

The much praised state of nature, to tell the truth is not very attractive, compared to the life led by civilized people. It is better to enjoy the paintings of the gentle Correggio and the skilled Poussin, the statues of Bouchardon, the jewel setting of Germain, better to live in rooms whose walls are covered with Gobelin tapestries, than to dwell in the garden which became famous because of the Devil and the apple.

One hardly can believe it! But at that time it was criminal to joke about our early ancestors' ignorance of the virtues of bathing or to make fun of the legend of Eve and the snake. And yet what right has a modern Dane like myself to be astonished at this, when as late as the year 1891 my own Danish government prosecuted the editor Henrik Pontoppidan because he had published in his paper a humorous variation of the story of the creation of Eve. But Denmark, unlike Holland and Switzerland, never was a country in which one could expect to find freedom in religious matters.

Voltaire sent *Le Mondain* to the Bishop of Lucon. When the Bishop died the same year, it was found in one of his drawers; copies were circulated and soon the poet was informed that he was to be seized for punishment.

Thus his flight became a necessity. Emily wept bitterly when they parted. Only one consideration made a short separation desirable: certain puritanic and malicious relatives of the mistress of Cirey resented her living with Voltaire while her husband was at the wars, and they threatened to send the husband a letter of complaint. Although the Marquis had not the least resentment and always kept the same friendship for his wife and for Voltaire this interference on the part of outsiders might have put him in a difficult position.

13

Voltaire traveled via Brussels to Antwerp, thence to Amsterdam and Leyden. In Holland he was safe, and he was welcome; here he could watch over the printing of his books and make corrections on the spot. Just then his great work *Eléments de la Philosophie de Newton* was being printed.

All Madame du Châtelet's efforts were bent on stopping the persecution of Voltaire. She induced her friends to apply to the Treasurer, Monsieur de Chauvelin, and she herself made a naïve attempt by confessing frankly to him how indispensable Voltaire had become to her. In December, 1736, she writes to her friend d'Argental: "The Treasurer knows the bond that unites us; he is aware that my friend's desire for a quiet life with me will hold him in check. Now, what pleasure can he find in filling our lives with bitterness!"

The warm-hearted woman saw her problem in keeping Voltaire from being careless. She recognized that restraint was the condition upon which they might have a happy future. But she suffered tortures trying to restrain a poet and writer of Voltaire's incalculable temper. Paris was still avid for copies of *Le Mondain,* when the rumor of the hundred times more dangerous *Pucelle* started.

A month later Madame du Châtelet writes to d'Argental: "At every moment I have to save him from himself and I use more diplomacy in guiding him than the Vatican does to subdue all Christendom."

When Voltaire reached Brussels, he found the rumor circulated by Jean Baptiste Rousseau, that he had come with the sole purpose of preaching atheism. For this reason he stayed only one day, so his admirers had *Alzire* performed that evening. Madame du Châtelet writes of that to d'Argental: "His laurels follow him everywhere. But what good is all this honor to him! Real happiness in obscurity would be worth far more. How vain is mankind, how blind the soul!" The last she says in a Latin quotation:

O vanas hominum mentes! o pectora cæca!

Of course on this journey Voltaire traveled under an assumed name. He was Monsieur Révol, merchant. He received his letters under this name, and had them addressed to the firm of Ferrand Arty in Amsterdam, and to the banker Hellin in Leyden. True, his incognito was harder to preserve than a king's.

In Leyden crowds collected to see him; twenty young Englishmen of the Court of King George visited him in a body. In Amsterdam, where he lived with a book-dealer named Ledet, he was flooded with tributes from all sides. One of the municipal authorities translated *La Mort de César* and dedicated the translation to him. His *Brutus* had long since been translated into English; now the translation of *Zaïre* was staged in York Buildings, which one of Voltaire's enthusiastic admirers, Mr. Bond, rented for that purpose. Bond playing the part of Lusignan, and several of his enthusiastic friends in other rôles, gave an excellent performance. The sixty-year-old Mr. Bond having put his whole soul into the part he played, collapsed after the first performance and died at once. Such fanatic adorers of Voltaire were these amateurs, that they could not be scared off even by this incident; another at once took over the part of the deceased and the next day the tragedy was played again on the improvised stage, with a prologue in honor of the deceased and of the poet.

All these honors reported to Voltaire from England and those received daily in Holland, together with the job of proof-reading his book on Newton's philosophy, kept this susceptible poet and diligent worker so busy that he rather neglected the correspondence with his friend in Cirey.

How hurt she was by this is shown by a letter she wrote to d'Argental in February, 1737. It is so long that it is impracticable to quote it in its entirety. But no other document shows as clearly the depth of honest love in the character of the Marquise.

In the first pages she assures d'Argental of her absolute confidence. She knows his heart. She reproaches herself for letting Voltaire depart, though she does not mention his name; but she had thought it impossible to keep him at Cirey without the knowledge of the government. Now she wants d'Argental to tell her by what subterfuges he might be able to stay there. Could he stay with her under a different name? That would be embarrassing for him. But if d'Argental thought it necessary it would be done. Could he stay at Cirey openly? One thing in its favor is that just now very few people from Champagne are likely to be run across at the castle. Besides she finds it better for them to be together in Cirey than anywhere else. It would be best if he returned there. No inconveniences would be entailed by this, unless her malicious relatives should carry out their threat and write "that wretched letter" to Monsieur du Châtelet. When he is not at Cirey she cannot watch his conduct so well, and show him the pitfalls that open under him as soon as he misbehaves. Then she gives vent to the fears which clutch her tortured heart, the fears that he may never return at all. In her letters she has reproached him so fiercely that he either answered coolly and formally or not at all.

"I have just received a letter which makes me fear that he will not return; I am very depressed about it. Now I must confide to you the worst: I fear that he feels far more guilty toward me than toward the ministry. Now we shall see if he comes; but I repeat I do not think he will, and I swear to you that I do not believe my strength capable of bearing it. I shall lose him for once and all, don't doubt it! But who can save him from his own will! I have nothing to reproach myself with; that is one consolation, but a very poor one. I was not born to be happy. I do not dare to ask anything of you; but I wish you would try one last attempt to touch his heart. Write him that I am very ill, that I want to let him know it, and that he owes it to me to return, at least to prevent my death. I assure you that after all this is no exaggeration; for the past two days I have had fever. My wild imaginings can kill me if this keeps up for two more days.

"I deserve far more sympathy than ever before. It

is humiliating for me to have to complain about him; it is a torture I never knew before. If you still have a little pity for me, write him; he will not risk having to blush before you. I ask you for this on my knees.

"He sends me the first proofs of this miserable book *Eléments de la Philosophie*. I tell you he thinks only of that. But he will be ruined if it is published in Holland. If he must be ruined he ought at least to know what dangers he is running. On my knees I beg you, write him emphatically, that, if he will not give in and return, he is hopelessly lost; this is my firm belief. If, as you say, his life's happiness or unhappiness depends on his reasonable and careful behavior, he must not be left to himself for even a moment.

"If you had seen his last letter you would not judge me harshly. Its signature is formal, and he calls me Madame. This is so oddly different from old times that my head was dizzy. Write to him at Brussels!

"Monsieur du Châtelet is nagging me to go with him to the wedding of the Princess (Elizabeth-Therese) in Lorraine; but I do not want to. A wedding and a Court would make me desperate. The place which speaks to me of our friend, is the only place I can live."

The letter is much longer and pictures the torture with which Madame du Châtelet pays for having let herself become so attached to a man that he became everything to her, while she means only something to him, not everything, especially not when he was traveling with "his mistress, glory," as Saint-Lambert said of Jean Jacques Rousseau.

Emily could never get used to his absence. Another time she writes:

"I am one hundred and fifty miles away from my friend and it is twelve days since I have heard from him. Excuse me, excuse me! But I am in a terrible state.

"Two weeks ago I was in torture if I let two hours pass without my seeing him; I wrote to him from my room to his. And now two weeks have gone by, and I don't know where he is or what he is doing; I haven't even the sad consolation of sharing his misfortune. Forgive me for boring you with my lamentations; but I am too unhappy!"

She could no more get used to his ambition, his love of glory than she could to these absences. She saw that fame was and remained his real mistress, his dearest beloved. But she could not believe that he was willing to risk obvious dangers, only to be read and admired by the public. One should read the following very characteristic fragment of a letter:

"If a friend, whom he had known for twenty years, had asked him for the manuscript, he would have refused; and he sends it to someone he has scarcely met, a prince! Why in the world put his security in someone else's hands, so unnecessarily? It must be out of pure, foolish vanity (there is no other word for it): to show his metaphysics to a man who cannot appreciate it and is bound to see in the work nothing but its indiscretions! Any man who has no more sense than to blurt out his secret deserves to be betrayed. But I, what have I done to him that he should make my life's happiness dependent upon this Prussian? I tell you I am beside myself."

Poor woman! It was not easy to be unmarriedly wedded to Voltaire, and it is not surprising that in the course of a decade her love for him was exhausted, even though no other woman ever filled his mind or obscured Émily in his eyes.

14

Even when he had grieved her so much by addressing her as Madame and signing his letter formally, he nevertheless promptly granted her request, interrupted his corrections on the book on Newton and quickly returned to Cirey; there he was forgiven at once and—like an insect sensing danger—played dead. He had his letters addressed to him there under the name of Madame d'Azilli.

When Monsieur du Châtelet went to Paris, where he had to interview Cardinal Fleury, Voltaire and Madame du Châtelet gave him letters for d'Argental. Voltaire writes in his:

"I have not dared to write you since I came again to Cirey, and you will understand that I have not written to anybody. I confess to you that, had it not been for the friendship that called me back, I would have spent the rest of my days in a country where I am at least safe from my enemies. . . . In France I can expect nothing but persecution; that is all the reward I shall get here. I should avoid living on French soil, were it not that the tenderness and the great qualities of the one who draws me back cause me to forget that I am here. . . . I make myself a voluntary slave, to live with her beside me. Everything else amounts to nothing. . . . I have always told you that even if my father, my brother, or my son were the Prime Minister of a despotic state, I would leave the state the next day. . . . But Madame du Châtelet, of course, is more to me than father, brother and son."

Madame du Châtelet, on the same occasion wrote a long letter, which begins thus:

"Our friend sends you, my dear friend, a melancholy letter; but his situation is really abominable. You know that his temper is passionate; but his love for you is passionate, too. I dare to take upon myself the responsibility for his continued careful behavior, at least as long as I am so happy as to have him where I can speak to him. . . . I believe that the return of your friend has saved him from a trap into which he was just about to be betrayed by his customary goodness and politeness. Please do not say anything about that in your letters to me as I show them to him; but just repeat your advice to him, to be cautious about having *Newton* printed in France, and to keep *La Pucelle* locked with a hundred keys."

Two daughters of Voltaire's sister had become fatherless and he and his brother took charge of them. Voltaire would have liked to marry the older of them to a son of Madame de Champbonin, a near relative, whom he esteemed highly and who had settled in Cirey with him. But the young girl preferred to choose for herself. She married, as told above, a young officer who had become military intendant. They visited Cirey shortly after their marriage.

For those who are familiar with Madame du Deffand's and Madame Delaunay de Staël's spiteful descriptions of Madame du Châtelet, it will be of great interest to read that this young niece, angry at seeing Voltaire estranged from her and her family by his relations with the Marquise, says vicious things about her and the establishment at Cirey. The young woman writes naïvely:

"I am desperate; I believe him lost to all of his friends; he has fettered himself so that, it seems to me, he will never be able to break his chains. They live in an awful, inhuman solitude. Cirey is situated four leagues (two and a half miles) from the nearest habitation, in a region where one sees nothing but mountains and untilled land. They are deserted by nearly all of their friends and have almost no one from Paris with them.

"That is the life the greatest genius of the century is leading—true, it is with a woman who is highly talented and very pretty, and who employs every conceivable trick to hold him.

"There are no ornaments she does not wear, and no passage from any of the greatest philosophers she cannot quote, to please him. Everything will be lost; He seems more bewitched than ever before. He has furnished a nice apartment for himself with a darkroom for physical experiments. The theatre is very pretty; but no comedy is ever played because there are almost never actors. (Only nine months later Madame de Graffigny writes that within twenty-four hours the inmates themselves rehearsed and played thirty-three acts, of tragedy, comedy, and opera.) But all traveling stock companies that come within six miles have orders to appear at the chateau. Everything possible was done to get hold of one of these during our visit; but the best we got was marionettes, though on the whole they were rather good ones. We were given a splendid reception."

Voltaire, as we saw, interrupted the printing of his *Eléments de la Philosophie de Newton* in Holland, hoping to get permission for the publication of the book in France. But the chancellor, d'Aguesseau, an educated man of no character, thought it impious to criticize Descartes who, although it was not long ago that he, too, was exiled, had now been declared infallible. Voltaire wrote: "Apparently a poor Frenchman is not allowed to express his belief in the proven existence of a general gravitational force, or of a vacuum in space, or that the earth is flat at the poles, and that Descartes' theory is absurd." Cautious of book-sellers, he refused to give Ledet the end of his manuscript and thought he had thus secured himself against the possibility of the book's coming out without his sanction, in case the government refused to give its permission.

He had not reckoned with the slyness and greediness of the book-seller. The latter engaged a mathematician to finish the manuscript, and published it as if all of it were by Voltaire. In order to increase the sales he went so far as to supplement the title *Eléments de la Philosophie de Newton* with the sub-title: *mis à la portée de tout le monde* (made understandable for everyone), which Abbé Desfontaines cleverly misread as *mis à la porte de tout le monde* (shown the door by everyone).

Even Voltaire's worst enemies, the editors of the ecclesiastical journal in Trevoux, acknowledged the astonishing ability he showed in this work, to make clear the most difficult and obscure things. As they remarked, Newton had been buried for twenty-seven years in the warehouse of the publisher who had dared to print his work; but now with Voltaire's explanation he was resurrected. Newton knew how to measure, calculate, and weigh, not how to talk. Thousands of English, German, Hollandish, Russian scholars had probed into his depths, had penetrated the dark, interpreted understandingly, explained intelligently, and produced admirable works. But these distinguished men, also, had not known how to talk, except academically. Newton remained a secret whispered by the initiated among themselves. Then came Voltaire, and Newton was understood; all Paris echoed Newton, stammered Newton, studied Newton, got acquainted with Newton.

15

At that time Voltaire had numerous troubles. The publisher Jore had caused him much anger and had gone so far as to attack his honor. Finally Jore wrote a letter of apology, begging to be forgiven and declaring that he had acted as he had under the influence of Voltaire's enemy (probably Abbé Desfontaines), "of the enemy whom you very well know " Another, similar case was that of Demoulin who speculated in the grain market for Voltaire. Demoulin cheated him out of 24,000 livres and then had the impudence to threaten him with the "surrender of his secrets," if he complained. Only when he saw that Voltaire could not be intimidated, he had his wife write and ask forgiveness. Voltaire, who never grieved over the loss of money, forgave the debt, but demanded a letter in which Demoulin had to apologize for his impertinent threats.

These attacks by Jore and Demoulin meant nothing to Voltaire. He was far more hurt by the stubborn attacks of Abbé Desfontaines.

Of the work on Newton, Desfontaines wrote:

"It would be ridiculous for a philosopher to give up philosophy late in his life, to take up poetry. But, on the contrary it is quite all right for a poet at such an age to turn his back on verse in order to become a philosopher. It is disgraceful for an old man to want to be a poet (*turpe senes vates*). I am not one of those who find it unreasonable that Monsieur de Voltaire has finally grown tired of rhyming his thoughts and measuring his words, and that he is trying to ennoble his mind by rising to the heights of philosophy. But it is a pity that he has allowed himself to be taken in by this Newtonianism which is bad physics and is rejected by all good thinkers in Europe. Besides, one has to be a born geometrician or physicist to make any real headway in these sciences, just as one has to be a born poet to take honors on Parnassus."

And he goes on: The first successes Voltaire has had in science have filled him with such joy that he thought he could teach others. But he was no good as scholar and he has chosen a path which is only leading him astray.

How impudent the Abbé becomes is best shown by this: He writes that in his *Eléments* Voltaire gave a rule for dividing an angle into three parts with a pair of compasses; as a matter of fact the book does not say a word about it. He evidently did not read the book.

Finally Voltaire lost patience with him and wrote a short pamphlet entitled *Le Presérvatif,* in which he takes up the various criticisms of the Abbé point by point, and proves about thirty faults and errors. Not content with the purely literary quarrel, he also takes up, in order to hit Desfontaines the more surely and deeply, his personal relations with him. But as he was in no position to start a feud with a Desfontaines, and as for various reasons he always tried to assure himself of anonymity, he induced a certain Chevalier de Mouhy to let his name appear on the pamphlet, the title page of which showed Desfontaines kneeling in the prison at Bicêtre being beaten black and blue by a lusty fellow with a lash.

This Chevalier de Mouhy, one of the numerous starved literary adventurers of that time, had long received financial support from Voltaire. He got a yearly stipend for literary correspondence with which he supplied the poet. As always in such cases Voltaire was so naïve as to believe his authorship was hidden by leaving the responsibility to a dummy. Actually this was impossible, as the decisive point of the pamphlet permitted no doubt that Voltaire was behind it all.

In the twenty-seventh section of the book, the author is made to say that as Desfontaines in his *Observations sur les Ecrits Modernes* had attacked Monsieur de Voltaire and had boasted of a letter which Voltaire was supposed to have written him, the author had taken the liberty of writing to Monsieur de Voltaire, although he did not know him personally, and had received the following answer:

"I have known Abbé Guyot Desfontaines since 1724, when Monsieur Thiriot introduced him to me as a former Jesuit, who had therefore done some studying. I welcomed him as I welcome all who interest themselves in literature. Fourteen days later I was surprised to receive a letter from him dated from the prison in Bicêtre where he was confined. I learned that three months before had been in le Châtelet for the same crime of which he was now accused. . . . I was fortunate enough at that time to have several influential friends whom death has since taken away from me. Ill as I was, I hurried to Fontainebleau to throw myself at their feet; I plead with them; I saw everybody. Finally I succeeded in having him freed and having the charge against him dropped, thus saving his life. I secured permission for him to go to my friend, the President de Bernières, in the country. He moved out there with Monsieur Thiriot. Do you know what he did when he got there? He wrote a libel against me. He even showed it to Monsieur Thiriot, who forced him to throw it into the fire. He asked my forgiveness, insisted that the libel had been written before he entered the prison of Bicêtre. I was weak enough to forgive him, and this weakness won me a deadly enemy, who wrote anonymous letters against me and sent twenty libels against me to Holland. This is a part of what I have to tell you about him."

Voltaire could have added that it had been Desfontaines who had denounced his *Le Mondain* to the government.

What he said here was the pure truth; but it was sufficient to enrage Desfontaines and to kindle in him a desire for revenge. In the same year he published, anonymously like Voltaire, his viciously offensive, lying and vulgar reply, called *La Voltairomanie, ou Lettre d'un jeune Avocat.*

That Voltaire wrote *Le Préservatif* was certainly not in conformity with the ideas of Emily. It stirred her contempt that he should waste time and strength in engaging with the rabble. When he wrote a play to attack Desfontaines—*L'Envieux,* in which Ariston, representing Voltaire, is very noble, and Zoïlin, representing Desfontaines, extremely vulgar—she hoped devoutly that it would never be performed at

the Théâtre Français. And it was not. It was submitted anonymously and rejected by the actors who
did not imagine who the author was.

16

Desfontaines—except for Jean Baptiste Rousseau
—stands first of the group of the professional haters
and attackers of Voltaire, a large number, notably:
Fréron, La Beumelle, Nonotte, Saint-Hyacinthe,
Clément (le Dijon), and many others.

The most important among them belong to the
literary class of spongers, who through insatiable
envy attack some great personality and make their
living by their hatred. Envy inspires such people,
gives them, sterile as they may be in themselves, a
certain fecundity, sometimes even a little wit, and
always that constant malice, that gift of distortion
which makes a writer widely read. Externally, too,
their hate gives them a certain position; the public,
capable of but little judgment, regards them as the
"opponents" of the one whom they attack, just as a
sort of anti-Pope—incredible as it sounds—gets himself thought of as equal to the Pope.

The hostile parasites who sucked Voltaire's blood
were of various kinds. None of them had any honor,
except the hard-headed and ignorant Jesuit Nonotte,
a pedant whose name has been made a word of the
French language by Victor Hugo. Most detestable,
because of his unbounded impudence, was perhaps
La Beaumelle, who knew Denmark before he knew
France, and who in his youthful self-conceit had insulted Holberg before he insulted Voltaire. The one
who had the most brains was Fréron, who owed his
chief notoriety to Voltaire's passionate defence. He
did not lack wit. Also, he was the only one who had
something, that—with some good will—could be
called talent. He had an unmatched perseverance.
The number of volumes he published as a magazine
editor is prodigious, outnumbering even Voltaire's
output. But of all Fréron wrote nothing has lasted
but a few taunts against Voltaire.

17

Guyot Desfontaines was born in 1685, at Rouen, studied and taught under the Jesuits, became tired of it, and took shelter with the powerful Cardinal d'Auvergne. He was a sort of court fool for the clerical prince who patronized literature. Desfontainės obtained the position of a priest in Thérigny, Normandy.

But celebrating Mass was not his idea of pleasure; and he gave this up to practise the literary profession. He wrote an ode on the foolish use made of life, and several bad psalms, and a "critical" essay expressing his disgust with French poetry.

La Motte, too, had expressed himself against poetry in general, and had advanced arguments which are often repeated in the history of literature. He calls versification a mechanical and ridiculous business: everything could be said just as beautifully and effectively in prose; the only sensation of pleasure verse can give is that of a difficulty overcome; the art of the rhymester is like the art of the mountebank.

La Motte, however, wrote his tragedy *Ines de Castro* in verse, and it had a success; Voltaire said of it that it was "one of the most interesting dramas on the stage." Its verses, it is true, were not harmonious, and Desfontaines criticized the play severely. Voltaire's criticism was more humorous. When La Motte, speaking of *Œdipe,* said to him: "It is the finest theme in the world; I must put it into prose," Voltaire answered: "Do that; and in return I shall put your *Ines* into verse."

We have seen that Desfontaines stole and published Voltaire's *La Ligue,* thinking that the poet would not dare to claim his rights as author, and that he interwove verses of his own. But in order to see Desfontaines in the full light, one must know that he had the coolness, while in prison, to write a pamphlet criticizing the very verses smuggled into *La Ligue* by Desfontaines himself.

Desfontaines had just taken over France's oldest critical review, the *Journal des Savants,* when he had

the misfortune to mistake a chimney-sweep for
Cupid. He was caught, you remember, and came very
near to death at the stake. One feels the vast difference between the modern attitude toward sexual ab-
normalities and the morbid interest of the eighteenth
century. Not only was the punishment horrible; but
we are amazed at the freedom with which it is referred to and joked about, in literature. One need
only read two epigrams by Jean Baptiste Rousseau.
Here is one:

> En un marché passaient avec maint sbirre
> Deux Florentins que pour crime on brûla
> Crime galant tel que l'aurez pu lire
> Du beau Catulle et de Caligula.

Another starts:

> Un vieux paillard qu'à Rome on accusait
> De pratiquer l'amour antiphysique
> Vit à Paris un prestre qu'on cuisait
> Pour mesme cas dans la place publique.

And both end with jokes which hardly bear repeat-
ing. In the last poem it is emphasized that what is
called crime in Paris, is, in Rome, a matter of which
nobody thought anything.

We have seen that the stake was inevitable for
Desfontaines when Voltaire saved him and the death
penalty was changed to exile.

Desfontaines wrote to him:

"I will never forget how infinitely I am obliged to
you. Your heart is worth even more than your head,
and you are the most active friend a man ever had.
The zeal with which you came to my aid honors me,
somehow, more than the malice and hatred of my
enemies has shamed me by the unworthy treatment
I had to suffer."

And he begs Voltaire to complete the rescue by
having recalled the *Lettre de cachet* which exiled
Desfontaines eighteen miles from Paris.

Voltaire's goodness went so far that he wrote a
petition for the annulment of the exile. When the
matter dragged, he secured for Desfontaines permission to stay at the country seat of President de Ber-

nières, and continued his efforts to effect his read-
mission to Paris.

A second time Voltaire saved Desfontaines from
imprisonment, which threatened because in the preface of a book on the trial of Père Girard and the
pretty Cadière he said some sarcastic things about the
directeurs de conscience and the parliaments.

Nevertheless, his attitude toward Voltaire remained
that of a man who was not indebted to him for anything. In *Observations critiques sur le Temple du
Goût* he attacked that poem. Voltaire answered him
anonymously, but annihilatingly, in his *Discours sur
l'Envie:*

> Cent fois plus malheureux et plus infâme encore
> Est ce fripier d'écrits que l'intérêt dévore,
> Qui vend au plau offrant son encre et ses fureurs,
> Méprisable en son goût, détestable en ses mœurs . . .
> Chacun, avec mépris, se détourne de toi;
> Tout fuit jusqu'aux enfants, et l'on sait trop pourquoi.

Every week Desfontaines published his *Observations* on the new books, and never again praised
Voltaire.

Desfontaines suggested that it was Voltaire's aim
to give a low estimate of the most famous writers,
in order to appear himself the perfect author. A silly
accusation, as Voltaire's criticisms of his predecessors, though free, are none the less admiring.

In a letter to Cideville (September 20, 1735) Voltaire says in grim jest: "I regret having freed him
from Bicêtre and the Place de Grève. In the end it is
better to burn a priest than to leave him free to bore
the public."

Simultaneously with the student performance of
La Mort de César, the play was printed—without
Voltaire's knowledge and consent—and with numerous errors. Desfontaines wrote a damning review of
it, which reveals his superficial education: He
seriously reproaches Voltaire because all characters
of the play say thou to each other, as if they were
equals. Desfontaines seems to think that the Romans
knew the polite "vous." He writes of Brutus: "This
Roman is more like a Quaker than a Stoic [he apparently does not know that Quakers never carry

any weapons] and expresses the feelings of a monster rather than those of a hero." Plan, sequence, dialogue, style, thoughts, he insists are cut to the pattern of the English theater. Nothing in it really was in the least English.

Sensitive to criticism as Voltaire always was, he stooped so far as to write to Desfontaines, and this attempt to disarm and win the scoundrel by flattery is painful: he even asked the critic to let him know what mistakes he and his friends found with his works, so that he could correct them in the new edition.

But Desfontaines broke the armistice. Count Algarotti was about to go on an expedition, with Maupertuis, Clairaut, and several others, to Lapland to investigate whether the earth was flat on the poles or not, and before his departure Voltaire wrote him a private letter, a copy of which fell, owing to carelessness, into the hands of Desfontaines. He wished to publish the poem. Voltaire refused his consent. Desfontaines did it just the same. At the end of the letter Voltaire paid homage to his Emily in a way permissible in a private letter only:

> Allez donc, et du pôle observé, mesuré,
> Revenez aux Français apporter des nouvelles.
>   Cependant jé vous attendrai,
> Tranquille admirateur de votre astronomie,
> Sous mon méridien, dans les champs de Cirey,
> N'observant désormais que l'astre d'Emilie.
> Echauffé par le feu de son puissant génie,
>   Et par sa lumière éclairée,
>   Sur ma lyre je chanterai
> Son âme universelle autant qu'elle est unique;
> Et j'atteste les cieux, mesurés par vos mains,
> Que j'abendonnerais pour ses charmes divins
>   L'Equateur et le pôle arctique.

The way in which the physical charms of Emily were praised as a possession which the poet would not exchange for all knowledge about the equator and the pole, aroused Monsieur du Châtelet as well as his wife. They were both about to write to the Chancellor of the Exchequer when the circumstance that Desfontaines was threatened by a far greater danger made them generously withhold their accusation.

It was the French Academy which attacked Desfontaines with all its power. In a pamphlet attributed to Abbé Ségui, were certain sharp invectives against the Academy, these were ascribed to Desfontaines; he swore on his honor in a letter read to the Academy that he had no part in the libel; but when cross-examined in court, he had to confess the authorship; he had sold the pamphlet to the publisher Ribou for three louis d'or.

Voltaire, not liking the Academy because it had not accepted him as member, was of the opinion that Desfontaines had good reasons for ridiculing it. But on learning that Desfontaines was in danger of being arrested and perhaps of ending his life as a galley slave, he wrote on January 29, 1736, from Cirey to Abbé Asselin: "I hear that Abbé Desfontaines is in trouble, and therefore I forgive him. If you know where he is, send him to me. I could be of help to him and he could learn from this kind of revenge that he should not have mocked at me."

Shortly before he had written the following biting verses on Desfontaines in the *Ode on Ingratitude:*

> C'est Desfontaines, c'est ce prêtre,
> Venu de Sodome à Bicêtre,
> De Bicêtre au sacre vallon,
> A-t-il l'espérance bizarre,
> Que le bûcher qu'on lui prépare
> Soit fait des lauriers d'Apollon?
> Il m'a prit l'honneur et la vie,
> Et dans son ingrate furie,
> De Rousseau lâche imitateur,
> Avec moins d'art et plus d'audace
> De la fange où sa voix coasse
> Il outrage son bienfaiteur.

With the aid of powerful protectors Desfontaines obtained his freedom. And when he spoke with warmth and admiration of Voltaire's tragedy *Alzire,* which had had so great a success on the stage, Voltaire for the time being omitted in his ode the stanzas on Desfontaines.

Desfontaines' criticism of Voltaire's drama *L'Enfant prodigue* was somewhat unfavorable, but moderate. But while Desfontaines was thus being careful not to reveal his hatred, he forced Voltaire by his denunciation of him as author of *Le Mondain* to flee from his refuge in Cirey.

Then followed the foolish review of the book on Newton, Voltaire's anonymous publication of the pamphlet *Le Préservatif,* and Desfontaines' equally anonymous polemic *La Voltairomanie,* a collection of the crudest insults interwoven with the cleverest lies.

18

La Voltairomanie begins with a statement, by a young lawyer who is supposed to be the author, that Abbé Desfontaines is too firmly resolved to maintain the mildness and moderation he had always shown toward Voltaire, to stoop to answer his nasty and infamous pamphlet. He has left the matter to the young lawyer who so far has tried his poor eloquence only at the bar, but who is armed by the righteousness of his cause to appear against the bold writer to whom nothing is holy, neither morals, nor decency, neither truth nor religion. Voltaire is again and again exposed by his ignorance and senselessness. Abbé Desfontaines, whom he dared to attack, is a man of honor and a great writer. Voltaire's *Henriade* is a chaos with more grammatical mistakes than the book has pages; his *Charles XII* is a bad novel, written by a confused ignoramus who took the tone of a chatterbox; his *Eléments sur la Philosophie de Newton* is the argument of a school-boy who in his deep ignorance stumbles at every step—the book had exposed its conceited author to derision in France as well as in England; his *Philosophical Letters,* with their impudent remarks about religion, have been burned by a wise decree of Parliament.

Therefore, the lawyer continues, this author's life consisted, quite properly, in a series of chastisements. During the Regency he got a well-deserved beating in Sêvres. Then followed the famous flogging in front of Sully's palace. Still another bastonnade took place in London, where he was beaten by an English publisher (this is pure imagination) so that he had to beg for permission to return to Paris.

It is incredible, he says, that Voltaire has dared to warm up a disgraceful old accusation against Desfontaines, the falseness of which he himself once confessed (more pure imagination) in an apology that the deceased President de Bernières had ordered him to write. The President, though not Voltaire's friend—how could such a man be the friend of a peasant's son!—was a great gentleman who out of kindness let him stay for some time in his own house, but showed him the door in 1726, when Voltaire behaved impudently toward the Count de Rohan on the occasion of a chance meeting at the Opera.

Desfontaines, through the "lawyer's" mouth, denies positively that when he was in Bicêtre he wrote anything against Voltaire. Of Thiriot, he writes:

"Monsieur Thiriot is a man who is respected by honest people as much as Voltaire is abhorred by them. Against his will he still clings to the loyalties of an old friendship of which he is ashamed, but which he is too weak to break off altogether. Monsieur Thiriot has been asked by Voltaire to testify that Desfontaines wrote at Bicêtre a pamphlet against Voltaire and of course he had to answer that he knew nothing about it. So we have Voltaire concerned: the abbé's visit to President de Bernières took place in the holidays in 1725. If there exists a pamphlet against Voltaire printed in that year, let him show it! If he tries to answer that Abbé Desfontaines himself threw it into the fire, let him produce witnesses! For, so much is certain, that Voltaire is not to be trusted on his bare word. Monsieur Thiriot, he says, induced Desfontaines to throw the writing into the fire. And Monsieur Thiriot declares the story is untrue. Monsieur Voltaire therefore is the most rascally liar that ever existed."

19

Madame du Châtelet on this occasion proved herself a brave and sympathetic friend. As we can see from her letters to the Count d'Argental, she was firmly resolved to keep Voltaire from knowing about the libel, fearing that his peace might be disturbed and his health upset. On the other hand it was impossible to leave it unanswered. It wouldn't do for Voltaire to defer the matter to Thiriot and have Thiriot leave him in the lurch. In this embarrassing situation she herself composed a reply which, as she flattered herself, was written with more moderation—though with less wit—than if Voltaire had done it. If one reads what she wrote, moderation does not seem to be exactly the outstanding feature.

In a private letter to d'Argental she says:

"My greatest wrath, I confess, is against Thiriot, and there is nothing I would not do to force him to this declaration which he owes to his friends' honor and to his own. I have written him already with my best ink, and if he does not now give Monsieur de Voltaire complete satisfaction, I will follow him to the end of the world to get it."

Meanwhile, however, the humorous and at the same time touching situation arose that, while Emily was doing everything in her power to keep the existence of the pamphlet a secret from her friend, he had already received and read it without saying a word about it to her, for fear it might hurt her too deeply.

Both believed that Thiriot was the only one who could testify to the existence of that (supposedly) burned pamphlet; for Thiriot, during his last stay in Cirey, had spoken specifically and with the greatest indignation about the occurrence, and that indignation was, as he saw, entirely shared by those present! Now he gave the Marquise such a lukewarm answer that she burned with anger. He wrote that he had recently been questioned over and over as to the circumstances surrounding a certain happening, i.e. that he had compelled the Abbé to burn the pamphlet; that he had invariably answered that he recalled the matter, but that he had forgotten the exact circumstances under which it took place, and hence it was impossible for him to give any account of them that after so many years this was not surprising. All he could remember was that at the house of Bernières the conversation had turned to some polemic against Voltaire, a thing of forty or fifty pages, which Desfontaines showed him, and which Thiriot requested him to burn. He has forgotten when the pamphlet was written, and what its title was.

One sees from this answer Thiriot's cowardly attempt not to fall out with either Desfontaines nor Voltaire.

With the unbounded patience of his loving heart Voltaire still could not be angry with Thiriot. He assured him with the most touching expressions that he was not to break with Desfontaines, but only to write another, warmer, letter to Madame du Châtelet:

"In the name of our friendship, write her something that will make her heart more glad. You know the firmness and generosity of her character; she regards friendship as so strong and sacred a thing that to allow the least bit of politics to enter it seems to her a crime. . . . You seem to think it dishonorable to retract, to take back your statements. But is it not dishonorable to refuse to join in a fight for a friend? Is it not a still greater shame to flee in the midst of a battle? Friends who have known me for two days are burning to defend me, and you leave me in the lurch, you, a friend whom I have cherished for twenty-five years! . . . But, my friend, does one live only to eat a good supper? Does one live for himself alone? Is it not a fine thing, to vindicate one's taste and the choice of one's heart by standing up for a friend?"

In strong contrast to Thiriot's detestable scampering away was Madame de Bernières' behavior. In the most clear and uncompromising phrases she declares, in a letter for publication, that all statements made with regard to Voltaire's position at her house were lies and inventions. He was not merely tolerated there, but on the contrary had been a trusted friend and daily companion. Furthermore he would not accept their hospitality without reimbursement, and he had paid for his own and Thiriot's board.

Enlightening in regard to the situation in Cirey as well as in regard to the conception of the eighteenth century of the right of the individual to dispose of himself, is the way in which the most manly character in Cirey, the husband of Emily, the Marquis du Châtelet, interfered, first turning to Thiriot, then to Desfontaines, whom he alone knew how to force to his knees.

One must recall how deeply Thiriot was indebted to Voltaire. The sale of the *Lettres Philosophiques* had brought him over two hundred guineas; he had secretly spent the whole amount he had collected for the subscription of the *Henriade,* money which Voltaire had to return to the subscribers when the book was forbidden. Only a year before (1738) Voltaire had slipped fifty louis d'ors into his portmanteau, when he returned from Cirey to Paris. And he, who had intercourse with Desfontaines, without a protest permitted the latter to accuse Voltaire of dishonesty in the publication of the *Henriade,* although he knew that the only two cheats in the whole affair were Desfontaines and himself.

The Marquis du Châtelet was no great stylist; but he was a man. He wrote from Cirey (January 10, 1739) to Thiriot:

"Monsieur, the extraordinary friendship I feel for Monsieur de Voltaire, as well as the friendship he, as I know, feels for you and of which he has given you considerable proof, induces me to demand that you discharge your obligation to this friendship. Your letters, which I have seen, in which you speak of the pamphlet shown to you by Abbé Desfontaines at the house of President de Bernières, in Rivière-Bourdet, do not allow me to believe that you can have had any part in what is said about the matter in a new pamphlet, entitled *La Voltairomanie.* But as this pamphlet attacks Monsieur de Voltaire in other important points, the letters of which I speak are not sufficient to fulfill what you owe to truth and to Monsieur de Voltaire; and I am sure that you will without hesitation do what the laws of decent society require of you. So you must kindly write me a letter following approximately the enclosed outline. You know that this outline contains nothing but the strict truth, and I leave it to your feelings to add anything your heart and the gratitude I have observed in you, will dictate. You are under a greater obligation than anyone else, to defend the good name of the man whom Abbé Desfontaines accuses of rapacity, who, however, as you know well, has spent his life in giving pleasure to his friends, so that he is as well known for his generosity as for his writings.

"Regarding the lapse of memory which you claim to suffer in this affair, that can be shown a sham by printing the letters which are in the possession of Monsieur de Voltaire. These are to be worked up into a clear memorandum which all his friends, among whom I have the honor to count myself, have advised him to send to the Chancellor and to publish. In addition to the respect which you will earn by playing the part of a man and a true friend in this matter, you will win the full esteem of the one who calls himself, Monsieur,

"Your devoted and obedient servant,

"CHÂTELET."

La Voltairomanie was a great success in Paris. Although the pamphlet had been printed secretly in Holland, two thousand copies were sold in two weeks. In private circles Desfontaines did not deny his authorship; he read it to his friends, including some who were also friends of Voltaire, as Abbé Prevost, and Algarotti.

The lawyer, who was supposed to be the author of the pamphlet, gave him no trouble, because he did not exist. But Voltaire's position toward the pretended author of his own pamphlet was not so comfortable. For, the latter existed in flesh and blood. Monsieur de Mouhy, who had served as dummy and had made a very tidy sum out of the pamphlet, began blackmailing Voltaire with the threat of breaking his silence.

Mouhy and the Abbé Moussinot, Voltaire's regular representative, implored him to come to Paris, and fight the matter to a finish. Not because of the danger which a visit to the capital involved, but more probably because of his jealousy over Clairaut's presence in Cirey, Voltaire remained there. One day when

Madame du Châtelet and Clairaut, in spite of repeated summons, did not appear for supper, because,
deeply absorbed in the solution of a mathematical
problem, they had locked themselves up to be undis-
turbed, Voltaire ran up in a rage and with one kick
broke open the door.

He had not the necessary coolness to leave behind
a young rival.

There is no indication that Thiriot could be driven
from his detestable reserve. The letters he wrote
were returned to him by Madame du Châtelet, including his answer to her husband's letter, which was
so unsatisfactory that she was afraid that if the Marquis saw it he would go to Paris and challenge him.

Desfontaines was summoned before the police
commissioner; but when the latter saw Voltaire's
letter in *Le Préservatif*, which was such an attack on
Desfontaines' honor, he did not show any inclination
to intervene. He suggested that Desfontaines should
offer to apologize for *La Voltairomanie* if Voltaire
would do the same for *Le Préservatif*.

But Madame du Châtelet's pride rebelled at this.

To end the matter, the Marquis went to Paris, went
to Desfontaines and forced from him the following
declaration:

"I herewith make it known that I am not author of
the pamphlet entitled *La Voltairomanie*, that I absolutely disapprove of it, that I regard everything said
in it about Monsieur de Voltaire as slanderous, and
that I should consider myself dishonored had I even
the least part in writing it, as I entertain for Monsieur
de Voltaire the feelings of respect which his talents
deserve and which the public brings him with such
good reason."

20

From now on Desfontaines was on the down grade.
His journal *Observations* was put under surveillance
and censured, and at the slightest personal attack
was in danger of being suppressed; hence it necessarily became steadily more colorless and boring.

But, like all scandal-writers, he was forced to write

something sensational. He picked a certain Abbé Gourné, Prior of Taverny, who in 1741 had published the first number of a *Géographie*. Desfontaines found pleasure in attacking it in two or three articles. The Prior was not at all content to suffer in silence: he replied, charging that Desfontaines had received money from certain Paris publishers to make the *Géographie* a failure, and he insisted that Desfontaines had said to him:

"I could easily stop the publication of your work— a matter which is for you so important. But I respect you and would like to put you under obligation. But you must help me a little. I live on my pen and as a critic I am the scourge of authors. Woe to him who does not write as I please!"

The Prior took this to mean he would have to give Desfontaines a free copy of his work. But the reviewer demanded seven copies, four louis d'ors, and a manuscript containing the history of Reims Cathedral. In return he promised to praise the *Géographie* at the expense of all other geographies. For the subsequent write-ups he would be content with his seven copies and one louis d'or: "I am, as you can see, not expensive, and I shall do you a friendly turn."

Gourné refused. Whereupon Desfontaines conspired with three booksellers to spread a rumor that Gourné's *Géographie* was finding no buyers. Should the Prior then insist on the contrary that he had sold and was still selling many copies, he was to be charged with violating the laws concerning the book trade.

When Gourné made all this public, Desfontaines complained to the police. The Prior's house was searched and the Prior put under arrest. Gourné now brought complaint to the Parliament, but at the same time Desfontaines sued him in the court of Châtelet. The Prior, however, obtained a resolution of the Parliament, which halted the court proceedings. The case, therefore, did not come to trial; and in October, 1743, Desfontaines' franchise for the publication of his *Observations sur les écrits modernes* was revoked.

To this extent Voltaire was revenged; true, the authorities had not intervened for his sake but on behalf of the French Academy, which Desfontaines had challenged a second time by writing in the preface of his translation of Vergil: "It offends me more to hear a haughty crowd of people being praised than to see Augustus treated as a god by Ovid and Vergil."

This vague, unspecific allusion, added to the discourse in which Desfontaines had, seven years before, mocked the Academy, under an assumed name, was the last straw. Prior Gourné was only an excuse.

Desfontaines did not believe himself lost altogether. He began a new periodical, *Jugements sur les Ouvrages nouveaux.*

In 1745 he fell ill with pneumonia which developed into dropsy. He repented his sins and died.

21

Madame du Châtelet was a greater and more independent spirit than most women of her time, or of later times. She had none of the systematic prudery of the *"triste"* nineteenth century, and none of its hypocrisy. Nevertheless she cannot be called typical of the eighteenth century. She was thoroughly feminine, but without coquetry. Although a woman who could be absorbed by a single great passion, she was not of the spirit of her generation, not surreptitious like Mademoiselle de l'Espinasse or emotional like Mademoiselle d'Aïssé, but of a frankness that was shameless in the eyes of some.

Emily, in her mental outlook, in her learning, and in her feeling for Nature, was nearer the Italian women of the year 1500 than the French of 1740.

Like certain eminent ladies of the Renaissance she was shameless without being unchaste. She did not mind being seen naked by a lackey; she did not regard him as a man.

Madame du Châtelet's valet, Longchamp, tells in his memoirs of his first day in her service. In the morning when he and his sister, who was the chambermaid, entered the bedroom of the Marquise, Madame du Châtelet pulled back the coverlets and got up:

"While my sister was getting a chemise ready, Madame, standing in front of me, let her shirt fall down to her feet and stood there, naked as a marble statue. I was stupefied and did not dare to look at her, although, trained at the Court in Lorraine, I had had more than one opportunity to see ladies change their shirts; but not like this. As soon as Madame was dressed she ordered her supper, she ate only once a day, which was to be attended by two persons only, the Duc de Richelieu and Monsieur de Voltaire. . . . Several days later she rang the bell while she was in the bathtub; my sister was otherwise occupied and could not answer. Madame du Châtelet told me to take a kettle of boiling water that stood on the fire and pour it into her bath; the water had become too cold. When I approached her I saw that no salts had been added to the bath water, for it was very clear and transparent. The lady stretched open her legs so I could pour the boiling water more easily without scalding her. When I began to pour my glance fell on what my eyes had not sought. Bashful and standing as far off as possible, with my head turned away, I was so unfortunate as to have my hand tremble, pouring the water at random into the tub. 'Look out!' she cried boisterously, 'you are burning me!' So I was forced to look more closely and longer than I had wished. . . . I was not accustomed to such lack of constraint in the ladies I had served formerly."

Hypatia, in antiquity, surely used more restraint in front of a slave, learned and free from prejudice as she was. There was a certain modesty about a Greek intellectual in ancient Egypt as well as in Hellas, which was lost in the neo-classicism of the eighteenth century.

Hypatia knew Homer and Plato but not mathematics and physics. Madame du Châtelet did not feel the ameliorating influence of the Greeks, but on the other hand she had mastered the mathematical knowledge of her time. Although she never alluded in society to her mathematical abilities, at times she made use of them at the card table to solve the problems that arose. This, however, did not prevent her losing a fortune in Fontainebleau at the Queen's card table one unlucky evening.

22

It has already been mentioned in the Overture that Voltaire's *Eléments de la Philosophie de Newton* was not an extract from Newton's *Principia* but an independent development of his discoveries in optics and astronomy. In its original edition (1738) the work was dedicated to Madame la Marquise du Châtelet, with a poem and a brief letter. The dedication was further elaborated and altered in 1741, and in 1745 it was replaced by the more important epistle which begins with the enthusiastic words:

"Madame!

"When first I put your name at the head of these *Philosophical Elements* I was studying with you. Since then you have soared to such a height that I can no longer follow. Now I am in the position of a grammarian who would subject Demosthenes or Cicero to an examination in the art of speech. I offer simple rudiments to one who has plumbed all the depths of higher geometry and who has given us our only translation and explanation of Newton. This philosopher won all the honor he deserved during his lifetime; he caused no envy, for he had no rival. The learned world was his apostle; the rest of the people admired him without making claim of understanding him. But the honor you gave him is doubtless the greatest he ever received."

The work which then and later was highly esteemed by experts for its clear exposition of difficult philosophic, physical and astronomic truths, is introduced by a metaphysical argument, the first deistic chapters of which were at that time well suited to pave the way for the book, but today act as a deterrent to reading it. They contain nothing but pure theology, today so obsolete—the supposedly rational theology of the eighteenth century, which was as bare of logic as the speculative dogmas of the nineteenth century. Now and then, though, one feels vivid flashes of Voltarian sagacity. Take, for instance, the reflections on freedom of will. But where with remarkable clarity he elucidates Newton's discoveries in optics and physics, he stands at his height as an enlightener and educator. Here he popularizes the new ideas, the law of gravity, the universal force of attraction, the refraction of light rays; and he attacks the errors of his time.

But he was not content to stop at the description of the ideas of other scholars.

23

In 1738 the Academy of Sciences in Paris announced a prize contest for the best essay on the *Nature and Diffusion of Fire.*

Voltaire was eager to use the knowledge he had acquired from his ambitious natural science experiments and studies in Cirey, in a way which would draw public attention. The year before he had tried to find out from Maupertuis what prize contest the Academy of Sciences was planning. He said a friend of his was anxious to know. When the problem turned out to be so well suited to his studies and experiments, he promptly set to work on his paper.

In Cirey he had a dark-room and a laboratory containing a physical apparatus and the best chemical equipment the time afforded. He was the first to carry out an experiment, indicated by Newton, to prove that the reflection in a prism does not come to an end when the glass is surrounded by a vacuum instead of by air.

He tried to determine the nature of heat. He performed experiments, using every resource known at the time: first a balance, then a Réamur thermometer and a Munschenbroek pyrometer, not a modern heat-meter, but a measure by which one could observe how heated bodies expand.

Even about the progress of forest fires he made experiments on a large scale, expensive though they were.

Strangest of all—as mentioned in our first chapter

—was his observation that the same amounts of different fluids, such as oil, water, vinegar, of different temperatures, do not take an average temperature when mixed.

As Voltaire in pursuing his ideas regarding the oxidation of metals and the compound nature of air would have had to discover oxygen, he stood on the threshold of the discovery of the specific heat of matter. These experiments of Voltaire's, at a time when—as Condorcet, and later Dubois-Reymond remarked—chemistry in France had not even reached the stage of belief in the calory, have won him the highest esteem of natural philosophers of the present day.

24

The Marquise du Châtelet took part in the competition without letting on to Voltaire. In a letter to Maupertuis, of June 21, 1738, she begins by reproaching him for having gone to Saint-Malo, instead of Cirey, where she had counted on seeing him, and where he would have found the peace he longed for; indeed, peace had ruled there for three years; there he could have enjoyed alternately solitude and the company of two people who admired and loved him as he deserved. Then, after a discussion of how well he would get along with Frederick the Great, whom he later, to Voltaire's anger, so completely won, she informed him:

"I believe that you must have been very surprised at my keenness to compose an essay for the Academy. I wanted to test my ability incognito; for I flattered myself that my secret would be kept for ever. Monsieur du Châtelet was the only one I told, and he has kept such a close mouth that he didn't even tell you about it when he was in Paris. I was unable to do any experimenting, because I was working without the knowledge of Monsieur de Voltaire. The idea came to me only one month before the work had to be sent in; I could work at night only and I was further handicapped by a lack of experience. Voltaire's essay, which was almost finished before I began on mine, infected me with the idea of competing in the same line. I began to work without knowing whether or not I would send in my essay and I said nothing to Monsieur de Voltaire because I did not want to blush for an action which I feared would displease him, especially since in my essay I opposed nearly all of his ideas. I confessed it to him only when I saw from the newspaper that neither he nor I had received a share in the prize. It seemed to me that a defeat shared with him would be honorable. Later I learned that his entry and mine, too, were among those admitted to the contest. That you, therefore, would read it was a thought which stimulated my courage.

"Instead of being angry at my secrecy, Monsieur de Voltaire thought only of being of use to me, and as he was quite satisfied with my work he asked me to have it printed. I hope to bring this about, especially if you would be so good as to write a line to Monsieur Dufay and Monsieur de Réaumur for me. Monsieur de Voltaire has written to both. Monsieur de Réaumur has answered with exquisite courtesy. . . . I am not surprised that you were pleased with Monsieur de Voltaire's essay; it is rich in sagacity, instructive experiments and tests. Nothing of that sort appears in mine and it is very natural that you have no recollection of it. Perhaps, if you were the one to read it, you will recall it if I tell you that it was essay number six, and stated that fire has no weight, that it is possibly neither spirit nor matter but a substance of an unknown nature, like the empty space whose existence can also be taken as proven but whose composition defies us."

The prize was divided between three other contestants, among whom was a mathematical genius, the then thirty-one-year-old Euler. The Marquise as well as Voltaire received honorable mention, and the Academy had their treatises printed after the three that had received the prize. But although among the judges were men like Réaumur and Dufat, as science has developed it is clear that Voltaire deserved the prize ever more than Euler and far more than the other two winners. One of these two, the Jesuit Lozeran de Fiesc, believed in the vortex of Descartes.

The third prize-winner, one Count Créquy, was a Cartesian also, and as the Academy was Cartesian, the success of the victors could easily be explained.

Madame du Châtelet's essay, written in eight nights during which she slept only one hour each, contained something thought extraordinary by the scholars of later times. She supposes that the colors of a spectrum contain heat in varying degrees, red being the warmest, and violet the coldest. Forty years later Rochon proved that she was right.

Voltaire ascribed his and the Marquise's defeat to the superstition of the Cartesian vortex. In a letter to Maupertuis, whom he politely calls his and her instructor, he says:

"You admit that it is funny. It is cruel that these confounded whirls should prove stronger than your pupils. . . . The essay on fire, composed by Madame du Châtelet, is full of things that would do credit to the greatest physicist, and she would have won the prize, were not this senseless and ridiculous phantom, the vortices, haunting their erudite heads."

The Academy consented to print the two essays. They appeared with a preface which said that both essays gave evidence of extensive research, wide acquaintance with the best physical works, and were full of true observations; moreover, No. 6 was written by a lady of high rank, Madame du Châtelet, and No. 7 by one of "our most prominent poets." Emily asked in vain, in a letter to the Academy, to remain anonymous: "I have a thousand reasons for asking it." Apparently she had only one, that it was supposed to be ridiculous for a woman to be learned.

Voltaire and she, by the way, were the objects on this occasion of a strange endorsement. A prior in the Sorbonne, who gave a lecture on Newton and his doctrine before a learned assembly, added a eulogy on Voltaire and Madame du Châtelet, which contained the following expressions: "Newton's system is a maze, through which Monsieur de Voltaire has found his way by the aid of a thread which was put into his hands by the modern Ariadne. The Theseus and Ariadne of our own time are the more deserving of praise, for those in the Greek legend burned for each other in a sensual love only, while these feel for each other an intellectual love only."

25

Voltaire's numerous essays on natural science, some in the *Dictionnaire philosophique,* some in *Singularités de la Nature,* bear witness to his independence of mind, which does not fear to question the decision of an authority, nor to confess to himself the limitation of his own knowledge.

However, as we have seen, his inclination to believe in the obvious sometimes made it impossible for him to understand truths a little deeper than the obvious, and led him to scoff where he should have seen that he was face to face with truth.

In his *Singularités de la Nature* he has a typical chapter (the twelfth) on shells and the theories for which they are responsible. He says that one sometimes comes across heaps of mussels, or petrified oysters, on high land. From this it has been claimed, in spite of the law of gravity, and in spite of the known level of the sea, that several million years ago the whole face of the earth was covered by the ocean. Although the waves never reach higher than fifteen feet above the coasts, it is argued that the sea covered mountains of 18,000 feet height. True, nobody denies that in the course of centuries great changes have taken place on our earth. It is physically possible— and involves no serious contradiction of the Bible— that the island Atlantis, as Plato describes, disappeared nine thousand years before his time. But that is not proof that the sea created the Caucasus, the Pyrenees and the Alps. It is said shells have been found on Montmartre and near Reims. But as to high mountains, he doubted it. He had had people search for them on St. Gotthard and on St. Bernard; but none were discovered.

One physicist had written to him that he had found a petrified oyster shell on Mont-Cenis. He is forced to believe it, and is only surprised that such shells were not found by the hundred. The lakes near by abound in large mussels whose shells are very like those of the oyster. And now comes Voltaire's comic explanation of these findings:

"Is it, after all, so fantastic to suggest that there were countless pilgrims, with mussel shells on their hats, who wandered on foot from San-Jago in Galicia and from all other provinces to Rome? They come from Syria, Egypt, Greece, as well as from Poland and Austria. . . . One solitary oyster found on Mont-Cenis, therefore, does not prove that the Indian Ocean once covered all the land in our hemisphere."

He set his heart upon hygiene in an epoch when it had no consideration. In his little story *Le monde comme il va,* in which he makes the sage Babouc his mouth-piece, it is told how the wise man came to Persepolis (Paris) and what impression he received of the church-goers there:

"Babouc mixed in a mob, consisting of the ugliest and dirtiest of both sexes; this mob hurried with dull expressions into a great, gloomy hall. The constant murmur, the unceasing movement he observed, as well as the money some paid to be allowed a seat, at first made him think that this was a market where straw chairs were being sold; but when he saw several women fall on their knees and stare straight ahead it was clear to him that he was in a temple. Sharp, rough, ugly voices resounded under the vault . . . , so that he stopped his ears; but soon he was also tempted to stop his nose, when he saw laborers with hoes and shovels enter the temple. They lifted a large slab, and to the right and left they threw earth from which came a pestilential odor. Then they put a body into the opening and on top they replaced the stone. 'How,' said Babouc, 'these folks bury their dead in the same place in which they pray to their God! Can it be, they fill their temples with corpses! In that case I am no longer surprised at the pestilences which prostrate Persepolis so often. The rottenness of the dead and the smell of the living who pack into this place are sufficient to poison the globe.' "

Considering how pleased Voltaire's ancestors were

at the distinction of being buried in churches, one can feel the progress that had taken place with him.

26

Mademoiselle d'Issembourg d'Happoncourt came from a prominent and meritorious family. Her father was a Major in the guard of the Duke of Lorraine. Her mother, Marguerite Callot, was the grand-daughter of the famous painter and engraver, Jacques Callot. She was born in Nancy in 1695. At a very early age she was married to a chamberlain of the Duke of Lorraine, Huguet de Graffigny, a rough and violent man, who in his fits of uncontrolled temper almost beat her to death. We can still read a touching letter she wrote to her father, begging him to free her from this marriage.

She succeeded in obtaining her liberty, but after her separation she was so poor that she had but a few hundred francs. She had become companion of the young Mademoiselle de Guise, when Voltaire arranged the latter's marriage with the Duke de Richelieu; the Duchess, however, did not tie her so firmly to herself that she could not make a rather extended visit in Cirey. Not until the year 1820 were the letters put in order and published, which she had written to her friends from Cirey.

These letters are highly interesting in themselves; for they describe with the greatest accuracy everything that their writer did, saw and heard. We can share her experiences. Daily occurrences, quarrels, etc., are reproduced in such a way that one can almost hear the voices of the participants, listen to their mannerisms and their jokes. We hear Voltaire's reading of his writings, listen to one dramatic performance after another, both on the stage and off.

The tone of these letters is absolutely intimate; all persons to whom or about whom Madame de Graffigny writes, are called by their nicknames, of which the most popular have three or four. Most of the letters are addressed to a friend of Madame de Graffigny's youth, the harmless, phlegmatic Devaux. Devaux had been given a position as reader with King Stanislaw in Lunéville, at an annual salary of two thousand thalers. The story is that when Devaux was proposed to Stanislaw as a reader, he said: "What in the world do I want with a reader? I have about as much use for one as my son-in-law [Louis XV] has for a father-confessor."

Devaux is humorously pictured by King Stanislaw's almoner, Abbé Porquet, in a short poem which begins:

> Le ciel te prodigua tous les défauts qu'on aime;
> Tu n'as que les vertus qu'on pardonne aisèment;
> Ta gaieté, tes bons mots, tes ridicules mêmes,
> Nous charment presque également.

In the letters Devaux is called Panpan or Panpichon. Madame de Graffigny uses the familiar pronoun in addressing him, as she does with all her friends. Among these is Saint-Lambert, later so celebrated as the author of *The Seasons* (*Les Saisons*), and also later on Voltaire's as well as Jean Jacques Rousseau's successful rival with their chosen ladies. In the letters he is called *le petit saint*.

The main figure is a cavalry lieutenant, Leopold Desmarets, the lover of Madame de Graffigny. Her letters to him were perhaps too passionate; at any rate, they have disappeared. But the extant letters to her friends reveal the lady's warm heart, and the unlimited gift of observation that later distinguished her *Lettres peruviennes*.

An unbounded admiration for Voltaire drew her to Cirey. To be near him, hear him talk, sit next to him, is paradise for her. In the first weeks of her stay she enjoys this happiness thoroughly.

Her letters often refer to Voltaire as "your idol" (for Devaux, too, adored him); superciliously she calls the Marquis *le bonhomme;* the Marquise is usually *le nymphe.*

27

Upon her arrival on December 4, 1738, at two o'clock in the morning, the Marquise received her

very well; but Madame de Graffigny remained only
a minute in the former's bedroom, then went up-
stairs to her own: "One moment later appeared, who?
. . . Your idol with a little candle in his hand, like
a monk. He said a thousand courteous things to me;
he seemed so glad to see me that he kissed my hands
ten times and showed a touching concern over my
health. His next question was of you: it took a quarter of an hour. He says he loves you with all his heart.
Then he spoke to me about Desmarets and Saint-
Lambert, and finally went to give me time to write
you. Now it is done. Good night, the mail goes tonight."

The day in Cirey is divided thus: between half-past
eleven and half-past twelve everyone is notified that
the coffee is served. It is taken in one of Voltaire's
rooms. The conversation lasts until twelve or one.
Noon in Cirey is called coach-men's lunch hour but
M. du Châtelet, Madame de Champbonin, the stout
good-natured cousin of Voltaire, and her son, are
apparently counted among the coach-men, for they
eat at this time. But the Marquise, Voltaire and Madame de Graffigny remain seated, until Voltaire
makes a deep bow and asks the others to go. Thereupon everyone retires to his room. At four o'clock
there is sometimes a little refreshment for which,
however, Madame de Graffigny does not appear if she
is not expressly called. At nine o'clock in the evening
comes the chief meal—for which Voltaire is always a
little late because he cannot tear himself away from
his dictation to his secretary—and everyone sits there
until midnight: "My God! What a supper! It is always a feast of Damocles. All pleasures are brought
together here, but oh! The time is so short; nothing
is missing, not even the sword above my head; for
time, that flees, is this sword. . . . To be let absolutely alone all day, and then be able to enjoy good
company, that is the life for me."

Voltaire lets her have various of his writings to
read, when she is alone; *Mérope,* the still unpublished
tragedy, and the manuscript of *The Century of Louis
XIV,* which Madame du Châtelet does not wish Voltaire to finish—she thinks he should devote himself

to science and leave history alone—and which she
therefore keeps locked up. He has to ask her to let
Madame de Graffigny have the part of the manuscript
that he has already done. He also gives her his commentary on the comedies of Molière, which he had
prepared as an introduction for the new de luxe edition of Molière, but which was not used because the
Chancellor of the Exchequer, who is said to be his
most spiteful enemy, ordered Monsieur Lasserre to
furnish the introduction for the work.

Voltaire always makes the visits he has to make
upon his guests without sitting down; he is always on
the point of leaving; is it not one of his favorite
sayings, that people are over-addicted to wasting time
in idle talk, time, mankind's most precious gift?

The guest is more than a little indignant at the
tyranny Madame du Châtelet imposes on Voltaire.
In vain do Madame de Champbonin and Madame de
Graffigny explain to her the enormity of the crime of
locking away *The Century of Louis XIV*: "He is dying
of desire to finish it, and says that it is the work
that gives him the greatest satisfaction of all. All
she can say to justify herself is that there is nothing
to be gained by writing a book which would be forbidden publication. I urge him to write for his own
satisfaction in the immortality he will win. He answers that he is sure to finish the book, but not here.
She is driving him crazy with her geometry." Here
Madame de Graffigny is interrupted in writing by
Voltaire, who wants to read *Mérope* to her.

She gives a vivid picture of the enjoyment Madame
du Châtelet apparently gets from feeling and letting
others feel her power over the rare bird she has
caught. It showed itself in a love of crossing him,
which was essentially a feminine lust of power, that
found its satisfaction in trifles.

Voltaire, for instance, comes in to read them *Mérope*. Madame du Châtelet has the caprice to ask him
to put on another coat: "It is true, his coat was not
neat; but he himself was nicely powdered and wore
fine laces. He gave ample reasons for not wanting
to change the coat right then; the others are less
warm and he easily catches cold. In the end he rang

for his valet to go fetch him another suit. But the valet was not to be found, was out for the moment, and Voltaire now thought he could let the matter go. But no: the nagging began anew. Then Voltaire got excited; furiously he spoke to her in English, and left the room. He was sent for; but he returned the message that he had colic, and thus *Mérope* came to naught."

Madame de Graffigny goes on to tell how the Marquise asked her to go down and bring him back. As long as she and Madame de Champbonin were with him, he was laughing and in a good humor; but as soon as he reëntered the room of the Marquise, his features clouded, and pretending his colic, he took a seat in a corner without speaking a word. The moment the lord of the house left the room, "the two sulkers began to speak to each other in English, and a minute later *Mérope* reappeared." Naïvely Madame de Graffigny adds: "It is the first sign of love I have noticed since I came; indeed, their behavior is admirable; but all the same, she does make life a little hard for him."

Madame de Graffigny prefers Voltaire more and more to the mistress of the house: "Voltaire is always delightful and always thinking of my entertainment. His attentiveness is untiring; he is so fearful that I might be bored. This fear is quite superfluous. Bore oneself with Voltaire!"

Madame du Châtelet's brother, the Abbé of Breteuil, pays her a short visit. He is very courteous, gallant and witty; his presence makes the suppers still more festive. The picture of this company grows quite vivid with the details into which Madame de Graffigny goes in her descriptions. After supper Voltaire begins to get angry because Emily wants to stop him from drinking a glass of Rhine wine he had filled for himself. Then he does not want to read aloud from *Jeanne,* as he had promised. By much jollying Breteuil and Madame de Graffigny finally succeed in breaking down his resistance. Then the Marquise, too, being in just the right mood for teasing, can resist no more; the result is a fusillade of humorous retorts which ends with the reading of a

canto from *Jeanne,* which, however, does not seem
any more entertaining than Voltaire's witty conversation.

Another evening Voltaire gave a magic lantern
exhibition and accompanied the pictures with a talk
which had everyone doubled up with laughter. He
described the entire circle of the Duke of Richelieu,
then told the story of Abbé Desfontaines, going on
from there to one anecdote after another, and ending
up with a perfect imitation of the dialect of the
Savoyards.

Voltaire told one story about how his valet, by
dint of copying his employer's poems, had become
persuaded that he was a wit and poet himself. Voltaire gave a few comic examples of this manservant
poetry and told how the valet had by and by acquired enough self-confidence to correct things that
he found faulty. Thus Voltaire had begun writing
the verse

> Ah! croyez-moi, mon fils, voyez mes cheveux blancs,
> La triste expérience est le fruit des vieux

when an interruption called him away before he
could add the word "ans." The valet, finding that
this did not rhyme, copied the verse in this form:

> Ah! croyez-moi, mon fils, voyez mes cheveux bleus,
> La triste expérience est le fruit des vieux.

In Voltaire's presence some of his guests once
asked him to recite a selection from his master's
works. He said he could remember only the one
passage from *Jeanne,* in which her person is described. This passage had taken the following shape
in his memory:

> Trente-deux dents brillent à fleur de tête;
> Deux grands yeux noirs, d'une égale blancheur,
> Font l'ornement d'une bouche vermeille
> Qui va prenant de l'une à l'autre oreille.

Madame de Graffigny was much moved by Voltaire's forbearance and susceptibility in his attitude
toward criticism. Emily had ridiculed his tragedy
Mérope, which she could not abide. Madame de Graf-

figny could feel that he was hurt by her mockery. She herself admired the tragedy with the exception of one scene which did not please her. She told him in private. He thanked her heartily for her objections, and said: "I am glad that you speak to me frankly; you are right, there is something uncommonly trenchant in your criticism." And the good lady adds: "Really, I'm telling you, it's only poor writers who are haughty; the good ones have a sane vanity. He listens to unfavorable criticism, but he likes praise and is not ashamed to admit it."

One night it occurred to Madame du Châtelet to ask Madame de Graffigny if she had had any children. One question led to another and finally the poor lady was brought to the point of telling her life story, which was new to the mistress of the house as well as to Voltaire. "Oh!" she exclaims, "what a good heart!" The pretty lady laughed in order to keep from crying; but Voltaire, "this humane Voltaire burst into tears. He is not ashamed of his sympathy. I wanted to stop; but it was impossible; I was asked again and again to go on. They were so moved that my reserve proved to be of no avail. Finally I had to cry myself."

It was only gradually that she learned the extent of Voltaire's attentiveness toward her. His valet came at frequent intervals to ask if she needed anything. Finally she noticed that Voltaire had ordered all his servants to wait upon her just as upon himself. They were his, not the house's lackeys who served her. She writes with amiable simplicity: "Judge for yourself if it is possible to love your idol sufficiently!"

She describes the way in which Voltaire himself is waited upon at supper. The valet does not budge from behind his chair, and his lackeys hand him everything he needs, just like pages when the King's friends sit at the table; but all this is done without pomp or ceremony. "So true it is that choice spirits know to preserve their proper dignity, without putting on ridiculous affectations."

Madame de Graffigny made every effort to get her friends invited to Cirey; most of all, of course, she wished to present Desmarets, who finally came. But his arrival brought the poor woman a bitter disappointment. For, he had hardly more than arrived when he told her that he no longer loved her.

Just as assiduously as Madame de Graffigny was trying to secure an invitation for Desmarets to come to Cirey, Saint-Lambert was trying to win admission through her. And she, loyal friend, praised him in such glowing terms that Madame du Châtelet finally yielded: "I must tell you that this morning I lay such siege to the lady of the house that she finally committed herself about Saint-Lambert. She is willing to have him come, but he must understand the condition is that he remain in his room and lead the life which is lived here. I have given her such positive assurance of this that she now wishes very much to see him as well as Desmarets here."

It is strange to see how reluctant Emily was at first to receive Saint-Lambert, who nine years later was to become her lover.

Before very long Madame de Graffigny's idyllic existence in Cirey was to come to a rude end. But so far everything was still carefree and gay. Madame du Châtelet took long rides on horseback, Voltaire went hunting. At the theater several merry farces were played, among them one by Voltaire that can be found among his works under the title of *L'Exchange,* a jolly little play in prose.

28

Madame de Graffigny had spent about three or four weeks in Cirey, happily content, when one late evening Voltaire entered her room to tell her that he was lost and that his fate was in her hands.—"Lord, help me, how is that?" she asked.—"How is that?— There are numerous copies of *Jeanne* in circulation. I must leave here at once, I don't know where to go, Holland or perhaps still further. Monsieur du Châtelet is going to Lunéville. You must write at once to Devaux and tell him to get hold of these copies. Is he to be trusted to do that?"—She assured him that she would do everything in her power to prove her devotion to him, and that she was very sorry that this had

to happen during her stay with him.—"No excuses!"
he exclaimed bitterly. "You are the very one who sent
those copies out." In vain she protests that she has
never copied so much as a single line.—"Enough,"
answers Voltaire, "Devaux assures me that it was you
who sent *Jeanne* into the world."

Her head was whirling; she could make nothing of
all this, could only reiterate, what was the truth, that
these copies of *Jeanne* did not come from her. But he
insisted most emphatically that Devaux had read
Jeanne to Desmarets, that Madame de Graffigny is
sending copies to everybody, and that Madame du
Châtelet had the proof of this in her pocket.

For the poor woman the entire matter was incomprehensible; she could only see the anger and indignation without being able to explain how this misunderstanding had come about.

Of course, it was not easy to explain. To understand, one must know that the suspicious mistress of
Cirey had the bad habit of reading all she could of
the letters written by her guests as well as all those
addressed to them before they were distributed.

Now the unfortunate and innocent Madame de
Graffigny had truthfully reported to her friend the
impression she had got from Voltaire's reading of a
canto from *Jeanne,* which seemed to her especially
amusing and witty; shortly thereafter Madame du
Châtelet had opened a letter from Devaux which,
referring to this, contained the unfortunate words:
Le chant de Jeanne est charmant. The distrustful
Emily saw this as proof that this passage had secretly
been sent to Devaux;—Voltaire did not doubt this,
but on the other hand he did not want to reveal the
way he had found out about it, and he angrily accused the guest of the house, who could not imagine
what it was all about.

Madame de Graffigny did not succeed at once in
convincing him. He ordered her to demand back the
original and all copies. At his order she began to
write; but as she could not demand back what she
had not sent, she asked Devaux for some explanation
and information about the dangerous copies. When
she handed Voltaire the finished letter, he threw it

away, with the words: "Pfui, Madame, one should
be honest and straightforward with a poor wretch
whose life and well-being are at stake, as mine are."

This embarrassing scene lasted at least an hour;
but it was nothing compared to what was in store for
the poor misunderstood lady. Madame du Châtelet
stormed furiously into her room and hurled at her
again all the accusations Voltaire had made before.
Then she took a letter out of her pocket, held it
toward her now silent guest, and said: "See here the
proof of your infamy. I took you here not out of
friendship, but out of pity, and you betray us. You
stoop so low as to steal a manuscript from my desk
to copy it."

Madame de Graffigny could say nothing but, "Be
quiet, Madame, I am too unfortunate to be treated so
unworthily."

Voltaire took Madame du Châtelet around her
waist and drew her to a safe distance from the accused, for she was approaching her guest so excitedly
that a physical assault had to be feared.

For a long time the poor woman could find no
words; then she asked to see the letter, which was
refused. "Then show me at least the sentence that so
accuses me." And then she was shown the few unimportant words: "The canto from *Jeanne* is charming."

With infinite relief she told the simple truth: that
she had described in a letter the delightful impression she had received by listening.

Voltaire was intelligent enough to believe her, to
understand the mistake that had been made. But the
furious mistress of the chateau would not back down
from her assertions, although Voltaire gave her a
long talking-to in English, and asked her in French to
say that now she believed her guest.—They left at
three o'clock in the morning, leaving Madame de
Graffigny on the verge of nervous hysteria.

When daylight came, she was ill and desperate.
Nothing would have been more natural than an immediate departure. But the poor creature had not
enough money with her to hire a coach to take her to
the nearest city. She had to stay where she was, humiliated and abused.

It was small consolation that Voltaire afterward tried to make up for the incident. (Madame du Châtelet could never bring herself to the point of making a hearty apology for her silly attack.) The poor lady spent several wretched months at the the place to which she had come so joyfully and which she now longed so desperately to leave. She could not even give her friends an accurate account of the incident, for she knew that every one of her letters was spied into.

This foolish little incident shows us, among other things, in what crises Voltaire's life was spent, because he could not resist writing things that exposed him to danger, and because he could not refrain from reading these things to a hundred people, would even send copies to a half dozen trusted friends, putting himself at the mercy of their discretion.

29

In running through Madame du Châtelet's letters one can see from her complaints, every time Voltaire leaves her on one of his "unnecessary" journeys, how essential his presence is to her, how unhappy she is without him, doubly unhappy when she is tormented not only by his absence but also by his negligence in sending her assurances of his health and his affection. November 23, 1740, she writes to Richelieu from Paris:

"I have been cruelly rewarded for all I have done at Fontainebleau; I have adjusted the most difficult matters; I have obtained for Monsieur de Voltaire the right to return to his country openly. I won him the good will of the Ministry and paved the way for his acceptance by the Academies. And do you know how he repays such zealous devotion? He informs me curtly that he has gone to Berlin, knowing perfectly well that he is piercing my heart, and leaves me in a state of indescribable torture which your heart alone can understand. . . . I hope to be dead soon. . . . And would you believe that the thought that is uppermost in my mind when I feel that my grief will kill

me, is the terrible sorrow my death would bring to
Monsieur de Voltaire. . . . I cannot bear the idea
that the memory of me will one day cause him unhappiness."

In another letter, later in the same month, after
telling the Duke what unbounded friendship she feels
for him, she writes: "But this does not cure me of the
unrestrained passion which is the cause of my present unhappiness. It is easy to say: 'That is not possible.' I have an answer that is to the point: 'It is,
and will remain so all my life, even though you de-
plore it.' "

To d'Argental she writes, on October 15, 1743, from
Brussels:

"I doubt if anyone has ever been more in love and
more desperately unhappy. Just think when Monsieur
de Voltaire could and should be back here . . . he
goes from Berlin to Bayreuth, where he surely has no
business; he spends a fortnight there, without the
King of Prussia, and without writing me a single
line. He returns to Berlin and stays there another
fortnight, and who knows! perhaps he would stay
there all his life if it were not that business now recalls him to Paris. Then, he writes me four casual
lines from an inn, without letting me know what he
was doing in Bayreuth and without mentioning his
return . . . and this little note is all I have had from
him since September 14, a full month."

Contrast these letters to those in which Voltaire
at the same time explains to Frederick quite firmly,
though politely, that he could not stay with him because it was impossible for him to abandon his friend.

To further his purpose, Frederick constantly jeers
at the poet. He likens Voltaire to Rinaldo in Armida's
arms, robbed of his strength by his love, unable to
tear his way out of the net his own senses have spun
around him.—So, for instance, in his letter of June
20, 1742, in the clumsy lines which smell, so to speak,
of tobacco and stale beer:

> Enfin ce Bork est revenu
> Après avoir beaucoup couru.
> Entre les beaux bras d'Emilie
> Il m'assure vous avoir vu,

Le corps languissant, abattu,
Mais toujour l'esprit plein de vie.

Voltaire explains in his answer (July, 1742) that it
is not love but friendship that binds him:

Vous prenez pour faiblesse une amitié solide,
Vous m'appelez Rénaud, de mollesse abattu,
Grand roi, je ne suis point dans le palais d'Armide,
Mais dans celui de la Vertu.

Frederick says bluntly and tactlessly:
"You are offended because I believe you capable
of a passion for the Marquise du Châtelet; I thought
I should be earning your gratitude by thinking so
well of you. The Marquise is pretty and loveable—
you are susceptible. She has a heart—you have feelings; she is not of marble and you have lived together
for ten years. Are you trying to tell me that you
spoke all this time, to the most delightful woman in
all France, of nothing but philosophy? In this case,
my dear friend, you must have played a very sad
rôle. I did not think that pleasure was outlawed from
the Temple of Virtue, in which you insist you live."
Voltaire replies in a rhymed letter to these questions, and sadly but emphatically he refers to his age,
which excludes him from the joys of love:

Ah! vous m'avez fait, je vous jure,
Et trop de grâce et trop d'honneur
Quand vous dites que la nature
M'a fait, pour certaine aventure,
D'autres dons que le don du cœur.
Plût au ciel que je l'eusse encore
Ce premier des divins présents,
Ce don que toute femme adore
Et qui passe avec nos beaux ans!
J'approche, hélas! de la nuit sombre
Qui nous engloutit sans retour;
D'un homme je ne suis que l'ombre,
Je n'ai que l'ombre de l'amour.

30

Madame du Châtelet wrote a short essay on *Happiness*, from which one may know her almost as well

as from her letters. To be happy, she says, one must have discarded his prejudices and retained his illusions. One must be high minded; one must enjoy good health, and have keen tastes and enthusiasms. Our only problem in this world is to experience agreeable sensual pleasures and reactions.—It is, as may be seen, the theory of Voltaire's *Le Mondain*. One should give his life a fixed direction and follow it without sorrow and without remorse. One should know his starting-point and his goal, and try to scatter flowers on the path.

Where she speaks of her tastes and enthusiasms, she admits her love of gambling, but dwells especially upon her urge to study: "Of all passions, the desire for knowledge is the one which contributes most to happiness, for it is the one which makes us least dependent upon each other." Love she calls "the greatest of the good things that are within our grasp, the only one to which even the pleasure of study ought to be sacrificed. The ideal would be two individuals who would be so attracted to each other that their passion would never cool or become surfeited. But one cannot hope for such harmony of two persons; it would be too perfect. A heart, which would be capable of such love, a soul which would be so steadfast and so affectionate, is perhaps born once in every century; it seems, as if the creation of two such souls in the same generation is beyond the power of God."

But she believes that an affectionate and sensitive soul can be happy with the mere pleasure of loving. Here she was thinking of herself; for in a letter she says: "I was happy for ten years in the love of the one who had conquered my soul, and those ten years I spent in perfect communion with him, without a moment of anger or languishing. When age and illness had reduced his affection, a long time passed before I noticed it; I loved for two; I spent my whole life with him, and my trusting heart enjoyed the ecstasy of love, and the illusion of believing itself to be loved. It must be said I have lost this happy state. It was not without many tears that I did so."

Voltaire, for his part, said a hundred times that he

became happy only at Cirey. He cared less about the material and sensual happiness than about the quiet joy of living, which he found in the solitude beautified by his friend. "Do not tell me that I work too much. These tasks are trifles for a man who has no other occupation. If the mind has been shaped in the mould of fine literature for a long time, it adapts itself to this work without trouble or effort, just as one has no difficulty in speaking a language which one has studied a long time, or as the hand of a musician runs easily over the keys of a piano. . . . I am trying to lead my life in accordance with my situation without painful passion, without envy, with much knowledge, with a few friends. . . . We must force our minds into all kinds of forms. It is a fire entrusted to us by God; we must nourish it with the best we can find. We must let every conceivable phenomenon enter into our being, open all the gates of our souls to knowledge as well as to emotional experience. Provided it does not try to enter in confusion, there is room in the soul for a whole world."

One can see, Madame du Châtelet's best side was human, while Voltaire, at his best, was pure mind.

There exists a letter from Emily to d'Argental, in which she describes herself from the physical side. "I have," she says, "good health, but I am not robust. There are things that surely would destroy my health, for instance, wine or any kind of liquor. I have denied myself these since my early youth. But I have an ardent disposition, so I spend my mornings steeping myself in baths."

This ardent disposition was matched at first by Voltaire's. But in the course of years, when constant sickness had undermined Voltaire's health, the two became altogether different. Voltaire began very early to feel old. In France of the seventeenth and eighteenth century a man over forty was considered old. The ridiculous old Arnolphe in Molière's *L'Ecole des Femmes,* who is so foolish in trying to win himself a young wife, is forty-two years old. When Voltaire entered the second half of the forties, he began to refer to himself in his letters as an old man.

While he had, mentally, preserved his greatest

vigor while he even felt an increase of his intellectual
capacities, he seems to consider that he has arrived
at a time of life when friendship has to replace passion.

In sharp contrast to most other artistic geniuses
who have kept young physically as long as intellectually, Voltaire scarcely had reached the age of forty,
when he regarded love as a passion for which he was
too old; his forced resignation and renunciation he
expressed in a lovely poem in July, 1741. The poem is
entitled *À Madame du Châtelet:*

> Si vous voulez que j'aime encore,
> Rendez-moi l'âge des amours;
> Au crépuscule de mes jours
> Rejoignez, s'il se peut, l'aurore.

> Des beaux lieux, où le dieu du vin
> Avec l'Amour tient son empire,
> Le Temps, qui me prend par la main,
> M'avertit que je me retire.

"We must," he says, "leave passion to youth. We
have two minutes in which to live. One of these minutes may be devoted to prudence."—He certainly is
an old man, although just forty-six years old, when
he says:

> De son inflexible vigueur
> Tirons au moins quelque avantage.
> Qui n'a pas l'esprit de son âge,
> De son age a tout le malheur.

> Laissons à la belle jeunesse
> Ses folâtres emportements;
> Nous ne vivons que deux moments;
> Qu'il en soit un pour la sagesse!

Not, indeed, that the speaker is content with his
premature old age, or wants to boast of it, as Cicero
in *De senectute* boasts. On the contrary, this condition is death, worse than death:

> On meurt deux fois, je le vois bien:
> Cesser d'aimer et d'être aimable,
> C'est une mort insupportable.
> Cesser de vivre, ce n'est rien.

But, while he was grieving over the loss of the
sweet indiscretions of youth, he was given, as he says,

one consolation. Down from the heavens came friendship, to take the place of love:

> Du ciel alors daignant descendre,
> L'Amitié vint à mon secours;
> Elle était peut-être aussi tendre,
> Mais moins vive que les Amours.

Madame du Châtelet, at that time thirty-four years old, and having a temperament which "was like fire," could not change into an old woman at the same time. The transition from love to friendship with her was not demanded by Nature, as with Voltaire; and it therefore is not surprising that a number of years later she was carried off by another man.

From now on. however, she is a friend, only, to Voltaire, and during the thirty-seven years he has still to live, no other woman appears within his horizon. The time is past, when he could know the joy and pain of loving, and soon, too, will be gone the time when he could be inspired or enthused by a woman.

From now on, Truth is the sole object of his desire, Humanity the sole object of his adoration. Justice has become his only bride and Fame the only mistress with whom he travels and lives.

A soldier is not fit for marriage. It is unbecoming for a missionary to be married. From now on Voltaire becomes more and more the soldier and the missionary. The Templars were at the same time monks and knights, soldiers and priests. Half soldier, half priest, Voltaire henceforth is a new kind of Templar or rather Grand-master of the Order of Templars, which during his lifetime slowly formed and looked to him as its leader.

END OF VOLUME I